# Dickinson

# Dickinson

*Selected Poems and Commentaries*

## HELEN VENDLER

*The Belknap Press of*
Harvard University Press
CAMBRIDGE, MASSACHUSETTS
LONDON, ENGLAND
2010

Emily Dickinson's poems are reprinted by permission of the publishers and the
Trustees of Amherst College from *The Poems of Emily Dickinson: Variorum Edition*
and *The Poems of Emily Dickinson: Reading Edition*
edited by Ralph W. Franklin, Cambridge, Mass.: The Belknap Press of
Harvard University Press. Copyright © 1998, 1999 by the President and
Fellows of Harvard College. Copyright © 1951, 1955, 1979, 1983 by the
President and Fellows of Harvard College.

Library of Congress Cataloging-in-Publication Data
Dickinson, Emily, 1830–1886.
[Poems. Selections]
Dickinson : selected poems and commentaries / Helen Vendler.
p.   cm.
Includes bibliographical references and index.
ISBN 978-0-674-04867-6 (alk. paper)
1. Dickinson, Emily, 1830–1886—Criticism and interpretation.
I. Vendler, Helen, 1933–   II. Title.

PS1541.A6   2010
811'.4—dc22        2010007090

IN MEMORY OF JOHN KEATS

Should any one call my dedication of Chatterton affected,
I answer as followeth:
'Were I dead, sir, I should like a Book dedicated to me.'

—Keats to his publisher,
with the original preface to *Endymion*

# Contents

# A Note on the Text

Quotations of Emily Dickinson's poems are drawn from *The Poems of Emily Dickinson: Variorum Edition,* ed. Ralph W. Franklin (1998), but are cued to the poem numbers of Franklin's *Reading Edition* (1999). Following the text of Franklin's *Reading Edition,* the poems reprinted here retain Dickinson's dashes and capitals, using a shorter dash than the full modern one (her own dashes differ in length). I have included all of her dashes when quoting entire lines but not when quoting phrases; and I have placed my own punctuation (commas, periods) outside the quotation marks to preserve the integrity of Dickinson's own punctuation. I have allowed her misspellings to stand, with a few exceptions: in order to avoid confusing readers, I have printed "upon" for her characteristic "opon," and I have regularized her punctuation of possessives, since she normally writes "it's" for the possessive "its" and "your's" for "yours," etc. I have inserted apostrophes (to make her "cant" into "can't," for example), and I have added a grave accent (not in Franklin), when an "-ed" which is normally silent is to be pronounced aloud, thus sparing the modern reader the impression of a metrically defective line.

In 1955, Thomas H. Johnson published the first scholarly edition of Dickinson: *The Poems of Emily Dickinson: Including Variant Readings Critically Compared with All Known Manuscripts.* Johnson took as his copy-text the earliest fair copy of a poem; Franklin, in contrast, takes as his copy-text the last fair copy. Either decision can be defended. The debates about the best editorial presentation of Dickinson's handwritten poems are acute and still in flux.

The identifying numbers of the poems cited throughout are those assigned by Franklin. However, I have given at the end of each Commentary the number of the poem in Johnson's edition (J) for the convenience of readers who may own the Johnson but not the Franklin.

Throughout the Commentaries in this book, the identifying numbers of the 150 poems (listed in the table of contents) which have received a full

Commentary bear an asterisk when the poem is mentioned. Other poems, when mentioned in a Commentary, bear no asterisk; they are, however, included in the Index of First Lines that follows that Commentaries.

Quotations from the letters of Emily Dickinson are drawn from *The Letters of Emily Dickinson,* ed. Thomas H. Johnson and Theodora Ward (1958). Such quotations are cited in parentheses by letter-number, preceded by L.

Biblical citations are taken from the King James Version, the text Dickinson would have known.

# Dickinson

# Introduction

## Dickinson the Writer

Emily Dickinson (1830–1886) bequeathed to us nearly 1,800 poems; in some passionate years she wrote almost a poem a day. Like all capacious writers, she baffles complete understanding: to enter her poetics entirely a reader would have to know by heart (and by ear) all her poems. Ideally, too, her reader should possess the King James Bible as firmly as she did, and should have read the poetry of the English past as fervently as she had: she knew Shakespeare, Herbert, Vaughan, Milton, Wordsworth, James Thomson, Keats, George Eliot, Emily Brontë, Elizabeth Barrett Browning, and others. She had also read the famous male and female American poets of her day, mentioning in her poetry and letters Longfellow, Whittier, and Bryant. (She even mentioned Whitman, but only to say she had not read him, having heard that he was "disgraceful.")[1] Yet readers worldwide, even when they have lacked her background, have flocked to her poems, responding to her candor, her grief, and her wit. This selection of 150 poems by Dickinson, accompanied by a short Commentary on each, aims to bring readers to a deeper acquaintance with Dickinson the writer, the inventive reconceiver and linguistic shaper of her perennial themes: nature, death, religion, love, and the workings of the mind and of thought. This is a book to be browsed in, as the reader becomes interested in one or another of the poems commented on here.

The Dickinson household received the literary magazines of the day, and it was in one of these—the *Atlantic Monthly* of April 1862—that Dickinson read an article entitled "Letter to a Young Contributor," written by Thomas Wentworth Higginson. Desperate for a literary eye to look at her poems, the

---

1. *The Letters of Emily Dickinson,* ed. Thomas H. Johnson and Theodora Ward (Cambridge, Mass.: Harvard University Press, 1958), 3 vols., L 261.

thirty-two-year-old Dickinson (representing herself as younger in the art of poetry than she actually was) wrote a letter (unsigned) to Higginson asking him to tell her whether her poetry "breathed" (L 260). She enclosed four poems on separate sheets of paper, and added, in a small envelope, her calling card. This brave act began her most important literary correspondence. Dickinson later told Higginson he had saved her life by responding to her plea.

Higginson, seeing the eccentricity of Dickinson's poems, made (as she might have expected) editorial suggestions that she gracefully acknowledged but did not obey. When he hinted that she might be seeking publication, she said that publication was as foreign to her mind "as Firmament to Fin - " (L 265). Even so, her longing for an audience is manifest in such poems as "This is my letter to the World" and in her dissemination of much of her verse in private letters. Her sense of her own genius led her to write to Higginson, "If fame belonged to me, I could not escape her - " (L 265). But Dickinson's suspicion that her poems would not please publishers was ratified when, after her death, her first editors emended her poems considerably—not only by substituting accepted punctuation for her running dashes and regulating her metrics, but also by flattening her uncommon diction and censoring her bolder speculations. In sending scores of poems to her extended family and friends, she carefully selected, among her poems, those that she allowed to be "published" in this intimate way; she did not forward her more irreligious poems, nor her most macabre or explicitly erotic ones. It was not until 1955 that a three-volume scholarly edition of Dickinson's poems by Thomas H. Johnson appeared, and not until 2007 that Johnson's chronology was corrected by the ingenious work of Ralph W. Franklin (who determined from watermarks and pinholes the order of the sheets of paper that Dickinson had folded and sewed together in the little booklets now called "fascicles"). My texts here follow, and are cued by poem number to, Franklin's one-volume *Reading Edition* (1999); readers wishing to see the many arresting variants of the poems, some of which I quote in the Commentaries, should consult Franklin's three-volume *Variorum Edition* (1998).[2]

---

2. Franklin's *Manuscript Books of Emily Dickinson,* in two volumes (Cambridge, Mass.: Harvard University Press, 1981), reproduces chronologically and in their original order the manuscripts of the poet's forty sewn fascicles and fifteen unsewn "sets," all presenting copies of poems of which

In choosing the 150 poems for inclusion here I wanted to exhibit many different aspects of the poet's work as a writer, from her first-person poems to the poems of grand abstraction, from her ecstatic verses to her unparalleled depictions of emotional numbness, from her comic anecdotes to her painful poems of aftermath. I have included many of the familiar poems, but I have wanted to make space, too, for daring poems that have rarely been anthologized or taught in school, and so have not reached a large general audience. There are poems of varying achievement here, the lesser ones included to show the conventional or occasional Dickinson, the greater ones to sustain her right to fame.

Dickinson the writer: How do we characterize her? She is epigrammatic, terse, abrupt, surprising, unsettling, flirtatious, savage, winsome, metaphysical, provocative, blasphemous, tragic, funny—and the list of adjectives could be extended, since we have almost 1,800 poems to draw on. What surprised (and still tends to surprise) readers was that Dickinson's mature poems were all so *brief.* Many of the writers admired by Dickinson had embarked ambitiously on epics, dramas, long narratives, sonnet sequences, and dramatic monologues, yet Dickinson never attempted such genres. Her tenacity in keeping to a miniature form caused some readers, even in the twentieth century, to patronize her work. She seems to have asked herself that fundamental question of the choice of size—why such short poems?—and answered it in a remarkable lyric, "Ashes denote that Fire was - " (*1097). Her poems, she says—defending their reduced form—are the Ashes of a previous conflagration that destroyed "the Departed Creature" now dead (although that Creature, at death, had briefly "hovered" over the Ashes of her former self). To understand the vanished Creature of whom the Ashes are the residue, one must become a Chemist, and deduce from the remaining Carbonates the nature of the person consumed by the Fire:

> Ashes denote that Fire was -
> Revere the Grayest Pile
> For the Departed Creature's sake
> That hovered there awhile -

---

she had discarded prior drafts, although revisions continued to be inscribed in some of these fair copies.

Fire exists the first in light
And then consolidates
Only the Chemist can disclose
Into what Carbonates -

The original Creature was first illuminated by the "light" of some revelation; the revelation then kindled into a fiery conflagration, and the conflagration ended in a consuming. What is left does not resemble the past earthly being of the Creature: the Fire has done its work, leaving only the Ashes, the cremated "Carbonates" that we find in the poet's pages. (Dickinson may have borrowed her Ashes and her deathbed from Shakespeare's Sonnet 73, recalling the fire "That on the ashes of his youth doth lie.") Dickinson calls on us, as the forensic Chemists of verse, to reconstruct from a small heap of Ashes—her poem—the self originally nourished and then consumed by the light of insight and the Fire of emotion.

How is one to set about that reconstruction demanded by the artist? Because Dickinson is a poet of implication rather than of statement, she consistently provokes the reader's intelligence into puzzled and active response. Although she may make distinct opening statements—"Renunciation - is a piercing Virtue - " (*782); "I cannot live with You - " (*706); "I heard a Fly buzz - when I died - " (*591)—those explicit statements generally lead to later lines more perplexing both in language and in import:

Renunciation - is the Choosing
Against itself -
Itself to justify
Unto itself -

Who is "itself" and why is it called "it"? Is it single or dual? How can "itself" choose "Against itself - "? Why is the choice so abstractly, even algebraically, expressed? What does such a choice lead to? And so the reader is led, here as elsewhere, into a thicket of speculation.

Dickinson's verse was, in the past, sometimes considered amateurish because it is for the most part constructed within a single frame, the "childish" four-line stanza of hymn-meter: 4 beats, 3 beats, 4 beats, 3 beats, with a single rhyme-sound linking lines 2 and 4. There are variations on this base (such as 3-3-4-3), but Dickinson rarely writes in pentameter or a consistent tetrameter. (Yet see the wonderful tetrameter of her dramatic sunset, "Blazing in Gold and quenching in Purple" (321); there are such metrical experiments scattered throughout her poems, and my Commentaries point them out.) Because of the near-omnipresence of Dickinson's hymn-meter, her ingenious and meaningful variations in rhythm and syntax within that frame have often passed unnoticed. We can view her marshaling of syntax, for instance, in "Bloom - is Result" (*1038), in which the Flower, to arrive at Bloom, must work intelligently and forcefully on many fronts: it needs

> To pack the Bud - oppose the Worm -
> Obtain its right of Dew -
> Adjust the Heat - elude the Wind -
> Escape the prowling Bee -

(This is comic, with its "prowling" Bee—but it is also mock-epic in its list of various dangers: the unjust opposing forces, the oppressors, the predators, the authorities' refusal of necessary sustenance.) To represent the Flower's struggle, Dickinson adjusts the Flower's successive efforts to the length of the poem's lines: in each of the four-beat lines there are two peremptory infinitives and nouns; and in each of the three-beat lines, one infinitive and one noun. After the first incisively monosyllabic verb, "pack," the poet lines up all her verbs into two-syllable form, each (as she was well aware) presenting some form of a Latin prefix—*ob* ("against"), *ad* ("toward"), and *ex* ("out"): op-pose, ob-tain, ad-just, e-lude, es-cape. By the end, the marshaling of the Flower's duties reads like a military field manual entitled, "Procedures Necessary To Achieve Victory." If we recall the ancient pun of "poesy"/"posy," we can also view this stanza as an allegorical manual for the construction of a viable poem. As we pursue its allegory, we intuit behind it a set of hinted-at procedures necessary to make a poem "bloom":

> To pack the Line - oppose Cliché -
> Obtain its right of Song -

Adjust the Pace - elude the Coarse -
Escape the lurking Wrong -

We can see why Dickinson (like so many earlier poets) was drawn to the symbolic plane of the Flower: its maneuvers could present a light sketch of the strenuousness of self-authentication, which elsewhere—as in "Shall I take thee, the Poet said" (*1243)—she treated on an exalted religious plane, rewarding the Poet with a Vision endorsed by Cherubim, those angels nearest the seat of God.

Dickinson chose a secluded life; she never married, and lived till her death with her parents and her sister Lavinia in the family house in Amherst, Massachusetts. Only after her death, with the posthumous publication of her poems, did others become aware of her as an author. However, Dickinson knew that poetic influence does not die with the death of the writer. In one of her startling openings, she gestured away the importance of personal death:

The Poets light but Lamps -
Themselves - go out -

But—she continues—if "vital Light" is given off by those surviving Lamps, "Each Age [becomes] a Lens / Disseminating their / Circumference - " (*930). Her own "Lamps," from their first publication through the present, have shone through four such "Age[s]," interpenetrating ones, which might be named "The Age of Publication," "The Age of Biography," "The Age of Editing," and "The Age of Commentary." The poems appeared, from 1890 on, in several volumes but in regrettably emended versions; only in 1955 did Thomas H. Johnson establish a reliable text of the poems with variants.[3] Jay Leyda's book *The Years and Hours of Emily Dickinson* (1960) and Richard Sewall's 1974 biography securely established for the first time the main life-events, family relations, and Amherst context of the poet. These books gave rise to a flood of commentaries, further stimulated by Ralph Franklin's work on the manuscripts and his revisionary edition of the poems (1998). The bio-

---

3. *The Poems of Emily Dickinson: Including Variant Readings Critically Compared with All Known Manuscripts,* ed. Thomas H. Johnson, 3 vols. (Cambridge, Mass.: Harvard University Press, 1955).

graphical, the editorial, and the critical endeavors continue vigorously at present, and I have been very grateful, in teaching Emily Dickinson's poetry and in writing about her, for the invaluable publications, over the past fifty years, of modern editors and critics.[4] Interested readers will deepen their knowledge of Dickinson as they go beyond this restricted set of poems and the accompanying brief Commentaries. Yet I hope, by focusing here on Dickinson the writer—inventor of a new form of poetry on the page—to emphasize, more than thematic studies can do, Dickinson as a master of a revolutionary verse-language of immediacy and power.

As the "Lens" of each Age has disseminated the circumference of her "vital Light," Dickinson has come to be more securely placed in her historical moment. Critics have compared her poems to those of other nineteenth-century writers, male and female, who also treated the topics to which she constantly returns. This scholarly and critical work has served to intensify our sense of the way Dickinson differs from those contemporaries in her force of will, her skeptical mind, her idiosyncratic imagination, and her ceaseless wresting of language to her own purposes. And although she has been much imitated, one can distinguish Dickinson from her imitators by her unmatched capacity for concentrating, into a small poem, an unqualified passion, an intricate and often counterintuitive logic, a keen analytical penetration, and an unpredictable vision. Precisely because she was so conscious of the tradition of lyric in which she worked, Dickinson was particularly concerned to distinguish her own conception of poetry, and her manner of expression, from that of others. She borrowed from Shakespeare, for instance, the idea of poetry as an essential fragrance remaining after the death of its natural source in the flower, but whereas he saw it (in Sonnet 5) as "distilled," she saw it as a painful "gift of Screws - ":

> Essential Oils - are wrung -
> The Attar from the Rose

---

4. A substantial bibliography of such work in English is available in Fred D. White, *Approaching Emily Dickinson: Critical Currents and Crosscurrents since 1960* (Rochester, N.Y.: Camden House, 2008), 195–213. "The Emily Dickinson Lexicon" is an online resource offering a concordance—still under revision—of all of Dickinson's uses of any given word.

Be not expressed by Suns - alone -
It is the gift of Screws -

[*772]

My Commentaries here draw attention above all to the imaginative and linguistic "Screws" that Dickinson applied to emotional experience in order to extract and frame its essence. Although I provide paraphrases of difficult passages, what I most want to bring into view is the manner in which Dickinson's ardor and grief found words, sentences, phrases, enigmas, proverbs, impersonations, scenarios, and strategies adequate to the sequence of human emotions, personal and impersonal, that she was impelled to bring into visibility. She told Higginson that when she said "I" she meant "a supposed person"—that she intended her constructions to be relevant to others' experience (L 268). It is tempting to read the poems as direct reports from Dickinson's own life, and to forget that a poem, no matter how personal its origin, always requires a selection from, and a linguistic attitude toward, that personal source. It is hard, but necessary, to keep in mind that there are always two Dickinsons on every page: the "Representative" speaker and the poet who is creating her. I use the word "Dickinson" for both, trusting the reader to understand when I mean the speaker and when I mean the creator of the speaker, that alert conscious author of the speaker's lines. Dickinson's deliberate "naïveté" and consistent use of a first-person speaker are strategies to make us forget the intricate shaping accomplished by language and art. We can read backward from the "Ashes" to the conjectured "Fire" and the "Creature" consumed by it, as the poet suggested, but those readings remain our constructions deduced from the never-changing but ever-rich words of a particular poem. As she said about her own search for poetic structures:

For Pattern is the Mind bestowed
That imitating her
Our most ignoble services
Exhibit worthier.

[1219]

Supremely aware of the embarrassments, crudities, and shames of raw life, Dickinson counted on her aesthetic Patterns to make more worthy on the page what may have been ignoble in experience. Dickinson made ignoble service "worthier" by a devotion to the discipline of "Pattern" that in earlier times would have been exerted in the discipline of the soul.

Choosing patterned abstraction in part to be "Representative" and to "Exhibit worthier" her emotional and intellectual material, Dickinson also found abstraction congenial to her deep wish for privacy. In her commitment to the abstract, she obeyed her own injunction (in *240, Version A) to "Deal with the soul / As with Algebra!" (*She* would offer a symbolic *x* and *y,* and *we* were to supply our own personal variables.) Although she sometimes did write the sort of first-order poem that reads like a transcription of a life-event, such as a vigil around a deathbed, more often she found a second-order "algebraic" equivalent for emotional occasions, whether rapturous or troubling. Often, her symbolic equivalents arise from emotional torture:

> Before I got my eye put out -
> I liked as well to see
> As other creatures, that have eyes -
> And know no other way -

> [336]

But often, too, her symbols are generated by transports of joy, especially in the revelation of love:

> To My Small Hearth His fire came -
> And all My House a'glow
> Did fan and rock, with sudden light -
> 'Twas Sunrise - 'twas the Sky -

> Impanelled from no Summer brief -
> With limit of Decay -
> 'Twas Noon - without the News of Night -
> Nay, Nature, it was Day -

> [703]

On her second-order symbolic plane, events do occur, but they present themselves, like the savaged eye-put-out, surreally: "In Winter in my Room / I came upon a Worm / Pink lank and warm" (*1742). We are immediately forced to become interpreters of the encounter: What are we to understand when the poet says of the Worm (turned snake) "He fathomed me - "? The energy of decoding that Dickinson ignites in us is testimony to her resourcefulness of expression, and yet the decoding to which we are compelled remains necessarily a reduction of the whole, which is restored only by a return to the shaped words and sounds of the poem.

One of the exhilarations in reading Dickinson arises as we become acquainted with the almost illimitable set of templates on which she mapped her poems:

> the temporal scale of years, seasons, hours, and minutes;
> a circular geometry of center, circumference, and the "spokes" connecting them;
> a vertical scale extending from "under the beetle's cellar" to the stars;
> a horizontal scale extending from the East of dawn to the West of sunset;
> geographic coordinates stretching from New England to the poles;
> a cultural plot of myth, with subsets of Greece, Rome, Jerusalem;
> a spectrum of foreignness by way of Europe, Asia, Africa, and India;
> a grid of time, space, and temperature, voiced in notches, gauges, degrees, steps, and plunges;
> a scale of population, from a single person to a mob;
> a theory of belief ranging from prayer to despair;
> a pathology of emotion stretching from insensibility to derangement.

The list could be continued. These ingredients, taken one by one, are mainstays of lyric. But what disorients Dickinson's reader is the way that the poet maps these templates or grids one upon another, enabling her to leap from plane to plane:

> From Blank to Blank -
> A Threadless Way
> I pushed Mechanic feet -

> [484]

The enigmatic "Blank" could arise from a number of grids: it could be a trackless waste, a benumbed sense, or a sightless passageway; the "Threadless Way" suggests the mythical labyrinth; the "Mechanic feet" imply that the self is plotting itself on a grid of machinery; the "push" implies a forward advance, but one made in numb ignorance. If we are reading as the poet directs, we find ourselves dizzy from following in her footsteps, putting our own kinetic impulses in the exact positions assumed by hers—footing a blank gap, hands empty and unguided, pushing our will to set our feet going, the feet themselves stiff and unresponsive. Like "From Blank to Blank - ", its famous counterpart "After great pain, a formal feeling comes - " (*372) recklessly mixes grids of this sort:

> The Feet, mechanical, go round -
> A Wooden way
> Of Ground, or Air, or Ought -
> Regardless grown,
> A Quartz contentment, like a stone -

Can a way of "Ground" be "Wooden"? What sort of "contentment" lies in an immobile crystal lattice? Imitating imaginatively, in our own body, the feeling-state that would generate such successive metaphors, we experience the mechanical Feet, the path of Ground no longer springy with life but wooden; the path that seems made of insubstantial Air; the path of Anything-you-can-think-of ("Aught," spelled by the poet "Ought"); our glassy unreceptive stare; our stony stoic "contentment." Only after pressing our senses to follow in Dickinson's wake can we return to the structuring words themselves, tethering them to their preceding and following companions on the page.

Even when Dickinson is more explicit, her images can remain for a time mysterious, as when she opens a poem with a series of incompatible similes without identifying the actual "it" that they purport to illustrate:

> 'Twas like a maelstrom, . . .
> . . . . .
> As if a Goblin with a Gauge -
> . . . . .
> As if your Sentence stood - pronounced -
>
> [*425]

Just as she likes the abstracting use of "it," she likes the use of verbs unmarked by tense or number or mood. Substituting infinitives for active verbs, she guarantees a more universal plane:

> I never saw a Moor.
> I never saw the Sea -
> Yet know I how the Heather looks
> And what a Billow be -

> [*800]

If we try to substitute "is" for Dickinson's final "be," we are made to realize that "is" need not be the only possible substitution: Dickinson's last line could be rewritten as "[I know] what a Billow *might be -* " or *"should be - ".* These would work as logically as "is" (especially since the poet has never seen the Sea). We are compelled to find a different reason for the anomalous "be": Dickinson knows these unseen objects (Heather, billow) on a Platonic plane, where they are ever the same—the abstract Idea of the Heather, the unchanging Idea of the Billow. "Be," in its temporal immobility, is one of the many Dickinsonian verbs that point our eyes to the timeless realm of Type, rather than the changing field of Instances.

Just as she loved the stimulus of teasing riddles, Dickinson was drawn to provocative definitions: "'Hope' is . . ." (*314); "One and One - are One - " (497); "This was a Poet - " (*446); "There are two Ripenings - " (*420). She also sought to catch her reader's attention by opening her poems with questions—"Dare you see a Soul at the 'White Heat'?" (*401)—or exclamations —"Civilization - spurns - the Leopard!" (*276)—or paradoxes—"My life closed twice before its close" (*1773). The incessant physical "Drama in the flesh - " (*279), combined with her austere but equally dramatic self-inspection, generated lurid scenarios of torment as well as exalted vistas of speculation.

What did Dickinson do to individualize, within her poems, the genres she had inherited from the long history of lyric? The nature poem, the prayer, the elegy, and the love poem were all familiar kinds to readers of poetry. By what forms of vivacity could she resurrect them? "I see - New Englandly - ", she said (*256), and her provinciality became her great resource in reinventing nature writing—to which we might add "human-nature writing." She observed like a Linnaeus the human fauna of her Massachusetts village, finding ample subjects for satire, from the "Gentlewomen" of "What Soft - Cherubic Creatures - " (*675) to the "afflictive" "Presbyterian Birds" of the churches (1620). She had a personal flower garden, enabling allegories such as the energetic "Bloom - is Result - " (*1038) and the chilling "A Visitor in Marl - " (*558). She scrutinized, throughout the year, the surrounding fields and hills, adorned by Nature and populated by "Nature's People" (*1096)—birds, snakes, crickets, hummingbirds, butterflies, beetles, squirrels. She "never saw the Sea - " (*800), but she had the sky always overhead, day and night, ornamented with the sun, the stars, the moon, and (on at least one spectacular occasion) the Northern Lights. Storms visited her Massachusetts village, and so did floods; frost and snow came in their turn. And she also took an interest in the more curious manifestations of nature: a cocoon, a lightning bolt, a diamond. In her hands—by a figure or an adjective—the staples of nature poetry are transformed. The lightning is a "yellow Fork" (1140); a "Silver Fracture" indicates the surface of a winter river (950); the snow "Heaves Balls of Specks, like Vicious Boy" (622). She comes by stealth upon her reader, beginning a list of common things and then pitching it into an unnerving other. Her bland summary of things seen in nature, for instance, is at first an anodyne one:

> "Nature" is what We see -
> The Hill - the Afternoon -
> Squirrel -
>
> [721]

And just when we are becoming lulled by this conventional list, what do we encounter following Dickinson's genial "Squirrel"? "Eclipse." Pure darkness. Or she will praise the "Bronze - and Blaze - " of the Northern Lights (*319) and then, just when we might expect an echo of "The heavens declare the glory of God" (Psalm 19), Dickinson announces that the auroras' majestic indifference to herself engenders in her a self-deceiving pose desiring to resemble their majesty, a false grandeur that "Infects my simple spirit / With Taints of Majesty - ". (In the 1896 *Poems,* "Infects" and "Taints" were removed, and in their place the editor put "It paints" and "tints": Dickinson's surprises were not always welcome ones.) Dickinson's nature poetry alternates disturbingly between tenderness and violence, and is almost always a vehicle for an observation on human life: "Nature, like Us is sometimes caught / Without her Diadem - " (*1121).

Dickinson, like other writers of religious poetry, encountered the special difficulties enumerated by Dr. Johnson in his life of Edmund Waller: "Omnipotence cannot be exalted; infinity cannot be amplified; perfection cannot be improved." Yet omnipotence, infinity, and perfection (together with their cognate subjects immortality and eternity) are among Dickinson's most frequent subjects. Religious texts—the Hebrew Bible, the New Testament, Christian liturgical ritual—offered Dickinson her only metaphysical vocabulary; my allusions in these Commentaries are to the King James Version of the Bible, the one she knew. She never found a congenial substitute for religion as a system of order (as others of her era adopted Darwinian evolution, or as later skeptics would ally themselves to psychoanalysis or Marxism). Yet her intellectual honesty forbade her taking Jesus as her savior (as all her fellow students in her college did); as an adult, she ceased to attend church with her family.[5] Her remarks about religion and its preachers were often wry, as in "He preached upon 'Breadth' till it argued him narrow - " (1266), but her remarks about Jesus are sympathetic; it was a consolation to her that human beings had at last conceived of a Deity capable of suffering. Her conviction that certain abstractions—Virtue, Love, Hope—were as real (on an invisible plane) as visible objects and persons were (on the material plane) could locate no ground except in the transcendent realm claimed by Christianity. But the theological faith, hope, and love identified by Saint Paul eluded her attempts at firm definition; hope, lacking an identifiable object (such as an afterlife), "sings the tune without the words - " (*314); faith "slips - and laughs, and rallies" when questioned (*373); and as for love, it not only seemed inapplicable to God, that "Burglar! Banker! - Father!" (39) but was also inevitably

---

5. In 1873, her father wrote on a card, "I hereby give myself to God," and signed and dated it (L 389, note).

frustrated in life—"Born - Bridalled - Shrouded - / In a Day - " (*194). Yet
the lexicon of Christian belief, toward which she bent her minute attention
and ceaseless investigation, never ceased to appear in her verse. We can say of
her writing what she said of the light shed by Death on judgment:

> 'Tis Compound Vision -
> Light - enabling Light -
> The Finite - furnished
> With the Infinite -

> [*830]

The Christian promise of personal Immortality was the doctrine that
most tempted her: one of the last dated poems printed by Franklin (1683)
says that "every way we fly / We are molested equally / By immortality." The
thought that on the Last Day she would be reunited with those she had loved
was so moving to Dickinson that she wrote some of her most gripping poems
about that imagined reunion:

> Of all the Souls that stand create -
> I have Elected - One -
> When Sense from Spirit - files away -
> And Subterfuge - is done -
> When that which is - and that which was -
> Apart - intrinsic - stand -
> And this brief Drama in the flesh -
> Is shifted - like a Sand -
> When Figures show their royal Front -
> And Mists - are carved away,
> Behold the Atom - I preferred -
> To all the lists of Clay!

> [*279]

Considered against the usual hymns envisaging "Jerusalem the Golden" as it
was described in Revelation, this poem is sharply irreligious; God does not
figure in it, nor do the evangelist's joys of heaven. On the Last Day, with
no celestial apparatus mentioned, only two figures stand visible: Dickinson

and her beloved. The vocabulary of the heavenly reunion is not "Golden" but dry: we hear such technical terms as "Elected" "Subterfuge," "intrinsic," "Drama," "Atom," "preferred." Although impossible without the Christian imaging of the Last Day, this poem could not have been written by a Christian believer: "In the resurrection they neither marry nor are given in marriage," says Jesus (Matthew 22:30). All of Dickinson's poems that resort to Christian imagery and language rework Christianity in some way—intellectually, blasphemously, or comically: see, for instance, her poem drawing on Longfellow's "Courtship of Miles Standish," "God is a distant - stately Lover - " (*615), for her joke on the doctrine of the Incarnation. And along with the New Testament, the poet read with fascinated intensity the Hebrew Bible, the Old Testament (as she would have called it). In her poems, she often embedded, with a mocking impudence, its plots and promises:

> Abraham to kill him
> Was distinctly told -
> Isaac was an Urchin -
> Abraham was old -
>
> [*1332]

And Dickinson reshaped the pious Christian idea of death—in which the resolved and virtuous soul, at peace with itself and God, expires without protest—into many macabre reinventions of elegy. Death was for her the great mystery in which spirit was extinguished and the corpse became a thing dishonored: in her axiomatic phrase, "Dust is the only Secret" (166). Gazing upon a corpse in an open coffin in "Oh give it motion - " (1550), she constructs a morbid fantasy of reanimating it, step by step, in a backward parody of the steps of God's creation of Adam. Death was the wall she could not breach, the veil she could not lift. A corpse is laid out by mourners, "And then an awful leisure was / Belief to regulate - " (*1100). Belief, as she knew, cannot be "regulated" or controlled; it is present or it is not. To Dickinson, Death was the unintelligible riddle: "And through a Riddle, at the last - / Sagacity, must go - " (*373). Dickinson's own sagacity, which was intellectual and independent, engaged in a lifelong standoff with that riddle. The incomprehensible extinction of human beings by Death provoked from her one poem after another, elegy upon elegy.

Dickinson succeeded brilliantly in outstripping her American poetic contemporaries (with the exception of Whitman) in writing of both nature and death; as for her defiant critique of Christianity and her uninhibited scrutiny of its concepts, it is unequaled among other poets of her day. Dickinson's most acute remark on God is made in the wake of contemplating the powers of the human brain:

> The Brain - is wider than the Sky -
> For - put them side by side -
> The one the other will contain
> With ease - and You - beside -
>
> The Brain is deeper than the sea -
> For - hold them - Blue to Blue -
> The one the other will absorb -
> As Sponges - Buckets - do -
>
> The Brain is just the weight of God -
> For - Heft them - Pound for Pound -
> And they will differ - if they do -
> As Syllable from Sound -
>
> [598]

Her first two stanzas here are unremarkable in their Romantic claim that the Brain is capable of containing or absorbing, in its fullness, not only vast natural phenomena (Sky, sea) but also the human being perceiving those phenomena—"and You - beside - ". But the first two stanzas clearly exist for the sake of the third, when Dickinson forsakes natural phenomena in order to examine the concept of God. What is the relation of the Brain to the Divine? Abandoning metaphors of containment and absorption, she turns to the significant power of each of her two entities: the Brain and God. They weigh the same, she says—as we can see when we lift them, using our two hands as two pans of a scale: "Pound for Pound" they are equal. The Brain is said not to contain the Divine nor to absorb it—merely to equal it in weight. But do we not feel a difference between the two weighed things? Yes—and the difference is language. God, through Nature, utters Sounds, but human language alone is voiced in Syllables. The Poet exists to reframe in intelligible Syllables the unintelligible Sounds ascribable to God. This boast—that Syllables are better than Sounds, and that therefore the Brain is superior to God—presumes a Divinity who is exceeded in power by Humanity. Dickinson's sacrilegious worship of the Syllable may remind us of Whitman's equally sacrilegious worship of the Body: "If I worship any one thing more than another it shall be the spread of my own body, or any part of it" ("Song of Myself," Canto 24). Both poets are compelled to inquire into what—if not religion—is worthy of reverence. Their answers, though far apart in substance, are united in their repudiation of the conventional superiority of the Divine Creator to the Human Creature.

It was when she treated the third of her obsessive concerns—love—that Dickinson's desire to write outside cliché met its greatest difficulties of realization. Love came to her as a surprise - "I thought that nature was enough / Till Human nature came" (1269)—and her early poetry of love threatened to rest in the pathos of sentiment:

> Poor little Heart!
> Did they forget thee?
> Then dinna care! Then dinna care!
>
> Proud little Heart!
> Did they forsake thee?
> Be debonnaire! Be debonnaire!
>
> [214]

She relied at first not only on sentimental expression but on italics, as in "If *He dissolve*," where she dispatches an envoy with a message to her beloved:

> Say - that a *little life* - for *His* -
> Is *leaking - red* -

*His little Spaniel* - tell Him!
*Will He heed?*

[251]

Such a hapless falling-back on italics to carry the emotional impulse of the poem shows the younger Dickinson at a loss for a better means to convey distress. Her ultimate arrival at a stern poetry of heartbreak is a brilliant achievement for a woman brought up within the sentimental conventions of female love and marriage. Her preferred version of the love poem is, in her mature work, the poem of love lost:

> I cannot live with You -
> It would be Life -
>
> . . . . .
>
> I could not die - with You -
>
> . . . . .
>
> Nor could I rise - with You -
>
> . . . . .
>
> So we must meet apart -
> You there - I - here -

[*706]

Such is the skeleton of her most famous love poem, as erotic deprivation becomes one of her most profoundly explored subjects. After the marital fictions of "Title divine, is mine. / The Wife without the Sign - " (*194) and "I'm "wife" - I've finished that - / That other state - " (225), Dickinson recognized the axiom motivating her tireless refreshing of her verse: "Perception of an Object costs / Precise the Object's loss - " (1103). Each individual loss prompted her to new invention; and, as Dr. Johnson said (again, in his life of Waller), "The essence of poetry is invention." But Dickinson's forms of invention might not have pleased Dr. Johnson: he continues by asserting that the pleasure given by poetry "proceeds from the display of those parts of nature which attract, and the concealment of those which repel the imagination." Dickinson certainly writes within the sphere of the attractive, but she does not deny the sphere of the repellent. In her search for equivalents of the suffering inherent in love, Dickinson went so far as to imitate, in her dactylic rhythms ("Gush after Gush, . . . / Scarlet Experiment!"), the successive arterial spurts of pulses of blood from a dying lark "split" by her lover's accusation of infidelity:

> Split the lark - and you'll find the Music -
> Bulb after Bulb, in Silver rolled -
> Scantily dealt to the Summer Morning
> Saved for your Ear, when Lutes be old -
>
> Loose the Flood - you shall find it patent -
> Gush after Gush, reserved for you -
> Scarlet Experiment! Sceptic Thomas!
> Now, do you doubt that your Bird was true?

[*905]

Although this love poem participates in the female lyric tradition of love-suffering, its outraged tone is anything but conventional. And although "The Soul has Bandaged moments - " (*360) participates in the female Gothic tradition of the macabre, Dickinson's plot is more explicitly sexual than we might expect. As the woman speaker suspects her lover of infidelity, he is replaced in her mind by a doppelgänger. In her torment of suspicion, she feels "some ghastly Fright come up / And stop to look at her - " and

> Salute her, with long fingers -
> Caress her freezing hair -
> Sip, Goblin, from the very lips
> The Lover - hovered - o'er -
> Unworthy, that a thought so mean
> Accost a Theme - so - fair -

[*360]

Such encounters with the uncanny take numerous forms in Dickinson as she meditates on the interior specters that haunt the mind (see *407, "One need not be a Chamber - to be Haunted - ").

Instead of using ordinary punctuation, Dickinson chose (for the most part) to place, in her own fair copies, a dash between phrases or even between single words. (She did resort to conventional punctuation, often, in sending poems to friends.) Her dashes served a multitude of purposes. Sometimes, as in "I cannot live with You - " (*706), the dash becomes an enactment of separation: "You - here - I - there - ". It is evident that a comma ("You, here, I, there") would not produce the same effect of painful distance. Or the dash can indicate a break in continuity, as the poet revises a first utterance to a second thought, creating a semi-parenthesis: "For you served God - you know - / Or sought to - ". An ominous dash can correct a narrative: "We passed the Setting Sun - // Or - rather - He passed Us - " (*479). The dash becomes especially significant when it concludes a poem. Dickinson was certainly willing to use forms of normal punctuation, such as the question mark and the exclamation point, when they were appropriate—"Dare you see a Soul at the 'White Heat'?" (*401) or "Gay, Ghastly, Holiday!" (*341). She was equally willing to close with a period when she was inscribing a finished event:

> The Robin for the Crumb
> Returns no syllable
> But long records the Lady's name
> In Silver Chronicle.

> [810]

But Dickinson's concluding punctuation was almost always the dash. What does a final dash convey? Often a state of suspended being: "First - Chill - then Stupor - then the letting go - " (*372). Sometimes a state of continuing action: "Narcotics cannot still the Tooth / That nibbles at the soul - " (*373). Elsewhere, the concluding dash broadens into infinity:

> When Bells stop ringing - Church - begins -
> The Positive - of Bells -
> When Cogs - stop - that's Circumference -
> The Ultimate - of Wheels -

> [601]

In short, each final dash is an invitation to the reader to ponder what it may imply. Because many of Dickinson's manuscripts were lost, our only authority for some poems is a transcription made by a recipient or by one of Dickinson's early editors. In such cases, conventional punctuation may appear, but we cannot be sure it is Dickinson's own. Consider the famous undated poem, its manuscript lost, "My life closed twice before its close" (*1773). As we have it in a transcription by Mabel Todd (herself working from a transcribed copy), it contains a semicolon, commas, and two periods:

> My life closed twice before its close;
> It yet remains to see
> If Immortality unveil
> A third event to me,
>
> So huge, so hopeless to conceive
> As these that twice befell.
> Parting is all we know of heaven,
> And all we need of hell.

Perhaps—as seems likely—Dickinson's original manuscript may have read:

> My life closed - twice - before its close -
> It yet remains to see
> If Immortality unveil
> A third event to me -
>
> So huge - so hopeless to conceive -
> As these that twice befell -
> Parting - is all we know of heaven -
> And all we need - of hell -

As we compare the two possibilities, which seems more Dickinsonian? And what inference does a final dash allow that Todd's terminal period does not? A closing dash assumes a hell still continuing into the present, as the pang of parting goes on in the mourning soul. Although this case is purely speculative, in Dickinson's own manuscripts her processes of thought are secreted not only in her words, but also in her enigmatic dashes.

When we encounter for the first time a poem by Dickinson, we feel that something—as yet unanalyzed—is persuading us to value this arrangement of words and sounds. We find ourselves enabled either to recognize or to remember a human sentiment—or a human presentiment:

> Presentiment - is that long shadow - on the Lawn -
> Indicative that Suns go down -
>
> The notice to the startled Grass
> That Darkness - is about to pass -

[487]

Reading "Presentiment - " we may insert our own experience into Dickinson's symbolic "algebra," and feel the threatening intimation of an end—betrayal, disease, death—that is approaching us. After reading Dickinson's words, we can scarcely see a long shadow on the Lawn without recalling not only the startled Grass and the Darkness it fears, but also the foreboding Latinity of the abstract "Presentiment." The more we read this poet, the more she fills up our atmosphere—natural, intellectual, moral—with her abstractions crossed with her images, with her unexpectedly conversational tones, from grave to gay. After being persuaded by a poem, we begin to ask ourselves how the poet has made it unforgettable, our curiosity launching us into an analysis that persuades us once more, this time in an aesthetic way, of the sentiment governing the poem. In entering Dickinson's poems through both their sentiments and their strategies, we become bearers of her "Slant of light" (*320), of that "internal difference - / Where the Meanings, are - ".

# Selected Poems and Commentaries

✄✄✄ ✄✄✄ ✄✄✄

# 23

> In the name of the Bee -
> And of the Butterfly -
> And of the Breeze - Amen!

This light—but blasphemous—little poem parodies the Trinitarian formula of baptism, initiated by Jesus' commandment to his disciples that they should go forth baptizing all nations "in the name of the Father, and of the Son, and of the Holy Ghost" (Matthew 28:19). That formula relies on an established doctrine (the Trinity), but Dickinson relies—as we first think—on simple alliteration to bind her poem together: Bee, Butterfly, and Breeze make up a natural spring "trinity." But there were other B-nouns that Dickinson could have used: if alliteration were all she was after, she could have said "Bird" in lieu of "Bee," or "Buttercup" in lieu of "Butterfly." We have to look a little more curiously at the import of her three successive nouns.

Dickinson has assumed here the authority of the minister who inaugurates a ritual with his "In the name of the Father" and ends it with his "Amen." As the representative of God, he holds the highest spiritual rank in any nineteenth-century Christian town, surpassing that of magistrate or mayor. It is Dickinson's conviction of her intellectual and aesthetic authority that enables her to stand, however whimsically, against the church, and offer Nature as a better object of worship than the Trinity. The authority of the poem is so sweetly exerted that its sting is felt only after its charm: this mixture of comedy and satire is characteristic of many of Dickinson's early poems.

Dickinson's first editors thought that this short invocation couldn't be a complete poem. Making one poem out of three poems transcribed by Dickinson on a single page, they tacked this little tercet onto the end of their compound assembly. And in fact such a short poem raises the question of what counts as a poem at all. Using "In the name of the Bee - " as our example, we could say that what a poem needs above all is imagination. In this tiny poem we see a first, second, third, and fourth effort of imagination.

First: the poet invents the idea of a parody of a Christian form of words, while retaining a trace of its source in its closing "Amen." And second: the poet decides on the three nouns to be substituted for the three Persons of the Trinity. And third: the poet has to make her trinity of nouns "mean something" in relation to one another (as Father, Son, and Holy Spirit are related). While Bee and Butterfly are named and capitalized living beings (as are the Father and the Son), the Breeze is a motion of air (as was the Holy Spirit at Pentecost). And fourth: the nouns chosen must have a "spiritual" quality, must be symbolic as well as "real"; the Bee (for Being), the Butterfly (Psyche, the resurrected Soul), and the Breeze (the Spirit) all fit that criterion. While the imagination is doing its work, a parallel investigation is being carried out by the ear, creating a link of sound—Bee, Butterfly, Breeze—to substitute for the "familial" links of the Trinity.

Dickinson keeps a secular Sabbath in the open fields, her ear open to the bee's hum, her eye open to the butterfly's flight, and her skin open to the caress of the spring breeze; but she sanctifies them by making them "match" the Christian Trinity. It is her own imaginative effort that Dickinson is "baptizing" here, calling on the authority of Nature, not of God.

[J 18]

# 32

The morns are meeker than they were -
The nuts are getting brown -
The berry's cheek is plumper -
The Rose is out of town.

The maple wears a gayer scarf -
The field a scarlet gown -
Lest I sh'd be old fashioned
I'll put a trinket on.

We see here the look of a Dickinson list before it becomes cryptic, or wild, or eccentric. Nonetheless, the list migrates oddly from category to category: time of day; high-up fruit of nut tree; ground-low fruit of berry vines; an absent flower; a vertical tree; a horizontal field. We can't at first deduce the idea generating this heterogeneous series. But then enlightenment arrives: we are following Dickinson's eye as she goes out on an early-morning walk. She notices first the altered behavior of the morning, with its "meeker" sun, and the comparative tells us she is looking back to a now-vanished season, summer. She looks up at the darkening nuts, then down to the "plumper" berries (both elements suggesting Keats's Autumn, who arrives "to plump the hazel shell / with a sweet kernel"); she grieves at the absence of the Platonic Form of the summer Rose that used to adorn the rose garden. Then the comparative returns, this time one of color; she has gone (like Keats) beyond the kitchen garden and rose bed, and now looks up at the reddening maple, then to the horizontal field, scarlet (with fallen leaves?). The berry's plump cheek may be that of a baby of unspecified gender, but the Rose is a lady, and so are the maple and the field, with their "gayer" scarf and scarlet gown. The comparative "gayer" is asserted in favor of the season's livelier hue, to compensate for its parallel initiating comparative, the "meeker" behavior of the sun. Dickinson's list, like Keats's list at the opening of "To Autumn," is one of directed motion from domestic surroundings to an agricultural field, as the poet explores the new qualities ushered in by a change of season.

As a consequence of her observations, Dickinson decides that she should participate in the new fashion of self-adornment. Will she don a "gayer" scarf? Will she acquire a vivid new "gown"? Her conclusion mediates between the meek and the gay: a trinket is a sign of gaiety, but of a minor sort—a meeker sort, one could say. She satirizes the impositions of fashion on women, but admits she notices the vagaries of its rules; she agrees to observe the new mode, but without ceding to its flamboyance. "Trinket" is an example of Dickinson's characteristic understatement; a trinket is neither encompassing like a scarlet gown nor a substantial accessory on the order of a "gayer scarf." "When fashion changes, I notice, and I'll even obey, but I'll conform in my own New England way; I'll concede to a trinket, but won't go all the way to a scarlet gown." Rebuking the extravagance of noticeable accessories and intensifying color, she defines the plane on which she will live.

Dickinson's economy is such that she implies, rather than states, the sequence of actions generating the order of the list. She casts the poem as an informal report to an absent friend who knew the earlier look of the scenery, when the mornings were bolder, the berries smaller, and the nuts paler. We can imagine reproaches made to Dickinson for her "old-fashioned" plainness of dress—or her "old-fashioned" hymn-meter style. This defense of her own fashion suggests that in her poems we'll find "trinkets" of modernity that have never turned up in ancestral hymns. Her wry self-portrayal as a wearer of a single piece of modest jewelry is the fruit of the unexpected word "trinket." Its last syllable, "-et," makes the word a diminutive, and yet jewelry is, in its essence, adornment: purely decorative, it lacks the utilitarian function of a scarf or gown. The whole point of the difference between other "people" and herself would be lost if Dickinson announced that she would put on a utilitarian pair of new gloves. And despite the apparent superiority of the energetically fashionable maple and field, Dickinson's small joke is that the maple wears a GS ("gayer scarf"), the field an SG ("scarlet gown"): they are obedient to the same conventions, only reversed; and it's a short jump from "scarf" to "scarlet." Only "trinket" both escapes and—with its "-et" echoing "scarlet" —participates in the graphic and phonetic atmosphere with which Dickinson surrounds high fashion.

Dickinson's comedy notwithstanding, one sees that she loves Nature's ever-changing scene, and in part the poem asserts that if there are losses (the brighter sun, the beautiful Rose) there are also gains in gaiety. Yet for all this balanced evaluation, there is a large void in the middle of the poem. The autumn beings are continuous with their former selves—they are merely meeker or plumper or gayer. But the Rose does not appear in a lessened or heightened form of herself: where she was, there is nothing. Loss often prompts human assertions of compensation; but for the disappearance of the Rose, no compensation can be imagined. However mildly Dickinson puts it ("The Rose is out of town"), that absence defeats all the neighboring "sensible" attempts at illustrating the qualities of the season. The Rose is Eros, always—poets are conscious of the anagram—and we see here a plainspoken elegy for Eros.

This poem, which is more ingenious than it first appears, maintains the same rhyme-sound throughout. It exhibits a perfect chiming in "brown," "town," and "gown," but is plainer in its dress, like Dickinson, in its closing simplified "on."

[J 12]

# 90

An altered look about the hills -
A Tyrian light the village fills -
A wider sunrise in the morn -
A deeper twilight on the lawn -
A print of a vermillion foot -
A purple finger on the slope -
A flippant fly upon the pane -
A spider at his trade again -
An added strut in Chanticleer -
A flower expected everywhere -
An axe shrill singing in the woods -
Fern odors on untravelled roads -
All this and more I cannot tell -
A furtive look you know as well -
And Nicodemus' Mystery
Receives its annual reply!

Dickinson did not use titles, and when we see that her first editors headed this poem "April," we can wince at the degree of foreclosure a title brings. The aesthetic point of this list-poem is to keep the reader guessing as a blank canvas is filled in, piece by piece. "An altered look" could be said of the approach of any season. We are not quite sure when "Tyrian" purple might be introduced to the village—at sunset? A "wider" sunrise does not resolve our uncertainty about Dickinson's subject—it might imply summer. A "deeper" twilight might signify winter. The "vermillion foot" of the presiding goddess might be implied in an autumn leaf. Even the "purple finger on the slope" could have to do with spring heather or sunset. But soon Dickinson abandons such riddling invitations to thought, and offers, after her fly and spider, a character indubitably associated with spring: Chanticleer with his "added strut" (like his predecessor in Milton's "L'Allegro," who "stoutly struts his dames before"). "Ah," we say when we come to the radiant line "A flower expected everywhere - ", "the poem is about spring." Yes—but its most conspicuous quality so far has been its maintenance of its opening riddle, drawing the reader into its abstract but unexplained sights of alteration, amplification, and deepening. Dickinson's riddle is rendered null when "April," as a title, heads the poem. And "April" is by no means coterminous with "spring."

We see the resemblance between this list and the parallel one in "The morns are meeker than they were - ", while noting the greater variety and sophistication here. As Dickinson's awed and awakening consciousness brings a happiness to her six lines of natural scenery, we think we are entering a single outdoor landscape. But with the intrusion of the flippant fly (and his alliteration), we are jolted tonally and spatially into another sphere entirely. The fly is very funny, and, with his companions the diligent spider and the strutting rooster, tells us that spring wakes domestic merriment as well as natural grandeur. The happiness rises to its zenith in the plenitude of "A flower expected everywhere - ". "Everywhere" satisfies all expectation.

It is like Dickinson to kill the flower, so to speak, as soon as she has introduced it. It is actually a tree, cousin to the flower, that is killed by "An axe shrill singing in the woods - " as the forester's weapon commits tree-murder with insouciance, singing as it works. The penultimate item in Dickinson's puzzling list is the mysterious "Fern odors on untravelled roads - ", with its hint of an undiscovered country for which she yearns. And the list ends with her mysterious "furtive look" spied by the conspiring addressee, a lover whose own "furtive look" completes the circuit of spring's erotic glances between human beings. The Gospel of John (3:1–21) tells the story of how Nicodemus, a Pharisee, not wanting to be observed by other Pharisees, came by night to where Jesus was. Perhaps this secret quester is the origin of Dickinson's rare use of "furtive," a word which appears in the finished poems only here, although she once considered it for inclusion, but rejected it, in "The inundation of the Spring" (1423, J 1425).

With the introduction of Nicodemus, Dickinson can join her mysteries of spring to the mystery of internal rebirth. To Nicodemus, Jesus says: "Except a man be born again, he cannot see the kingdom of God." After Nicodemus counters, reasonably enough, "How can a man be born when he is old? Can he enter the second time into his mother's womb, and be born?" Jesus replies, "Except a man be born of water and of the Spirit, he cannot enter into the kingdom of God." Natural species, "born again," return in spring in identical form; so if one entertains doubts (as Dickinson did) of a rebirth in Jesus, one finds "Nicodemus' Mystery" sufficiently and literally answered by the annual reawakening of the natural world. It is startling to find Nicodemus, summoned from his wholly other context in the Gospel, keeping company with the flippant fly and Chanticleer. We thought we had "solved" Dickinson's descriptive riddle when we encountered the flower expected everywhere, but we hadn't. Dickinson's natural riddle is a spiritual riddle as well: How is one to find a rebirth of the spirit and of desire? Rather than sending Nicodemus to baptismal water and the spirit, Dickinson sends him to the expected flower (and the rest of her list, comic as well as tender). We can hardly tell whether she is naturalizing the spiritual or spiritualizing the natural; often the two converge in her mind. The "vermillion foot" is surely no human foot, but rather the rosy foot of Spring; yet it, like the alliterating purple finger, casts a "human" color on the landscape, preparing the arrival of the human "look."

The poem binds its surprising variety of list-items closely together by housing them in couplets (a form not only primitive, like the first season, but intellectual, like Nicodemus' question and Jesus' reply). We could scarcely associate Chanticleer and the "flower expected everywhere" if they didn't rhyme; but once we see the rhyme, we see Dickinson's union of the humorous and the vernal.

[J 140]

# 122

These are the days when Birds come back -
A very few - a Bird or two -
To take a backward look.

These are the days when skies resume
The old - old sophistries of June -
A blue and gold mistake.

Oh fraud that cannot cheat the Bee.
Almost thy plausibility
Induces my belief,

Till ranks of seeds their witness bear -
And softly thro' the altered air
Hurries a timid leaf.

Oh sacrament of summer days,
Oh Last Communion in the Haze -
Permit a child to join -

Thy sacred emblems to partake -
Thy consecrated bread to take
And thine immortal wine!

Although the poem was cast, in all of Dickinson's fair copies, into six stanzas, its rhyme shapes it into three parts, rhyming (except for lines one and two) *aabccb:* "Bee . . . plausibility . . . belief"; "bear . . . air . . . leaf"—two tetrameter couplets, each followed by a trimeter which binds, by its rhyme, every two stanzas together, making three double-stanzas. Because Dickinson does not repeat this strategy, the form remains unique.

The poem goes in and out of direct address to its "Indian Summer" (the title the first editors gave it). Dickinson addresses the season as "Oh fraud," "Oh sacrament," and "Oh Last Communion"—epithets summing up in brief the evolving course of her feelings. She begins remotely, describing the season in the third person: "These are the days . . . These are the days." But she cannot remain fixed in her "objective" critique of what she initially calls "The old - old sophistries of June - " (as if June, seeming to promise eternal skies of blue and gold, were a philosopher manipulating the truth) and secondly names as "a mistake" (as though June were a prophet in error). Defending the wisdom of bees against Keats's pity ("until they think warm days can never cease"), Dickinson vigorously asserts that they were not deceived, that the season's "fraud" (as if Indian Summer is a plausible swindler) cannot "cheat the bee."

But what of herself? Abandoning her resentment that she was so deeply deceived by the "sophistries" of June that she could at first see only a "fraud" in their brief autumn recurrence, she admits gratitude for the unexpected return of a departed and despaired-of warmth. Like the birds, she takes a "backward" look; with her usual determined objectivity, she substitutes that adjective for her pathetic earlier variants "final" and "parting," since neither "backward" (merely directional) nor "parting" (sentimentally anthropomorphic) declare termination as "final" does.

The poem turns on the "until" of stanza 4, ushering in the certainty that fall has come, as seeds "bear witness" to the disappearance of flowers, and the "timid leaf," afraid of the experience of falling, "softly . . . hurries" to the ground as the fall wind shakes the boughs. Why must Dickinson now turn into a child? Because only a child can feel the innocent religious belief which the adult skeptic cannot share. As a child, the poet can resume her faith in the sacrament of the Eucharist, in which the bread and wine are emblems of Christ's body and blood. Taking her "Last Communion," she will "partake" in the religious emblems and "take" consecrated bread and immortal wine, while her adult self looks on in tender memory of the child's trust. For her original choice of "break," Dickinson substitutes "take," dropping active participation in the breaking of material bread in favor of a more neutral verb derived immediately from its preceding cousin, "partake." In this "Communion," because it is a virtual one, she can "partake" of emblems, but cannot "break" actual bread. The poem's permitted fantasy of childlike belief ingeniously both contradicts and ratifies the earlier adult awakening from Nature's sophistical promise of eternal joy (in spring, in love, in youth). Yes, she can dream again, in the autumn haze, of untroubled belief, but it is not available to her except in nostalgic remembrance.

Why does Dickinson make her six-stanza poem also a three-part one (by rhyme) and a two-part one (turning on the hinge-word "Till")? The six-stanza shape represents the six temporal segments of her evolving plot, from "These are the days" to a "last Communion"; the three rhyming-units (introduced by "These are"; "Oh fraud"; and "Oh Sacrament") track her emotional changes from objectivity through resentment to yearning; and the solemn binary shape, divided by the "Till" to which the seeds bear reliable witness, leads us to—and from—the cusp where the balm of Indian Summer returns to the "altered air" of true autumn. Dickinson often combines two or more "shapes" in a single poem to alert her reader to the separate import of each superimposed division, each of which is real, and each of which bears meaning, so that we are here reading three poems at once: a poem of six parts, another of three parts, and another of two parts.

The closing rhyme of "join" and "wine" is legitimated by earlier poetic practice, while the slant rhyming of "back," "look," and "mistake"—in the midst of other, perfectly conventional rhymes—is pure Dickinson. The monosyllabic and disyllabic rhyme-words are conventional, too, but the "unbalanced" rhyme of the monosyllabic "Bee" with the five-syllable "plausibility" enacts the difference between the frankly real and a complex deceptiveness.

[J 130]

# 124

Safe in their Alabaster Chambers -
Untouched by Morning -
And untouched by noon -
Sleep the meek members of the Resurrection,
Rafter of Satin and Roof of Stone -

Grand go the Years,
In the Crescent above them -
Worlds scoop their Arcs -
And Firmaments - row -
Diadems - drop -
And Doges - surrender -
Soundless as Dots,
On a Disc of Snow.

The second stanza of this famous poem exists in three versions (given be-
low). Because Dickinson's most recent editor, Ralph Franklin, takes as his
"reading text" the last version of each poem, he has line 4 begin with "Sleep"
—derived from a copy sent by Dickinson to Higginson in 1862—rather than
"Lie," as in the last copy the poet made for herself, transcribed in Fascicle 10
around 1861 (the first version, using "Sleep," was transcribed in Fascicle 6,
about 1859). It seems to me that Dickinson may have substituted "Sleep" in
Higginson's copy because the conventional religious phrase is "to fall asleep
in Christ." In 1 Corinthians 17–18, Paul says, "And if Christ be not raised,
your faith is vain. . . . Then they also which are fallen asleep in Christ are per-
ished," implying that the Christian dead *will* be awakened from their sleep:
their faith is not vain, since Christ was resurrected. Dickinson doubted that
the dead would be raised; that is why, presumably, she eventually rejected her
1859 exact allusion to Paul for an allusion that—by substituting "Lie," the
conventional opening verb on a gravestone, "Here lies"—refutes Paul on res-
urrection, and emphasizes instead the buried body. I believe that the poem
should be anthologized in the future with "Lie." (The poem was printed in

the *Springfield Daily Republican* in 1862; that version used the word "Sleep" and redoubled the effect of that "Christian" word by bearing a Christian title, "The Sleeping," which implies a resurrection.)

It is not merely Dickinson's revision of "Sleep" to "Lie" that makes this poem blasphemous. The second stanza of the original poem, as transcribed in Fascicle 6 (but not present in Franklin's *Reading Edition*), is deeply ironic, since nature's sounds cannot reach the "stolid" dead:

> Light laughs the breeze
> In her Castle above them -
> Babbles the Bee in a stolid Ear,
> Pipe the sweet Birds in ignorant cadence -
> Ah, what sagacity perished here!

Dickinson's transcriptions of the sounds made by happy and "ignorant" natural forces (the breeze's laugh, the Bee's babble, the sweet Birds' piping) with the description of the region inhabited by air as a "Castle"—give nature's aristocratic if unconscious personages supremacy over the "stolid" deafness of the corpses underground. The ironic epitaph—"Ah, what sagacity perished here!"—also refutes Paul's assurances of resurrection. His obliterative alternative to resurrection—the dead are "perished" if Christ is not raised—is quoted exactly in the last line of the stanza. "Sagacity" perishes, but nature's laughing ignorance, perpetually resurrected, lasts forever.

When, in 1861, Dickinson's sister-in-law Susan criticized the second stanza, Dickinson sent her a new version of the poem, substituting "Lie" for "Sleep" in the first stanza, and writing an entirely new second stanza which speeds exhilaratingly out from the provincial cemetery of the first stanza to a universe of cosmic time and space that reveals the utter insignificance of the dead (even if they are Monarchs or Doges):

> Grand go the Years - in the Crescent - above them -
> Worlds scoop their Arcs -
> And Firmaments - row -
> Diadems - drop - and Doges - surrender -
> Soundless as dots - on a Disc of snow -

Dickinson never put her dash-pauses to better use. Each one implies a questioning mind seeking the right phrase, as it observes event after event. The world above the dead is now not a natural paradise, but a forbidding unreachable zodiacal "Crescent"; Worlds other than ours are inventing their orbits, scooping them in air; plural Firmaments (by contrast to our single one) row in the ocean of space. And when a queen (more likely here than a king, to serve as female counterpart to the unquestionably male Doge) dies, what happens to her diadem? It drops from her sinking head. And what happens to Venetian power? It surrenders to the superior force of death. Dickinson binds together her sequences of deaths by interwoven alliteration (first "d" for Death, then "s," perhaps for cessation) to emphasize their inevitability: "Diadems drop . . . Doges . . . dots . . . Disc; surrender . . . Soundless . . . snow." Just as her "d" words—with the exception of "drop"—include "s" ("Diadems," "Doges," "dots," "Disc"), her "s" words (except for "snow") include "d" ("surrender," "Soundless"). The braid of extinction is woven too tight for anyone to escape its grasp.

But why the dots and the Disc? These are Dickinson's most oblique abstractions. Her field of snow is, as a disk, circular in shape, and perhaps alludes here to "The (apparently flat) surface or 'face' of the sun, the moon, or a planet, as it appears to the eye" (*OED,* s.v. "disk," 4a). Our planet, seen from afar, in the Arctic light of death, is rather like our full moon—a white disk, frozen into snow. On it have fallen "dots," tiny miniatures of the shape of the disk—like fallen drops of rain on snow (almost colorless, almost indistinguishable from the Disc's surface, and soon to disappear). In the cosmic distance, human deaths, even the fall of crowns, cannot be heard. The world-altering effects of a change of earthly government are insignificant to the cosmic observer-from-afar. Dickinson's imagination, as many have remarked, is at its most powerful when it moves out into cosmic circumference.

But Susan did not like this tremendous substituted second stanza ("It does not go with the ghostly shimmer of the first verse as well as the other one"). Although Susan tried to persuade Dickinson to drop both second stanzas ("the first verse is complete in itself; it needs no other, and can't be coupled"), Dickinson, persisting, sent a new version of the second stanza (eventually transcribed into Fascicle 10) with the note, "Is *this frostier?*" The poet's conviction of the deadness of the dead, that they are "eclipsed" rather than "sleeping," brings a new chill to the Alabaster Chambers, which now lack any satin-lined comfort. The Chambers are so cold that the echoes of spring zephyrs, encountering them, undergo rigor mortis, and the aristocratic alabaster has mutated into memorial marble, with frosted windows forbidding sight and a numb door that can never open:

> Springs - shake the Sills -
> But - the Echoes - stiffen -
> Hoar - is the Window - and numb - the door -
> Tribes of Eclipse - in Tents of Marble -
> Staples of Ages - have buckled - there -

Just as the pious townspeople thought they were "safe" in their graves, so these "tribes" thought they were nomadic, their burial "tents" pitched temporarily until they could move to heavenly mansions, where they could "[shine] as the stars for ever and ever" (Daniel 12.3). Instead they are eclipsed, and their cloth "tents," in rigor mortis like the spring echoes, stiffen to marble. Not only that; the dead have not moved for ages. Like the "stapled feet" of those awaiting execution in "They put Us far apart - " (*708, J 474), they are fastened, by immemorial metallic staples, in their tombs. Susan's reaction to this stanza is not recorded, but Higginson in 1890 printed, in the *Christian Union,* the whole first version and appended this second substituted stanza, commenting, as Franklin tells us, that the stanza struck "a note too fine to be lost."

Dickinson went on to revise this newly substituted stanza, but although she transcribed the revision into Fascicle 10, there is no record of her sending it to Susan. The revision, with its Arctic landscape, becomes even more frigid and threatening and absolute than its predecessor, not allowing, within its total sealed silence, even a stiffening echo of resurrected birdsong. Although Dickinson concedes that spring in the Arctic produces some motion, as a warmer sun allows frosts to "unhook" and icicles to "crawl" out from caverns, human death is irreversible; no sun will rise to light its midnight or warm its chill:

> Springs - shake the seals -
> But the silence - stiffens -
> Frosts unhook - in the Northern Zones -

Icicles - crawl from polar Caverns -
Midnight in Marble -
Refutes - the Suns -

Although Dickinson pluralizes "Sun" into "Suns" (perhaps to avoid the possible Christian pun "Sun/Son"), there could be no firmer repudiation of the resurrection than this perpetual and permanent Midnight that will not allow successive Suns to rise. The Suns here (normally rising predictably every morning) resemble supposedly impregnable philosophical propositions (such as Edgar's "The worst returns to laughter" in *King Lear*). But the logic of death "refutes" them permanently and conclusively (there is no such thing as a temporary or merely apparent refutation).

The pious Christian belief that one is "safe" in one's death chamber is articulated with mordant irony in Dickinson's first line. We know this because the speaker of the poem immediately corrects this naïve faith with her own counter-remark that being "safe" entails total separation from all life, even that of the Sun: the dead are "untouched" by Morning light and "untouched" by noon warmth. Although they are patiently "meek," willing to await the great morning that will mean Resurrection, that morn will never come. In their past faith, they thought themselves members of one spiritual assembly, the resurrective gathering of the Last Day; but now each lies in an isolated tomb. The Amherst cemetery where Dickinson now lies is full of Dickinsons—and those "meek members of the Resurrection" must have seemed to her like ancestors and cousins. She alone distinguishes herself from the family flock—the unbeliever commenting on the deluded faithful.

[J 216]

# 129

Our lives are Swiss -
So still - so Cool -
Till some odd afternoon
The Alps neglect their Curtains
And we look farther on!

*Italy* stands the other side!
While like a guard between -
The solemn Alps -
The siren Alps
Forever intervene!

It is hard to imagine why Dickinson's first editors entitled this poem "Alpine Glow": the Alps in it don't glow, although perhaps the blocked *"Italy"* might, if only one could get there. Dickinson frequently imagines something opaque impeding vision or access. Here, while the blocking Alps are obscured by mist, one cannot even speculate about what lies beyond; but when they let down their guard, and forget to draw the curtain over their landscape, one can see, beyond the passes, an ecstatic vista. The still, cool, white life of an Alpine region remains untroubled until one senses a possible warmth. If only one could traverse the mountains! These Alps, in their monumentality, resemble the Decalogue, which "intervenes" between ourselves and our desires: "Thou shalt not" say the *solemn* Alps. But just as the thing forbidden is the most desired, so the peaks are also the *siren* Alps, resembling Homer's sexual sirens luring seamen to destruction. The binding sound between the two stanzas is "s": "Swiss" and "still" introduce the sound as one of propriety and quiet. But those adjectives are then confronted with the contradictory adjectives "solemn" (denoting moral authority and duty) and "siren" (denoting transgressive sexual appetite).

The moral poles of the poem are thus set before us in three sentences, each of which ends with an exclamation mark. The first expresses the excitement of unobstructed vision after the clouds lift; the second the exalted vision of an Eden that could be ours had not God's flaming sword (Genesis 3:24), here transmuted into the secular Alps, barred us from it; and the third denotes the exclamatory despair elicited by the damning word "forever." *Paradise Lost* promises us that our loss of Eden will last only until a "greater man" —Milton's "Son of God"—shall "restore us, and regain the blissful seat." Dickinson offers no such promise; our banishment is permanent.

After the proper iambs of the first stanza, the dactylic *"Italy . . . !"* comes like a shout of discovery; but it is immediately rebuked by the flaming sword of a counter-dactyl, "While like a [guard between]," and the rest of the poem subsides into the iambs of its beginning. At first the Alps seem feminine to Dickinson: they "neglect their Curtains" as she might herself. But then, as they turn into "a guard" paralleling the fearful "Cherubims" of Genesis at Eden's gate, they are masculinized. Their two alliterating adjectives—a "solemn" authority, a "siren" seductiveness—repeat the tension between the masculine and the feminine, but ascribe them both to the single moral realm of forbidding and the forbidden. Just as Dickinson has "rewritten" Genesis here, she will also, a bit later, rewrite her past despair into a hope of an erotic Eden. In a poem firm in recurrent trochees, taking its metrical signature from its governing trochaic noun, "Eden," (205, J 211), she writes:

> Come slowly - Eden!
> Lips unused to Thee -
> Bashful - sip thy Jessamines -
> As the fainting Bee -
>
> Reaching late his flower,
> Round her chamber hums -
> Counts his nectars -
> Enters - and is lost in Balms.

The rhythmic pattern of the first stanza, 3-3-4-3, changes in the second stanza to 3-3-2-4, Dickinson's last two dashes enacting the gradual penetration of the flower by the Bee.

[J 80]

# 134

Did the Harebell loose her girdle
To the lover Bee
Would the Bee the Harebell *hallow*
Much as formerly?

Did the "Paradise" - *persuaded* -
Yield her moat of pearl -
Would the Eden *be* an Eden,
Or the Earl - an *Earl?*

This is one of the early poems that was not entered into a fascicle; it is complete (in pencil), but not "preserved" in ink, perhaps because of Dickinson's judgment on its quality. Another Eden poem, it begins with an already anthropomorphized "lover Bee" and a willingly uncinctured flower (a "girdle" here is merely a belt). But Dickinson goes on to the actual human realm, introducing an "Earl" and his female "Paradise." The bourgeois taboo on premarital sexual intercourse—not from fear of pregnancy but from fear that the man will lose respect for the woman—is the object of Dickinson's mocking satire. Social shame always attached itself conventionally (as in *The Scarlet Letter*) to the no-longer-virginal woman; no one seemed to wonder whether a woman would respect a "fallen" man, or whether the world should condemn him as it does her.

After implying that nobody would pose the absurd question of the first stanza (because in the society of nature there are no sexual morals or conventions, let alone any "hallowing"), Dickinson comes to the human instance, which she locates at the highest English aristocratic rank, that of Earl (the word, and the consequent rank, perhaps prompted by the necessity of finding a rhyme for "pearl"). If the man is an Earl, and the woman, by convention, has to be idealized beyond the man, what can we name her but "Paradise," the highest concept of habitation? Like the twelve gates of Paradise, to which Dickinson consciously alludes, the woman manifests herself (enclosed in her "moat") as a single pearl: "And the twelve gates were twelve pearls: every several gate was of one pearl" (Revelation 21:21). After asking—in accordance with convention—whether a voluntarily compliant woman, loosing her own "girdle," would still, after intercourse, be an "Eden," Dickinson advances to the never-posed question of whether premarital intercourse would ever disgrace an Earl. She knows that the social world, allowing its presumably libertine aristocracy wide freedom of behavior, would not dream of barring from its drawing rooms an unchaste Earl.

The archness of the two parallel ironic questions lightens the solemn terms normally employed by church and family to argue the importance of virginity. The intensity of the italic *"hallow"* suggests the church; the italicized *"persuaded"* suggests the social form of courting; the italicized *"be"* raises the philosophical question of a change in existential status after intercourse; and the italicized *"Earl"* queries the moral stability of rank. The trochees mimic the usual intonation of an interrogative auxiliary verb—"Did ... Would ... Did ... Would"—while the precisely parallel syntax of the two stanzas superimposes the second (supposedly rational) query onto the absurd first one. Dickinson's original editors mildly named this poem "Possession"—a neutral word for a poem proposing such a subversive view of sexual activity, in which the woman and man are no more guilty than the Harebell and her Bee. Questions without answers will remain a favorite resource for Dickinson.

[J 213]

# 138

> To fight aloud, is very brave -
> But *gallanter,* I know
> Who charge within the bosom
> The Cavalry of Wo -
>
> Who win, and nations do not see -
> Who fall - and none observe -
> Whose dying eyes, no Country
> Regards with patriot love -
>
> We trust, in plumed procession
> For such, the Angels go -
> Rank after Rank, with even feet -
> And Uniforms of snow.

To gather a firmer sense of Dickinson's preferred way of treating her theme (the heroism of unobserved lives), we might compare her poem to a sonnet by Hopkins that deals with the same theme and that exemplifies it in the humble (but eventually canonized) Jesuit doorkeeper Alphonsus Rodriguez. Like Dickinson, Hopkins resorts to a military comparison:

> Honour is flashed off exploit, so we say;
> And those strokes once that gashed flesh or galled shield
> Should tongue that time now, trumpet now that field,
> And, on the fighter, forge his glorious day.
> On Christ they do and on the martyr may,
> But be the war within, the brand we wield
> Unseen, the heroic breast not outward-steeled,
> Earth hears no hurtle then from fiercest fray.

Compared to these vaulting lines, how plainspoken—even childish—seems Dickinson's style in its primer-iambics: "To fight aloud, is very brave - ". We shall have to see what she does with that voice as the poem evolves. Like Dickinson intuiting angels, Hopkins closes with reference to another, spiritual, realm that honors these quiet heroes: God estimates such a life rightly, and He

> Could crowd career with conquest while there went
> Those years and years by of world without event
> That in Majorca Alfonso watched the door.

We notice that after his martial octave, Hopkins has grown much more plain-spoken in his close, telling us that the earlier flashing exploits of diction and syntax belong to the active life; to the contemplative life (after a last salute to the martial as he transfers its vocabulary to the saint's career crowded with conquest) belongs more properly the plain style suitable to a world without event.

Looking back to Dickinson, we see that her comparison of two kinds of gallantry, the "loud" and the silent, is phrased first positively (*"gallanter"*) and then, to our surprise, negatively, as though she were making a negative from a positive print. The active hero's triumphs are seen by nations; his fall is observed by comrades; his death is regarded by his country "with patriot love." The silent hero or heroine, who faces a powerful cavalry of woe within, lives a life of subtracted homage: there are no nations watching such victories, no comrades mourning this fall, no proud Country meeting dying eyes with a gaze of grateful love. The childish speaker of the first line is, we see, speaking the naïve language of outward fights; the speaker of the second stanza has decided to negate the myth of the war hero and his popularity. There is by now a standoff: if Dickinson cannot use military language without complicity in its manner of evaluating heroism, to what language can she resort? To the language of luxury, we see with astonishment—as legions of angels ("Rank after Rank," angels to archangels to seraphim) pay homage in "plumed procession"—the most literary phrase in the poem, characterizing the angels by their downy wings, a sign of their regality. The uniforms of armies are always colored—Dickinson has noticed—with hues of smart pride, but the angels need no such advertising of their affiliations or energies. Pure among the pure, they are almost transparent in their "Uniforms of snow," unobtrusive in the gliding of their "even feet."

The anaphora of anonymity binding together stanzas 1 and 2—"Who charge . . . Who win . . . Who fall . . . Whose dying eyes"—is, as I have said, first positive and then negative, but it all refers to the silent heroes or heroines. To drop the anaphora—as Dickinson does in her last stanza—is to turn away from characterizing the silent inner warriors by relative clauses of any sort. She shifts her gaze from the earthly realm of disregard to a heavenly one of reward, where processions that honor the dead are composed not of soldiers and brass bands, but of legions of angels. "We trust," says Dickinson, and we recall Tennyson's "we trust" in *In Memoriam,* the word "trust" always arriving with an admixture of doubt:

> O yet we trust that somehow good
> Will be the final goal of ill . . .
>
> Behold, we know not anything;
> I can but trust that good shall fall
> At last—far off—at last, to all,
> And every winter change to spring.

But whereas Tennyson ends his canto in despair (as "An infant crying in the night"), Dickinson maintains her trust. The change from her initial "I" ("But *gallanter,* I know") to a final collective "we" ("We trust, in plumed procession") enables the turn to religious trust: her voice becomes that of a nation, rather than that of a single poet. To ratify the union of the two voices, she gives the rhymes associated with her closing "we" ("go" and "snow") the same vowel sound as that of the rhymes linked to the opening "I" (with its "know" and "Wo"). She, with her subtle ear, did not do such things unconsciously: the mutation of "I" into "we" is marked as a fusion rather than as a distinction.

[J 126]

# 165

I have never seen "Volcanoes" -
But, when Travellers tell
How those old - phlegmatic mountains
Usually so still -

Bear within - appalling Ordnance,
Fire, and smoke, and gun -
Taking Villages for breakfast,
And appalling Men -

If the stillness is Volcanic
In the human face
When upon a pain Titanic
Features keep their place -

If, at length, the smouldering anguish
Will not overcome,
And the palpitating Vineyard
In the dust, be thrown?

If some loving Antiquary,
On Resumption Morn,
Will not cry with joy, "Pompeii"!
To the Hills return!

This poem tells of "a pain Titanic" repressed by the one suffering it, a pain expressed by no change of feature on the "human face" of the sufferer. Dickinson had been reading Keats: his *Hyperion* (published 1820) describes (in Book II, lines 22–28) the vanquished and fallen Titans convulsed with pain. The strongest of them exhibit a "Volcanic" convulsion. They

Were pent in regions of laborious breath;
Dungeon'd in opaque element, to keep
Their clench\`ed teeth still clench'd, and all their limbs

Lock'd up like veins of metal, crampt and screw'd;
Without a motion, save of their big hearts
Heaving in pain, and horribly convuls'd
With sanguine feverous boiling gurge of pulse.

Under the apparently unmoved face of Dickinson's protagonist boils the maelstrom of blood evoked by Keats, resembling the seething magma of a volcano preparing for eruption. It is this kind of eruption that Dickinson prophesies for the sufferer, when the "smouldering anguish" will lay waste the "palpitating Vineyard" and throw it in the dust. This seems a poem of erotic loss or betrayal undergone, followed by a subsequent great effort at suppression. Dickinson writes, in "I shall not murmur if at last" (1429, J 1410) of a similar repression in her own case, as she conceals a secret from her intimates (in a poem addressed, but apparently not sent, to her friend Catherine Anthon):

> Divulging it would rest my Heart
> But it would ravage theirs -
> Why, Katie, Treason has a Voice -
> But mine - dispels - in Tears.

Even treason is permitted utterance; but like the girl mentioned by Viola in *Twelfth Night* who "never told her love, / But let concealment, like a worm i' the bud / Feed on her damask cheek," Dickinson's speaker in "I shall not murmur if at last" and the sufferer in "I have never seen 'Volcanoes' - " are destroyed by the secret they harbor.

In several poems, Dickinson compares the inner life, implicitly or explicitly, to a Volcano. Her meditation on "A still - Volcano - Life - " (517, J 601) ends with the hideous consequences of an eruption: the "hissing Corals" of the Volcano, those "lips that never lie," in a single action "part - and shut - / And Cities - ooze away - ". But in the earlier "I have never seen 'Volcanoes' - " Dickinson can still imagine a happy ending. (In envisaging it, she "blasphemously" redefines the action of the last day, from "resurrection"—an act performed by God on the passive dead—to "resumption"—an act by which the dead actively take back, by themselves, their living bodies.) On "Resumption Morn" Pompeii too shall reappear, summoned not by the trumpet of Gabriel but by the voice of "some loving Antiquary" (perhaps the lover whose death or permanent absence caused the intolerable pain under the stoic human face). He will "cry with joy," calling his beloved Pompeii to return to her ancient hills, now permanently immune to harm.

This complicated poem voices its last three stanzas in a long hypothesis, which would read, in paraphrase: "If it is not serenity one sees on this human face, but rather repression of pain, will not, at length, the smouldering anguish overcome the stoicism, and destroy the palpitating heart behind that face? And if that is so, will there not be, on the Last Day, some loving Antiquary, who will summon with joy his 'resumed' Pompeii?" What, we ask, necessitates Dickinson's convoluted phrasing of the possible future narrative of the broken heart? The syntax attempts to coerce the listener into a "Yes"— "Yes, the anguish will eventually burst into flame and lay waste the beating heart, but Pompeii will live again, along with her loving Antiquary, and they will be together once more." But Dickinson, with her ever-present doubt of an afterlife, can make no such confident prophecy of what is to come; instead she must resort to her hypothetical speculations and her imagined "Resumption Morn."

When we have seen the proliferating hypotheses of the last three stanzas, we are better placed to understand the two stanzas preceding them. These purport to represent what the stay-at-home speaker has been told by Travellers about eruptions: that the mountains, usually quiescent, actually bear within them something resembling not only the most appalling engines of military destruction but also the mythical dragons breathing fire on villages and eating men. The mountains are doubly animated by these comparisons: they are weapons of destruction ("Fire, and smoke, and gun - "), but they are also monsters "Taking Villages for breakfast." The strangest move Dickinson makes in stanza 2 is to affix the same word, "appalling," to both Ordnance and Men. The word appears as two different parts of speech, adjective and verb: appalling Ordnance is appalling Men. This exact reciprocity of attack and response compounds fire and victim into a single consuming and consumed dyad, a fusion reinforced in the same stanza by the grim rhyme of "gun" with "Men."

Dickinson's affectation of ingenuous naïveté ("I have never seen . . . those old - phlegmatic mountains . . . Taking Villages for breakfast") disappears once she experiences a real volcano in her heart, from which the legend takes on violent actuality. As she attempts to prophesy (in her uncertain hypotheses) her own future, her language becomes ever more convoluted, her allusiveness ever more complex (passing from the vineyards of the living Pompeii laid waste by Vesuvius, to the archaeological excavations of the buried city, to a correction of the Christian fable of Resurrection). Her "naïve" beginnings are almost always a foil to a sophisticated end.

[J 175]

# 181

A *wounded* Deer - leaps highest -
I've heard the Hunter tell -
'Tis but the extasy of *death* -
And then the Brake is still!

The *smitten* Rock that gushes!
The *trampled* Steel that springs!
A Cheek is always redder
Just where the Hectic stings!

Mirth is the mail of Anguish -
In which it cautious Arm,
Lest Anybody spy the blood
And "you're hurt" exclaim!

Behold a mirthful member of the household—volatile, resilient, pink-cheeked, gushing with expressiveness. What is the cause of this outward display of social animation? It is that she lives in anguish, hectic with fever, smitten and trampled, close to extinction from pain—but does not want the sympathy of others. So that her suffering will not be perceived, she assumes an attitude of mirth, concealing from the world the fatal wound that is bleeding still. Five exclamation marks italicize the unnaturalness of her condition. "How," she wonders, "can they not know what I am truly feeling? Haven't they been told, as I have, that an unnaturally high leap is, in a deer, the sign not of vitality but of a death-throe? Haven't they read in the Bible how the desert rock had to be smitten by Moses before it gushed forth its water? Can't they imagine how a convex shield, fallen from a dead soldier and trampled by the cavalry, springs back again and again? Don't they know that a hectic flush on the cheek is the sign of consumption? How can they not guess the lethal cause when they see me so unnaturally, reactively gay?" But lest they intuit the truth, and utter a word of sympathy, she arms herself with the chain mail of mirth—and succeeds too well in making herself invulnerable. It would be easier to die from the already-inflicted wound than to wear this sort of social armor forever.

Dickinson's adverbial use of "cautious"—"Anguish cautiously arms itself with the mail of Mirth lest anyone spy her wound"—caused a persistent series of misprints, corrections, and substitutions (the word appears successively as "cautiouns," "caution," "cautious" ("corrected" by the printer to "cautions"), "cautious," "caution." It was not until 1945, with the appearance of the Dickinson collection *Bolts of Melody,* that the poem achieved its permanent correct form. This little editorial vagary, extending over fifty-five years, represents one of the many difficulties posed to editors by the Dickinson materials. Dickinson's peculiarities of grammar, here a subjunctive ("Arm") to replace a normal present tense ("Arms"), did not make the first editing easy.

In my paraphrase of the poem, I wrote, "She arms herself with the chain mail of mirth," but that is not quite accurate. The lines offer an allegorical Mirth: "Mirth is the mail of Anguish - ". "Anguish" is the "it" of the next line: "In which it [Anguish] cautious[ly] Arm[s] [itself]." The two lines together act as an aphorism summing up, in general terms, all the excessive display (leaping, gushing, springing) that has gone before. Dickinson might well have continued to the end, as she often does, in that aphoristic mode. Instead, the poem reverts acutely to the domestic scene and the possibility of excruciating sympathy that lurks there. The colloquiality of "You're hurt!" hurtles against the dry epigram, "Mirth is the mail of Anguish - ", as actual blood invades the mental determination to conceal. Just as the Hunter, the Deer, and the Brake lend some actuality to the beginning, so the visible blood does to the close; in between, as the sufferer seeks for more exempla—the Rock, the Steel, the Cheek—she never attempts even a sketchy narrative of the sort animating the little fable of the wounded Deer. In the exempla, everything is already over: the Rock has been smitten, the Steel has been trampled, the Cheek is already diseased.

The most noticeable stylistic gesture in the poem is the persistence of feminine endings ("highest, gushes, redder, Anguish") which take their sonic cue from the crucial two-syllable *"wounded."* The anomalous "masculine" end-words are *"death"* and "blood"—both, one might say, truncated, lacking, by design, the final weak syllable common to their four counterparts. The abrupt cessation of life is stated by the monosyllable *"death,"* threatened by the monosyllable "blood."

[J 165]

# 187

Through the Straight Pass of Suffering
The Martyrs even trod -
Their feet upon Temptation -
Their faces - upon God -

A Stately - Shriven Company -
Convulsion playing round -
Harmless as Streaks of Meteor -
Upon a Planet's Bond -

Their faith the Everlasting Troth -
Their Expectation - fair -
The Needle to the North Degree
Wades so - through Polar Air -

In the middle of this poem we see a scene of celestial danger: a Planet hangs in the sky, within the bonds of its orbit, when suddenly there streaks by it the unloosed energy of a Meteor. This convulsion of matter does not hurt the Planet, however; unharmed, the Planet continues on its way. Dickinson was always aware of "Convulsion playing round - ", whether the convulsion was one of illness or death, grief or loss, rage or madness, doubt or fear. Electricity animates the atmosphere whenever she is in a state of high excitement, and the lulls in that electrical storm, occasioned by natural beauty or warmth of feeling, were moments she prized. Still, the vibrations of her nerves made her constantly alert to their oscillating state between anxiety and pleasure—or to their deadness, when pain numbed them. Convulsion seemed to her to inhabit the air she lived in, and she emerged from its worst onslaughts badly shaken. She envies those Martyrs whose faith preserved them from spiritual harm when they encountered violent Meteors—the headsman's axe, the burning grill—but that envy is mixed, here, with an unwillingness to share the martyrs' "Polar Air." She chooses Martyrs as her topic, rather than Saints, because they are "witnesses" (the etymology of their category), public saints, if you will. Others watch them, and are edified, as they suffer in extremis. Their faith is open to inspection even unto death.

Like the angels "with even feet" who go in plumed procession for the unsung dead of the inner life in "To fight aloud, is very brave - " (*138, J 126), the martyrs walk with "even" tread. Nothing disturbs them, nothing affrights them. They have conquered Temptation, now vanquished under their feet; but if there was a struggle in that victory, no trace of that conflict now remains. Their conquest of evil seems frictionless, their faith unmixed with fear. George Meredith, contemplating, like Dickinson, the impassive serenity of celestial power, bitterly criticized a painting by Raphael that he saw in the Louvre. In it, Saint Michael is spearing the dragon Lucifer:

> In Paris, at the Louvre, there have I seen
> The sumptuously-feathered angel pierce
> Prone Lucifer, descending. Looked he fierce,
> Showing the fight a fair one? Too serene!
> . . . . .
> Ah Lucifer, when men the fiend do fight,
> They conquer not upon such easy terms.
> Half serpent in the struggle grow these worms,
> And does he grow half human, all is right.

Raphael's canvas teems with "convulsions" around the serene Saint Michael: in the background, we see a burning city; behind Saint Michael, there are monsters and scenes of hellish torment. These sufferings have no effect on the meditatively calm and youthful Saint Michael, as the dragon screams under his spear.

Dickinson's Martyrs travel with fortitude toward a nonastronomical Heaven. Unlike the natural sky, Heaven has no threatening meteors. The Martyrs are sinless: shriven, they have been absolved of any sins of their past. They are stately; they seem not to know the meaning of agitation. Their Thermopylae is "the Straight Pass of Suffering," but instead of remaining trapped in agony, they emerge from that pass facing God. Their confident faith that expectation will be rewarded and their adherence to the "Everlasting Troth" of God's care baffle Dickinson, and cause her to search around for a comparison that will make their actions more intelligible to her. The compass that serves as her metaphor is almost destroyed, conceptually, by her description of it. A compass needle does not "wade" through any medium; it always points effortlessly to the North. But to progress to the pure, and even inhuman, Polar Air of the divine requires effort (Dickinson is thinking of the almost insuperable difficulties of Arctic exploration); the Martyrs "wade" through suffering as if through a deep current. God awaits them at the Pole; the Martyrs have a single aim, His presence. They always know the direction in which to go, no matter what suffering they must endure in making their way to Him. Their internal compass is always set to the Polar chill of sacrificial death, and their eyes are on their goal.

I have been speaking of the Martyrs in the present tense, coerced into such presentation by the cunning of the poem. At the beginning, the Martyrs certainly are creatures of the past, their verb tense ("trod") conveying their legendary past existence. But as the poem advances into the second stanza, the atmosphere around them is voiced in the present participle, which we interpret as "convulsions [ever] playing round." And in the third stanza, Dickinson's suppression of the copula that would have defined temporality draws attention away from the pastness of the Martyrs and gives them a certain eternal witnessing: "Their faith [was then, as ever] the Everlasting Troth, / Their expectation [was then, as ever] fair." And the closing metaphor—employing in "wade" the present tense of perpetual and unvarying forward progress—gives us the Martyrs before our eyes, their struggle continuing, their steadfast faces turned toward a superhuman ideal. Dickinson's imagination both states their pastness and implies the perpetuity of their example, contrasting them with more secular martyrs of present suffering.

[J 792]

# 194

<table>
<tr><td>

Title divine - is mine!
The Wife - without the Sign!
Acute Degree - conferred on me -
Empress of Calvary!
Royal - all but the Crown!
Betrothed - without the swoon
God sends us Women -
When you - hold - Garnet to
    Garnet -
Gold - to Gold -
Born - Bridalled - Shrouded -
In a Day -
"My Husband" - women say -
Stroking the Melody -
Is *this* - the way?

             [194 A: 1861]

</td><td>

Title divine, is mine.
The Wife without the Sign -
Acute Degree conferred on me -
Empress of Calvary -
Royal, all but the Crown -
Betrothed, without the Swoon
God gives us Women -
When You hold Garnet to
    Garnet -
Gold - to Gold -
Born - Bridalled - Shrouded -
In a Day -
Tri Victory -
"My Husband" - Women say
Stroking the Melody -
Is this the way -

             [194 B: 1865]

</td></tr>
</table>

Version A (1861): four exclamation points; one italicized word; question mark as closing punctuation. Version B (1865): *no* exclamation marks, *no* italicized word; *no* definitive closing punctuation, merely another dash. Franklin's decision to print not the first but the last version of each poem in the *Reading Edition* gives the reader, in this case, virtually a different poem from the first, 1861 version. The first version is hyper-excited, a series of triumphal exclamations (when they are not boasts). The second version deletes all punctuation except dashes, and states, in "Tri Victory - ", the implication of all the exclamation points. Four years after sending Version A to Samuel Bowles (with a message: "*Here's* - what I had to 'tell you' - You will tell no other? Honor - is its own pawn - "), Dickinson sent Version B to her sister-in-law Susan, with enough time between the versions (and perhaps enough disappointment) for a cooling-down of mind and poem. (The first version, with its insistently elated punctuation, seems to me closer in spirit to the defiant words of the poem, and so I print it here beside its later, more composed, variant.) What Samuel Bowles made of this claim and its cryptic accompanying message, we do not know. Nor do we know to whom Dickinson was "Betrothed"—or why she was "Shrouded" the same day she was "Bridalled." Or why "Shrouded" should, in its deadness, make up part of a "Tri Victory - ".

The middle part of the poem offers a picture of a conventional wedding: the bride and groom hold hands, juxtaposing their twin rings (each, garnet and gold) as the bride experiences that "Swoon" (of joy, of accomplishment, of sexual satisfaction) coming from, or given by, God to women on that occasion. No such divine blessing sanctions Dickinson's betrothal (as she imagines—or recounts—it in the opening of the poem). Instead, at her macabre invisible marriage, she receives three things: a Title (Wife), a Degree (that of Empress), and a rank (Royal). But she also lacks three things: "the Sign" of marriage (the wedding ring), the Crown due her rank, and the divinely sent and sanctioned "Swoon" of carnal satisfaction that Brides commonly receive. So far, the poem has shown "My wedding" in Part I, "Their wedding" in Part II. The third part sums up Dickinson's inhumanly compressed erotic life: "Born - Bridalled - Shrouded - / In a Day - " (a striking epigram spoiled, it seems to me, by the bald announcement "Tri Victory - " that was added in 1865). The three past participles of the epigram show a life finished even as it is begun, since its day of birth into bridal joy is also the death-day of that joy, as the wedding dress (not mentioned in either marriage description but inevitably springing to mind) turns into the (equally white) shroud that replaces it. Dickinson's self-epitaph, inscribed as the whole tale of her life, "ought" to end the poem. But in her characteristic desire for symmetry, after summing up her paradoxical wedding in condensed form for her tombstone, she turns once more to the conventional marriage, inserting into her poem not the "I, So-and-so, take thee" of the ceremony itself, but its aftermath in the language of the new-married bride, saying for the first time, "My Husband." Dickinson cannot ever say these words aloud—it is her greatest deprivation. She could do without the Title, the ring, and the Crown, even without the Swoon; but she wants the phrase, those words loved so much (in such complex ways of pride, possession, claim, boast, increase) that when wives pronounce them they "stroke" the Melody as they enunciate the words. Since the words "My Husband" are devoid of Melody in any ordinary sense of the word, their Melody when they are spoken by women is conferred solely by intonation. Dickinson tries out in the poem what it would be like to say the forbidden phrase, asking her reader to listen, and to pronounce on the authenticity of the two forbidden words from her lips, so unused to them: "Is *this* [the phrase pronounced aloud and pointed to by the illustrative "*this*"] the way?" The confirmation has to be pronounced by someone not herself, who will judge her conformity, as she says the phrase, with the usual way of "Stroking the Melody - ". The poem ends, in this version, with an emphasized turn to a witness (another missing ingredient in her marriage ceremony), and a real question. All this becomes considerably more pallid with Dickinson's later removal of the italics and the question mark: it loses its original urgency, as did the opening of the poem, when its exclamations (deprived of their exclamation marks) were turned into observations.

I have not so far mentioned the outrageous claim Dickinson makes in describing her new state: she is "Empress of Calvary!" The degree of "cognitive dissonance" (as we say) between these two terms is shocking. Granted, the words "King of the Jews" were affixed to Christ's cross (John 19:19–20: "And Pilate wrote a title, and put it on the cross. And the writing was JESUS OF NAZARETH THE KING OF THE JEWS"). The mere mention of Calvary parallels her "Title" to that of Jesus. If He is King of the Jews, She is, so to speak, his royal consort in suffering, Queen of Calvary. She too hangs on a cross, if an interior one, and Her suffering is like His. Why "Empress" instead of "Queen"? Jesus' title sets him as the ruler of an ethnic group, the Jews; her "Title divine" will outdo his, naming her as the ruler of an entire Empire. This self-aggrandizing self-crowning (it is the only time she names herself "Empress") is "objective," the title having been bestowed on her by Divinity. Fate has placed her in this extraordinary marriage, just as Jesus was placed on the cross by others, his "royalty" conferred by Pilate, commanding the inscription. Dickinson mentions God and Jesus here in her usual unorthodox (not to say blasphemous) way. God's function is to send women divine titles and the sexual "Swoon"; Jesus is seen to lack a female consort on Calvary, a lack which Dickinson will immediately supply.

The irregularity of form in this boast squares with its excited utterance:

the lines vary from monometer ("In a Day" could be read as a single anapestic foot, although it is probably a dimeter) to tetrameter ("Acute Degree - conferred on me - "). This Dionysian variation (when compared to Dickinson's common hymn-meter) almost demands the expressive exclamation marks to confirm its ecstatic origin. Even the rhyming, beginning in couplets, breaks down after three couplets into unrhymed line-endings ("Women . . . Garnet . . . Gold . . . Shrouded") before ending, not in the couplets of its beginning, but (in Version A) in an oddly rhymed quatrain: "Day . . . say . . . Melody . . . way." (It was the lack of an ear-rhyme for "Melody" that presumably suggested to Dickinson that she insert the extra line in B, "Tri Victory - ".)

Dickinson was severely limited, given the brevity of both her lines and her poems, in representing the ecstatic, the Dionysian, and the sublime (all of which usually demand length of utterance). Though we may flinch today at "Empress of Calvary!" we can see at least that Dickinson (in her first version of the poem) was working on every technical level—rhyme, rhythm, punctuation, structure, imagery—to convey ecstatic disruption. Instead of a "coherent" binary structure—"My marriage versus Their marriage"—she makes a "disorderly" four-part one—"My Marriage, Their Marriage, My Extraordinary Day, Their Utterance." Her daring (assimilating Calvary to her own purposes) and her modesty (the humble double ring of "Garnet to Garnet - / Gold - to Gold - ") cohabit in the poem, marking the distance between her transcendent, if ringless, exaltation and the simple sign of twin rings in common marriage.

The most unexpected feature of this boast-poem is the absence of the first person. We see no such form as "I am an Empress," "I'm royal," or (as in 225, J 199) "I'm 'wife' . . . / I'm Czar - I'm 'Woman' now - ". The conviction that her exaltation has been divinely decided makes Dickinson able to claim that the divine Title "is mine," that the Degree is "conferred on me." Only that conviction allows her to name herself "Empress of Calvary." As she thinks up that designation in her small upstairs bedroom, she displays to us the unconfined sense of huge expanses of time and space natural to her imagination.

[J 1072]

# 204

I'll tell you how the Sun rose -
A Ribbon at a time -
The Steeples swam in Amethyst -
The news, like Squirrels, ran -
The Hills untied their Bonnets -
The Bobolinks - begun -
Then I said softly to myself -
"That must have been the Sun"!
But how he set - I know not -
There seemed a purple stile
That little Yellow boys and girls
Were climbing all the while -
Till when they reached the other side -
A Dominie in Gray -
Put gently up the evening Bars -
And led the flock away -

This exquisite little poem—eight lines for the sunrise, eight for the sunset—affirms by its calm structural symmetry the order of the "old dependency of day and night" (as Wallace Stevens says in "Sunday Morning"). And it affirms by its absence of white space that the whole process of sunrise and sunset is a seamless whole. Although its first editors called it "A Day," it is precisely day—the period between sunrise and sunset—that Dickinson omits. In its original fascicle version, the poem was copied in four quatrains with white space in between them. Franklin comments that in the fascicle "Dickinson drew a horizontal line between the second and third stanzas, as though she considered making separate poems." I think she drew the line after stanza 2 because she thought of putting a white space only there, separating the poem into two separate eight-line stanzas, one for sunrise, one for sunset—the median choice between four quatrains, where she began, and one long sixteen-line poem, where she ended.

As I've written elsewhere *(Poets Thinking)*, Dickinson chooses, as her metaphor for the fine gradations of dawn's progress, the "ribbons" by which the sun rises. She then presents a sequence of four "ribbons" (each metaphorically representing one chromatic half-step in sunrise): the town steeple bathed in Amethyst light, the news of sunrise spreading as fast as Squirrels run, the Hills emerging from the morning mist, and the dawn chorus of the Bobolinks. Her gaze is wide enough to imply that no aspect has been omitted, scanning (in synecdoche, substituting the part for the whole) the town, the animals, the landscape, and the birds. "I'll tell you," says Dickinson, with absolute confidence in her ability to narrate the birth of the day. Ah—but what of the death of that day? "But how he *set,* I know not!" (Version A, the italics emphasizing the truth that whereas rising is a present visible miracle, setting is a future mystery). The end of life is indescribable because unknown—and through Dickinson's sudden withdrawal of certainty, we recognize that the poem concerns life and death, as well as sunrise and sunset. Her fantasy of sunset—in which little Yellow boys and girls climb continuously over a purple stile—ends in an allusion to the Twenty-Third Psalm: but instead of being looked after by Jesus, the good shepherd, this little Yellow flock are shepherded by "A Dominie in Gray," and after they reach the other side, the Dominie (schoolmaster) changes the purple stile into a series of "evening Bars," as the children are gathered into a fold from which they can never return. Dickinson is content to leave this imprisonment a soft implication in "Bars" (borrowing the word's visual meaning from a clause in Keats's "To Autumn": "While barrèd clouds bloom the soft-dying day").

In an arresting later poem, "Who is the East?" (1085, J 1032), Yellow and Purple are more obscurely expounded: their state depends on an Atlas-like middle man, variously named "He . . . / That carries in the Sun" and "He . . . / That lets Him out again." This "He" himself (mighty enough, supposedly, to carry the Sun) is nonetheless sharply limited in power: "if He can" is the fulcrum on which each metamorphosis (Yellow to Purple, Purple to Yellow) turns:

> Who is the East?
> The Yellow Man
> Who may be Purple if He can
> That carries in the Sun.

Who is the West?
The Purple Man
Who may be Yellow if He can
That lets Him out again.

The East is (naturally) colored Yellow, because it is where the Sun comes up. The West is (naturally) colored Purple, because it is where sunset takes place. But, having the usual human desire for difference, Yellow prays to be Purple, and Purple prays to be Yellow. If the Carrier of the Sun into the East were able, he could carry the Sun out, and the East would turn Purple. If the imprisoner of the Sun in the Yellow East could release him, the Sun could go visit the West, and the Purple Man could turn Yellow. The emphasis on "if He can" suggests that He can't: Death cannot be reversed, Purple Sunset cannot be changed into Yellow Sunrise. As Keats says, "The sacred seasons might not be disturbed," even by a "primeval God" (*Hyperion,* I, 293). For Dickinson, the hope of a resurrection is as vain as hoping that the West could turn Yellow.

"Who is the East?", concluding in an enigma, is cousin to "I'll tell you how the Sun rose - ", but it wrenches the mind away from that poem's gentler panorama of sunrise and sunset. As the little Yellow children of the Sun pass the Purple Stile of Death, they enter a Stygian twilight foretold by the Dominie's Gray and the evening Bars. Everything nonetheless is as it should be: the little flock are obedient to their gentle shepherd of souls. The acute "wrungness" of "Who is the East?" comes from Dickinson's recognition that Purple can never return to Yellow, and that a gentle fantasy is no substitute for tragic reality.

[J 318]

# 224

An awful Tempest mashed the air -
The clouds were gaunt, and few -
A Black - as of a spectre's cloak
Hid Heaven and Earth from view -

The creatures chuckled on the Roofs -
And whistled in the air -
And shook their fists -
And gnashed their teeth -
And swung their frenzied hair -

The morning lit - the Birds arose -
The Monster's faded eyes
Turned slowly to his native coast -
And peace - was Paradise!

In its step-by-step list, the tale of the Tempest resembles in method "I'll tell you how the Sun rose - ", (204), but instead of finding ways to describe the awakening delights of the sunrise, Dickinson invents symbols for the hellish changes taking place in a world suddenly overcome by a fearful storm. The nightmare she recounts has something of the painter Henry Fuseli's gleeful grimness, populated as it is by nameless "creatures," minions of the storm: some lay siege to the town Roofs, chuckling as they land or whistling in the air; others shake their fists and gnash their teeth like ogres; still others, like Shelleyan Maenads, swing their frenzied hair. One of the problems raised by Dickinson's description of the Tempest is the poem's passage from the singular to the plural and back again: although the singular nouns, literal and metaphorical, Tempest and Monster, are easily enough assimilated to each other, it is the host of nameless "creatures" that give pause: like Spenser's allegorical "Errour" (*Faerie Queene* I), Dickinson's Monster has generated a horde of evil children, who by elvish harassment multiply on all sides the effects of their parent's assault, "chuckling" (the best word of the middle description) as they carry out their torments.

The most surprising word in the departure of the Tempest (put to rout by the light of morning and the rising of the bird-chorus) is "faded." The storm had hitherto been imagined in terms of utter Black: now we are asked to imagine that a demonic light has all along dwelt in the Monster's eyes, a hellish glare perceived only as it fades into the light of the rising sun. Defeated, the Monster turns his weakened eyes homeward, and with him his Hell (with its gnashing of teeth) departs, as the day (rewriting the story of Genesis) restores Paradise after the vanquishing of Satan and his retinue.

The introduction of the "awful" and awe-inducing Tempest uses violent verbs not usually associated with human beings (who cannot "mash" the air, or cloak Heaven and Earth from view). The witnesses of the onset of the storm are the appalled "gaunt" clouds, knowing, in their fewness, that they are overmatched. The "spectre's cloak" inserts the appropriate Gothic touch for this overshadowing of the world by darkness. In this Dickinsonian spectral spectacle of air and clouds and blackness, the true goblin chill arrives with the onslaught of the anthropomorphisms of stanza 2, since the chuckling and whistling and shaking of fists and gnashing of teeth and swinging of hair are taking place not in the air among the clouds, but on the very Roofs, shaking every townsman's security. The anthropomorphism of stanza 2 is "catching": through it, the overseeing Monster of stanza 3 is generated by the quasi-human activities of his assistants, who have inserted him into the human scene and rendered credible his hellish eyes. The over-generous assessment of the restored world as "Paradise" demonstrates the human capacity to repress, even forget, the Monster's ability to return from his "native coast" whenever he wishes.

[J 198]

# 232

He forgot - and I - remembered -
'Twas an everyday affair -
Long ago as Christ and Peter -
"Warmed them" at the "Temple fire."

"Thou wert with him" - quoth "the Damsel"?
*"No"* - said Peter - 'twasn't me -
Jesus merely "looked" at Peter -
Could I do aught else - to Thee?

Dickinson invokes, as an analogy to her own feeling of being forgotten, the forgetting by Peter of Christ's prophecy concerning him. (Among the accounts of the incident in the synoptic gospels, the closest to Dickinson's version is that of Luke 22, the only one that contains Christ's "look" at Peter.) After the Last Supper, Jesus speaks to Peter:

And the Lord said, Simon, Simon, behold Satan hath desired to have you, that he may sift you as wheat: But I have prayed for thee, that thy faith fail not: and when thou art converted, strengthen thy brethren. And he said unto him, Lord, I am ready to go with thee, both into prison, and to death. And he said, I tell thee, Peter, the cock shall not crow this day, before that thou shalt thrice deny that thou knowest me. . . . [Jesus undergoes his agony in Gethsemane, reproaching his disciples—among whom Matthew's Gospel mentions Peter—and urging them not to sleep, but to watch and pray. After Judas identifies Jesus with a kiss, Jesus is taken to the high priest's house.] And Peter followed afar off. And when they had kindled a fire in the midst of the hall, and were set down together, Peter sat down among them. But a certain maid beheld him as he sat by the fire, and earnestly looked upon him, and said, This man was also with him. And he denied him, saying, Woman, I know him not. And after a little while another saw him, and said, Thou art also of them. And Peter said, Man, I am not.

And about the space of one hour after, another confidently affirmed, saying, Of a truth this fellow also was with him: for he is a Galilaean. And Peter said, Man, I know not what thou sayest. And immediately, while he yet spake, the cock crew. And the Lord turned, and looked upon Peter. And Peter remembered the word of the Lord, how he had said unto him, Before the cock crow, thou shalt deny me thrice. And Peter went out, and wept bitterly.

This piercing story of human failure and repentance finds a place in American verse not only in Dickinson but also in Elizabeth Bishop: in her "Roosters," the whole story is summed up in the Latin inscription *Gallus canit, flet Petrus*—"The cock crows, Peter weeps." (Bishop had probably read Dickinson's poem.)

For Dickinson, the Bible had a story, and a language, to fit every situation; one had only to take thought and it would arise in one's recollection. Her quoting, within "He forgot - and I - remembered - ", of significant phrases from the gospel narrative ("temple," "fire," "damsel") suggests an initial immersion in the original accounts; but then a mischievous nativism takes over, as a New England Saint Peter replies roundly to the Gospel "Damsel" (the word drawn not from Luke, but from Matthew 26:69): *"No'* - said Peter - 'twasn't me - ". Rewriting the Bible was one of Dickinson's constant amusements—but the gaiety with which she invented the retort of her rustic Peter should not blind us to the seriousness with which she searched the Gospels for life-commentary. Here, the gospels tell her she should forgive the person who forgot her, since Jesus did not repudiate Peter. Indeed, when the "young man" at the empty sepulchre, Christ's own messenger, tells the Marys (in Matthew 28) to bring news to others that Christ is risen, the only name he mentions is that of Peter: "But go your way, tell his disciples and Peter that he goeth before you into Galilee." Peter is entirely forgiven, both by the look from Jesus and by his designated place of primacy among the disciples.

Dickinson distinguishes the two stanzas of the poem by initially referring, in the third person, to the "sinner" who forgot her—"He forgot"—and then swerving, at the end, to the second person (direct address) to ask that sinner: "Could I do aught else - to Thee?" This change of reference enacts the forgiveness she has learned to extend. At first, since the man has played her false in some way, she speaks *of* him, not *to* him; but after Jesus' "look" at Peter, she too can "look" (grammatically speaking) directly at the offender, calling him "Thee," and announcing, in her closing question, that she has followed the example of Jesus. She leaves it to the sinner whether, after receiving her "look" that resumes discourse between them, he will go out and, following Peter's example, "weep bitterly." Omitting the heartbroken Peter at the end of the Gospel story, Dickinson forces a remembrance of him upon her addressee, who must, if he heeds the tale's close, repent his forgetting.

Dickinson conflates, for brevity, two moments in the gospel story. In the first, Jesus rebukes the Jews who take him captive by reminding them that although he taught daily in the Temple, they did not take him there, but have come furtively, in the night, to capture him; in the second, the servants of the high priest build a fire in the hall of the high priest's house (or palace). Dickinson places the fire in the Temple, perhaps in the conceit that any place where God is located becomes a temple from that fact alone. The rhyming of "(af)fair" and "fire" puts us in the realm of "pure" slant rhyme. The trochaic tetrameters allow for great emphasis, when needed, on the first syllable of the lines: "*He* forgot"; "*Thou* wert with him"; "'*No*' - said Peter."

[J 203]

# 236

Some - keep the Sabbath - going
   to church -
I - keep it - staying at Home -
With a Bobolink - for a
   Chorister -
And an Orchard - for a Dome -

Some - keep the Sabbath, in
   Surplice -
I - just wear my wings -
And instead of tolling the bell,
   for church -
Our little Sexton - sings -

"God" - preaches - a *noted*
   Clergyman -
And the sermon is never long,
So - instead of getting to
   Heaven - at last -
I'm - going - all along!
          [B, 1861, Fascicle 9]

Some keep the Sabbath going to
   Church -
I keep it, staying at Home -
With a Bobolink for a
   Chorister -
And an Orchard, for a Dome -

Some keep the Sabbath in
   Surplice -
I, just wear my Wings -
And instead of tolling the Bell,
   for Church,
Our little Sexton - sings.

God preaches, a noted
   Clergyman -
And the sermon is never long,
So instead of getting to Heaven,
   at last -
I'm going, all along.
      [C, 1862, sent to Higginson]

The "regularized" version of this famous poem that was sent to Higginson
(and that appears in Franklin's *Reading Edition*) uses only one dash in its in-
ternal punctuation, deleting or replacing the other internal dashes of the fas-
cicle version. Given Dickinson's own usual preference for her dashes, and her
use of them in the fair copies she bound in fascicles, I think this poem should
be anthologized with the fascicle dashes intact. Dickinson tones down, for
Higginson, the broad satire of line 9: she removes her quotation marks from
the name of God and her italics from the word "noted." Higginson had, after
all, begun his professional life as an ordained minister, and his preference
would have been for a conventionally punctuated poetry.

Although the poem is written in the 4-3-4-3 meter of the ballad stanza, from the very first line the smiling anapests begin to confer their lilt on the iambic voice. The penultimate line in Version C has three anapestic feet:

˘ ˘ / ˘ / ˘ ˘ / ˘ ˘ /

So in stead | of get | ting to Heav | en at last

And the purest iambic line is:

˘ / ˘ / ˘ /

Our lit | tle Sex | ton sings.

As the anapests keep bubbling up into the iambs, Dickinson of course is imitating her chorister, the Bobolink, whose very name has a bounce to it. A renegade from the church, the poet is not surly but instead cheerful in her secular (and preferred) Sabbath. As the poet works out the analogies between her own form of church and service and the conventional Christian ones, she enumerates the treble of the chorister (her Bobolink), the dome above the worshipers (the branches of her orchard), the surplice (her wings), the bell (her singing Sexton), the preacher (God), and the sermon (her poem). The preacher (at undue length) promises an eventual heaven; but she, in her orchard listening to birdsong and writing her "sermon," is already there, in a natural heaven formed by God's second scripture, "the book of the creatures," in which God is known not only through his Word but also through his works: "So - instead of getting to Heaven - at last - / I'm - going - all along!" Her assumed "wings" are not those of an angel but those of a bird; she sings as her own choir, just as the Bobolink sings in grassy fields.

Dickinson's reluctance to attend church may have been caused in part by her nervous difficulty in leaving the house and meeting strangers; she knew that her life "exempt from public haunt" was, in one aspect, a form of adversity in which she was held captive. When Dickinson was composing "Some keep the Sabbath," the Duke's speech on "the uses of adversity" in *As You Like It,* Act 2, scene 1, may have crossed her mind:

Sweet are the uses of adversity,
. . . . .
And this our life, exempt from public haunt,

Finds tongues in trees, books in the running brooks,
Sermons in stones, and good in every thing.

. . . . .

I would not change it.


Dickinson's poem announces a comparable natural religion to balance her private isolation.

Dickinson's refusal to keep the Sabbath in a conventional way generated two poems in Wallace Stevens's work: the boisterous "Ploughing on Sunday" (in which the speaker engages in the sort of "servile work" that was prohibited on the Sabbath) and "Sunday Morning," Stevens's sequence examining the consequences for humanity of a loss of belief in the Resurrection and an afterlife.

[J 324]

# 238

How many times these low feet staggered -
Only the soldered mouth can tell -
Try - can you stir the awful rivet -
Try - can you lift the hasps of steel! -

Stroke the cool forehead - hot so often -
Lift - if you care - the listless hair -
Handle the adamantine fingers
Never a thimble - more - shall wear -

Buzz the dull flies - on the chamber window -
Brave - shines the sun through the freckled pane -
Fearless - the cobweb swings from the ceiling -
Indolent Housewife - in Daisies - lain!

When Higginson published this poem in the *Christian Union,* he gave it a conventional elegiac Latin title, "Requiescat"—a shortened version of the phrase *Requiescat in pace,* "May she rest in peace." The poem contemplates a Housewife now dead, but formerly diligent in her work: sewing, darning, mending (while wearing a thimble); regularly airing out the house by opening the windows; cleaning the window panes vigorously to remove spots; and sweeping away cobwebs as far aloft as the ceiling. But the point of the poem is not her former diligence, nor yet her present "indolence": the point is the suffering she underwent in life, never to be revealed now that her mouth is "soldered." Dickinson's hyperbole replaces the embalmer's stitching with a harsher permanent "soldering" of the lips; and the casket becomes a dungeon from which the corpse will never be freed, attached as it is by an "awful rivet" and bound as it is by unremovable "hasps of steel." Dickinson, imagining the moment after death, feels how useless now are the mourner's earlier tender gestures—stroking the fevered forehead, lifting the hair, taking the hand: the forehead is cool, the hair listless, the fingers stony.

Dickinson never lacked for ways to represent that most difficult of subjects, Death. Here, she imposes on it an odd temporality: stanza 1 looks briefly back at life's suffering (to give us a living body with uncertain feet), and then fastens on the torture of being riveted in place, one's feet stapled by hasps of steel, one's mouth soldered. The corpse feels none of these things, but Dickinson, having momentarily imagined the living body, sinks with it into the coffin, suffers its feelings of dreadful confinement. After a flashback to the moment of death and the mourner's now futile services, the poet's gaze widens to the house of which the dead woman was the house-wife; in every corner, on every pane, the house shows signs of neglect. No one has opened the window in the room where the woman died, and the flies attending dissolution are still trapped there, their "Buzz" emphasized in the reversed initial foot; on that window there are "freckles"—a kind word for spots of dirt; and from the ceiling swings a cobweb, no longer afraid of a dangerous broom. The flies buzz, the cobweb swings, the sun bravely shines through the spotted pane. Finally, Dickinson imagines the woman after burial, "in Daisies - lain," and makes a mock-inscription for her tombstone: "Indolent House-wife!" No epitaph could be more untrue to the life that lies buried here.

Dickinson's disordered sequence of time panels—the pictures of painful life, the torturous confinement in a casket, the deathbed, the posthumous neglect of the house, the corpse after burial, the ironic epitaph—seems to represent the back-and-forth of the mind of a mourner after a recent death, wake, and funeral. "I knew she suffered—but at the wake, seeing her fastened down in the coffin with her mouth stitched shut, I realized that her life-struggle will never be told. How horrible a coffin is, in its straitened dimensions, for a being so recently sentient! How useless I felt at the deathbed, when our small attentions to her were no longer possible! How neglected the house seemed after her death—how quickly her immaculate cleaning was undone! And now—never again to rise to her characteristic humble activities—she lies beneath a bed of Daisies in the graveyard." An ordered temporal narrative—of deathbed, embalming of the corpse by the undertaker, the wake, the return of the mourners to the woman's house the night before the burial, their last memories of her in life, and then the burial with its afterlife of ornamental daisies—would not represent the disquieted musing mind of a bereaved friend or relative. The reader has to "straighten out" the narrative in the reading.

I have called this a "narrative," but not all its speech acts are narrative ones. In the first two stanzas, there are many adjurations: "Try - "; "Try - "; "Stroke";

"Lift - ". And there are questions: "Can you stir"; "Can you lift." These vain efforts—all are vain—reenact the powerlessness of the mourner who is directly addressed: she cannot lift the heavy hasps of steel; she cannot even lift the weightless listless hair. (After the double "can you," the line "Lift - if you care - the listless hair - " almost inevitably rings in the ear as "Lift - if you can - the listless hair - ", assimilating the hair to the other unliftable challenges. "If you care" is an eerie phrase, sounding almost like "If you dare." "Stroke" and "lift" are humane words; but once it is mentioned that the mourner could "handle" the stiff fingers, we are out of the realm of caring gestures. ("Handle" was of course generated by the corpse's unmentioned "hand.") The inserted mini-narrative of the surrounding nonmourners—the flies, the sun, the cobweb—ironizes the parallel narrative of mourning; it displays a set of actions indifferent to the mourner's vain wish to stir the rivet and lift the hasps.

In the Gospel of Luke (10:41–42), Jesus is asked by Martha to instruct her sister Mary (who has been listening to Jesus) to help her prepare a feast. "And Jesus answered, and said unto her, Martha, Martha, thou art careful and troubled about many things: But one thing is needful: and Mary hath chosen that good part, which shall not be taken away from her." In the volume of Dickinson's verse published in 1890, this poem was given the title "Troubled about Many Things," as though it repeated (in its recollection of the diligence of the dead woman) Jesus' rebuke to Martha. The first editors of Dickinson turned this portrait of two neighbors—a woman who staggered from suffering before she died, and a mourner who wishes fruitlessly to lift the rivets and hasps of death from the corpse—into a Christian morality tale.

The strong trochaic tetrameters and their syntactic inversions—"Buzz the dull flies"—enable Dickinson to emphasize the initial exclamations and adjurations in the lines of this poem. With its emotional disturbance carried by these insistent first words, and its various recollections mirrored in its tangled temporalities, the poem has nonetheless room for an aesthetic distance in remarking the indifference of flies, sun, and cobweb. The dying Keats said to his friend Severn, "I feel the daisies growing over me." Dickinson, imagining the grave of the dead woman, covers it with daisies, Keats's "simple flowers of our spring."

[J 187]

# 240

Bound a Trouble - and Lives will bear it -
Circumscription - enables Wo -
Still to anticipate - Were no limit -
Who were sufficient to Misery?

State it the Ages - to a cipher -
And it will ache contented on -
Sing, at its pain, as any Workman -
Notching the fall of the even Sun -

"Bound"—used as a verb ("to set boundaries to, to limit")—is obsolete, according to the *OED,* and causes the first difficulty here for a reader, who knows the word as the past participle of "bind." Dickinson's language here is so compressed that the first act of a commentary should be to let in some air. In expanded form, the sentences would say: "If you can set a boundary around a trouble, people will be able to bear it; a circumscribed space of time enables the (sane) endurance of woe. Always anticipating pain is intolerable—were there no limit set on suffering in an infinite extension of sorrow, who would be strong enough to bear Misery? But if you tell Misery the exact number of Ages that its agony will continue, it will be content to go on aching; it will sing at its pain as a workman sings at his work, notching time, hour by even hour, on a tally-stick, until, at the going down of the evening Sun, his workday comes to an end." We infer that Dickinson is the one experiencing hopelessness as she suffers a pain that seems to have no foreseeable termination.

The speech acts of the poem are various. They consist of three hypotheses and one proverb, each representing a result of thought:

1.  Hypothesis 1 and result: [If you] Bound a trouble, Lives will bear it;
2.  Proverb: Circumscription enables Woe;
3.  Contrary-to-fact hypothesis and result: If there were no foreseeable limit to anticipation, who could bear the Misery?

4. Mathematical version of Hypothesis 1 and result: If you tell Misery the exact number of the Ages during which it will have to bear Woe, it will ache on, contented; it will sing (which is Misery's work) while suffering, just as the Workman sings at *his* work, waiting for the known end of his workday, marking off, notch by notch on a stick, each successive hour as the Sun declines.

It can be seen from this sketch that stanza 2—in its arrangement as hypothesis and result—very closely resembles, in its structure, stanza 1. The chief difference between the two lies in the further refinement of time in the second stanza—into *exact* numbers for the length of suffering, into a *foreseen number* of notches until the *known* hour of release. Both stanzas are generated from Dickinson's (invented) "proverb": "Circumscription enables Wo." The proverb reveals, in its three words, the usefulness to the poet of the genre of the proverb: it joins together—often, as here, by an expressive verb—an emotional or physical state and a positive or negative result (compare, for a positive example, George Herbert's "Repentance": "Fractures well cured make us more strong"; or, for a negative example, "A rolling stone gathers no moss"). Dickinson "rewrites" the genre of positive proverb in this poem by refusing to provide the end-state of emotional health that we expect ("Circumscription enables Stoicism"); instead, she tells us that in the place where unbearable woe was, circumscription puts bearable woe. (One is reminded of Freud's assertion to an analysand's mother that the most he could promise to achieve for her homosexual son was "ordinary unhappiness," in lieu of neurotic unhappiness: "Circumscription" promises ordinary woe instead of intolerable woe.) Dickinson's mathematical side has been somewhat neglected; in fact, many of her resolutions, as in this poem, depend on numerical exactness (in *409, for example, "I've known her - from an ample nation - / Choose One - "). Here, the obsessive need to know the precise dimensions of woe determines her demand to be able to "notch" the anguished hours as they pass, in expectation of a foreseeable time of cessation.

The 1863 version of "Bound a Trouble - ", printed above, is a revision, in the right direction, of its earlier 1861 transcription. Both have almost the same second stanza, but in the earlier version the first stanza is both exclamatory and—especially in its fascinating if melodramatic third command ("Deal with the soul / As with Algebra!")—surprising:

> Bound - a trouble -
> And lives can bear it!
> Limit - how deep a bleeding go!
> So - many - drops - of vital scarlet -
> Deal with the soul
> As with Algebra!

Dickinson enjoys having her dashes represent, drop—by—drop—, the exsanguination of the bleeding heart. The drawn-out phrase, "So - many - drops - ", as an amplification and specification of the preceding more general "bleeding," needs a metaphysical tourniquet. In Algebra, one "solves an equation" by determining an exact number that can correctly replace *x*. The vastness of the soul presents innumerable *x*'s of pain to the sufferer; but if you can ascertain, and disclose to the bleeding heart, the *specific* number of drops of blood that it will have to shed before its suffering is ended, drop-by-drop turns manageably into a reassuringly terminal "50" (or "60" or "100"—it doesn't matter; the equation has been solved). In a way, all of Dickinson's poetry is an attempt to fix precision (often by instrumental means—a compass, a plumb line, a tally-stick) on a maelstrom of emotion. (The turmoil, in both versions of the poem, generates "wrong" rhyme-sounds, linking the fatal "go" with the potentially resolving "Algebra," and circumscribable "Wo" with limitless "Misery.")

We notice that what is missing in this early version of stanza 1 is the elegantly turned proverb that dominates Dickinson's revision: "Circumscription - enables Wo - ". Geometry enters with the Latinate abstraction "Circumscription," which Dickinson "yokes violently together" (as Dr. Johnson said of the Metaphysical Poets) with the brutally Anglo-Saxon "Wo," as though the sedate act of the mind in envisaging a limit could render bearable the pangs of the heart. The first version, we recall, was organized solely by exclamatory exhortations:

Bound a trouble and lives can bear it!
Limit how deep a bleeding [of many drops of blood] may go!
Deal with the soul as with Algebra!

These are (as a court would say) "excited utterances" by someone who is afraid she will bleed to death if no limit is set to her loss of blood. Dickinson's first versions are often purely expressive, as this one is, of her own woe. But in her second versions, as has often been remarked, we can see evidence of her taking thought, referring her own trouble to a wider application (proverbs, for instance, are meant to be universally applicable). In the revised version, the exhortations are reduced to two: "Bound a Trouble" and "State it the Ages," with neither bearing an exclamation mark. To Dickinson, the finding of an aphorism is a satisfying way to articulate (and relieve) pain.

Why does Dickinson invent the final "Workman" as a way to conclude a poem about the apparently infinite ravages inflicted by a bleeding wound? There are two reasons: paid work (unlike most things in life) has always had a predetermined extent, so it responds metaphorically to the desire of Misery for a limit; and singing as one works is a powerful poetic trope, represented most sympathetically in Wordsworth's poem "The Solitary Reaper":

> Behold her, single in the field,
> Yon solitary Highland Lass!
> Reaping and singing by herself;
> Stop here, or gently pass!
> Alone she cuts and binds the grain,
> And sings a melancholy strain;
> O listen! For the Vale profound
> Is overflowing with the sound.
>
> . . . . .
>
> Whate'er the theme, the Maiden sang
> As if her song could have no ending;
> I saw her singing at her work,
> And o'er the sickle bending.

Dickinson takes it upon herself to rewrite this (lately much criticized) portrait of a natural integration of work and expressive song. Her workman, like the reaper, is governed by sun-time; but while Wordsworth's reaper seems to take this condition as natural, Dickinson's Workman feels the burden of his stated hours. By substituting "pain" for the expected word "work" in "Sing, at its pain, as any Workman," Dickinson makes it clear that the soul's work, in a state of Misery, is pain. It will "ache on" to its conclusion.

One further question: although the poem's sufferers start off as human beings ("Lives"), Dickinson then drops the human plural in deciding to allegorize Woe as "Misery," speaking of it henceforth as "it." ("Trouble" is an "it," too, but it is endured by "Lives.") "The soul" in the original version is the indirect object of the imperative "Deal," making "the soul" the antecedent of "it" and "its" in the second stanza: "State it the Ages . . ." For Dickinson, "soul" and "spirit" often take the gender of their possessor, as in "The Soul selects her own Society - " (*409, J 303) and in "The event was directly behind Him" (1724, J 1686), when a bullet "let His Flesh / Centuries from His Soul." She did not often think of the Soul as an "it"—but see "With Pinions of Disdain" (1448, J 1431) for one such use; the Soul appears more often in her poetry as an animate thing. When Dickinson saw "the soul" (in her original version of "Bound - a Trouble - ") becoming the antecedent of the pronoun "it," she may have resolved to seek a noun to which "it" is more suitable—and therefore obliterated the word "soul" entirely in the second version, leaving the more generalized Platonic idea "Misery" as the antecedent of "it."

A poem such as "Bound a Trouble - " ought to suggest to us why Dickinson often prefers to be resolutely cryptic. What does she gain—for herself, for art—by making her poem difficult, not only in lexicon and syntax, but in apparent incoherence (the sudden intrusion of the human Workman into a discussion carried on in an atmosphere of abstraction, the peculiar idea of "notching" the fall of the sun, the strange description of the sun as "even")? She ensures, first of all, that the casual reader will dismiss the poem as one "making no sense." She chooses her readers by their willingness to enter her anarchy—the anarchy that caused her conventionally educated readers such as Higginson to raise an eyebrow. Yet education alone—although indispensable for reading some of the poems that are resistant to interpretation—does not serve. As Stevens says (in "Man Carrying Thing"), a poem must resist the intelligence *almost* successfully. To resist the intelligence is a quality we might ascribe to higher mathematics—and we admit to ourselves readily that we are unable to penetrate such formulations. But verbal artifacts can resist the intelligence too, and can set puzzles that the casual reader will not feel competent to solve. A poem that seems to use only perfectly simple words— "bound," "workman," "notching," "even"—should, the reader feels, be easy to understand. Even an abstraction such as "circumstance" is usually obvious in context. Dickinson sits in a transparent house with no visible door, enjoying the self-selected sympathizers who can slip inside the glass. Those who find a poem unintelligible are incompetent not so much through class or education as through a lack of imagination. Dickinson was always prepared to admit those who could imagine their way into the situation enacted in the poem; and by sending her poems to friends and relatives (many of whom were women with little higher education), she asserted her own confidence that readers of the poems needed no special preparation.

[J 269]

# 243

That after Horror - that 'twas *us* -
That passed the mouldering Pier -
Just as the Granite crumb let go -
Our Savior, by a Hair -

A second more, had dropped too deep
For Fisherman to plumb -
The very profile of the Thought
Puts Recollection numb -

The possibility - to pass
Without a moment's Bell -
Into Conjecture's presence
Is like a Face of Steel -
That suddenly looks into ours
With a metallic grin -
The Cordiality of Death -
Who drills his Welcome in -

Dickinson sent the double-length third stanza (without the other two) to
Higginson in a letter; and it certainly makes a poem in itself. Without warn-
ing, a dreadful possibility appears before us—the hint, say, of a fatal diagno-
sis. Even the possibility of meeting Death is like . . . What *is* it like, asks Dick-
inson? It is like encountering the face of a skull—but not a corruptible skull
of bone. Instead, it is the immortal Platonic Form of a skull—a face made of
steel, which instead of eyeholes has some organ that can "look," and instead
of a skull's human teeth has teeth of steel, bared in a "metallic grin." We of
course refuse to welcome such a guest; but he, insisting on entering our
house, lifts, with a dreadful "Cordiality," one of his awful steel instruments (a
drill in this version—but an alternative reading gives a nail) and, pretending
that we are welcoming him, bores a bodily entrance for himself.

What does this hideous encounter with the Face of Steel have to do with stanzas 1 and 2? Those introductory stanzas narrate a hair's-breadth escape from death. You are traversing a "mouldering" granite Pier which, the moment you have crossed it, crumbles; a second more on its surface would have dropped you too deep in the ocean for anyone to rescue you. This narrative is framed, fore and aft, by two versions of post-traumatic response. The first version is an "after Horror" that is coterminous with your whole being ("that 'twas *us* - "); the second version is active repression that "puts Recollection numb."

As she often does, Dickinson begins with a story of "real life" and then retells it as abstraction. Here, the abstraction—with its gothic steel face, metallic grin, and drill—is more successful than the initial, more realistic narrative (as Dickinson herself may have thought in sending only the third stanza to Higginson). The single-stanza abstraction of the skull-as-Death is coherent; but the two-stanza narrative is finally incoherent. It includes a Horror, a Pier so mouldering that it has become an assemblage of Granite crumbs, a Savior without obvious antecedent, a proverbial Hair, an imagined Fisherman, a Thought-profile, and numbness. It is always dangerous to indict Dickinson for incoherence, because some connection one has not yet perceived may light up coherence where incoherence was thought to be. The best thing in stanza 1 is "the Granite crumb," Dickinson's favorite sort of paradox; the best thing in stanza 2 is the idea that one can see a Thought either in full face or in profile. In stanza 2, we see a profile, but in stanza 3, Dickinson allows the full (metallic) face of the Thought of Death to turn its chilling look in our direction. (Keats connects a profile view of allegorical figures to a full-face view in the "Ode on Indolence," which, since it was published posthumously in 1848, Dickinson may have read.)

[J 286]

# 256

The Robin's my Criterion for Tune -
Because I grow - where Robins do -
But, were I Cuckoo born -
I'd swear by him -
The ode familiar - rules the Noon -
The Buttercup's, my whim for Bloom -
Because, we're Orchard sprung -
But, were I Britain born,
I'd Daisies spurn -

None but the Nut - October fit -
Because - through dropping it,
The Seasons flit - I'm taught -
Without the Snow's Tableau -
Winter, were lie - to me -
Because I see - New Englandly -
The Queen, discerns like me -
Provincially -

Dickinson's statement "I see - New Englandly - " tends to be quoted by scholars as a serious announcement. It is that, in part, but it is also a humorous one, in which the poet indicts herself for the universal provinciality of vision that she takes as her topic here. The Queen, being English, would like Cuckoos, while Dickinson, being American, likes Robins; each nation favors its own landscape, flowers, climate, and birdsong. Dickinson's only explicit comparison is that of her Robin to the English Cuckoo—who pervades English poetry from "Sumer is icumen in, / Lhude sing cuccu" through Shakespeare to Wordsworth's "O cuckoo, shall I call thee bird, / Or but a wandering voice?" The nightingale is England's bird for "high art"; the cuckoo is homely, familiar, a sign of spring. Although England, like Amherst, has robins, they do not play the salient role accorded to cuckoos in earlier literature.

Instead of continuing her transatlantic comparisons, Dickinson ceases, after line 4, to illustrate English preferences, and colloquially lists her own attachment to "the ode familiar" (an unpretentious song), the Buttercup, Daisies, the Nut, and Snow. Only in the conclusion does she return to the transatlantic comparison, yet here she brings England and New England together not to contrast them, as before, but to liken them: both "discern . . . / Provincially - ".

Although Dickinson does not widen her remarks beyond preferences in nature, her subversive perception—that in every nation the inhabitants see provincially—can equally apply to food, religion, or politics. Dickinson, like Hopkins, prized distinction of species; a world without national differences would be boring. You are "Britain born," so you are Anglican; he is "Texas born," so he is a Baptist. But it is more clever to affect a harmless discourse of buttercups and nuts than to be explicit about national distinctions in politics and religion; those who understand will know that your relativism goes further than cuckoos.

How does Dickinson proceed in outlining her taste after citing her first criterion—the aesthetic one of "tune"—satisfied by the spring Robin? After music comes poetry ("the ode familiar" being the criterion there), followed by the sunny Buttercup of summer (because, as well as being a native of New England, that flower is a native of a minor Dickinsonian region, Orchards, where buttercups grow under apple trees). As for "Daisies," "Daisy" is the nickname Dickinson gives herself in the "Master" letters, written to an unknown beloved and found in draft form among her papers. Having done with the spring and summer, the poet continues into fall: the Nut in New England, as it drops, says that October has come, teaching the poet that "The Seasons flit." Never was the downward slide of temporality mentioned more lightly, and we soon discover the reason; being a New Englander, the poet loves the onset of winter, seeing its authentic sign in "the Snow's Tableau." This designedly decorative inner rhyme, and the French word "Tableau," together elevate prosaic New England winter into the realm of European art.

The irregular rhyming in stanza 1 mimics free rumination; but having declared herself entitled to her own preferences, Dickinson moves to assertive rhyming in stanza 2: first . . . "fit . . . it . . . taught," with inner rhyming in "Nut" and "flit"; and then the amusing inner rhyme confined in a single line, "Snow's Tableau"; and finally a left-right closing bow of four rhymes together: "me . . . Englandly . . . me . . . Provincially." Naturally, Dickinson's irony lies in the fact that any person who concedes that she "sees provincially" has left the provincial stance behind.

[J 285]

# 259

A Clock stopped -
Not the Mantel's -
Geneva's farthest skill
Can't put the puppet bowing -
That just now dangled still -

An awe came on the Trinket!
The Figures hunched - with pain -
Then quivered out of Decimals -
Into Degreeless noon -

It will not stir for Doctors -
This Pendulum of snow -
The Shopman importunes it -
While cool - concernless No -

Nods from the Gilded pointers -
Nods from the Seconds slim -
Decades of Arrogance between
The Dial life -
And Him -

The Clock that stops (with spondees) in the first line of this poem is, by its shape, a species of grandfather clock, as we know from its possession of a pendulum, and from Dickinson's explicit declaration that it is not a mantel clock. It exhibits a dial-face (with gilded Hour Hand and Second Hand). But it is a miniature grandfather clock, set in a shopman's window, a "Trinket." At the same time it is an artificial puppet that "just now dangled still." It is also a dead human body that "will not stir for Doctors," and will not respond to the importunities of the Shopman whose window it has enlivened. This chilly poem is an example of Dickinson's imagination at its most agitated, finding metaphors for multiple aspects of dying and death. As she contemplates the corpse—having watched its quivering death agony—she wants to convey both the exquisite workmanship of the body and its inert cold rect-angular shape on the deathbed, its loss of all voluntary self-positioning, its indifference to the commercial world importuning it to resume its function, and its refusal to concede to the ministrations of doctors and "stir" once again. It has been taken over by a death daimon, whom Dickinson names "cool - concernless No." What does "N-o" do? He "N-o-d-s." (We under-stand, seeing this congruence, why Dickinson dropped her original verb for him—"stares"—and constructed her second, the repeated "No(ds)" gener-ated by the first, silent "No.") It is clear that the emotionless "No" belongs to the realm of "snow," from which the pendulum takes its present inertia, able neither as pendulum to "swing" nor as body to "stir."

The "puppet" has been created by "Geneva," the synecdoche for a watch-maker (the Enlightenment's "Watchmaker God" is not far away). But its life-activities have been controlled by a puppeteer-God, who, having manipu-lated his puppet into a last bow on stage, lets it "dangle," as though it had been hanged. Death puts paid to the notion that God created us as creatures of free will: no human will in the world can challenge Death's approach or overcome it by struggle.

The elegance of the poem is maintained by its unobtrusive rhymes, all of them perfect except for "pain" and "noon," in which the slant rhyme, adopted by Dickinson's intense sympathetic imagination, connects the wrenching ag-ony of the soul with its unnatural time of death. The rhythm of the poem also has a notable feature: if we temporarily regularize each instance of two short lines (at the beginning and end) into a single long one, creating regu-lar quatrains, we notice that recurring feminine rhyme-words in the odd-numbered lines alternate (visually) with masculine ones in the even-numbered ones. Among the odd-numbered lines, only "Decimals" in stanza 2 and "between" in stanza 4 have masculine endings. Otherwise, in those odd-numbered lines, we hear the constant final trochees associated with femi-nine rhyme: "Mantel's," "bowing," "Trinket," "Doctors," "[impor]tunes it," and "pointers." Because the poem (until its last stanza) is largely iambic, we instinctively add the "extra" syllable of these "trochees" to the last iambic foot of the lines in which they appear, without taking particular note of them. When we come to the even iambics that constitute stanza 3, we think we have arrived permanently at a deathly inertia; but those regular iambics are there to prepare for the shock of the merciless initial trochees following them in stanza 4. The earlier repetition of the trochaic rhythm ( ′ ˘ ) in the five odd-numbered end-words cited above has (as we see only in hindsight) prophesied the savage turn in rhythm of stanza 4 into arrogant dactyls and trochees, assaulting us as "cool - concernless No - // Nods from the Gilded pointers - / Nods from the Seconds slim - ".

    ′   ˘   ˘ | ′ ˘ | ′  ˘

Nods from the Gilded pointers -
Nods from the Seconds slim -
Decades of Arrogance

With the arrival of the word "between," the poem begins its subsidence into its final iambics of deadness:

  ˘   ′ | ˘  ′|˘ ′ |  ˘   ′

between / The Dial life - / And Him -

The poet anthropomorphizes the Clock-face and its numerical Figures, and sees the twelve-hour span of time—during which the Hour Hand completes the passage from the numeral 12 to the numeral 12 again—as a circle of 120 "Degrees." And the Second Hand has its own sixty "slim" Seconds within each Degree. When the "pointers" for the hour, the minute, and the second coincide at midday, at the numeral 12, the Clock marks "Degreeless noon," the hour of death. I think Dickinson does not have death take place at "Degreeless midnight" (equally accurate as a description of the Clock-face at twelve), because the Trinket-Body's agonized consciousness of Death is all-important; at midnight, Death could come, unrecognized, in sleep. The consciousness of the "Trinket," sensing its end, feels "awe"; the Figures (numerals) bend over in pain, making them look like hunchbacks; and then, in a mysterious phrase, they "quiver . . . out of Decimals" before the moment of death. Dickinson seems to use "Decimals" to mean (as the *Dickinson Lexicon* suggests) "an amount measured in tens," as the Clock-face is marked off in increments of ten spaces. When "Degreeless noon" strikes, mortal beings "quiver" out of their places on "the Dial life" into nothingness. The antithesis between "pain"—so human, so wrenching—and "Degreeless noon" —so geometrically inhuman—brings together the two halves of Dickinson's chief metaphor, the dying human being and the circular "Dial" representing (by analogy) lived life.

The "cool - concernless No" is supercilious; his "Decades of Arrogance" distance him from the Dial life—the life that was lived by the moving pointers and indicative Figures while they still had an intrinsic temporal relation to each other. When, with the expiration of the last second of life, the Pointers cease to move, "No" declares his power—which has in fact extended through all the decades of the mortal's life, even if never reflected on. "No" was merely awaiting his hour to assert his haughty superiority to the multifarious moments of "Yes" in body and spirit.

[J 287]

# 269

Wild Nights - Wild nights!
Were I with thee
Wild nights should be
Our luxury!

Futile - the winds -
To a Heart in port -
Done with the Compass -
Done with the Chart!

Rowing in Eden -
Ah - the Sea!
Might I but moor - tonight -
In thee!

Dickinson's arrangement of these lines in dimeter quatrains obscures their basic construction as rhyming couplets. We can see what is gained by the poet's dimeters if we write the poem out in couplets, in which it flows on easily:

Wild Nights! - Wild nights! Were I with thee
Wild nights should be our luxury!

Futile - the winds - to a Heart in port -
Done with the Compass - done with the Chart!

Rowing in Eden - Ah - the Sea!
Might I but moor - tonight - in thee!

The ecstatic pauses of wish, envisaged arrival, and active rowing are too easily subsumed in the couplets, and too rapidly arrived at. In the original, the phrase "Wild Nights" gains force from appearing twice in the first line and once more in the third line; and the anaphora in lines 7 and 8 (with "Done" heading two separate lines) would disappear in a tetrameter couplet. Dickinson's pauses, as they so often do, create a mind enraptured, pausing to evaluate its own emotions and its own language. At first, the voice seems to dream aloud, naming its desire, then pausing (after the dash) to pass to a higher register, denoted by the exclamation point, but not yet revealing what makes these exclamatory nights "Wild." The ecstasy is immediately modified by a contrary-to-fact supposition, "Were I with thee," and its imagined consequence in "should," the subjunctive form of "would." Leaping rapidly over the unsatisfactory absence of her lover, the speaker imagines the Heart's relief at finding repose in a harbor after a long sea-voyage threatened by the winds, which would be rendered "futile" by her lover's achieved presence. Those instruments of precision—Compass and Chart—have no portion in wildness, and the speaker will, once in port, discard them with full joy, relieved that she will no longer have to monitor her own navigation. Although this fantasized "port" is not yet available as a stopping place, its imagined presence turns the windy sea into an Edenic landscape of anticipation, and the lover and port coalesce in one haven which—in a surprising instant, "tonight"—brings fierce desire, not merely yearning, into view. Dickinson's first rhyme-word, "thee," is also her last, showing the magnetic pole around which the speaker's mind revolves.

I have said nothing as yet about "luxury." It comes as the answer at the end of the contrary-to-fact hypothesis: Wild Nights would be, were I with thee, our—what? Dickinson's choice of the identifying word "luxury"—with its overtones of indulgence, overabundance, and (with its Latin root *Luxuria*) lust—knowingly violates virginal propriety and thrift.

The speculation that the speaker of the poem must be a man—a critical interpretation deriving, with a coarseness foreign to Dickinson, from "moor . . . / In thee"—seems to me untenable; the poet's diction is that of female romance. Later, in "How sick - to wait - " (410, J 368), Dickinson, repeating much of the diction of "Wild Nights," once again imagines herself as a woman sailing in a boat, saying *One port - suffices - for a Brig like mine - // Ours be the tossing - wild though the sea - / Rather than a mooring - unshared by thee.*"

[J 249]

# 276

Civilization - spurns - the Leopard!
Was the Leopard - bold?
Deserts - never rebuked her Satin -
Ethiop - her Gold -
Tawny - her Customs -
She was Conscious -
Spotted - her Dun Gown -
This was the Leopard's nature - Signor -
Need - a keeper - frown?

Pity - the Pard - that left her Asia!
Memories - of Palm -
Cannot be stifled - with Narcotic -
Nor suppressed - with Balm -

"Myself the only Kangaroo among the Beauty" (L 268)—Dickinson, fearing how her eccentricities might be viewed by others, offered this ironically arch description of herself to Higginson in a letter of July 1862. Here, she is not a Kangaroo from Australia, but a captive Leopard from Asia imprisoned in "Civilization." This is one of Dickinson's poems to a "Master," here a "keeper" addressed by the honorific "Signor"—an Italian title used also in 270 (J 250) and 387 (J 429). Exotic felines—the Leopard, the Tiger—and their tropical homes strike Dickinson as just what is lacking in New England. Yet her Signor has spurned her—was it some fault of her own?

The Leopard speaks about herself in the third person, but speaker and Leopard are one. At first, the Leopard seems repentant, asking (as if talking about a child), "Was the Leopard bold?" (We are not so likely to use the word now in rebuke, but "Bold girl!" was a common form of harshness from a teacher in the nineteenth century.) The spurned Leopard, hanging her head, talking about herself in placatory babytalk-third-person, seems humbled. But soon she rises in self-defense: elsewhere, her golden satin coat was prized—in deserts, in Ethiopia (a country totally exotic to Americans of Dickinson's era). And then, in one of her startling revelations of relativism in taste, Dickinson has her Leopard, in an about-face, adopt the Signor's (implicitly racist) criteria: the Leopard knows that her customs are, like her face, tawny, not white; she knows that a northern taste might find her golden coat "Dun" and "spotted"; she is conscious of all this, but defends herself against "Civilization" by an irrefutable claim—this is her nature, she was born like this. Then why must she endure her keeper's frown?

There seems to be some attempt by her "keeper" to reconcile with the Leopard: to cure her homesickness and erase her memories of the past, he proffers narcotics; to sweeten her present life within his "Civilization," he offers "Balm." The Leopard, knowing such remedies useless, gives sudden voice to her wretchedness: "Pity - the Pard - that left her Asia!" Her memories can neither be "stifled" nor "suppressed," however inconvenient they may be to her Signor and the Civilization he represents.

Beast (and bird) fables are attractive to Dickinson as an ancient folk form —"homely," sanctioned by tradition, less stiff than her analytic allegory of abstractions. It is hard to imagine the "Asia" where there would be a tribe of Dickinsons under the palms; yet every exceptional person dreams of better company than that offered by her local context. This injured speech bears its intonation in all its initial accented syllables: "*Was* the Leopard - bold?" (implicitly contradicting an accusation by her keeper); "*Deserts* - never rebuked her Satin - " (nor Ethiopia her Gold), as she haughtily tells her Signor. The same initial emphasis pervades her concessive self-description registering how "ugly" she is by white standards: "Tawny - ", yes, admittedly; "Spotted - her Dun Gown - ", granted. Before these alien criteria she is ashamed of her spots and her dun garment, with a woman's shame at not being found beautiful. Apologetically she cites her incapacity to change: conscious as she is of her keeper's taste, *This* was nonetheless her nature. (We find, in "Need - a keeper - frown?" the idiom we know from "Coming through the Rye": "If a body kiss a body, / Need a body cry?") Does the offense warrant the response? Does the Leopard's offense warrant her keeper's scorn?

The keeper's attempts at placating her receive from her a commensurate scorn, conveyed by her emphasis on "Cannot" and "Nor" as the poem ends. Dickinson's expert use of metrical accent to create tone is never more in evidence than here, as the Leopard goes from mock-babyishness to proud self-defense, to apology, to pleading, to self-pity, to scorn. In effect, she gives us a metrical score for our reading aloud. The Leopard's closing stanza meaningfully rhymes the nostalgic Asiatic "Palm" with the keeper's vain "Balm."

In the "Master" letters, there are reminiscences of the Leopard's sentiments: "God made me - [Sir] Master - I didn't be - myself. I don't know how it was done" (L 233). And in the heartbroken last "Master" letter (L 248), Dickinson speaks of herself in the third person (as "Daisy") just as the Leopard does: "Perhaps she grieved (grazed) his taste - perhaps her odd - Backwoodsman [life] ways [troubled] teased his finer nature (sense). Daisy [fea(rs)] knows all that - but must she go unpardoned - teach her, preceptor grace - teach her majesty - ".

[J 492]

# 279

Of all the Souls that stand create -
I have Elected - One -
When Sense from Spirit - files away -
And Subterfuge - is done -
When that which is - and that which was -
Apart - intrinsic - stand -
And this brief Drama in the flesh -
Is shifted - like a Sand -
When Figures show their royal Front -
And Mists - are carved away,
Behold the Atom - I preferred -
To all the lists of Clay!

In her first version of the bold and exalted line 7, Dickinson wrote "And this brief Tragedy of Flesh," to which, after taking thought, she ultimately preferred "And this brief Drama in the flesh." Not everyone's life is a tragedy, she must have reflected; it was sentimental to project her own feelings onto the gathered multitudes of the entire apocalyptic scene. She was perhaps correct, but "this brief Tragedy of Flesh" is one of her rejected phrases that ought to be remembered.

The Protestant doctrine of Election taught that God had selected certain souls, from all eternity, as his Elect, and had predestined them to that status. (Others are damned for eternity.) Dickinson, imitating God, appoints her Elect—but, more discriminating than God, chooses only one. Her metaphor for multitude is "all the Souls that stand create," comprising everyone from Adam to the last person created: all those that will appear on the Last Day, those "lists" (armies) of Clay. ("List," in the military sense, is used of all those having one category in common: on the Last Day, their bodily mortality— Clay—is the one past thing that the throngs of resurrected Spirits will have in common.)

Dickinson's description of the Day of Judgment proceeds in steps. When their bodies died, the dead saw their sensual capacities, like an army, "file away" from their spirits. With the disappearance of the covering flesh, the possibility of "Subterfuge" (etymologically, that which flees under something else) departs; every truth of the spirit is made manifest. In the timelessness of Eternity, present and past are completed; each stands separate, seen now in their "intrinsic" and not contingent nature. Each of the souls present at the Last Day has had his or her own bodily "Drama in the flesh," which can be seen as "brief" only when one has left it behind—or rather when it has been "shifted - like a Sand" by divine power. The phrase is enigmatic: and the use of a peculiar singular for Sand resembles Dickinson's employment of the singular for Hay: "I wish I were a Hay - " ("The Grass so little has to do," 379, J 333). Her brief life, in retrospect, seems to her one Sand in the "Deserts of vast eternity" (Marvell, "To His Coy Mistress"), just as the beloved Elected Soul is called the singular "Atom - I preferred" among all the atoms gathered in "the lists of Clay."

The last of Dickinson's descriptions of the revelations of the Last Day— that it is the time "When Figures show their royal Front - / And Mists - are carved away"—borrows from the theory (ratified by some sculptors) that the figure which eventually appears from the stolid block of marble was "in the block" all along, and that the sculptor had only to carve away the excess in order to expose it. The liberated spirits of the Elect (no matter how humble their former brief drama) now shine forth as what they always were: royal, of the company of the King. In order for their glory to be visible, the earthly Mists obscuring that glory—as Mists obscure the sun—must be "carved away" by the Divine Sculptor, who reveals all.

The first two lines of the poem match the two last: the declaration of Election, and then the *Ecce Homo,* "Behold," pointing to that Elected One. In between, the poem unrolls as a list of adverbial clauses using "When" (with "when" sometimes being "understood," grammatically speaking); fully expanded, there would be, by my count, six "when" clauses illustrating the aspects of the Last Day. The grandeur implied by each slows the gradual unveiling by the poet of the various apocalyptic conditions. Descriptions of the Last Day are usually loud and highly colored: they include Gabriel's trump, the Resurrection of the Dead, the Pronouncing of Judgment ("Depart, ye accursed") and various frightening supernatural manifestations (as in Revelation). "If I were describing the Last Day," Dickinson implies, "this would be my narrative," and she produces a reduced but essential panorama. Once Sense and Subterfuge pass away with the departure of the body, a metaphysical stateliness commences, ending in Dickinson's broad gesture of "Behold!" God's choosing of his Elect is a ponderous act of Predestination; but Dickinson's bold version of choice declares only what she "preferred"—the verb intimating an act of taste rather than of morality.

[J 664]

# 284

The Zeros taught
  Us - Phosphorus -
We learned to like the Fire
By handling Glaciers - when a
  Boy -
And Tinder - guessed - by power

Of Opposite - to equal Ought -       Of Opposite - to balance Odd -
Eclipses - Suns - imply -            If White - a Red - must be!
Paralysis - our Primer dumb           [Version A, 1862]
Unto Vitality -
      [Version B, 1863]

Here is a translation into ordinary English: "Cold taught us *heat;* we learned to like *Fire* by handling *glacial ice* in our youth; and surrounded by chill, we guessed the existence of *Tinder* (kindling for starting a fire) by the power of Opposite to equal . . . anything at all." In other words, we learned desire from deprivation; we learned to like desire from our manipulation of destitution; we guessed the existence of something combustible because we knew that everything had its opposite, so our chill inability (so far) to ignite told us there was Tinder. Eclipses imply (an anterior presence of hot) Suns; Paralysis—in its cold dumbness (or numbness) is our first lesson in Vitality (of speech or feeling).

The poem concerns the passionate desire for heat (vitality, sun's warmth) felt by one who has been cold all her life. The more life forced her to handle ice, the more she learned to prize fever. Finally, she perceived from these ever more pressing unsatisfied desires an underlying truth: anything can be conjectured from its opposite. She has intuited, from living in her darkness, that there is a sun; she has been instructed in vitality by experiencing paralysis.

In her first version (A, above), Dickinson, wishing to illustrate the power of an opposite to balance something else, thought of mathematics. Even balances Odd. We guessed the existence of Tinder "by power / Of Opposite - to balance Odd - ". But Odd and Even are not opposites of the same sort as the emotional opposites of heat and cold, so the poet adds another analogy, this time one of color. White is the color of ice, red the color of heat: "If [there is a] White - a Red - [there] must be!" From her "snow," she guesses the existence of flame.

> And Tinder - guessed - by power
> Of Opposite - to balance Odd -
> If White - a Red - must be!

We need to ask why, from Version A, the poet cancels Even and Odd in favor of the power of Opposite to equal "Ought" (Dickinson's customary spelling of "Aught," meaning "Anything"), and why the images of white and red are canceled in favor of eclipse and paralysis. Needless to say, eclipse and paralysis are far more dramatic and provocative of thought than white and red; and the philosophical axiom introduced by the superlative "Aught"— "*Everything* has an opposite by which it may be defined"—is more analytically interesting than balancing even numbers against odd ones.

It was typical of Dickinson to go back into a poem when she was dissatisfied with the degree to which its contours matched those of the experience she wished to convey. "White" is a weak way of saying "ice," "snow," or "destitution." "Red" in its vagueness could imply blood (against the whiteness of the body) rather than heat. What did it *really* feel like (she asks herself at the point of revision) to be chilled, destitute, death-cold, speechless? It felt like a permanent eclipse, through which she could imagine, with sick yearning, a radiant sun; it felt like paralysis, a stroke depriving her of speech, making the body dumb. Wanting her formulations of emotional states to be precise, recognizable, and striking, she inscribes these revisions.

In "The Zeros" Dickinson utters a gnomic first line, intending not a lasting riddle (since the next two lines immediately explain the first), but rather a strikingly deviant use of language. "The Zeros" can be thought of as a climate, like "the tropics": such an Arctic zone, with its repeated inflictions of "zero at the bone" (see *1096, "A narrow Fellow"), creates a desire not merely for heat, but for self-ignition, a flare of glowing inner explosion. And in what element could that be found? Phosphorus. Dickinson's 1844 Webster says of phosphorus: "It burns in common air with great rapidity, and in oxygen gas, with the greatest vehemence." In "Who is it seeks my Pillow Nights" (1640, J 1598), "Phosphorous" [*sic*] signifies the fire and brimstone of hell, ascribing sinfulness—in a Christian view—to the passionate desire represented by "Phosphorus" in "The Zeros."

In "We play at Paste - " (282, J320) Dickinson, pondering how we learn to embrace and deploy our values, ends by saying that playing at "Paste" (costume jewelry, fabricated pearls) prepared us to embrace "Pearl"; our hands, by analogy "Learned Gem Tactics / Practising Sands - ". Such a poem presents learning as a gradual advance from the lowly to the exalted, and can therefore end on a positive note. The different kind of learning described in "The Zeros" is not learning by analogy; it is learning by opposites. And the bitter ending, in which one guesses at abundance while suffering destitution, envisages no "Gem" entering our paralyzed hands.

The striking first line of "The Zeros" is formulated on the basis of a more conventional remark such as "The tropics taught us (by contrast) the pleasure of winter." Arresting first lines are of course sought by all poets; as we recall characteristic ones, we see they may derive their power from various means: direct address ("Busy old fool"; Donne) or vigorous action ("I struck the board"; Herbert) or a memorable sight ("Behold her, single in the field"; Wordsworth) or a flight of fancy ("The Owl and the Pussycat went to sea"; Lear). Dickinson's first line, by comparison with these, is sublimely dry: zeros, phosphorus—a riddling chemical didactic epigram. The "punch" of epigram is dear to Dickinson as an opening gesture, especially when it can arrive in phosphorescent metaphor.

[J 689]

# 288

My first well Day - since many ill -
I asked to go abroad,
And take the Sunshine in my hands
And see the things in Pod -

A'blossom just - when I went in
To take my Chance with pain -
Uncertain if myself, or He,
Should prove the strongest One.

The Summer deepened, while we strove -
She put some flowers away -
And Redder cheeked Ones - in their stead -
A fond - illusive way -

To Cheat Herself, it seemed she tried -
As if before a Child
To fade - Tomorrow - Rainbows held
The Sepulchre, could hide.

She dealt a fashion to the Nut -
She tied the Hoods to Seeds -
She dropped bright scraps of Tint, about -
And left Brazilian Threads

On every shoulder that she met -
Then both her Hands of Haze
Put up - to hide her parting Grace
From our unfitted eyes -
My loss, by sickness - Was it Loss?
Or that Etherial Gain
One earns by measuring the Grave -
Then - measuring the Sun -

In a poem recalling, perhaps, Keats's "To Autumn," Dickinson describes the weeks when the goddess of Autumn (in myth, Demeter) arrives and then takes her gradual farewell. The poet, ill and confined to the house since Spring, has not seen Summer this year: she was striving against Death, in a struggle to see which of them will be (not "stronger" but) "strongest," since to lose is to be killed. When Dickinson recovers enough to go out again, she notes all the things that must have happened between Spring (when she last was out-of-doors and everything was "A'blossom") and the present: she, like Keats, goes "abroad" in Autumn, to "see the things in Pod," now that the flowers are gone. Just as Keats saw (as—he says—anyone can see) the goddess of Autumn pausing over her work of harvesting, so Dickinson sees Autumn at her tender compensatory work of substituting other attractions for those of Spring. As the "Summer deepened," while the poet strove with death, late "Redder cheeked" flowers (dahlias, zinnias) replaced the rosy blooms of Spring, as Summer tried to will herself into an unconsciousness like that of Keats's deceived bees, or his Fancy that "cheats," concealing the passage of time. Summer tries to "Cheat Herself" with the red flowers—and then Dickinson, in one of her cruelest similes, compares the way Summer deludes herself to the way one might hold up a Rainbow—in a vain attempt to hide the imminent Sepulchre—before a child doomed to die tomorrow.

After this harsh prophecy of death (deriving from her own past serious illness), the poet, able to be "abroad" once again, relents toward the seasonal change, and shows the goddess, although now deprived of flowers, still continuing her decoration of the world, bestowing new fashions on nuts, seeds, and leaves and dropping warm ("Brazilian") colors on every "shoulder" (shrubs, perhaps?) that she meets or (in one alternative) "could reach." In the last two stanzas, the goddess, like Keats's Autumn, disappears in a "Haze" of mists, sparing "our unfitted eyes" the anguish of her "parting Grace." ("Haze," "Veil," "Gauze" and other such words always hint, in this poet, at another "side" hidden from us.) Dickinson will echo this divine departure when she writes—in "As imperceptibly as Grief" (*935)—of seeing "A courteous, yet harrowing Grace, / As Guest, that would be gone" as "Summer made her light escape / Into the Beautiful - ".

A surge of gladness that she has not died in her life-or-death contest with pain overcomes the poet's resentment at having missed the Spring, and she is now prepared to sympathize with the earth-goddess, who persists in her decorations even with so little to work with: little Hoods for Seeds, bright scraps of Tint, "Brazilian" threads (decorative in their tropical colors, but still merely threads, just as the cloth is merely scraps, the Hoods minuscule). The awakening of Dickinson's mind to Autumn's creations puts strong activity in place of Summer's earlier weak verbs. While the poet suffered indoors, Summer had colorlessly "put . . . away" the earlier flowers; once Dickinson has come out to watch, the new season, Autumn, vigorously "dealt a fashion to the Nut," "tied the Hoods to Seeds," and "dropped bright scraps."

When the narrative begins, Dickinson, too weak to walk unassisted, "asked to go abroad"; her first wish is to "take the Sunshine in my hands." Those two hands, eager to grasp the warmth of the season, prophesy the appearance of the hands of Autumn toward the end, as she puts up her misty "Hands of Haze" before leaving. Once she has gone, the poet has to test her short glimpse of "things in Pod" against her loss, through illness, of earlier, and more beautiful, weeks of flowers. Was it loss—or rather, perhaps, gain? The compensatory move has been a frequent one in lyric; although Wordsworth loses the sight of the singing reaper, "That music in my heart I bore / Long after it was heard no more," and though he has lost "the glory and the dream" ("Ode: Intimations of Immortality"), he has gained the capacity to hear "the still, sad music of humanity" ("Tintern Abbey").

What has the poet gained from the loss occasioned by illness? She has learned how precious the experience of life is; she has measured the Grave and then measured the Sun. As in other mathematical endings by Dickinson, measurement is often the vehicle of conviction, and here the one measurement (of loss) is the exact equal of the other (of gain). Compare the poet's later statement that "Perception of an Object costs / Precise the Object's loss - " (1103, J 1071). (Dickinson's twenty uses of the word "precise" testify to her mathematical relish.) The Grave tells us the greater worth of life, a conclusion reinforced by the rhyming of "Gain" with "Sun." This is an "Etherial" gain, a mental one; however vast, it is not paralleled in the material world.

[J 574]

# 291

It sifts from Leaden Sieves -
It powders all the Wood -
It fills with Alabaster Wool
The Wrinkles of the Road -

It makes an even Face
Of Mountain, and of Plain -
Unbroken Forehead from the East
Unto the East again -

It reaches to the Fence -
It wraps it Rail by Rail
Till it is lost in Fleeces -
It deals Celestial Veil

To Stump, and Stack - and Stem -
A Summer's empty Room -
Acres of Joints, where Harvests
   were,
Recordless, but for them -

It Ruffles Wrists of Posts
As Ankles of a Queen -
Then stills its Artisans - like
   Ghosts
Denying they have been -
       [Version A, 1862]

It sifts from Leaden Sieves -
It powders all the Wood -
It fills with Alabaster Wool
The Wrinkles of the Road -

It scatters like the Birds -
Condenses like a Flock -
Like Juggler's Figures situates
Upon a baseless Arc -

It traverses yet halts -
Disperses as it stays -
Then curls itself in
   Capricorn -
Denying that it was -
       [Version E, 1883]

This poem describing a snowstorm nowhere contains the word "snow"; in this feature it resembles other "riddle-poems" by Dickinson, asking the reader to guess its unnamed subject. Of the five variants of this poem, Ralph Franklin prints, in the *Reading Edition,* the short three-stanza Version E (1883), but it is worth seeing, for purposes of comparison, Dickinson's earlier five-stanza Version A, sent to Susan Dickinson in 1862, and reproduced above. As critics have noticed, the longer version seems to owe some of its conduct and words to an unsigned essay, "Snow," (ascribed to Thomas Wentworth Higginson) in the *Atlantic Monthly* of February 1862. In transforming A into E, the poet reduced four stanzas to one, and changed most of the final stanza, while keeping the closing lines of E similar to those of A. When Dickinson decides to cut, it usually means that on rereading she notices that her imagination has digressed, in its love of play, from its basic aim. The three deleted stanzas are panoramic ones, extending the view of the snow (as Higginson does) beyond wood and road to mountain and valley, to fence posts and remnants of stripped agricultural fields where "Harvests" had taken place. Nothing is wrong, as such, with these stanzas; in fact, the strict lines of the "joints" where different fields abut each other come from the pure geometrical Dickinson. She must not have wanted a panorama, then, since she sacrificed, when cutting hers, even good lines and touching images (the ruffles of snow on the fence posts, the "Summer's empty Room - ").

What do her later additions reveal about what I've called her "basic aim"? The snow—as the first stanza tells us—smoothes out the characteristics of the landscape—the brown trees of the wood, the old ruts in the road. (Dickinson, like Higginson, alludes to Psalm 147:16: "He spreads the snow like wool.") The next three stanzas elaborate on this conceit of smoothing, but add nothing new. When the poet turns away from them to write a stanza that will *advance* the poem, she moves from the smooth white covering of the beginning to something far more active—a whirl of snow scattering like individual birds, then condensing into a "Flock." Versions C and D introduce a "juggler" whose materials are "Flowers," revised to "Figures" in E. The poem becomes ominous if we view the "juggler" creating this motion as God, the creator of the snowstorm. The "Figures" are then human beings, tossed by the will of God in "baseless" motion. The sinister implication of the juggler and his "Figures" is what the poem has been striving toward—a goal that the harmless beauty of the (canceled) panorama served only to impede.

The sheer unpredictability of the snow while the storm continues is the burden of the last stanza. After "scatters" and "Condenses"—verbs describing the physical appearance of a snow flurry in a whirl—the poem takes on verbs of wayward travel: the snow traverses, halts, disperses, or stays according to the will of its Juggler-Creator. Then, when he tires of his toying with snowy Figures, the storm vanishes, curling itself (like a beast in its den) in the winter zodiacal constellation—Capricorn—while pleading innocent to its disturbing visitation, denying its part in juggling hapless "Figures" in air.

The three stanzas of Dickinson's Version E are motivated by verbs, and it is in the verbs that the poet's thought is lodged. Her indication of a Creator is clearer in the 1862 B version, where the snow "stills its Artisans - like Swans - / Denying they have been." Snow has delegated its acts to its executive Artisans—but being Royal, these Artisans are "like Swans."

[J 311]

# 294

A Weight with Needles on the pounds -
To push, and pierce, besides -
That if the Flesh resist the Heft -
The puncture - Coolly tries -

That not a pore be overlooked
Of all this Compound Frame -
As manifold for Anguish -
As Species - be - for name.

In this riddle-poem depicting "Anguish," we are in the torture chamber of some Inquisitor, who has decided that the usual instruments of torment are not adequate. He has therefore invented a new one. It is a Weight (like those used to press to death martyrs such as the English Margaret Clitheroe, commemorated by Hopkins). But this Weight has Needles on its lower surface, the part that will come into contact with the victim's flesh. There are so many needles that they will pierce every pore on the sufferer's skin. The Weight applies its push; but if the victim resists, the Weight, in addition, "Coolly" tries puncture.

Ascribing agency to the Weight itself, as it proceeds from the torture of "Heft" to the torture of "puncture," Dickinson also ascribes intention: the Weight has invented its Needle-piercing in order "That not a pore be overlooked." Such devilish intentionality, so minutely pursuing its violence (scanning the body to find its smallest orifices), suggests madness in the agent who invented the Needle-pounds of the Weight. The "Compound Frame" that is being tortured is that uneasy combination of body and soul that we call a self. Although the torture is applied to the flesh—the pores of the body—its ultimate aim is to puncture with anguish the similarly porous surface of the soul. There is no more powerful word than "anguish" in Dickinson's lexicon. She uses it thirty-two times in her poems to describe excruciating physical or mental pain. Speaking of the agony in the Garden in "Proud of my broken heart" (1760, J 1736), Dickinson refers to "the strong cup of anguish brewed for the Nazarene." Agency is omitted in that passage, as in "A Weight," but we know that it is God who brewed that anguish, since Jesus prayed, "O my Father, if it be possible, let this cup pass from me: nevertheless not as I will, but as thou wilt" (Matthew 26:39).

Dickinson has conceived her imaginary torture instrument to describe what she feels is being done to her by some superhuman external force. She has done nothing to deserve the imposition of such extremity. Driven to explanation, she says that the self has as many pores through which to feel anguish as . . . as what? As Adam had names for all created species. Language is the greatest manifold in the poet's symbolic system. She associated anguish with the lost paradise, writing in "Better - than Music!" (378, J 503) of how in adulthood the story of Eden becomes "a legend - dimly told - / Eve - and the Anguish - Grandame's story - ". The slide from the oppression of Anguish to a prelapsarian joy—Adam's naming of all the animals—makes the end of "A Weight with Needles on the pounds - " a shock.

Genesis offers, as one of the images of plenitude associated with the Creation, God's invitation to Adam: "And out of the ground the Lord God formed every beast of the field, and every fowl of the air; and brought them unto Adam to see what he would call them: and whatsoever Adam called every living creature, that was the name thereof. And Adam gave names to all cattle, and to the fowl of the air, and to every beast of the field" (Genesis 2:19–20). The majestic linguistic power nascent in Adam interests even God: he brought the creatures to Adam *to see what he would call them.* What could be more "manifold" than Adam's linguistic invention, finding for *every* living species a name? Dickinson must have found reassurance in the biblical verses: God takes an interest in human linguistic creation, which must include her own. At the same time, she defies Genesis by adopting a modern scientific word—"Species"—for living beings. In rhyming the human "Frame" with "Name," the poet reiterates the power of language.

[J 264]

# 306

A Shady friend - for Torrid days -
Is easier to find -
Than one of higher temperature
For Frigid - hour of mind -

The Vane a little to the East -
Scares Muslin souls - away -
If Broadcloth Hearts are firmer
Than those of Organdy -

Who is to blame? The Weaver?
Ah, the bewildering thread!
The Tapestries of Paradise
So notelessly - are made!

Dickinson's relations with women were in some cases very close. But women often seemed to her stifled by convention and fashion: see "What Soft - Cherubic Creatures - " (*675). Most "Gentlewomen," she thought, had a "Horror so refined / Of freckled Human Nature - "; a Horror not excluding, one supposes, Dickinson's own nature, since in "Doubt Me!" (332, J 275) she called herself "a freckled Maiden," and in 267 (J 1737) she referred to her "freckled Bosom." She reveals other women's disquiet at her sometimes unconventional behavior, a veering of her weathervane. When, she says, her weathervane is "a little to the East" (perhaps a sign of an oncoming storm), it scares away women—whose souls, like their dresses, are made of Muslin. In her more disturbed moments, it is in men she finds support: Hearts made of "Broadcloth" (a fabric for men's suits) are firmer than Hearts made of "Organdy" (another delicate female fabric, like Muslin, or the "Dimity" of 675). In women, Dickinson could find friends to cast soothing shade on her "Torrid days": they would cool her exaggerations, her tempests. But women were alienated by her "Frigid" hours of mind, her frequent depressions. Men, apparently "higher" of temperature than women, could lift her depressions back to life-warmth, perhaps because, when she was young, she had instinctively taken refuge in her attachment to her father and her brother, Austin, who were closer to her heart than her mother and her sister, Lavinia. To her, men were figures of authority, ranging from her father to later acquaintances such as Benjamin Newton, Charles Wadsworth, Samuel Bowles, T. W. Higginson, and Otis Lord. Their warmer "temperature" had social backing in the convention that men had firmer hearts than women (the word "courage" comes from Latin *cor,* meaning "heart").

These reflections on the comparative reliability of women and men as friends make the poet wish to blame women for their insufficiencies of response. But she checks herself with the thought that just as it was her "nature" to be a "Leopard" (*276), so perhaps it was other women's "nature" to be formed of Muslin or Organdy. What Creator-Weaver made them so? Who can say how the "Tapestries of Paradise" are made? There are no records of the decisions made by that unpredictable Creator in weaving his "bewildering thread" of Broadcloth here, Organdy there. The later poem "What Soft - Cherubic Creatures - " blames women's deficiencies on their socialization into class snobbery, overrefined and timid female behavior, and intellectual weakness. Paradoxically, in this slightly earlier poem, Dickinson goes deeper, ascribing disparity of behavior to intrinsic gender distinctions, rather than to mere socialization. In the course of "A Shady friend," unable to bring herself to denigrate the very nature of women, she shifts her blame from women to God. Like men, women are one version of "Tapestries," those beautiful hangings woven for the castles of kings. And God's castle is Paradise.

In the poem, Dickinson has "Torrid days" and "Frigid hour[s]," implying perhaps that she experiences hysteria more frequently than depression, but she does not locate any temperate zone between. Her life seemed, in her mind, to speed from one extreme to another. After his first meeting with the poet, Higginson remarked (in a letter to his wife) on her exhausting intensity (which could probably relax itself only at home with family members, if then). Higginson was glad not to live near her; and she preferred eventually to sustain friendship by correspondence rather than by personal encounters.

She was expecting too much of friends, perhaps, in the way of help for her temperamental instability; and intuiting that, she directs the blame back at God, the creator of these human Tapestries. Beginning with a firm statement, "A Shady friend" slides into a hypothesis, and then into a tentative ascription of blame, ending in a bewildered exclamation at the inscrutability of causation.

[J 278]

# 312

I can wade Grief -
Whole Pools of it -
I'm used to that -
But the least push of Joy
Breaks up my feet -
And I tip - drunken -
Let no Pebble - smile -
'Twas the New Liquor -
That was all!

Power is only Pain -
Stranded - thro' Discipline,
Till Weights - will hang -
Give Balm - to Giants -
And they'll wilt, like Men -
Give Himmaleh -
They'll carry - Him!

Reducing the Himalayas to one compound mountain, endowing it with Giant status and a Giant proper name—Himmaleh (with the accent on the last syllable)—Dickinson writes a less stoic version of her theme in "We never know how high we are" (1197, J 252): the capacity to exceed one's own abilities. "I can wade Grief" allows the possibility of—in fact narrates the event of—Joy, an unexpected happening in a life that usually consists of wading through "Pools" of Grief. The poet has suddenly been given a drink of a "New Liquor," Joy—the "New" implying that there was an "Old Liquor" of tears, which eventually had accumulated into whole Pools of Grief. One doesn't usually have to "wade" through "Pools"; in fact, in another use of "wade" ("A Sparrow took a Slice of Twig"; 1257, J 1211), Dickinson conjoins it with the word "deepest." Like the "Polar Air" of "Through the Straight Pass of Suffering" (*187), Grief is an obstructive and hindering medium that one cannot step easily through. At every lifting of the foot, there is effort.

Routine becomes so unconscious a habit—even when it amounts to a daily passage through Grief—that a divagation from it wakes consciousness up into dizziness. The gay "little Tippler" of "I taste a liquor never brewed - " (207, J 214), who ranged freely through states of voluntary inebriation from "air" and "Dew," is an altogether different figure from the Dickinson undone by Joy here. "Joy" manifests itself as a sort of earthquake that "Breaks up" her feet and amuses each Pebble observing from the roadway as (she continues) "I"—and we expect the word "trip," but are tripped up ourselves on seeing "I tip - ."

Her stoic "Power" in her past struggle with Grief did not arise, she realizes, from physical strength; it was conferred by Pain, fortified by Discipline to the point where it could bear plural "Weights" (perhaps one on each side, like a laborer balancing two heavy baskets). What can Dickinson be thinking of when she speaks of her Pain as "Stranded"? Grief has stranded her feet in Pools, lesser bodies of water, which, having no current, can never reach the sea, the normal goal of land water. "Exultation is the going / Of an inland soul to sea - " (143, J 76), she had written, but that "divine intoxication" is forbidden her, isolated as she is in Pools. She perhaps remembered both of those earlier poems of intoxication and inebriation ("I taste a liquor" and "Exultation") in composing this poem of "drunken" Joy. Yet neither of the earlier poems framed Joy in habitual Grief, as "I can wade Grief" does.

By now, the poet has learned the rarity of Joy, and is well acquainted with the habitual collapse back into Grief. Her compensatory argument—that one gains strength through Pain—asserts that there is a sapping debilitation in Joy. Even Giants, when they are "lost in Balms," like the "fainting" bee of "Come slowly - Eden!" (205, J 211), will "wilt, like Men." But if they are "called to rise" by being given an overwhelming weight to bear—even so unspeakable a weight as the Himalayas—Giants become like Atlas and can carry the world on their shoulders, fitting their strength to their burden. We have by now left "drunken" Joy far behind: Dickinson never reverts to it, never expresses a hope of its return; it seems to have vanished beyond recuperation as she bends once more under the superhuman weight of Discipline. ("Discipline," here, has the religious meaning of interior self-regulation, not of discipline exerted from an external authority.)

"I can wade Grief" is not easy to scan. It seems composed of trimeters and dimeters, in no predictable order except for the trimeters that are the last four lines of each stanza, with their *abcb* rhyme. The lines preceding these (five in stanza 1, three in stanza 2) have an uncertain rhyme-scheme. The irregularity of step, once Joy tips the poet's gait, may perhaps lie behind the irregularity of meter.

[J 252]

# 314

"Hope" is the thing with feathers -
That perches in the soul -
And sings the tune without the words -
And never stops - at all -

And sweetest - in the Gale - is heard -
And sore must be the storm -
That could abash the little Bird
That kept so many warm -

I've heard it in the chillest land -
And on the strangest Sea -
Yet - never - in Extremity,
It asked a crumb - of me.

Dickinson's use of the word "thing" is worth thinking about. She employs it, according to the *Emily Dickinson Lexicon,* 115 different times and with seven distinguishable meanings. For our purpose here, it is enough to say that it is her single largest mental category, which can embrace named and unnamed acts, creatures, concepts, occasions, and so on. It is as though she begins each inquiry with the general question, "What sort of thing is this?" and then goes on to categorize it more minutely: a major thing or a minor thing, a present thing or an absent thing, a live thing or a dead thing—the word suits all subdivisions. However, because it is neutral (in age, sex, status, location), "thing" is also a peculiarly bloodless word, reducing all nouns subsumed in it to inspectable-at-arm's-length objects. Dickinson's relentlessly intellectual demand that experience be classified and defined leads to her inclination to place acts and feelings first under the rubric "thing," and then to track the "thing" back to specificity through various inner questions.

The first move she makes here, in wishing to describe the implications of the word "Hope"—which she puts in quotation marks to show us she is intending mention, not use—is to think of its aspiring nature: it has wings. "Hope" is "the thing with feathers." Only one "thing" has feathers: a bird. Why doesn't she simply say, "'Hope' is a bird"? After all, she does say so in the second stanza, calling it "the little Bird." But she is able to use the definite article there (instead of saying "a little Bird") precisely because she has already sketched it out, in her non-naming first stanza. The non-naming rhetoric makes a faux riddle of Hope's species, prolonged from "the thing with feathers" to the "thing's" location (in the soul), to its form of expression (a melody without words), and to a temporal extension (it never stops). The riddle-defining persists even in the two lines which introduce the second stanza. "The thing" sings both in Calm and in Gale (of course, since it never stops at all), but its voice, always sweet, is "sweetest" in the Gale. Superlatives are Dickinson's highest form of praise; and we now see the howling storm sweetened for the hapless sailor by the "thing" singing to him not just any song, but its sweetest song.

It is only with the foreboding thought—"But is there some Storm so sore that it can silence that song?"—that Dickinson can introduce "the little Bird." "Abash" means "to destroy the self-possession or confidence" of someone, and by admitting that Hope's persistence may not survive some killing Gale, the poem takes on the problem lurking in its former confident assertion concerning Hope: that it "never stops - at all." "How do you know that?" asks that part of the mind that William Blake named the "Idiot Questioner" (not an "idiot" at all, since the Questioner goes straight, as always, to the most dubious premise of the argument, indefensible here because life is not yet over and thus one can't say whether Hope persists forever). All the poet can do is retort with the history of Hope—it kept so many warm in the past—and reiterate her own experience of its omnipresence, whether in the Arctic land of depression or disappointment, or on the "strangest Sea" of uncharted isolation.

Abandoning the question of whether one can claim that Hope "never stops - at all - ", Dickinson sketches its sublime offer to exempt her from conventional reciprocity: it remains under her roof whether or not she ever repays it for its sustenance. Even "in Extremity"—when she asks the most of it—it never asks anything back, not even a crumb. In such a closing, Dickinson accompanies gratitude with irony: Can the power she claims for it exist in a "thing" that lives on air alone? (Hamlet to Claudius, Act 3, scene 2: "I eat the air, promise-crammed.")

The antithetical rhyming in "storm" and "warm" emphasizes the paradoxical (but uncertain) power of Hope's tune. The interesting thing about Hope's melody (probably derived from Keats's similar reflection on the nightingale) is that it is pure abstraction, applicable to anything at all. The song of Keats's nightingale is now an "ecstasy," now a "requiem," depending on what the poet is thinking about or how he is feeling. The abstract syntax of music—expressing emotion without recourse to ideational language—is the envy of poets, who must construct a new set of relations among words already long in use, hoary with past meanings. That effort by poets can be thought of as a purification of tribal language (Mallarmé, "Le Tombeau d'Edgar Poe": "donner un sens plus pur aux mots de la tribu") or, conversely, as adding a further encrustation upon common usage (Stevens, "Two Illustrations That the World Is What You Make of It": "Speech is not dirty silence / Clarified. It is silence made still dirtier"). Dickinson, after beginning the poem with a reversed first foot in order to emphasize the concept ("Hope") that she means to define, reverts to pure iambs in every foot of all remaining lines, exemplifying the even *continuo* of Hope's song through time.

[J 254]

# 319

Of Bronze - and Blaze -
The North - tonight -
So adequate - it forms -
So preconcerted with itself -
So distant - to alarms -
An Unconcern so sovreign
To Universe, or me -
Infects my simple spirit
With Taints of Majesty -
Till I take vaster attitudes -
And strut upon my stem -
Disdaining Men, and Oxygen,
For Arrogance of them -

My Splendors, are Menagerie -
But their Competeless Show
Will entertain the Centuries
When I, am long ago,
An Island in dishonored Grass -
Whom none but Daisies, know -

This brilliant poem on the Northern Lights (its riddle-nature destroyed by the first editors, who named it "Aurora") was surely in Wallace Stevens's mind when he composed his greatest sequence, "The Auroras of Autumn." Previous poets (Wordsworth in *The Prelude,* Coleridge in "The Rime of the Ancient Mariner," Christopher Cranch in "To the Aurora Borealis") had also taken notice of the Auroras; Dickinson was not inventing the topic. But she did it justice.

Dickinson's extraordinary response to natural phenomena is visible as she herself becomes porous to the Auroras, saying she is "infected" by the power streaming out of them. Her simple spirit takes on, from the Auroras, "Taints of Majesty"—but she judges this an unearned Majesty, one not produced by her own "simple" spirit, but illegitimately borrowed. (Her first editors, appalled by "Taints," substituted the anodyne "tints," while also changing the indicting "infects" to "It paints," making the lines read, "It paints my simple spirit, / With tints of majesty." How unsettling they found her perceptions, while still admirably trying to forward her "letter to the World"!) Temporarily allowing the "infection," Dickinson-as-flower takes on "vaster attitudes" and absurdly (and arrogantly) tries to "strut" on her fixed "stem," declaring that she—like the Auroras—needs neither Men nor Oxygen. Although she recognizes the preposterousness of her metamorphosis into a sky-wide Aurora, she cannot deny that it has happened, that the glorious phenomenon has been incorporated, momentarily, into her very being. Her self-mockery as flower balances her mega-self as Aurora, and it is not surprising that the inflation of self collapses immediately into yet more mockery.

It has not always been understood that the second stanza powerfully contrasts the poet's ironically named "Splendors" (her ill-assorted "Menagerie" of poems) and the genuine celestial splendors of the Auroras, against which a human artist can never hope to compete:

> *My* "Splendors" are "Menagerie" (a miscellaneous collection of
>     animals)—
> But *their* (the Auroras') impossible-to-compete-with Show
> Will entertain the Centuries
> [Long after I expire, an anonymous and unknown person].

The poet left two alternatives—and did not indicate a clear preference for one of them—for the noun in the last line of the poem, writing first "Daisies," and then, immediately under it, "Beetles." Johnson prints "Beetles"; Franklin prints the poet's first choice, "Daisies." I prefer "Beetles," and will explain why.

The two stanzas have two different rhyme-schemes. The first consists of thirteen lines and is written in quatrains, with the rhymes being significant: the Aurora "forms" itself so distantly that it gives (for all its Majesty) no audible "alarms" to those on earth; the simple "me" appropriates "Majesty"; and her "stem" takes on arrogance vis-à-vis "them" ("Men" and earthly "Oxygen"). The second stanza, by contrast, is less than half the length of the first;

it is a single six-line rhyming unit (with three meaning-bearing full rhymes: the "Show" of the Auroras continues for centuries, while long "ago" the poet was buried anonymously, and where she is, only the Beetles "know"). When Dickinson abandons one formal shape for another, as here, she implies a distinct opposition between the two: in the first stanza—rhythmically—three quatrains couch her admiration of, and identification with, the Auroras, while the second stanza's sestet embodies her subsequent admission of the superiority of their "Show" to any assembled "Menagerie" of hers, contrasting their longevity in the Universe to her own brevity and anonymity. And yet, there is in the close an implicit analogy between her "Splendors" and those of the Auroras: both are capable of entertaining a spectator's eye. She does not have the Auroras "impress" the Centuries—nor does she introduce a hyperbolic verb such as "stun," "amaze," or "astound"; no, the purpose of the Auroras is to "entertain." It as though the Creator and the Poet were both artists, and God had decided to "entertain" the Centuries with his "Show" in the heavens, while the poet, in a lesser way, entertains a briefer span of years with her circus "Menagerie."

I have not yet come to the greatest challenge posed to the poet by her topic: how to represent the ever-changing glories of the cosmic Auroras. She does not give a name (whether "Aurora Borealis" or "Northern Lights") to the phenomenon she sees; rather, she looks to the North and sees it transfigured by enormous waves of heroic light, with colors of archaic armor and of fire: "Of Bronze - and Blaze - / The North - tonight - ". Many theatrical descriptions of shape and movement might have followed in another poet's work (and do follow, in Stevens's sequence). But Dickinson's mind leaps to another plane altogether, leaving visual rendition behind in order to rise to the plane of aesthetic judgment. Four judgments follow, explaining what is so aesthetically satisfactory about this great celestial phenomenon.

The first employs one of the poet's characteristically hyperbolic understatements: the Aurora forms itself *so* adequately—to what? To its intrinsic ambition (think of all the ambitious works that fail to produce an adequate execution of their aims). The second, interesting, judgment is that the Aurora is "preconcerted with itself": all its aspects accord with each other, following its initial plan (think of all the works composed with no pre-planning, composed of heterogeneous parts yoked together). The third judgment concerns the enormous distance of the Aurora from "alarms": no "great shout" (Webster on "alarm") can frighten it, no message of approaching hostilities can affect it. The fourth judgment describes the Aurora's majesty: such grandeur exercises a "sov[e]reign" disregard of both the Universe to which it belongs and of the human being contemplating its display.

Dickinson aspired to the same sovereignty for her works: her wish was that they should become equal to their ambitions, concordant in their construction, unaffrighted by hostility, and indifferent to public approval. It is a measure of her intellectual closeness to natural phenomena that she could analyze the Aurora as a symbol of major aesthetic realization. She can span in one of her tiny lines ("To Universe, or me - ") the whole distance from the inaccessible cosmos to herself in Amherst, and would claim the same capacity for any human brain—which is, as she will later assert, "just the weight of God - " (see *598, "The Brain - is wider than the Sky - ", discussed above in the Introduction).

But after the sublimity of her opening meditation on the Auroras, and the self-mockery of her "contamination" by Majesty, Dickinson must descend from the celestial to the terrestrial. As Wordsworth wrote in the 1850 *Prelude* (V, 553–557), the Northern Lights are magnificently omnipresent— "Here, nowhere, there, and everywhere at once"—but the poet's body must finally concede to an earthly "somewhere," the grave. Dickinson's laden description of the site of her buried body as "An Island in dishonored Grass" implies that the presence of a dead object is an isolated betrayal of a surrounding sea of innocent grass, which is dishonored by the presence of a decomposing corpse. And the posthumous location of that disintegrating body is known only to—to whom? Here Dickinson pondered two words (as I have mentioned above), "Beetles" and "Daisies." Not only has she compared herself earlier to a flower when she mocked her own assumption of "vaster attitudes," but her nickname in certain poems is "Daisy," and "Daisies" was what she first wrote in transcribing a fair copy of this poem into Fascicle 13. If she lies in a cemetery among her peers, then, the place of her grave would be known to other "Daisies." In "How many times these low feet staggered - ", the "Indolent Housewife" was "in Daisies - lain!" (*238). And Dickinson had even jokingly imagined (in the youthful poem "If I should die - "; 36, J 54) herself and a friend lying in Daisies while "Commerce will continue" and the stock market still thrives: "'Tis sweet to know that stocks will stand / When we with Daisies lie - ".

But despite the claims of a conclusion with "Daisies," the poet mentions no visible daisies in the picture of her isolated grave in "Of Bronze - and Blaze - "; she mentions only the "dishonored grass." The macabre Beetles may be more logical inhabitants than Daisies of the "dishonored Grass" and of the grave. (Keats's "Ode on Melancholy" mentions the death-watch beetle as accompaniment to the initial temptation to suicide.) In another, later poem ("Under the Light, yet under," 1068, J 949) Dickinson places burial deep in the earth, "Under the Beetle's Cellar":

> Under the Light, yet under,
> Under the Grass and the Dirt,
> Under the Beetle's Cellar
> Under the Clover's Root . . .

Dickinson's 1896 editors of course preferred "Daisies" to "Beetles," but Johnson adopted Dickinson's alternative "Beetles." In her fair copy, Dickinson had placed a comma after "Daisies," as in Franklin's version reproduced above. After the alternative "Beetles," she placed her more characteristic dash, making the line read, "Whom none but Beetles - know - ". Although both comma and dash indicate a pause, normal grammar does not permit a comma between subject and predicate. By using her dash—which can denote a pause to consider what the next word will be—Dickinson avoids grammatical disquiet, and introduces, with the Beetles, a macabre note. Both choices—"Daisies" and "Beetles"—suggest the poet's final admission, as she faces the celestial Auroras, of her inescapable "dishonor," mortality.

[J 290]

# 320

There's a certain Slant of light,
Winter Afternoons -
That oppresses, like the Heft
Of Cathedral Tunes -
Heavenly Hurt, it gives us -
We can find no scar,
But internal difference -
Where the Meanings, are -
None may teach it - Any -
'Tis the Seal Despair -
An imperial affliction
Sent us of the Air -
When it comes, the Landscape listens -
Shadows - hold their breath -
When it goes, 'tis like the Distance
On the look of Death -

Inoffensively entitled "Winter" when it first appeared in print in 1890, this bleak poem has become one of Emily Dickinson's most discussed and most often anthologized works. One can't fail, in reading "There's a certain Slant of light," to recall her later poem that begins "Tell all the truth but tell it slant - " (*1263). The connection between light and truth is an ancient one, and the winter Slant of light offers, in its "Meanings," the powerful, if desolate, emotional truth in "Despair." The theological concept of Despair is less well known now than in the nineteenth century: modern readers hardly realize that it is one of the two sins that can prevent salvation (the other being Presumption—the belief that to be saved, one does not need to practice virtue). To despair means, etymologically, to give up hope (Latin, *spes*); and Despair, in this poem, is the last truth and the last lesson. No one can teach it anything.

But how might a poet represent the state of Despair? There are coherent precedents, such as Cowper's "The Castaway," offering an integrated narrative of perdition. Dickinson's words and images, however, are unsettlingly disparate: a Slant of light, Winter Afternoons, oppression, organ music in a Cathedral, Heavenly, Hurt, scar, difference, Meanings, teach(ing), Seal, Despair, an empire, affliction, Air, Landscape, Shadows, Distance, the look of Death. Since until the last two lines there is no explicit narrative, we try, as we first attempt the poem, to group the poet's effects of diction and imagery: we see that the Cathedral, Heaven, the (imperial) Seal, Air, and Despair belong to religion; while the Slant of light, Winter Afternoons, Landscape, and Shadows belong to a natural scene. One group so far unaccounted-for includes Hurt, oppression, scar, and affliction, a group we could put under the category "damage caused by another." And finally, there is the abstract group: difference, Meanings, Despair, Distance, Death.

For us to create such groupings is an artificial exercise, of course, but it serves to point out what diverse threads Dickinson can combine in her closely woven fabric of poetry. As she veers from light to Hurt, from scar to Meaning, from Seal to Despair, and from Landscape to Death, the poet depends on our agility to move as she moves, from one plane to another. After all, the poem itself tells us that for every outside phenomenon there is an inside equivalent: if a Slant of light, then Hurt; if a Seal, Despair; if Shadows, Death. The impossibility of firmly separating the sense experience of landscape from the spiritual experience of Despair is a central point of the poem. Is it a poem arising (as it seems to) from a natural perception which is then given symbolic import, or is it a poem that arises from internal Despair and then looks around the landscape for an equivalent image? We cannot really say. Sense experience is richly called up by the light, the season, the time of day, the heavy-to-lift weight of organ music, the scar, the seal, the landscape, and shadows. The symbolic is equally richly summoned by the religious diction, as well as by the abstractions, which cluster around the governing one, Despair.

In assuming there is still a heavenly Empire that can deal out imperial afflictions to human beings, the poem seems to invoke a notion of God's plan, his providential decisions for our own good. He changes our internal conceptual universe by means of his imposed "affliction." But this "providential" explanation of the purpose of the Heavenly Hurt is immediately negated by the word "Despair," which gives no credence to heavenly purposes of salvation. And the "internal difference" does not teach us anything improving, such as "Whom God loveth he chastiseth." The change to Despair is unteachable; it is a permanent Seal set on life.

In the summary final stanza, in which the light comes and then goes (all in four lines), we learn that the Slant of light is prophetic of its own disappearance. As soon as that late-afternoon light is seen, the Landscape listens for the footstep of night (as in Baudelaire's "Recueillement": "Entends, ma chère, entends, la douce nuit qui marche"). And the Shadows—whose very existence depends on the presence of that light—hold their breath in suspense, knowing that with their next exhalation they will vanish. And when this last light goes, everything sinks into visual unreachability—as if one were to look on the face of a corpse and receive no answering gaze, only "the look of Death," as the person is in an instant removed to an incalculable distance from life. Dickinson's closing animation of both Landscape and Shadows gives a pathos to their coming extinction, as Despair, in existential parallel with them, extinguishes spiritual hope.

"Breath" and "Death" are so frequently rhymed in poetry in English because we lack an adequate supply of words containing the end-sound of "Death" (one can evade the problem, of course, by using a slant rhyme such as "faith"). Dickinson wouldn't claim originality in rhyming "breath" and "Death"—but by almost-rhyming "listens" and "Distance" in lines 1 and 3 of the closing stanza, she distracts us from the conventionality of "breath" and "Death" in lines 2 and 4. She also takes pleasure in finding rhymes in which one rhyme-word hides phonetically within its mate—as "Air" hides in "Despair," and "are" hides in "scar." Although she ushers in the poem with her usual ballad stanza (4-3-4-3), the first stanza, naturally pronounced, does not fall easily on the ear (as one can ascertain by giving it, read aloud, four downbeats, in accordance with its theoretical trochaic prosody):

> *There's* a *cer*tain *Slant* of *light,*
> Winter Afternoons -
> *That* oppresses, *like* the *Heft*
> Of Cathedral Tunes -

When I have heard the poem read aloud, it is not with these accents. The more "normal" reading inserts anapests at the beginning of line 1, and at both the beginning and the middle of line 3:

> There's a *cer*tain *Slant* of *light*,
>
> . . . . .
>
> That op*press*es, like the *Heft*

The next two stanzas of the poem observe a form of the ballad stanza that regularly truncates the first line, creating a considerably more abrupt effect: 3-3-4-3. And the final stanza, as the light "comes" with its brevity and "goes" into final darkness, offers us a perfectly regular trochaic ballad stanza, 4-3-4-3. The first stanza of a poem usually sets its normative prosody, but only the last stanza in "There's a certain Slant of light" obeys the normative rhythm of a trochaic ballad stanza. Whatever we make of stanza 1, pronouncing it either with the possibilities delineated above or with some other, it does not introduce us plainly, as ordinary opening stanzas do, to a rhythmic mode that holds for the rest of the poem. The rhythm of the last stanza, in the feminine end-words "listens" and "Distance," presents a dying trochaic fall, "caught" from the earlier trochees "gives us," "Any," and "affliction."

Dickinson avoids making the spiritual life a domain unto itself by tethering it so completely to an expiring New England winter moment. In reading her, we constantly flicker between sense and spirit.

[J 258]

# 325

There came a Day - at Summer's full -
Entirely for me -
I thought that such - were for the Saints -
Where Resurrections - be -

The Sun - as common - went abroad -
The Flowers - accustomed - blew -
As if no Soul the Solstice passed -
That maketh all things new.

The time was scarce profaned - by speech -
The symbol of a word
Was needless - as at Sacrament -
The Wardrobe - of Our Lord -

Each was to each - the sealèd church -
Permitted to commune - this time -
Lest we too awkward - show -
At "Supper of the Lamb."

The hours slid fast - as hours will -
Clutched tight - by greedy hands -
So - faces on two Decks - look back -
Bound to opposing Lands -

And so - when all the time had failed -
Without external sound -
Each - bound the other's Crucifix -
We gave no other bond -

Sufficient troth - that we shall rise -
Deposed - at length - the Grave -
To *that* New Marriage -
Justified - through Calvaries of Love!

There exist several versions of this poem. *Scribner's Magazine,* when it published the poem in 1890, omitted the fourth stanza, presumably for its blasphemous intimation that this spiritual communion between the speaker and her lover was a rehearsal of the heavenly banquet, a rehearsal kindly "permitted" so that they would not be awkward at the heavenly "Supper of the Lamb." (The stanza was restored in book publication.) There is a significant difference between the version of the poem printed by Franklin in the *Reading Edition* and the revised script of the earlier Version C, in which stanza 2 reads more explicitly:

> The Sun - as common - went abroad -
> The flowers - accustomed - blew -
> While our two Souls that Solstice passed -
> Which maketh all things new.

Dickinson may have reflected that it was more logical to say that everything in Nature went on as usual as if *no* soul were having an extraordinary revelation than to say that Nature's routines continued *while* the couple made their silent vows.

"Behold I make all things new," says God from His throne in Revelation (21:5). Drawing on this apocalyptic text, Dickinson conflates the longest day of the year, the Summer solstice ("a Day - at Summer's full - ") with Revelation's disclosing of all things and changing all that went before, and with the Resurrections that will occur on the Last Day. One could scarcely find a conflation more powerful. And this Day is one of both marriage and separation: the lovers' unspoken vow of mutual fidelity is taken with the eventual discovery that they will never meet again, as the parting for each of them becomes a crucifixion (each takes the other's Crucifix, binding it on as a sign of suffering and sacrifice). The speaker's fullness of joy is permitted to last unbroken for four ecstatic stanzas.

The lovers need say nothing; their moment together creates a shrine, and anything coming from the outside would destroy its sacredness ("profane" means, from the Latin *profanus,* "outside the temple"). Commenting on the needlessness of words, the poet makes a small joke: at the Eucharist, where the bread and wine represent the body and blood of the Lord, nobody demands the actual body-garment of Jesus, his "Wardrobe." So in this silent marriage, there is no need for the usual words of the marriage vows, which would be an unnecessary clothing to the communion of souls. "Each was to each the sealèd church" (the adjective must be pronounced "sealèd" to keep the meter). We may be helped to understand this religious metaphor by the corresponding passage in "My Worthiness is all my Doubt - " (791, J 751) in which Dickinson explains that since there is no one higher than God, He must, when He needs repose, "stoop" to one of his creatures. Thus, she may justify her lover's "stooping" to her, as her "Undivine" Soul becomes an Abode for the contentment of her lover, who is one of the Elect. And once he enters it, that Abode, housing the Sacrament of his presence, becomes a Church:

> So I - the Undivine Abode
> Of His Elect Content -
> Conform my Soul - as 'twere a Church,
> Unto Her Sacrament -

In "There came a Day - at Summer's full - ", each of the lovers is unto the other the "sealèd" church of final communion, because there can be no sacramental marriage in the flesh.

Why, asks the poet, were she and her beloved granted such a day of resurrection, revelation, and length of hours, a day entirely for the two of them? It was, she conjectures, to prepare them for their eventual reunion in heaven. Four stanzas of supernal joy, and then exile, generating in the poem a reproach to desire as excessive, "greedy," since it longs for permanent physical union. Two ships appear, each taking one of the lovers, who look back at each other from the two decks, knowing they are bound to opposing lands. (We are likely to think—in wondering what makes the lands *opposing*—of the later poem "I cannot live with you" (*706), with its comment, "You - served Heaven - You know, / Or sought to - / I could not - ".) Soundless, the lovers exchange crucifixes, signifying their bond in suffering; silent, they give no verbal promise. "Until death do us part" is already presumed in the exchange of fatal crucifixes. It need not be uttered.

The poem ends with a faith in resurrection, once the Grave has been "Deposed" (as a usurping sovereign is "deposed" when a rightful King is re-established on the throne). The "New Marriage" has been guaranteed by the lovers' parallel crucifixions, their "Calvaries of Love!" Dickinson introduces very deliberately the powerful theological concept of "Justification" (by faith, by works, an issue of Christian debate); not only does she appropriate, in "Justified," that weighty word, but she dares to pluralize the ever-singular "Calvary," the scene of the Crucifixion of Jesus. This blasphemy—that the lovers' crucifixions replicate in identical detail that of Jesus—confirms her defiance of the conventional God. Her rhyming of "word" and "Lord" in the third stanza is parodic, incorporating the Johannine "Word" into this erotic "Sacrament"; and she shows what can defeat the "Grave" by slant-rhyming that grim word with the exalted closing word, "Love."

The rhythm is that of the conventional ballad stanza, but twice—for the sake of the content—Dickinson distorts by addition or subtraction. Had stanzas 4 and 7 kept the 4-3-4-3 shape of the ballad stanza, their lines would have been arranged as follows, with "commune" rhyming with "Lamb":

> Each was to each - the sealèd church -
> Permitted to commune -
> This time - lest we too awkward show -
> At "Supper of the Lamb."

and

> Sufficient troth - that we shall rise -
> Deposed - at length the Grave -
> To *that* New Marriage - justified -
> Through Calvaries of Love!

Dickinson retained her "mislineation" in both stanzas in all versions of the manuscript. But *Scribner's Magazine,* when it published the poem in 1890, moved "Justified" to the end of the third line of the stanza (as above), refusing to countenance the poet's truncation of the meter of the third line. We can easily see why, in each case, Dickinson "mislineated" her stanza: the drama of "this" emphasized the singularity and nonrecurrence of the moment ("commune - this time"), and the triumphant announcement of the New Marriage dominates its dimeter line, as "Justified" turns the final line into a grand closing pentameter.

[J 322]

# 330

He put the Belt around my life -
I heard the Buckle snap -
And turned away, imperial,
My Lifetime folding up -
Deliberate, as a Duke would do
A Kingdom's Title Deed -
Henceforth - a Dedicated sort -
A Member of the Cloud -

Yet not too far to come at call -
And do the little Toils
That make the Circuit of the Rest -
And deal occasional smiles
To lives that stoop to notice mine -
And kindly ask it in -
Whose invitation, know you not
For Whom I must decline?

Dickinson makes the hoop that signifies union not a wedding ring, but a Belt with a Buckle that decisively snaps shut. The Belt preexisted the lover's use of it: it is "the" Belt, not "a" Belt (and perhaps it arises as a humble "New England" substitute for the royal claiming of a deer-beloved by a collar—see Sidney's "Whoso list to hunt"). An effect of verisimilitude arises from the parenthetical aside to a friend ("I heard the Buckle snap - "), which leads to a second aside: her sovereign folds up her lifetime, she tells her friend, "as a Duke would do / A Kingdom's Title Deed - ". We are thus prepared for the final remark to the friend (when the friend invites Dickinson to a closer relation than they have hitherto had), "know you not / For Whom I must decline?" Because "He" has claimed the poet's exclusive intimacy, she cannot extend it to another person (although she is permitted domestic "little Toils" which do not infringe upon her deep attachment to her Lord). He is a Duke; she is his Kingdom—and the exaltation of that relationship makes all others seem insignificant, although she continues in the small tasks that take her around the Circuit of others. She even (as hidden royalty) deals "occasional smiles" to those who think her a deprived person—to "lives that stoop to notice mine - / And kindly ask it in - ".

The poet's masquerade is the stuff of folktale: that of the housebound Cinderella who is in reality a princess. The only excuse for Dickinson's so dignifying her hidden self is that through being "buckled" to an "imperial" Other, she has become not royalty but "Henceforth - a Dedicated sort - / A Member of the Cloud - ". There may be an echo here (in "dedicated") of the comparable moment of vocation in Wordsworth's life, as he returns at dawn from a dance:

> I made no vows, but vows
> Were then made for me; bond unknown to me
> Was given, that I should be, else sinning greatly,
> A dedicated Spirit.
>
> [*The Prelude* (1850), IV, 334–337]

A comparable celestial "Cloud" occurs in "I got so I could take his name - " (292, J 293), in which Dickinson says that when she shapes her hands "Petition's way," her "Business - [is] with the Cloud, / If any Power behind it, be." Ever skeptical of "the other side" (that lies beyond the mortal veil), she yet was certain she had a duty in the world that had nothing to do with "the Rest." We meet, in this poem, four Dickinsons: the humble one doing "little Toils" in the routine "Circuit" of the Household; the spiritual "Member of the Cloud" who has business with a celestial Realm; the hidden Duchess who deals out royal smiles; and the poor spinster whom others take pity on, thinking that she needs invitations. Nobody understands her declining of those invitations, because they cannot see the imperial power to whom she belongs. Dickinson's rapid substitution of one of these four "selves" for another contributes to her account of living on a different plane ever since she "heard the Buckle - snap - ".

There is wit in the rhyming of a practical noun—"Title Deed"—with the remote and vaporous "Cloud," as there is also wit in rhyming two spheres of the poet's life: the private domestic "Toils" and the public social "smiles." Although the poem consists of four rhymed quatrains, these are amalgamated into two eight-line stanzas, to demonstrate the two lives that the poet lives. In the first we encounter her as she is royally bound to her invisible Possessor; in the second, we find her reticently bearing her unrevealed secret into her social context.

[J 273]

# 337

Of nearness to her sundered Things
The Soul has special times -
When Dimness - looks the Oddity -
Distinctness - easy - seems -

The Shapes we buried, dwell about,
Familiar, in the Rooms -
Untarnished by the Sepulchre,
The Mouldering Playmate comes -

In just the Jacket that he wore -
Long buttoned in the Mold
Since we - old mornings, Children - played -
Divided - by a world -

The Grave yields back her Robberies -
The Years, our pilfered Things -
Bright Knots of Apparitions
Salute us, with their wings -

As we - it were - that perished -
Themself - had just remained till we rejoin them -
And 'twas they, and not ourself
That mourned -

This passionate lament for "sundered Things" advances slowly on its topic. What are the Things that have been cut asunder from our Soul? The next name Dickinson gives the Things is "The Shapes we buried," so we know that the sundered Things are the dead; and the dual plurals ("Shapes" and "Things") make the object of lament a collective one. In one respect it is a collective lament, too, as it passes, with the coming of the second stanza, from the abstract universal ("The Soul") to the collective "we" (maintained throughout the poem until we encounter the last stanza's wonderful mixed plural/singulars—having it both ways—of "Themself" and "ourself"). In one lightning stroke, however, the poem is invaded, in line 8, not by general Things and Shapes but by a haunting particular: right in the middle of a stanza, an angelic silver "Playmate," "untarnished" by the grave, appears to memory. Yet he is, for all his shining self, a "Mouldering Playmate," one long in his sepulchre.

At this point in the poem, Dickinson has already begun the rapid flicker back and forth between the remembered playmate of her childhood and the mouldering corpse: "Untarnished" (alive), "Sepulchre" (dead), "Mouldering" (dead). He comes "In just the Jacket that he wore - " (alive), but the Mold immediately encroaches once again; the jacket has been "Long buttoned in the Mold" (dead). There follows a flicker back to youth in "Since we - old mornings, Children - played - ", undone by an immediate flicker back to the grave, as poet and playmate, ever since the death of the playmate, are "Divided - by a world - ." Dickinson's unerring management of the rapid flickering of consciousness between fact and regained memory, as the dead "Things" of the opening become the "Children" of the past, is the most original aspect of the poem.

As, like the Playmate, all those buried Shapes come alive, their insubstantial, but overwhelmingly real, existence in the "mind's eye" must be asserted, and Dickinson does not disappoint. Turning to a grand declaration of memory's form of resurrection, Dickinson declares that the grave is not the end of her "pilfered Things": they come back as "Bright Knots of Apparitions" (derived, probably unconsciously, from Henry Vaughan's "Bright shoots of everlastingness" in "The Retreat"). This characterization of the revenants stresses, first, radiance ("Bright"); second, intercaught threads ("Knots"); and third, a visionary quality ("Apparitions"). The ghosts, like a *corps de ballet,* move in and out of their "Knots," those interactions during life reproduced in memory's luminous scene. And in her rendition of the perfect eidetic encounter of present life and resurrected persons, Dickinson's revenants can "Salute us," with their wings, like the Gabriel of the Annunciation. At such a moment, the dead are in the ascendant, welcoming us to their realm, as if we were the ones who had perished, and they, in the afterlife, were waiting there for us to join them, suffering from our absence, being the mourners rather than the mourned.

Turning time inside out in such a manner, so that the remembered dead are more living than the mourning Soul, Dickinson replaces the "Things" back into the familiar "Rooms" they occupied in life, before Death—who comes "as a thief in the night" (1 Thessalonians 5:2)—removed them, taking, in its "Robberies," the poet's "pilfered Things." When they return, and the poet is no longer divided from them by "a world," the earlier "Dimness" of her earthly sight turns to "Distinctness," making the former visual obscurity seem the "Oddity."

On what base does Dickinson ground the tone of certainty in her yearning proclamation, "The Grave yields back her Robberies - / The Years, our pilfered Things - "? She borrows that tone from the prophets, but alters their future tense ("The dead shall be raised") into the immediacy of her present tense, voicing gratitude for the "special times" of "nearness" to the dead bestowed by acute moments of memory. She also borrows (and rewrites) the authority of the biblical metaphor calling Death a thief. And she denigrates Time as a "pilferer"—the sort of petty thief who is always caught, and whose spoils are returned to their owners.

Dickinson's "mislineation" in the closing stanza allows us to "perish" in the simile of its first line, and then to pass to the (pentameter) memorial preservation, where "Themself - had just remained till we rejoin them - ". Not "Themselves"—a plural to match "Things" and "Shapes" and "Knots"—but the single one of them who was the most beloved to "ourself"; we have been mourning that singular presence until memory changes the grave into bestower, not thief. The penultimate line is a tetrameter, the last a striking monometer: "That mourned - "

[J 607]

# 340

I felt a Funeral, in my Brain,
And Mourners to and fro
Kept treading - treading - till it seemed
That Sense was breaking through -

And when they all were seated,
A Service, like a Drum -
Kept beating - beating - till I thought
My mind was going numb -

And then I heard them lift a Box
And creak across my Soul
With those same Boots of Lead, again,
Then Space - began to toll,

As all the Heavens were a Bell,
And Being, but an Ear,
And I, and Silence, some strange Race
Wrecked, solitary, here -

And then a Plank in Reason, broke,
And I dropped down, and down -
And hit a World, at every plunge,
And Finished knowing - then -

Dickinson frames this famous account of a mental breakdown, indistinguishable from death because it so obliterates consciousness, in a single-sentence paratactic narrative, a tale in which the parallel clauses are joined mainly by successive "and's." Here there are twelve "and's," ten of them heading individual lines, the other two occurring medially in stanzas 4 and 5. And there are words and phrases that imply "and" as well: "treading - treading - "; "beating - beating - "; "then" (appearing both with and without "and"); "again"; "began to toll"; and "at every plunge." After the horrible repetition of attack after attack on "Reason," Dickinson divides herself into the corpse and the "Mourners." As she is figuratively buried, in an intolerably prolonged "Funeral," Dickinson remains an active analyst of her own situation; she mourns herself as repetitively as she is attacked. Her mental affliction is so intense that it becomes almost physical ("it seemed / That Sense was breaking through - " into mental space).

In "After great pain" (*372) Dickinson observes that "The Nerves sit ceremonious," and here her inner faculties, the "treading" Mourners, are eventually, in slow individuality, "seated" at the funeral. At the moment when some relief might be offered to the mind as the "treading" stops, an assaultive "Service" begins, beating and beating at her until she fears that her mind will become not deaf, but "numb"—a worse affliction than deafness. (And "numb" suggests "dumb.") Nor, when the Service stops, is she allowed quiet: once again the awful treading resumes, this time with the heavy step made by "Boots of Lead." Her analytic self watches, but her threatened self is now in "a Box," her coffin being taken to its grave. We do not particularly notice the verb "creak" at this moment (a floor in a church might well "creak" under Boots of Lead), but the word is, as Dickinson places it, a foreshadowing of the disintegration to come.

Once the proprieties have been observed—the Funeral, the Mourners, the Service, the Drum-voice of the preacher, the carrying-out of the coffin (no more than a rude "Box") by the pallbearers—Dickinson passes from "objective" analysis to an enacting of the terrible isolation endured by those who are mentally ill. She does not accompany her coffin to the grave; instead, she hears her death knell occupying all of space, as the Heavens become a Bell, and she—no longer "I" but "Being"—becomes a corresponding receptacle of the tolling spaces, an Ear. The tolling is the last sound she hears. When silence replaces hearing, a new hypothesis surges up, that of a shipwreck which leaves behind only two survivors, herself and Silence—who represent a "strange Race" (she, now dumb, belongs to the race of "Silence") in an eternal island solitude. Even that companionship with Silence turns out not to be the end of the narrative—although Dickinson's editors, in the 1896 *Poems,* did not publish the final stanza, perhaps thinking it entirely too explicit.

In line 10, Dickinson wrote first "Brain," and then, drawing brackets around "Brain," wrote "Soul." Corporeal madness seems indubitably a disease of the brain—yet how do we represent not a physical disease but a spiritual illness? In the course of her self-analysis, as spectator to her own funeral, the poet offers no hope (there were many medical nostrums for ordinary madness, but none for spiritual death).

She did not leave herself "Wrecked" on her island, nor does she live in a stasis with Silence as her companion. Instead, her detached analytic state, too, is "Wrecked," as the ominous earlier "creak," betraying the instability of the Soul's floor, wreaks its eventual havoc: "And then a Plank in Reason, broke, / And I dropped down, and down - ". With this line, Dickinson seems to admit a physical component to her "funeral": as life is to the body, so Reason (in its analytical capacity) is to the Brain. Without the support of Reason, madness replaces sanity. As Dickinson sought to name the location of her suffering, she began at "Brain" (line 1) and mutated into "mind" (line 8), then "Soul" (line 10), then "Being" (line 14), enumerating first a corporeal lodging, then an intellectual one, then a spiritual one, and finally a totality including all the others. The "Plank in Reason" breaks without any assistance from her, and she drops in successive stages without (at first) any contribution from her own will.

In a remarkable change of course in the last two lines, Dickinson begins to aid in her own extinction. As she drops through the universe, she hits a World at every (voluntary) "plunge" (replacing an earlier alternative, the more involuntary "Crash") and "Finished knowing" (with "Finished" replacing "Got through"). "[I] Finished" seems an act of will ("I finished gardening at dusk"), whereas "got through" is often said when one is unconscious of active participation ("I got through the operation and into recovery"). At the last moment, with "Finished," Dickinson reclaims agency in her own obliteration, before leaving madness for a merciful unconsciousness.

The extraordinary inflexibility of the rhythm, with its stolid "treading - treading - " from line to line, tetrameter to trimeter, is broken by only one irregularity, that of line 5, which "should" be a tetrameter, but is truncated into a trimeter as the "Drum" of the Service interrupts the narrative. If Dickinson had not made the meter so insistently percussive, we would not "feel" the Funeral she "felt."

[ J 280]

# 341

’Tis so appalling - it exhilirates -
So over Horror, it half captivates -
The Soul stares after it, secure -
To know the worst, leaves no dread more -

To scan a Ghost, is faint -
But grappling, conquers it -
How easy, Torment, now -
Suspense kept sawing so -

The Truth, is Bald - and Cold -
But that will hold -
If any are not sure -
We show them - prayer -
But we, who know,
Stop hoping, now -

Looking at Death, is Dying -
Just let go the Breath -
And not the pillow at your cheek
So slumbereth -

Others, can wrestle -
Yours, is done -
And so of Wo, bleak dreaded - come,
It sets the Fright at liberty -
And Terror's free -
Gay, Ghastly, Holiday!

At one extraordinary moment in this poem, Dickinson declares her atheism, choosing firm (if frigid) Truth over religious Delusion, secular (if unaesthetic) Despair over theological Hope. "The Truth, is Bald - and Cold - / But that will hold - ". She is certain of the Truth, but gestures briefly and dismissively to those who need illusion: "If any are not sure - / We show them - prayer - ". She then reasserts her own affirmation, as one of a company: "we, who know." This manifesto occupies lines 9–14 of this twenty-four-line poem, and it is visibly preceded by a prelude, and followed by a coda. The prelude declares that "the Soul" now knows the worst, and is therefore secure; a long suspense has ended, rendering Torment "easy" (by contrast to the former suspense). Shakespeare had written, "The worst returns to laughter" *(Lear);* Hopkins, retorting, asserted, "No worst, there is none. . . . / More pangs will, schooled at fore-pangs, wilder wring." But Dickinson, unlike them, stops decisively at "the worst," sure that nothing more at all—whether "laughter" or "more pangs"—can occur. At the revelation of "the worst," the Soul becomes giddy with hysteria at the snapping of the previous tension: the news, so appalling, insanely "exhilirates." It is so much beyond Horror that it "half captivates." (Dickinson finds any new psychological state in itself fascinating, no matter what hideous event precipitated it.) We begin to realize that the poem seems to be written, unusually for Dickinson, in rhymed couplets—a tight form that continues through the first three stanzas, but is then dropped in favor of more irregular rhymes, as we'll see. The relaxation of the first nervous laughter of the mind facing the worst is mimicked in the gradual resolution of the meter of the opening two stanzas, in which two pentameters decline into two tetrameters, which themselves decline into four trimeters (5-5-4-4-3-3-3-3). (The third-stanza manifesto, seen above, continues rhyming in couplets that compose a weirdly truncated "ballad" quatrain, 3-2-3-2, followed by a dimeter couplet.)

Dickinson seems indeed to have finished her poem as she pronounces her first-stanza epigram: "To know the worst, leaves no dread more - ". What is left to say? She resorts to a flashback: she was afraid, for a long time, to confront the possibility of "the worst"; as it passed through her mind she would merely "scan" it, not "grapple with it." But now she has wrestled with the Ghost (as Jacob wrestled with God in Genesis 32:24–30, a passage to which she often alludes), and has bested it by her struggle: the incessant, abrading "sawing" of Suspense has ceased. To insert a word such as "sawing" in the context of Horror, Ghost, and Torment is characteristic of Dickinson's drawing even the most extreme states into a New England (or otherwise homely) metaphor. The whine of the saw in the ear, the jagged edges of the saw in the flesh, the whole couched in the "kept on" of relentlessness—what else could so well convey the torture of prolonged suspense concerning one's ultimate destiny?

We have seen the third-stanza central manifesto ("The Truth, is Bald - and Cold - ") and its flashback-prelude in the first two stanzas. Just as Dickinson seemed at first to have contrived an ending for her poem in line 4, so she now seems to have contrived a second ending in the despair closing the manifesto: "we, who know, / Stop hoping, now - ." But there is more to say. Now that "Wo" has already come (line 21), what will follow? Dying—as we might have expected. Dickinson offers advice: See how easy it is! You have only to "let go" of your breath (and by posing her interlocutor with cheek on pillow, she even imagines a deathbed): "Looking at Death, is dying - ". She has reverted to her default stanza-form, the quatrain, but altering the hymn-meter to 3-3-4-2. Having laid her interlocutor on a deathbed, she can pronounce her at rest, in words reminiscent of a funeral: "Others, can wrestle - / Yours, is done - ". And something else is "done," over with, as well—and that is all the earlier "Wo" of torment, horror, suspense, and despair. Vanished forever is "bleak dreaded" woe; once death has come, the previous "Fright" and "Terror" flee the brain. Like a prisoner who has just been told his death date, the poet has nothing more on which to speculate. Her mind is suddenly "at liberty" in a ghastly way; its Ghost of hellish anxiety has been routed—but only by despair.

The curious construction of the concluding stanza is so irregular that it cannot be fitted into a pattern. It opens with two dimeters; *if* they are read as a tetrameter (which they are not) they match the following tetrameters: just as your wrestling is over, so is despairing Woe, which, once come, "sets the Fright at liberty." The stanza reads 2-2-4-4; and then what? Certainly something to rhyme with "liberty." Why not a parallel construction rhyming (ideally) with its synonym, "free"? Yes: an added dimeter, which would neatly make a couplet-conclusion, to match the previous couplet "done"/"come":

> It sets the Fright at liberty -
> And Terror's free -

But it is far from the poet's mind to depart from her poem with two such "positive" words as "liberty" and "free." With frenetic energy, she "celebrates" her liberation from Fright and Terror in a hideous third line flung at her couplet: "Gay, Ghastly, Holiday!" As a coda to her central manifesto, this last line has wrenched itself away from her attempt at lulling the "perturbèd spirit" to a "slumber," from the pronouncement that all is "done," from her announcement that she has conquered the Ghost and vanquished the fears and terrors that accompanied him. But the Ghost returns with a vengeance in "Ghastly," and this "posthumous" "Gay Holiday" of hysteria is revealed hyperbolically as worse than not knowing the worst, worse than despair, worse than being dead.

[J 281]

# 348

I would not paint - a picture -
I'd rather be the One
Its bright impossibility
To dwell - delicious - on -
And wonder how the fingers feel
Whose rare - celestial - stir -
Evokes so sweet a torment -
Such sumptuous - Despair -

I would not talk, like Cornets -
I'd rather be the One
Raised softly to the Ceilings -
And out, and easy on -
Through Villages of Ether -
Myself endued Balloon
By but a lip of Metal -
The pier to my Pontoon -

Nor would I be a Poet -
It's finer - Own the ear -
Enamored - impotent - content -
The License to revere,
A privilege so awful
What would the Dower be,
Had I the Art to stun myself
With Bolts - of Melody!

This poem (which provided the title, *Bolts of Melody,* for the widely read 1945 selection of Dickinson's poems) meditates, in three eight-line stanzas rhymed in quatrains, on the "sister arts" of painting, music, and poetry. (Keats's "Ode to a Nightingale," on music, and "Ode on a Grecian Urn," on sculpture, are poems of this genre that Dickinson would have known.) Keats (and others down to our own day—such as John Ashbery, in "And Ut Pictura Poesis Is Her Name") have made an explicit comparison between nontemporal visual art and inescapably temporal poetry, in Keats's case to the (temporary) disadvantage of poetry: the Urn can "express / A flowery tale more sweetly than our rhyme." But Dickinson revises the topic of comparison between the sister arts: she asserts that it is better to be the audience than to be the artist. She carries out her putative theme with respect to painting, music, and poetry—but because of her witty and beautiful descriptions of the various arts, we cannot help believing that it is an artist who is speaking to us.

With respect to painting and poetry, she focuses on the creator of the art; but with respect to music, she focuses not on the composer but on heard (instrumental) music. In each case, she represents her own response when she encounters art: in the stanza on painting, she wonders how the artist's creative "fingers feel"; in the stanza on music, she imitates the transcendental passage of melody through the air; and in the stanza on poetry, she represents the reverence of the audience toward an art that, like Jove's thunderbolts, can stun.

Dickinson is careful to give each stanza an individual atmosphere. The first two stanzas begin in strict synchrony: "I would not do X; I'd rather be the One who . . ." But after the beginning, they diverge. In the first, the viewer is active: I'd rather be the one to "dwell on" the picture, to "wonder" how the painter's fingers feel. In the second, the listener is passive, raised to the ceilings by the sound of the cornet and, once in the air, "endued [invested as a] Balloon"; the musical instrument is the agent: she is transported (as she remarks in amazement) "by but a lip of Metal." In the third stanza, on poetry, the formula changes; the poet, by synecdoche, becomes an "Ear" (as Keats implicitly does in the "Nightingale" stanza beginning "Darkling I listen"), and lists the conflicting adjectives characterizing that listening Ear: "Enamored - impotent - content - / The License to revere." (These adjectives are separated for meditation by dashes, like the earlier "rare," "celestial," and "stir.") She had wondered how the painter's fingers felt in making his picture, paradoxical in its effect of sweetness and torment, sumptuousness and Despair (she knows that this is the nature of all art, in which the sweetness and sumptuousness of achieved form coexist even with themes of torment and despair). She does not, however, express any desire to paint a picture herself; nor, in the stanza on music, during its dreamy floating over land and sea (with the Cornet as the pier where her Balloon-skiff, her "Pontoon," is tethered), does she express a wish either to create music or to play (or be) an instrument. But when she arrives at "Nor would I be a Poet - ", although she is still claiming that to be audience is better than to be author, her desire to have the revered License, the privilege, of being a Poet, is transparently evident. In a closed-circuit drive of composition, she becomes a Jove stunning herself with "Bolts" of melody. The reward is an incalculable "Dower," a treasure beside which all worldly treasures are dust—see "My Reward for Being - was this - " (375, J 343).

After its uninterrupted flow of iambic trimeters (mostly) and tetrameters (lines 3, 5, 19, and 23), keeping its wishes a pleasant fantasy, the poem suddenly becomes wonderstruck in the two initial reversed feet of lines 22 and 23, foretelling the closing exclamation mark: "*What* would the Dower be, / *Had* I the Art to stun myself / With Bolts - of Melody!" The two earlier responses—to painting and to music—elicited no such reversed feet and no such exclamation marks. Dickinson relished, we can see, the feast of vocabulary opened up by the three arts. She took care in her diction, sometimes making it more distinct ("the Ceilings" was previously "Horizons"), sometimes making it more evocative (scrutinizing the more workaday "upborne," "upheld," and "sustained," before reaching the archaic and aristocratic "endued").

[J 505]

# 351

She sights a Bird - she chuckles -
She flattens - then she crawls -
She runs without the look of feet -
Her eyes increase to Balls -

Her Jaws stir - twitching - hungry -
Her Teeth can hardly stand -
She leaps, but Robin leaped the first -
Ah, Pussy, of the Sand,

The Hopes so juicy ripening -
You almost bathed your Tongue -
When Bliss disclosed a hundred Toes -
And fled with every one -

Keats wrote, in his "Epistle to John Hamilton Reynolds," of the "eternal fierce destruction" within nature, where he saw

The Shark at savage prey - the Hawk at pounce,
The gentle Robin, like a Pard or Ounce
Ravening a worm.

Keats's dismay (which stems in part from a projection of this view into human life) is not Dickinson's: she contemplates—with considerable glee—her cat stalking a bird. She condenses her observations of the cat's actions into nine vivid verbs: "sights," "chuckles," "flattens," "crawls," "runs," "increase," "stir," "stand" (used of teeth!), and "leaps." This is a cinematic technique, resembling in its segmentation those "flip books" where incremental action gradually accumulates into serial motion. The entertainment of watching pure instinct displaying itself is, for Dickinson, emotion enough for a poem. She sees the unconscious "cruelty" of the cat without projecting its cruelty explicitly into human terms (except perhaps in "chuckles")—but she does fully anthropomorphize its disappointment: "Ah, Pussy[!]"

Pussy is not aerial; she is a denizen of the sand, whereas Robin—who has acquired a proper name as Dickinson perceives the species her cat is pursuing—is a denizen of the air. The contest is not an equal one: "She leaps, but Robin leaped the first - ". The interest lies not in the Robin's escape so much as in the cat's chase. It has some parallels with a human hunt, in which one sights the prey, then perhaps hides, then "flattens" oneself on the ground, or perhaps "crawls" to a more advantageous position. But Dickinson's little narrative quickly zooms into a purely feline hunt, where the cat (unlike us) can run without watching her step, as her eyes (unlike ours) can grow from their usual elliptical shape into staring "Balls." Amused, Dickinson watches as the cat's jaws begin to "stir" from dormancy into twitching; it is Dickinson who infers "hungry" from that twitch of the jaw. The next line is entirely peculiar: "Her Teeth can hardly stand - ". Stand in her mouth, so eager are they to begin to crunch? Or "Her Teeth can hardly stand" the suspense? In any case, the utterance is broken off by the final feline verb we have subconsciously been expecting all through the cat's increasingly tense maneuvers: "She leaps." (Dickinson may have borrowed, for her comic sympathy in "Ah, Pussy," something from Burns's address to the mouse: "But, Mousie, thou art no thy lane.")

The true anthropomorphizing begins with the introduction of human feeling into Pussy's "Hopes." Salivating so much that she almost "bathed [her] Tongue" in the ripening juices of anticipation, she sees—at that very moment—her hoped-for "Bliss" (the most human, and the most abstract, word in the poem) take flight. In considering the escape of the bird, Dickinson first considered whether to write "wings" or "Toes": but deciding for "Toes," she imaginatively keeps to the point of view of the cat (who doesn't understand wings, and perceives only that the bird can "run" faster than she can). The internal rhyme "disclosed"/"Toes" gives the Robin's flight a sudden lilt of take-off. The bird watches, frustrated of her prey, as those Toes defeat her:

> . . . Bliss disclosed a hundred Toes -
> And fled with every one -

We are acquainted with seven-headed monsters, or with the masses of progeny that they can disgorge, but nobody before Dickinson (except of course a cat) ever imagined a creature with a hundred rapid Toes.

This little picture of the cat as predator has a "happy" ending, as the bird escapes; but see, for a different result, the "Murder by degrees" in "The Whole of it came not at once - " (485, J 762), where a cat tortures and then kills a hapless Mouse:

> The Cat reprieves the mouse
> She eases from her teeth
> Just long enough for Hope to teaze -
> Then mashes it to death -
>
> [J 507]

# 355

It was not Death, for I stood up,
And all the Dead, lie down -
It was not Night, for all the Bells
Put out their Tongues, for Noon.

It was not Frost, for on my Flesh
I felt Siroccos - crawl -
Nor Fire - for just my marble feet
Could keep a Chancel, cool -

And yet, it tasted, like them all,
The Figures I have seen
Set orderly, for Burial,
Reminded me, of mine -

As if my life were shaven,
And fitted to a frame,
And could not breathe without a key,
And 'twas like Midnight, some -

When everything that ticked - has stopped -
And space stares - all around -
Or Grisly frosts - first Autumn morns,
Repeal the Beating Ground -

But, most, like Chaos - Stopless - cool -
Without a Chance, or spar -
Or even a Report of Land -
To justify - Despair.

As she opens her narrative, Dickinson first reveals, by implication, her confusing and terrifying present state: she stands in total blackness, in stifling heat, in freezing cold, immobile, locked in a Procrustean frame, her breath stopped. All these conditions are reported to her by her mind: but they are so thoroughly refuted by her senses, she doesn't know how to define them, except by negation of what her senses tell her. The baffling "it"—her condition—can't be Death, for the dead lie down, and she is standing up; it can't be Night, because the malicious Bells stick their tongues out at her, crying Noon; it's not Frost, because feverish tremors like parching winds crawl over her Flesh; nor can it be Fire, for her marble feet alone (as she becomes in her imagination a *gisant,* or horizontal tomb-statue) could chill the Chancel where she is buried. Coming to the end of her negative definitions, she begins to justify them: the morbid taste of her present selfhood feels like Death; her immobility is like that of corpses; her life has been "shaven" like the boards of the "frame" into which it has been fitted; in that living death, she cannot breathe, for she has no key to open the coffin.

As she goes on to finish the poem, she shows us that everything so far —all the intricate imaginings, and their even more intricate negations, and the self-justifying comparisons—have been delaying tactics, keeping at arm's length her true state, which she now confronts head-on. New descriptions replace the former ones: where she is, it is Midnight, and Time has stopped, while a vast black space, her new habitat, "stares" (like a threatening presence) in every direction. Or it is like the murder of nature's beating heart by judicial "Grisly frosts," which repeal the Ground's legal permission to live. But it was (she says, abandoning all her natural and human metaphors), most like Chaos. "Chaos" is that final unintelligibility of suffering that she has been avoiding by thinking she could analyze her state into metaphor (positive, negative, or cosmic). When Time had "stopped," it was still temporal, if suspended. But her Chaos is "Stopless": in it, there is not even a continuity that could be thought to have stopped. She was not wrong in thinking her feet could keep a Chancel "cool"—but the "cool" of Chaos is something prehuman; it has no Chancels, no tombs, no coffins. Nor does it have any possibility of change; it has no seasonal contingency of frost; it is without "a Chance" of survival.

Dickinson turns again to the state described in "I felt a Funeral, in my Brain," (340), where she and Silence were shipwrecked together. But in Chaos there are no companions; she is alone in the midst of an uninhabited sea. She has no ship's spar in sight, telling of a fellow sailor; nor can she justify her Despair by imagining that she could receive a report of even unattainable

Land. Chaos has no Eternity, not even an Eden; since there was nothing to hope for in the first place, there is nothing to be in despair about now. Dickinson is brave in facing a wholly indifferent Chaos as the place to which she has been brought by insupportable agony.

The only anomalous line in the poem, metrically speaking, is line 13, which instead of its proper four beats has only three. This seems deliberate: it is the line in which her life appears "shaven," diminished in its extent. The elaborately intellectual parade of negative and positive definitions is an evasive distraction from the hideous truth that Chaos is entirely beyond all defining. Even paranoia—evoking the inflictions of the jeering Bells, the crawling Sciroccos, the shaven life, the locked coffin—would be preferable to a causeless Chaos, in which cosmic indifference prohibits even Despair.

[J 510]

# 359

A Bird, came down the Walk -
He did not know I saw -
He bit an Angle Worm in halves
And ate the fellow, raw,

And then, he drank a Dew
From a convenient Grass -
And then hopped sidewise to the Wall
To let a Beetle pass -

He glanced with rapid eyes,
That hurried all abroad -
They looked like frightened Beads, I thought,
He stirred his Velvet Head. -

Like one in danger, Cautious,
I offered him a Crumb,
And he unrolled his feathers,
And rowed him softer Home -

Than Oars divide the Ocean,
Too silver for a seam,
Or Butterflies, off Banks of Noon,
Leap, plashless as they swim.

This bizarre little narrative has several notes characteristic of Dickinson: her cool eye, her unsparing factuality, her startling similes and metaphors, her psychological observation of herself and others, her capacity for showing herself mistaken, and her exquisite relish of natural beauty. The narrative begins with "Nature red in tooth and claw" (Tennyson)—and here we would add "beak." Like a news reporter observing low life, Dickinson talks of the hardened criminal she saw, who, thinking he was unobserved, committed murder and cannibalism on a hapless feeble creature, an "Angle Worm": like a savage, he "ate the fellow, raw." In the comic sequel, she shows herself now afraid of the criminal, feeling she must propitiate him or he might bite her in half, too. On the other hand, she has seen another side of the crass murderer: he drinks daintily a drop of Dew from the grass, and he makes way for a Beetle (whom he does not kill; on the contrary, he considerately steps aside). The narrator's approach frightens the bird, and he shows his alarm in his distinctly nonhuman "rapid" eyes—"like frightened Beads," says the poet, but who ever saw a bead that had taken fright? Two realms of diction—human and inhuman—crash up against each other in the "frightened Beads" (as they do not in the bird's metaphorically "velvet" head).

Dickinson apparently wrote two versions of the middle of the poem, in which the encounter between the narrator and the Bird takes place. In one, the Bird is cautious; in the other, it's she who is cautious. Here is the first, apparently as the poet sent it to Higginson, who published it after her death. In this version, there is no punctuation after "head," but there is a period after "cautious":

> He stirred his velvet head
>
> Like one in danger, cautious.
> I offered him a crumb

However, a copy the poet kept for herself has a comma, not a period, after "Cautious":

> He stirred his Velvet Head
>
> Like One in danger, Cautious,
> I offered him a Crumb

And the fair copy inscribed in a fascicle has both a period and a dash after "Head," and a comma after "Cautious":

> He stirred his Velvet Head. -
>
> Like one in danger, Cautious,
> I offered him a Crumb

Thus the different versions:

> "He stirred his velvet head like one in danger, cautious. I offered him a
>     Crumb"
> "He stirred his Velvet Head like One in danger, Cautious, I offered him a
>     Crumb"
> "He stirred his Velvet Head. Like one in danger, Cautious, I offered him
>     a Crumb"

Franklin prints the third option, in which the poet is the one in danger; this certainly accords best with Dickinson's comic side. So far, the poem has shown the encounter with ridiculous exaggeration, and the comedy is increased if the human being feels herself endangered by a Bird. After all, she saw him eat an Angle Worm. But perhaps she'll pass as unharmed as the Beetle did. Who knows?

In any case, the Crumb breaks the encounter, and the Bird flies off. What follows is the astonishing part of the poem. After seeing the Bird on the ground—as murderer and cannibal; then as delicately drinking and courteously making room; then as frightened—the poet finally sees him in his native element, the air. Grounded with Angle Worms and Beetles (and human beings), the bird is suspect and suspicious. Ah, but in the air! The gentle glide of the Bird into lift-off leaves the poet almost at a loss for words. How can she describe what he resembles at this moment? She draws first on two metaphors: he "unroll[s]" his feathers, as his collapsible wings unfold themselves; and he "row[s]" through the air more gently than Oars divide an ocean, a sea so calmly "silver" that no "seam" is visible as the water restores itself after the oars' passage. But there is an implied resistance in each of these media: the air resists the unrolling of the feathers, which requires effort; and the sea resists the Oars, which move only by dint of the labor of oarsmen.

As the poet admires the bird's graceful and effortless rising, she is compelled to a third metaphor: if not the unrolling of feathers in air, if not the motion of oars on the seamless silver sea, then what does the motion of the bird in flight remind her of? Searching through her repertoire of silent motion, she comes on butterflies: they swim in air so lightly that when they leap into their medium, there is no plash, not a sound. From what invisible Banks do the Butterflies leap into the invisible air? Banks of sunshine, Banks of Noon.

Does any participating reader, unrolling feathers and rowing in silver and swimming in sunshine with Butterflies, object pertinaciously, "But he *ate* the fellow, *raw!*" still insisting, with tenacity, on the Bird's savagery and the observer's (mock) horror? Of course not. This is a poem about aesthetic ecstasy obliterating the memory of savagery. What are we to make of this? "Why nothing, / Only, your *inference* therefrom!" ("As if some little Arctic flower"; 177, J 180). The two sides of nature—the cruel, the beautiful—stand here in the relation they often assume for Dickinson: the beautiful has the last word.

It may be, however, that the best sortie of the imagination here occurs in the "rapid . . . frightened Beads," the bird's eyes, and they are not "beautiful" in any ordinary sense of the word. Yet in their rapid, acid pain, in the poet's vivid observation, the "frightened Beads" have the rarer "beauty" of exquisite accuracy. Dickinson puts all her charm to work at the end of the poem, stifling both savagery and fear in the opulence of her "oh" sounds, accompanied by alliterating phrases: "rolled . . . rowed . . . Home . . . Oars . . . Ocean," followed by her light "silver . . . seam" and her buoyant "Butterflies, off Banks of Noon." In the synthesizing Dickinsonian imagination, the ocean's fish, which swim with splashing sounds, are by the one word "plashless," metamorphosed into a swarm of silently moving butterflies.

[J 328]

# 360

The Soul has Bandaged moments -
When too appalled to stir -
She feels some ghastly Fright come up
And stop to look at her -

Salute her, with long fingers -
Caress her freezing hair -
Sip, Goblin, from the very lips
The Lover - hovered - o'er -
Unworthy, that a thought so mean
Accost a Theme - so - fair -

The soul has moments of escape -
When bursting all the doors -
She dances like a Bomb, abroad,
And swings upon the Hours,

As do the Bee - delirious borne -
Long Dungeoned from his Rose -
Touch Liberty - then know no more -
But Noon, and Paradise -

The Soul's retaken moments -
When, Felon led along,
With shackles on the plumèd feet,
And staples, in the song,

The Horror welcomes her, again,
These, are not brayed of Tongue -

In this three-part poem, the Soul narrates the suspicion of infidelity. In part 1 her Lover has wounded her, and the Soul, wanting to hide the gash, bandages it. But the dreadful foreboding still haunts her, and, in a tour de force of gothic eroticism on Emily Dickinson's part, the Goblin of suspicion replaces the lover. Suddenly, in part 2, the suspicion lifts, and the Soul is violently ecstatic, bursting with liberated emotion, delirious with eros. In part 3, she is reimprisoned in suspicion, is once again led to her dungeon in shackles, her song as fettered as she. Those moments of Horror when the Goblin of suspicion caresses her again—when, after triumphing publicly in the ecstasy of renewed love, the Soul is forced once more into the abjection of jealousy—ah, she says, nobody tells about those times (compared with the way she "brayed" the good news of her liberation into renewed love). The speaker of this bitterly self-critical poem is mortified by having made an exhibition of herself in her explosive joy—bursting all the doors, publicly dancing like a Bomb, and swinging through the Hours for all to see. But she is equally ashamed of having tolerated the Goblin's ghastly seduction of her into suspicion: [It is] "Unworthy, that a thought so mean / [Should] Accost a Theme - so - fair - ", she says, lengthening out the stanza's final syllables with dashes as she regrets having besmirched a "Theme - so - fair."

We have no idea, when the poem opens, why the Soul has had to apply a Bandage to certain "moments." The hurt these moments inflict paralyzes her: she is held immobile in suffering as, to her horror, she is approached by an unnerving personification, Fright. The little narrative that follows is one of the high points of imagination in the poem, as Dickinson imagines an awful, if seductive, wooing by an unspecific creature. The Soul becomes terribly visible here, with real hair and lips, just as the previously allegorical Fright is made hideously visible by being turned into a mythical Goblin. The verbs of the narrative are increasingly assaultive as the Fright comes up to the Soul, stops, looks at her, salutes her (with his unnaturally long "fingers"—the first sign of his metamorphosis into a creature with a body), caresses her hair (which freezes under his touch, as though hair were living flesh), and then sips nectar "from the very lips" that the Lover himself had merely "hovered - o'er - ". (It is like Dickinson to make a Lover hover.)

Dickinson, at this moment, has "finished" what should have been her second four-line stanza. But to abandon the tableau with the Goblin's eerie lips upon those of the Soul seems to her disloyal: she adds the next two "superfluous" lines to apologize for entertaining "a thought so mean" about the Lover's love—but those disavowing lines are nonetheless caught in the Goblin's rhyme-scheme, "fair" echoing the quatrain rhymes "hair" and "o'er." Although we may not realize it, we have not yet seen the end of the suspicious, and suspect, goblin-thought.

The poem takes a fresh start in line 11, with "The soul has moments of escape - ", paralleling, as if quoting, and undoing, its opening line, "The Soul has Bandaged moments - ." The Soul seems newborn, as if the "Bandaged" moments have been obliterated, the "Goblin" routed. Escaping—we don't at first ask whence, thinking that the "escape" is metaphorical, and knowing only that the former place has "doors"—the Soul goes into a manic phase of freedom, bursting and dancing and swinging.

The simile "like a Bomb" is one of Dickinson's most extraordinary self-descriptions. In an 1862 letter to Higginson (L 271), Dickinson used the verb "explodes" to describe her reaction when she forced an unnatural discipline on herself: "I had no Monarch in my life, and cannot rule myself, and when I try to organize - my little Force explodes - and leaves me bare and charred - ". Her frequent implication of herself in such figures as the Volcano (in several poems) or the "loaded Gun" (*764) suggests that she was well aware of her potentially explosive "Force," and knew it was not "little." The word "Bomb" has only one denotation, always aggressive. Who knows what object the "Bomb" is headed for when it dances abroad? In any case, no "Bomb" is harmless.

Dickinson retreats from the Bomb to a safer metaphor, which we at first take as symbolic. She is, she says, like a Bee who has been long "Dungeoned" but is now delirious with joy as, liberated, he finds his Rose, and with her, "Noon, and Paradise." This ecstatic dénouement seems final—except that as the Bee sips nectar from his flower, we cannot forget that the Goblin sipped at the lips of the speaker.

There are few more disturbing endings to a Dickinsonian narrative than the last scene of "The Soul has Bandaged moments": the "Bomb," its winged feet shackled, finds itself being led toward reimprisonment in the Goblin's dungeon. The climactic horror—"staples, in the song"—comes as a blow because we had not been told earlier that there was a song at all: bombs and bees are not normally said to sing. The poem "should" end here, with the closing of the prison doors, as we realize that the Soul's earlier "escaping" was from a dungeon, and the "doors" she burst open were locked prison gates. What we took as metaphorical—"I burst open the doors and I escaped"—

is grimly literal, as are the shackles and the staples driven through the "feet" of the song. Dickinson had considered, as alternatives to these nouns, "irons" and "rivets." But those words, although synonymous (more or less) with "shackles" and "staples," have not the "binding secret" (Seamus Heaney's phrase in "Feeling into Words") of look and sound linking the final two fettering nouns, each with an initial graphic "s" and a final phonetic and graphic "les."

The poem ends with a two-line coda, separated by white space from the retaken Felon. The coda purports to be a cool comment, voiced from some position "outside" both sorts of moments—of miserable Bandages and unloosed Bombs. The coda appears retrospective: the "retaken moments," it says, too debasing to relate, are never "brayed of Tongue." One may boast when in the delusion of manic joy, but one never reveals the shackles of subsequent rehumiliation. However, these last two lines (like their earlier "extra" counterparts, lines 9–10) are bound by rhyme to what precedes them: "Tongue" is made to rhyme with "along" and "song," so that the poem ends with a six-line unit, rather than (as we had first thought) a two-line coda. The coda "belongs" by rhyme to the shackled Soul. Even though the Soul may affect, at the end, to take an ironic attitude toward her own suffering, we realize that the shackles and the staples are, even at the end, inflicting their own wounds, and that the tormented Soul will be seeking Bandages once more, in a constant fluctuation between joy and suspicion that will, it seems, never cease.

[J 512]

# 365

I know that He exists.
Somewhere - in silence -
He has hid his rare life
From our gross eyes.

'Tis an instant's play -
'Tis a fond Ambush -
Just to make Bliss
Earn her own surprise!

But - should the play
Prove piercing earnest -
Should the glee - glaze -
In Death's - stiff - stare -

Would not the fun
Look too expensive!
Would not the jest -
Have crawled too far!

This grim little poem tells us its true meter, trimeter, by its first didactic line: "I know that He exists." Like the equally didactic opening of "This world is not conclusion" (*373), this first line stops the poem dead, with a period, just when it has begun. It is a startling way to begin a quatrain, not to speak of a poem.

Dickinson emphasizes her trimeters so as to give spondaic weight to almost every syllable of the last appalling and alliterating suggestions:

> *Should* the *glee - glaze -*
> In *Death's - stiff - stare*
>
> *Would not* the *fun*
> *Look too expensive!*

The meter is odd: the second line of each stanza has a feminine ending: "silence," "Ambush," "earnest," "expensive." The slipping away of the final syllable in each second line leads us to think, at the beginning, that perhaps we will find the same soft ending in each fourth line as well, letting us down "gracefully" from each quatrain. No: the (mostly) spondaic fourth lines of each stanza hit their masculine endings with peculiar and uncompromising force: "He has hid his rare life / From *our gross eyes.*"

The rhymes are also odd: although the poem is printed as quatrains, and we have come to expect lines 2 and 4 of Dickinson's hymn-stanzas to rhyme, that does not happen in "I know that He exists." If the poem were written out according to its *rhyme,* without initial capitals in the middle of a sentence, it would look like this:

> I know that He exists. Somewhere - in silence - he has hid his
>     rare life from our gross eyes.
> 'Tis an instant's play - 'Tis a fond Ambush - just to make
>     Bliss earn her own surprise!
> But - should the play prove piercing earnest - should the
>     glee - glaze - in Death's - stiff - stare -
> Would not the fun look too expensive! Would not the jest -
>     have crawled too far!

Judging by rhyme, then, Dickinson is writing (mostly) in twelve-beat lines. She must have enjoyed making them look like little lines, when they were— at least when grouped by their rhyming—very long ones. Why would she— for this poem of irony at God's expense—so conceal her rhyming? "I know that he exists" looks, to the casual reader, like an unrhymed poem. As the eye scans the first stanza, it sees no rhyme; and unless the ear, hearing "surprise" in line 8, remembers "eyes" from line 4, it may not mark the presence of a rhyme at all, having just heard seven lines in a row with not a rhyme among them.

I think Dickinson's "jest" has to do with the maliciously self-concealing God in his game of hide-and-seek. Her rhymes are hiding, too, but they, unlike God, can be found. She jests honestly. Does God do so? The attempt to reassure herself in the light speculation of the second stanza, that God is merely waiting to "ambush" us as we enter heaven, does not last. The grotesque image of the death's-head stare puts "fond Ambush" out of the question. God's sadism in pretending he is available, and then not being so, turns out to be a Satanic attribute: the last jest is a serpent, crawling in evil glee. From her unequivocal opening assertion—"I know that He exists", followed by an equally unequivocal period—Dickinson tracks her wicked God, who by the end of the poem is indistinguishable from Satan.

[J 338]

# 372

After great pain, a formal feeling comes -
The Nerves sit ceremonious, like Tombs -
The stiff Heart questions 'was it He, that bore,'
And 'Yesterday, or Centuries before'?

The Feet, mechanical, go round -
A Wooden way
Of Ground, or Air, or Aught -
Regardless grown,
A Quartz contentment, like a stone -

This is the Hour of Lead -
Remembered, if outlived,
As Freezing persons, recollect the Snow -
First - Chill - then Stupor - then the letting go -


Hardly any commentator on Dickinson forgoes the satisfaction of writing about this famous poem. It bears, in its "Feet, mechanical," distinct resemblance to the "Mechanic feet" of "From Blank to Blank" (484, J 761; reproduced below), a poem which helps to illuminate its better-known sibling—and incidentally, with its final recourse to artificial blindness, to cast doubt on the cheerier critical readings of the ending of "After great pain":

From Blank to Blank -
A Threadless Way
I pushed Mechanic feet -
To stop - or perish - or advance -
Alike indifferent -

If end I gained
It ends beyond
Indefinite disclosed -

> I shut my eyes - and groped as well
> 'Twas lighter - to be Blind -

"After great pain" is a three-part poem, with the three parts disposed in gross disproportion. Part 1, the longest (unrolling down through "This is the Hour of Lead"), describes the numb "formal feeling" that a person experiences after a life-wound has caused such a deadening of the nerves that it may, at least to the sufferer, seem to prophesy oncoming death. The state described is one of prolonged psychic immobility consequent on the trauma which is the residue of "great pain." From the many sorts of reactive post-traumatic states that display themselves in life—anger, violence, bedridden bodily withdrawal, stunned mental paralysis—Dickinson chooses the fourth. (The poem is very specifically ungendered, and thereby universalized; but for ease of reference I'll call the sufferer "she.") Part 1 ends with the summary of the time undergone as "the Hour of Lead." Multiple implicit questions arise— Does this Hour always kill the sufferer? Or can one survive it? And if so, how is it remembered?—and these are all condensed into the three words of the single-line hinge of part 2: "Remembered, if outlived." (There is no better example of Dickinson's compression of several thoughts into the smallest possible container.) Part 3 tells, via an elaborate simile, how the sufferer will, in the future, recall this "Hour," if she survives it.

These three parts (as one might expect, perhaps) present the reader with several different metrical arrangements. The poem opens in a very orderly way, its first four lines comprising two pentameter couplets. It ends, in an orderly way, too, with its last four lines comprising two couplets—a trimeter couplet followed by a pentameter couplet—thus bringing the poem, metrically speaking, full circle. The "formal feeling" seems to be creating its own formal prosody. But this satisfying coherence is wrecked by lines 5–9, which appear on the page—in Dickinson's arrangement—as jagged and mostly unrhymed. One can of course rearrange these five irregular lines into a rhyming quatrain (4-3-4-4), written in couplets like the rest of the poem, by doing them conspicuous violence:

> The Feet, mechanical, go round -
> A Wooden way of Ground -

> Or Air, or Aught, regardless grown,
> A Quartz contentment, like a stone.

We might say, viewing Dickinson's stanza as it was inscribed by her, that something sinisterly disturbing has come to unsettle the "formal feeling." Nothing in lines 5–9, in her arrangement, "sits ceremonious": on the contrary. The sufferer is no longer sitting, but upright and—in some as yet unexplained way—in motion; her feet go mechanically round a track, so mindless of their surroundings that they do not know whether they are walking on a wood floor, a patch of ground, sheer air, or anything ("Aught") else. Going "round" suggests a circuit of duties—in the house, in the garden. But who knows? The sufferer doesn't notice. And she is alone: there are no observers or interlocutors. If she were inanimate, she would be best compared to a stone—or rather to a crystal of Quartz (which has an intricate interior formal lattice-structure, unlike a stone). She has grown so used to the numbness of her body and mind, that she convinces herself that this state is "contentment."

What is the purpose of Dickinson's "mislineation"? She is able at first to say, in a plausible tetrameter, "The Feet, mechanical, go round." Then something breaks down in the observing mind. It is as though another part of the mind is trying to force her to say what surface her feet are walking on. Attempting compliance, she says "A Wooden way." But "ways" are not usually "Wooden"; the word "way" (meaning "path") tends to be used of spaces out of doors. "Of Ground," she says more coherently—and then, with dull indifference, "Oh, on whatever you like—Air, or anything else." "Regardless grown," says the commenting part of the mind, in a line of its own, rather like Polonius commenting on Hamlet's purported madness. The ways of the Feet, the glance without a regard, lead to an attempt to penetrate the emotion on the face; but it is as impenetrable as stone, and, with a dark wit, the underlying emotion is dehumanized into what a stone—or perhaps something more organized, such as crystalline quartz—might feel if it were feeling content. This is a quite wrong reading of the emotion in question; the sufferer is overpowered by suffering with no rescue in sight, but is maintaining a stoic bearing to the world. The incoherence of inner desperation and outer compliance generates the ragged middle of the poem. The unnatural stumbling of the meter, while the feet of the sufferer are going their mechanical round, suggests the tottering of the psyche.

We return to part 1. The statuary of the Nerves-like-Tombs becomes the preparatory cemetery for the expiring Heart, anticipating, in its paralysis, the formality of funeral. The Heart, in fact, has already entered into the stiffness of rigor mortis. But the Heart still remembers the great pain of "Yesterday," and feels that Jesus' passion is its only parallel: "Was it He or I who was Crucified? And was it I, just yesterday, or He, centuries before?" The confusion of the moribund Heart speaks to the derangement of the mind that has produced that eerie "formal feeling," which, unsummoned, rules the corporeal and psychic economy of the one traumatized.

Yes: and what will this unnatural leaden hour of passivity-unto-death seem like in memory (if one survives to remember it in a later time)? It will be recollected, says Dickinson in a great and unexpected simile, as a set of stages. We have seen the "Hour" as something static, unchanging: the feet go round, the stoic face remains immobile, the nerves sit ceremonious, the sufferer has become indifferent to, "Regardless" of, the outside world. But this total stasis will be remembered—*if* outlived (and it is by no means certain that the episode of despair *will* be survived)—in terms of "first this, then that" (I distort lineation to show the import of Dickinson's "First . . . then . . . then"):

> As Freezing persons, recollect the Snow—
> First—Chill—
>     then Stupor—
>         then the letting go—

These are all *long* stages. As in Stevens's "The Snow Man" (which may owe something to Dickinson's poem), "One must have a mind of winter . . . / And have been cold a long time" in order to become a man made of snow. So as the mind wanders back, at a later moment, recollecting the frozen time, it will enact, in sequence, the stages of trauma: first the Chill (as the temperature of the heart and nerves descends lower and lower from its previous warmth); then, after the mind goes torpid, a prolonged Stupor (a state of having been stunned, rendered senseless); then an acquiescence to the Freezing, the letting go of one's own will to live. There is an absolute blank of memory between the letting go into unconsciousness and the possible revivification; after all, the revivification may not happen. "Remembered," used of those who have survived a disaster, means "retained in memory." "Recollect" means "to gather together the fragments" (here, staged serial fragments) of the past. Dickinson always knows the distinctions between etymologies.

Why does Dickinson append—to her extended picture of a trauma so total that it invades all parts of the body—the nerves, the eyes ("Regardless"), the heart, the feet, the visage—a recapitulation in terms of the fate of travelers lost in a snowstorm, who gradually sink into insensibility, and may or may not be rescued? Such a reprise, as we have seen, turns the stasis of the first several lines into timed stages—as though, in recollecting, one can't summon up all at once the paralytic result of such devastating pain, but must recall it phase by phase. But the reprise also gives us an ending suspended in uncertainty, which begins in time but ends—how? In the stasis of death? In the seriality of time? Dickinson will not prophesy the likelihood of the Soul's survival. If she does survive, she will remember. And remember slowly, and gradually, till she fully recollects the past "Hour of Lead" that preceded unconsciousness.

Why are there not two pentameter couplets at the end, to match the beginning? Because the uncertain state of the end—freezing to death or possible survival—is not the same as the immobile state of the beginning, with its total possession by the paralyzing "formal feeling." To remind us, however, that a hypothesis is only a hypothesis, and that a simile is only a simile, and that the poem—before hypothesis and simile—was an unrelenting picture of helplessness during and after pain, Dickinson ends the poem as she began it: with a pentameter couplet.

[J 341]

# 373

This World is not conclusion.
A Species stands beyond -
Invisible, as Music -
But positive, as Sound -
It beckons, and it baffles -
Philosophy, don't know -
And through a Riddle, at the last -
Sagacity, must go -
To guess it, puzzles scholars -
To gain it, Men have borne
Contempt of Generations
And Crucifixion, shown -
Faith slips - and laughs, and rallies -
Blushes, if any see -
Plucks at a twig of Evidence -
And asks a Vane, the way -
Much Gesture, from the Pulpit -
Strong Hallelujahs roll -
Narcotics cannot still the Tooth
That nibbles at the soul -

"This World is not conclusion" was placidly entitled "Immortality" in its early truncated publication in 1896 (which gave only lines 1–12, ending with the mention of Crucifixion). This initial group of twelve lines was not rejoined to its final eight lines (separately published in 1945) until Thomas H. Johnson's edition of 1955. The last eight lines vitiate the first twelve, which themselves slide further and further into skepticism: "Philosophy, don't know" any answer to this "Riddle," a gate through which even "Sagacity" must pass before being able to solve the riddle of whether there is another life after this one. "Ah, what sagacity perished here!" Dickinson had ironically remarked as she contemplated the inhabitants of the town cemetery, "Safe in their Alabaster Chambers - " (*124). Worldly wisdom was something she did not put much faith in.

The twenty lines of "This World is not conclusion" begin as strongly as possible, with a period after the first line. Not a doubt expressed. And before revision, line 2 had declared the existence of an afterlife: "a sequel stands beyond." In the revised version, Dickinson eliminates the temporality of "sequel," and asserts instead the existence of a Species not ourselves. The poet becomes the evolutionary Linnaeus preparing to describe this hitherto-unclassified "Species." She proceeds untroubled through line 8, but then documents again her second thoughts. Although she had first written "To prove it - puzzles scholars - ", she decides now that it is always folly to seek proof of the invisible, and substitutes "To guess it, puzzles scholars - ". She continues to review the version before her, and once again stops to revise at line 18: where the church's "Hallelujahs" once seemed "Sure," she now gives merely their aural power; they are "Strong." Her final revision is the most striking. She crosses out her "Mouse" from the closing lines, which originally said,

> Narcotics cannot still the Mouse -
> That nibbles at the soul -

As she revised, those lines seemed to her altogether too winsome an ending, something from an illustration in a book for children, where Mousie is shown nibbling at a wedge of cheese. The beast-fable Mouse vanishes, and in its place arises an allegorical Tooth, not killing its prey all at once but rather eroding the Soul's faith nibble by nibble, in a process excruciatingly slow, but affirmed by the poet's revisions even as she is making a fair copy for a fascicle. Any natural creature can be "stilled"; almost any trap will "still" a Mouse. But this deadly machine of perpetual motion—this unstillable gnawing Tooth—will win in the end.

What are the "Narcotics" that might (erroneously) be thought to still the nibbling Tooth of Doubt? The various antianxiety nostrums of religion—a presumed God, promises of an afterlife, heaven-sent angels guarding the souls of the faithful, the Eucharist—can quell the churchgoer's doubt only insofar as they dull the churchgoer's mind. The insidious logic of doubt remains in itself unaffected. When an unstillable machine—that unstoppable

Tooth—is at work within, no narcotic can be long efficacious; soporifics cannot outlast the will of the Tooth.

Like the first editors, we might doubt that the last two quatrains belong with the first three. Bafflement in onlookers (Philosophers, Sages, Scholars) is the topic of the first three quatrains; Faith, the topic of the next quatrain and a half; the Tooth, the topic of the last two lines. We know, after lines 1–12, that although onlookers may suspect the existence of a "Species" (or a "sequel") beyond this world, the only indication of it to them is what some men of faith—for example, Peter and Andrew, the crucified Apostles—have been willing to suffer to attain it. Baffled by the failure of external proof of that elusive "Species" beyond this World, the poet turns to the hope that we can ascertain an interior proof by consulting Faith within the Christian soul. But Faith proves an unsatisfactory and even foolish witness. Asked for proof, Faith slips, betraying doubt; queried on that slip, she affects to dismiss it with laughter, and rallies; but when one inquires into the nature of her "slip," she "Blushes, if any see - ", because that uncertainty will not stand up to inspection. If "Evidence" is requested of her, she has no sturdy staff to offer, but "Plucks at" a single twig as all she has to show; and if asked to give direction, she points to a weathervane, and indicates whichever way it happens to be blowing at that moment.

This demoralizing demonstration of the feebleness of individual Faith makes the poet turn to the collective faith of the church—where she finds empty Gestures in the Pulpit and noisy praises from the congregation. No reassurance is to be found there. Thus the appearance of the relentless Tooth. If Faith can move mountains, the Tooth can nibble them into nothingness.

Dickinson's mode of progress in inquiry is well demonstrated in "This World is not conclusion." She begins with the chief axiom of religion: the supernatural. She recites some of its tenets and its symbolic defenses to herself: there is an afterlife; there is the resurrected "Species" of fallen humanity redeemed; although invisible, the supernatural can be deduced from its effects, as we deduce, from the "positive Sound" of music, the preexistence of a score. All these assertions follow from the Christian premise with which she began: "This World is not conclusion." But reassertion takes her just so far. Having exhausted her store of doctrine, she finds herself, even if beckoned by its appeal, baffled by its elusiveness.

Finding doctrine insufficient, Dickinson turns to the wisdom of the ages. Can Philosophy help her to know whether there is an afterlife, full of the new Species of the redeemed? It shrugs. Can Sagacity help her? It declares the question a Riddle. Can scholars help her? To them, it is a puzzle—their guess is no better than her own. If abstractions offer no answer, can she turn to History? And here she finds a partial answer in human example: Jesus, the exemplar, has been followed through the ages by other heroic men, willing to bear, for their religious conviction, the sardonic "Contempt of Generations" as well as physical martyrdom. But who is to say they were right? Proof still eludes the poet.

Doctrine, wisdom, and exemplars having failed to convince her, Dickinson turns to Christian intimates of her own, hoping for enlightenment from their personal experience of conviction. As we have seen, she is scandalized by the frailty of their responses: they seem to be satisfied to join the church out of convention rather than conversion. But perhaps collective belief is stronger than individual faith? The church disappoints as much as its individual congregants do: from the Pulpit, she hears merely emphatic—but empty—oratory and the mutually reassuring noise of many voices, strong perhaps, but not "Sure." Doctrine, wisdom, exemplars, private profession of faith, and collective social pattern: Dickinson has exhausted her modes of inquiry. But it is relentlessly candid of her to exhibit them, one by one, and to display their failure. If all inquiry fails, then failure—continual, consistent, and inevitable—is the ultimate Truth. And Truth slides almost insensibly— in Dickinson's ear—into the awful "Tooth."

Never did a poem beginning with so firm a declaration decline into such permanent doubt. So much in Dickinson is reminiscent of George Herbert that we sense sharply, in a poem such as this, the endings she supplied to modernize his more confident map of the soul's psychology. There are unhappy endings in Herbert, where doubt gets the better of faith, but they never display Dickinson's conviction of the permanent instability of truth.

[J 501]

# 383

I like to see it lap the Miles -
And lick the Valleys up -
And stop to feed itself at Tanks -
And then - prodigious step

Around a Pile of Mountains -
And supercilious peer
In Shanties - by the sides of Roads -
And then a Quarry pare

To fit its sides
And crawl between
Complaining all the while
In horrid - hooting stanza -
Then chase itself down Hill -

And neigh like Boanerges -
Then - prompter than a Star
Stop - docile and omnipotent
At its own stable door -

This poem has received a good deal of comment because Emily Dickinson's father, a lawyer, was one of the backers of the (successful) effort to bring the railroad to Amherst; the eventual station lay not far from the Dickinson house. Those facts connect the social history of Amherst (and New England) to the poet's page. The association of progress with the coming of the "iron horse" generated other poems by Dickinson's contemporaries, of which Whitman's "To a Locomotive in Winter" is the best known.

At the same time, this poem has pleased children with its imaginative account of the train's journey. Responses to it as a poem have varied: to some it seems coy; to others it seems lightweight; and to those who are offended by the train's "peering" into the shanties of the railroad workers, it seems snobbish. Readers can't fail to notice that its opening statement is deliberately childish: "I like to see it lap the Miles, / And lick the Valleys up - ". Domhnall Mitchell, the best critic of the poem, has pursued the oddly difficult question, "To what sort of an animal is the train being compared?" It seems that it can lap, lick, feed itself, step, peer, pare rock, crawl, complain, create stanzas, chase itself, neigh, and stop. At the end of the poem it is, with its neighing, unmistakably an "iron horse"; but at the beginning, it resembles one of Dickinson's felines (cat, tiger, leopard), in any case something that can lick and lap and feed itself. It becomes strangely human midway, however, with its step, its peering, its paring of a Quarry, and its "stanzas." It really mutates into a horse only when it chases itself "down Hill"—but no sooner is it a neighing horse than it stops (as Mitchell remarks) like the Christmas star designating a stable. It is at once, says Dickinson, (summing up), both "docile" and "omnipotent." The latter adjective is properly used, of course, only of God: omnipotence, like omniscience, is among his attributes.

The two summary adjectives must have helped Dickinson generate the poem. "I must show it to be docile," thinks the poet, "but I must also show it to be omnipotent." (Those closing adjectives strike a reader as clinching a view that has been accumulating all along.) In its docile mood, the train can "peer"; in its omnipotent mood, it can "pare" a quarry down to size (as the shortening of lines 9 and 10 enacts the narrowness of the passage through the quarry-sides). The alliterative coordination of "peer" and "pare" (the only interesting rhyme in the poem) suggests how closely the two "moods" of docility and omniscience cohabit in the train, just as the alliterating pair "lap" and "lick" suggest, in turn, the gargantuan appetite of one who can "lap [up]" Miles, and the daintier appetite of one who merely "licks" the Valleys up. The train's "prodigious" omnipotence coexists with its fastidious opposite adjective, "supercilious" (which is a phonetic twin of "prodigious" in its "-ious" ending). Where else is the train "docile"? Where it complains against its journey, but obeys the route nonetheless: it has to "crawl" between the sides of the Quarry ("Complaining all the while"), and it has to stop where it has been told to stop, at its stable door. When else is the train "omnipotent"? When it can pare a Quarry, and chase itself down Hill, and neigh like Boanerges. (The "Boanerges" were the two disciples, James and John, to whom Jesus gave this name, which in Aramaic means "Sons of Thunder"; yet according to the poet's 1844 Webster, the word could also be used in the singular, as here, for a vociferous preacher.) When the train complains, it is both "docile" and "omnipotent": docile in following its uncomfortable route, but omnipotent in its invention of "horrid - hooting" stanzas to make its opinion known to all. Dickinson, in social exchanges in her earlier life (while she allowed them), was "docile," a "lady"; but in her room she was busy composing stanzas, often ones of satiric literary omnipotence. The train is Dickinson's self-parody, a bad poet. To this day, it still hoots its way through Amherst, with blasts upon its whistle in regular rhythmic succession, horrid "stanzas" indeed to the poet's ear, accustomed to the quiet of a small town.

[J 585]

# 401

Dare you see a Soul at the "White Heat"?
Then crouch within the door -
Red - is the Fire's common tint -
But when the vivid Ore

Has vanquished Flame's conditions -
It quivers from the Forge
Without a color, but the Light
Of unanointed Blaze -

Least Village, boasts its Blacksmith -
Whose Anvil's even ring
Stands symbol for the finer Forge
That soundless tugs - within -

Refining these impatient Ores
With Hammer, and with Blaze
Until the designated Light
Repudiate the Forge -

To show, in verse, a soul passing through flame, and beyond it to the "White Heat" of incandescence, is a daunting undertaking. In Dickinson's narrative, Fire's initial creation of Blaze is surpassed as the heated Ore, undergoing the Hammer of the Blacksmith, turns into Light.

There are four major acts of invention in the poem. The first is the summoning up of an observer, immediately invited—if he dares—to watch the spectacle of Heat becoming Light. He is warned to stay away from the immediate vicinity of the fire; he should approach no closer than the door (a door to what sort of building is not yet revealed), and to "crouch," subjected, just within it.

The second invention is the little narrative of the Ore, which we never see in its first, inanimate, and dark condition (as it appeared when it was excavated from the mine) but observe only in its medial, heated condition, when it becomes red (the Fire's own tint, its "common" color). The "vivid" Ore, already red when the poem begins, is imagined as engaged in a struggle with the refining Flame, which wants to retain it at the red stage, during which the Hammer of the Blacksmith will compel it into a useful object—a horseshoe, a sickle. That is the only aim of the Flame: once the Ore is "vivid," its dross has been sublimed away and it can be worked. The purified Ore, however, has an aim of its own; and once it has defied Flame's command that it remain red and useful, it "quivers"—the most revealing word in the poem—from the Forge, at whose door the observer, so inferior to Flame, must "crouch." When the Ore wins its battle with Flame, it transcends the common red and passes into its new state, that of Light. There the narrative of the Ore, Dickinson's second invention, would seem to end.

Dickinson's third invention, after she has created the observer and the Ore-narrative, is the distinction she establishes between an "anointed" and an "unanointed" state of the Soul. The first implies a designation made by some authority, often God in the Bible (who anoints a king, or an otherwise chosen person); the second (claimed by the Soul) is one that defies the authoritative divine appointing. There are only two other poems in which Dickinson uses the unusual (and irreligious) word "unanointed" (spelled by her with a double "n"). Dickinson's first use of the word, in the poem "The *Sun - just touched* the Morning" (246, J 232), depicts desolation: the deluded female Morning, visited by the male Sun, believes that he has come to stay and that she will be Queen to his King; at sunset, realizing his love was only temporary, she feels "*feebly - for Her* [vanished] *Crown -* / Her *unannointed forehead - / Henceforth - Her only* One!" Such youthful dismay at finding herself without the expected "Diadem" has entirely vanished by the time the poet can make a claim—in "Dare you see a Soul"—to autonomous "unannointed Blaze." Dickinson's third use of the word, after "Dare you see a Soul," occurs in a variant to a jauntily comic poem, "The Bobolink is gone - " (1620, J 1591). She sets the Bobolink among the dour "Presbyterian Birds," who are "opening the Sabbath in their afflictive Way." The joyous Bobolink contradicts their gloomy Calvinist music by interrupting them boldly: "from an unannointed Twig" (in a variant) "[He] shouted Let us pray." In the Bobolink's boisterous defiance, Dickinson dismisses entirely all nostalgia for official "anointing."

It would seem that the narrative of "Dare you see a Soul" should end once the Soul, quivering, has quit the Forge in the glory of "unanointed Blaze." But Dickinson at once begins—in her fourth enterprise of invention—an allegorical reprise of her plot (as if the presence of the word "Soul" in the first line had not already made the narrative allegorical). A hasty sketch of the "real-life" base for the symbolic allegory is quickly drawn: "Least Village, boasts its Blacksmith." The verb "boasts" was designedly introduced instead of its preceding variant, "has" (in Version A), establishing the importance of the Blacksmith to society. Dickinson's account of the Blacksmith's intensive shaping of intractable metal into formed objects (a contrast of nature and culture) is influenced by the poet's biblical knowledge of God as a spiritual "refining fire": "For he is like a refiner's fire . . . and he shall purify the sons of Levi" (Malachi 3:2–3). Symbolized by the "Anvil's even ring" under the afflictive Hammer, the "finer Forge / That soundless tugs - within - " will purge the Soul of impurities. Whenever Dickinson uses the word "tugs," it bears a childish connotation. Here, she suggests, by its odd inappropriateness to its context, how early the "still, small voice" (1 Kings 19:12) of conscience begins its severe task of purgation, "tugging" the child away from complacency to a sense of spiritual destiny.

To compose an ending for her second, allegorical narrative, Dickinson introduces three unexpected new insights. The first is that the Ores (with their initial admixture of dross) have been "impatient" to be purified. "Patient" comes from the Latin *patior,* "to suffer"; and in her use of "impatient," Dickinson asserts that the Ores were not merely passively undergoing the Forge's assaultive procedures, but rather longing for their completion. The second insight is that the "designated Light" (formerly the "unanointed Blaze") has accomplished its own anointing, its own appointment to an exalted status— the status of one who, having been purged, is "saved." Nothing in the poem has prepared us for Dickinson's third insight: that when the Soul has completed its voluntary passage through fire, and has subjected itself to the Hammer (a painful process euphemized in the earlier Anvil), it will "Repudiate the Forge - ". The word "repudiate" (from the Latin "to divorce," "to reject") dismisses any idea of gratitude to the Forge for what it has aided the Soul to accomplish. According to Paul (Colossians 3:9–10), the saved have "put off the old man with his deeds; and have put on the new *man,* which is renewed in knowledge." To reject, under the shaping of the Hammer, a past self (and its deeds) is the final move that the Soul will make when the refining is done. At that moment, having become a "new man," it can "Repudiate the Forge."

Twice—once in each telling of the story—Dickinson rhymes "Forge" and "Blaze," connecting as closely as possible the furnace of suffering and its incandescent outcome. By the second enunciation of the story, the invitation to an onlooker to dare to watch the process has been forgotten: the self-perfecting soul needs no audience as it completes its time of purgation and is (Paul again) "renewed in knowledge." Dickinson's refashioning of the Christian narrative of God's chastening purgation of the soul takes it into an entirely personal and secular sphere. Yet, paradoxically, the Bible remains the only location in which the poet can find sufficiently evocative symbols for her interior development. And the only suitable language for this difficult transformation is Latin: Latin roots underlie "vivid," "vanquished," "condition," "anoint," "forge," "refine," "impatient," "designated," "light," and "repudiate." With "Blaze," Dickinson might have been recalling its single most conspicuous use in English poetry, in Milton's *Lycidas:*

> But the fair Guerdon when we hope to find,
> And think to burst out into sudden blaze,
> Comes the blind Fury with th' abhorrèd shears,
> And slits the thin-spun life.

The attraction of the word "Blaze" is that even when used as a noun, its force as a verb brilliantly makes itself manifest, too.

[J 365]

# 407

One need not be a Chamber - to be Haunted -
One need not be a House -
The Brain has Corridors - surpassing
Material Place -

Far safer, of a midnight meeting
External Ghost
Than its interior confronting -
That cooler Host -

Far safer, through an Abbey gallop,
The Stones a'chase -
Than unarmed, one's a'self encounter -
In lonesome Place -

Ourself behind ourself, concealed -
Should startle most -
Assassin hid in our Apartment
Be Horror's least -

The Body - borrows a Revolver -
He bolts the Door -
O'erlooking a superior spectre -
Or More -

This poem—about the true spectres haunting the mind, so different from
the picturesque folktale ghosts that haunt houses—plays a game designed to
unsettle the reader. There are five stanzas, each of which tends to fall into a
comparison of "Material Place" and places within the mind. We expect, once
such a comparison is established, to find the terms remaining in the same or-
der with respect to each other.

Let me label as A the "external world" of Material Place, and as B the "in-
terior world" of mind, and track Dickinson's pattern (in two-line bits)

through the stanzas. On the left are the images of lines 1–2; on the right, the images of lines 3–4. And we see that Dickinson usually mentions the external world first, A preceding B:

|          | External | Internal |
|----------|----------|----------|
| 1: A, B  | Chamber/House | Brain/Corridors |
| 2: A, B  | External Ghost | [interior Host] |
| 3: A, B  | Stones/Abbey | One's own self |
| 4: B, A  | [Assassin in Apartment] | [Ourself concealed] |
| 5: A, B  | Body/Revolver/Door | superior spectre (or More) |

We perceive that in stanza 4 the pattern reverses itself: instead of first encountering Material Place, and then the mind, we encounter the spectre of the mind before external place: "Ourself behind ourself, concealed." This ingenious phrase "corrects" the previous Gothic presentation of the self pursued by Stones in a lonesome place (a ruined Abbey). The note struck there is one of picturesque pathos: the Place is "lonesome," and one is "unarmed." The poet thrusts in to repudiate that pathos with a didactic truth: "Ourself behind ourself, concealed - / Should startle most - ". "Startle" is a "cool" word, by comparison to "lonesome": and the self-concealing-itself-from-itself is a "metaphysical" concept rather than a Gothic one. A chiasmus links stanza 3 to stanza 4 at the crucial "reversal" of A and B: Place, Self, Self, Place. The presence of chiasmus always betokens conscious forethought, which here places the inner self as the fulcrum on which the poem turns. In stanza 4 Dickinson rhymes "most" with "least" to indicate the self as its own worst Horror, more to be feared than the "least" startling case—a stagy Gothic "Assassin" behind one's own front door. Earlier, too, Dickinson had used two other rhyme-words that match "most": the local "Ghost" and the "Host" (multiple warriors) of "superior spectres" threatened in the last line of the poem.

The poem begins with the impersonal "One," but the import of its first statement (with its Gothic "Chamber" followed by its non-Gothic corrective "House") tends toward the personal, as the poet begins her speculation on an inner terror within the labyrinthine "Corridors" of the resolutely anatomical "Brain." Not long after, the personal reference is continued in

"Ourself behind ourself" as the self is divided into two selves, one concealed, waiting to appall the other. In the final division, Dickinson seems about to repeat the old dualism of body and soul, as "The Body" takes precautions against invaders, while overlooking "a superior spectre"—its Soul. Yet Dickinson thinks one is mistaken to presume that only a single threatening spirit lies in wait: alluding perhaps to the seven devils cast out of Mary Magdalene (Mark 16:9) or to the Gadarene swine, with "more than two thousand" devils driving them to their deaths (Mark 5:8–13), Dickinson warns of a possible "More"—a host of spectres—waiting to torment the hapless haunted Brain. After all, the "unclean spirit," when asked his name by Jesus, answered, "My name is Legion: for we are many" (Mark 5:8–9).

Although "One need not be a Chamber" is written in 4-2-4-2 stanzas, Dickinson allows two striking exceptions, in the most sensitive locations in any poem: beginning and end. The poem opens with a declarative thematic pentameter, "One need not be a Chamber - to be Haunted - ", followed by a trimeter correcting "Chamber" to "House"; and it closes with an unexpected monometer (leaving blank continuing line-room for the "More" spectres that lie in wait). The spectres wandering the corridors of the mind cannot be stopped by revolver or bolts: one is helpless under their frightening invasions, and "More" of them may invade one's House at any time.

[J 670]

# 409

The Soul selects her own Society -
Then - shuts the Door -
To her divine Majority -
Present no more -

Unmoved - she notes the Chariots - pausing -
At her low Gate -
Unmoved - an Emperor be kneeling
Upon her Mat -

I've known her - from an ample nation -
Choose One -
Then - close the Valves of her attention -
Like Stone -

We might feel that Dickinson had already in effect composed this poem of absolute choice when she wrote, earlier in the same year, "Of all the Souls that stand create - / I have Elected - One - " (*279). Why does she need to change "all the Souls that stand create" into "an ample nation"? Why change the verb from "Elect" to "select" and "Choose"? Why name the beloved the "Society" of the Soul instead of "the Atom - I preferred"? What is the poet accomplishing in this second narrative of a final choice?

We recall that "Of all the Souls that stand create - " takes place on Judgment Day, when one can see and rank all created souls, all the "lists of Clay." The stunning description of the timeless eternal moment in that poem was never surpassed by Dickinson, but in "The Soul selects" she has redone the topic in humbler terms. She is no longer standing among the "Elect" in Eternity, surveying the ranks of the Saved; rather, she exists in ordinary time. The broad eschatological timelessness of the earlier poem is reduced to one lifetime; and the various "Souls that stand create," other than the beloved, are merely sampled in a single one, the highest-ranking on the (earthly) social scale: an Emperor. Instead of the hymn-meter of the Last Day, we find in

"The Soul selects" (except in the first line), a 4-2-4-2 arrangement, which catches us up short at the end of every two lines, in a long pause, as a door is shut, or eyes are closed. (The first line, like the first line in "One need not be a Chamber - to be Haunted - ," is a declarative pentameter, setting the theme.) The plane of discussion is human "Society" instead of all created souls; and it is from a restricted, if broad, secular group—"an ample nation" (not a hyperbolic "all the Souls")—that the Soul chooses. The Soul, Dickinson asserts as she descends from Eternity to time, does not possess only an eschatological destiny; she has a temporal one as well. Before she makes the eternal choice, she will need to make a choice in time.

There are two principal questions raised by the "The Soul selects": What is the necessity of the third stanza, which seems (to a casual reading) merely to repeat the first? And what is the function of the middle stanza? There appears to be no narrator in stanza 1, but there is an addressee, to whom a command is given: do not present any more candidates to the Soul. Before that imperative, the stanza has the quality of a universal aphorism: "The Soul selects her own Society, then shuts the Door." Yes, we agree; and we even agree that once she has assembled her own society, the rest of the world can be requested to present no more companions for her inspection. Her selected Society behind her shut door constitutes a "divine Majority." We still do not know how many Souls make up her selected "Society."

When we look down to the last stanza, which at first appeared to tell the "same story," we see many differences from stanza 1. To our surprise, we now encounter a speaking "I" asserting personal acquaintance with the choosing Soul, and telling us that in the case of at least some Souls, the chosen "Society" may consist of only one other person. The "divine Majority" must in that case mean a "Majority of Two" (an idea, in its difference from the proverbial "Majority of One," that must have entertained Dickinson). In the first stanza, the Soul "shuts the Door," a homely act taking place in a house. But in the last stanza, in the most unnerving image of the poem, the Soul closes "the Valves of her attention - / Like Stone - ". It is not much help to read that "Valves" replaced the word "Lids." Shutting one's eyes is easily seen as the spiritual equivalent of shutting a (material) door—but what is implied in closing "Valves"?

Dickinson had used the word once before, in "Besides the Autumn poets sing" (123, J 131), but there it carried its (here irrelevant) botanical sense of "the seed-vessel of a plant" (1844 Webster's). In his other definitions of "valve," Webster emphasizes that valves (in hearts as in pumps) are there to keep a flow unidirectional, to prevent its going backward. His third definition reads, "In anatomy, a membranous partition within the cavity of a vessel, which opens to allow the passage of a fluid in one direction, and shuts to prevent its regurgitation." Webster uses the same word ("shuts") as Dickinson; and since the word "valve" comes from the Latin for "folding doors" *(valvae),* it takes Dickinson back to stanza 1's "door." (Doors, however, are not unidirectional.) Some have thought of bivalves such as the oyster in connection with Dickinson's "Valves"—and the word "bivalve" is certainly in Webster's in both its botanical and anatomical meanings. Still, the valves of the heart furnish a far more probable meaning. Erotic "attention" requires the opening of the heart's passages; and when the object of that attention has entered the Soul's precincts, the heart can close its portals, never to reopen them. The comparison of the closed valves of the heart to impregnable "Stone" arises from the biblical contrast of hearts of flesh and hearts of stone. The most relevant citation, in terms of voluntarily attending and not attending, would seem to be Zechariah 7:12: "Yea, they made their hearts as an adamant stone, lest they should hear the law." Dickinson's Soul makes her heart as stone once love is satisfied, shutting out the pleas of other suitors.

What is the function of the stanza that links these two versions—the first, a general one, the last, a specific one—of the Soul's selecting her own Society? It exists to prepare us for the adamantine heart, by showing us the Soul's insusceptibility to temptation: "Unmoved," she watches the "Chariots" of (noble, classical, or biblical) suitors pausing at her humble "Gate." This Gate is part of the outer barrier that guards the perimeter of the house; inside the enclosure marked by the "Gate" is the "Door" leading to the inner "Valves" allowing entrance to the Heart. The Gate is not opened at all for the nobles borne by the "Chariots." One person, however, seems to offer enough temptation to be admitted at least through the Gate: he is the Emperor who kneels upon the mat outside the Soul's door (a "Rush mat" in one variant). Still "Unmoved," the Soul does not open her door even to the suitor ready to make her an Empress. (The phrase "she notes" is, in the grammatical sense, "understood" in line 3 of this stanza: "Unmoved - she notes the Chariots . . . /

Unmoved - [she notes whether] an Emperor be kneeling / Upon her Mat - "). Without the twofold presence of "Unmoved," we might be more surprised by the final irrevocable closing of the Valves of the Soul's erotic attention, once her chosen One has been admitted—past the Gate, past the Mat, past the Door, past the Valves, into the Heart itself.

In the first two stanzas, Dickinson's even-numbered lines close with four syllables, two iambic feet:

> Then - shuts | the Door -
> Present | no more -
> At her | low Gate -
> Upon | her Mat -

But in the last stanza, when the adamantine selection is made, the rhythm in the even-numbered lines shifts to spondees—two hard accents, two hard syllables, one after the other:

> Choose One -
> Like Stone -

Two Valves: two decisive and final shuttings of two unidirectional doors. And the final rhyme—"One" and "Stone," with "Stone" graphically enclosing its companion "One"—outlines the heart embracing the beloved within.

Oddly, since this poem is affirming, in the strongest possible terms, the selection of a permanent earthly beloved, the poet's early editors called it "Exclusion." Was "Selection" too peremptory a word for a female to use at that time?

[J 303]

# 420

There are two Ripenings -
One - of Sight - whose Forces spheric wind
Until the Velvet Product
Drop, spicy, to the Ground -

A Homelier - maturing -
A Process in the Bur -
That Teeth of Frosts, alone disclose -
On far October Air -

Like many of Dickinson's two-stanza poems, this one contrasts two things—here, two kinds of "Ripenings." We hear from Shakespeare's Edgar, "Ripeness is all" (said to his father, Gloucester, in *King Lear,* Act 5, scene 2). But how does one achieve "ripeness"? And is there more than one way?

In her first stanza, Dickinson takes as her metaphor the ripening of fruit (apples and peaches). This beautiful "Ripening" (which Dickinson knew very well, living in an agricultural town) ravishes three senses at once. Sight deduces, from the swelling apple, the existence of "spheric" forces that wind (as in winding yarn into a ball) the flesh of the fruit to its rounded perfection; touch reaches out to the velvety texture of the covering of the peach; smell takes in the seasonal "spicy" perfume of an apple orchard. The poem (like many others in Dickinson's work) owes something to Keats's classic "To Autumn," but Dickinson refuses Keats's infliction of a cider-press on the apples: they are allowed their natural course of life, dropping to the ground when they are ripe. Dickinson refers to the fruit by the strangely practical word "Product," in part because it allows her to give an agricultural aura to the fruit; see her later poem, "The Products of my Farm are these" (1036, J 1025). In this first stanza, Dickinson gives full value to this exquisite and profuse natural ripening, the one available to sight, touch, and smell.

Yet we sense her greater approbation of the hidden, second ripening: the forces here are not "spheric" but "maturing." We understand fully now her previous use of the word "Product," since she here introduces its invisible counterpart, "Process" (which, as Dickinson's chief interest, probably generated the alliterating "Product" in the first place). In retrospect, we realize that the "Forces" that Dickinson inferred in stanza 1 were part of a "Process" that invisibly compelled the apple into a visible spheric form, so that stanza 1, too, concerned a Process as well as a Product. The senses care only for the sensuously attractive products of nature's processes, but the mind is always more interested in investigating what is hidden; and so Dickinson now looks into a Process that produces nothing immediately appealing to the senses. If the senses pay any attention at all to the fruit of the chestnut tree, they perceive only the Bur, a dun product, odorless and spiky. But in October the Bur splits open, disclosing the glossy perfection of the (edible) nut hidden within the husk. Laconic, as so often, with respect to the savagery of nature and God, Dickinson lets fall the remark that it is the "Teeth of Frosts" that have caused the wound in the Bur; as the external body of the Bur falls away, it discloses the beauty and usefulness of the ripe kernel. The "October Air" of this revelation occurs "far" from the summer air in which the orchard fruits had their ripening, The chestnut's Process is "Homelier" because it brings to mind processes that take place inside houses—ones less showy, more ordinary, less remarkable, than external and visible events.

Dickinson opened a later poem with her prizing of the "nut," or "Kernel," that might exist within a kindred spirit (1081, J 1073):

> Experiment to me
> Is everyone I meet
> If it contain a Kernel?

Apples and peaches offer all their fleshly beauty without any searching: they do not have edible "Kernels." However, as Dickinson said punningly in "Experiment to me," to "meet" someone can yield the "meat" within, the nourishment that "is requisite / To Squirrels and to me." The interior ripening of the spirit is to be prized over the husk, which falls out of sight once its function has been fulfilled.

"There are two Ripenings - " may obliquely bear on gender. The usual way for women to bear ripe "fruit" is to give birth; but while that sort of "ripening" is, until birth, "out of sight," the rounding of the body allows us to deduce "spheric forces" at work, until eventually the Velvet Product drops from its producer. That biological ripening was not to be Dickinson's; her own "Process" produced poems as the Product of her "Homelier" single life. (And the poems had not the Velvet texture of peaches; they were irregular, spiky, like the Bur and like their author.) Her poetry, nonetheless, bears witness to the development of an extraordinary spiritual life. In spite of the plainness of the poet's existence, within it a secret Process occurs. The Soul—maturing only under the Teeth of chilled expectations, and aware of the approach of a wintry death after its October chastening—is "disclosed" only as the body is wounded by the "Teeth" of suffering, and will be fully revealed only in the apocalyptic uncovering of the Last Day.

[J 332]

# 423

The first Day's Night had come -
And grateful that a thing
So terrible - had been endured -
I told my Soul to sing -

She said her strings were snapt -
Her Bow - to atoms blown -
And so to mend her - gave me work
Until another Morn -

And then - a Day as huge
As Yesterday's in pairs,
Unrolled its horror in my face -
Until it blocked my eyes -

My Brain - begun to laugh -
I mumbled - like a fool -
And tho' 'tis Years ago - that Day -
My Brain keeps giggling - still.

And Something's odd - within -
That person that I was -
And this One - do not feel the same -
Could it be Madness - this?

Dickinson's most famous poem of the reiteration of suffering is "My life closed twice before its close" (*1773). The insult of repeated death-blows from "Immortality"—each one huge, each one inconceivable—leads, in that poem, to a succinct aphorism: "Parting is all we know of heaven, / And all we need of hell." "The first Day's Night" does not have the stoicism of its later sibling; on the contrary, it is, to my mind, Dickinson's most harrowing depiction of active mental suffering, and it ends not with an acid aphorism but with a question: "Could it be Madness - this?"

What threatens insanity here is a complete disruption of the continuity of the ego: it is not now what it was in the past. Or rather, the poet's present self and her past self "do not feel the same." The "Something" that is "odd - within" might be named, by a more ordinary writer, a "broken heart" or a "convulsion of dread"—some physiological or neurological equivalent of an emotion. But Dickinson's hazy vagueness at first allows no specification of her "Something," until (we realize) she admits a dire possibility in herself that until now she has refused to entertain: Madness. The mad (at least by nineteenth-century convention) have violently skewed perceptions and cannot use language coherently; Dickinson would expire as a writer were she to go mad. At its first publication, in 1935, this poem was stripped of its last two stanzas, which were not restored until 1947. A decline into hysteria and threatened madness was not an aspect of Dickinson's emotional life that her editor Martha Dickinson Bianchi wished to convey to the public. Nonetheless, the genius of the poem lies in its (originally suppressed) penultimate stanza, in which hysteria replaces language.

The poem begins with a resolute survivor of some disabling trauma, who courageously urges her Soul to resume her former song. The Soul explains, in reply, that her ruined instrument—one with a Bow and strings—has been damaged. Her strings are snapped, which is damaging enough, but her Bow has been "blown" to bits—or, worse than bits, "atoms"—by a sudden destructive explosion. There can be no more singing until the instrument is mended; and so all night the determined survivor repairs her Soul's snapped strings, and constructs a new Bow. When morning comes, her restored Soul will be able, she thinks, to sing again.

In describing her grief in terms of the First Day and the First Night, Dickinson borrows from Genesis (1:5): "And God called the light Day, and the darkness he called Night. And the evening and the morning were the first day." Dickinson makes this august allusion in order to broaden the measure of her own "first Day"—that of the devastating explosion—and of the first Day's Night—that of the mending of the instrument. The second catastrophe, "a Day as huge / As Yesterday's in pairs," recreates an apocalyptic final destruction. The survivor of the first destruction is undone—blinded—by the new reiteration of chaos, knowing she cannot again muster the force to retrieve her Soul's blasted, repaired, and now vanished strings and Bow.

It is at this point—seeing nothing further to live for with the disappear-ance of her singing Soul—that the poet falls into incoherent laughing and mumbling and "giggling." The deranged brain (here a physiological entity, not a spiritual one) can no longer form words, let alone a song. The inappro-priate response of hysteria—giggling at one's tragedy—indicates that the po-et's brain is refusing to articulate the unbearable second loss. The most des-perate words in this stanza are "still" and "giggling": the poet's brain began to laugh "Years ago - that Day," and it "keeps giggling - still." With its sinister punctuation of a period (always consequential in Dickinson when it replaces her customary dash), the long four-stanza sentence describing the undoing of a Soul comes to a halt, its last utterance ending in the hideous wrongness of the irrational and onomatopoetic "giggling."

There is a coda to the poem, following the period, which attempts a diag-nosis of the illness of the mind that has lasted for so many years. One can imagine many efforts, over prolonged time, to reunite the two halves of the self that stubbornly will not fuse. Dickinson describes such an effort in "I felt a Cleaving in my Mind - / As if my Brain had split - " (*867); "I tried to match it - Seam by Seam - ", she says, "But could not make them fit." To re-store the "person that I was" is impossible: too many years have passed in trembling and mumbling and giggling. And to take this dreadful subhuman creature of hysteria as one's real self is too frightening and humiliating to con-template. Unusually, this poem begins in the past tense and ends, in its coda, in the present. The tale is not complete; its future is uncertain.

The only true rhyme in the poem occurs in the first, hopeful, stanza, when the survivor of the terrible "thing" tells her Soul to "sing." That rhyme voices the consonance of hope. The rest of the rhymes are imperfect: "blown . . . Morn"; "pairs . . . eyes"; "fool . . . still"; and "was . . . this." The harmonious duet of singing voice and Bow will never be resumed.

Dickinson here uses one of her frequent variations on hymn-meter. In this variation, the first line is a trimeter (instead of the expected tetrameter): 3-3-4-3. The first trimeter is curt, with an implied stop, but the second one leads directly to its sequel:

> The first Day's Night had come - [*stop*]
> And grateful that a thing

So terrible - had been endured -
I told my Soul to sing -

We are relieved when we can relax, in line 3, into a full four-beat line, which, at its conclusion, glides smoothly into the following trimeter in a familiar cadence. The two incisive short lines beginning each stanza often have abrupt end-words: "snapt," "blown," "huge," "pairs," "laugh," "fool." But the final stanza, in the fearful present tense, can muster only weak end-words for its first two lines: in its "was" and "this," we hear resistance subsiding into an apprehensive query.

[J 410]

# 425

'Twas like a Maelstrom, with a notch,
That nearer, every Day,
Kept narrowing its boiling Wheel
Until the Agony

Toyed coolly with the final inch
Of your delirious Hem -
And you dropt, lost,
When something broke -
And let you from a Dream -

As if a Goblin with a Gauge -
Kept measuring the Hours -
Until you felt your Second
Weigh, helpless, in his Paws -

And not a Sinew - stirred - could help,
And Sense was setting numb -
When God - remembered - and the Fiend
Let go, then, Overcome -

As if your Sentence stood - pronounced -
And you were frozen led
From Dungeon's luxury of Doubt
To Gibbets, and the Dead -

And when the Film had stitched your eyes
A Creature gasped "Reprieve"!
Which Anguish was the utterest - then -
To perish, or to live?

Dickinson resorts to three successive similes, each offered in a two-stanza span, to explain the experience she narrates: the first is "'Twas like a Maelstrom"; the second, "As if a Goblin with a Gauge - "; and the third, "As if your

Sentence stood - pronounced - ". If a poet finds simile 1 insufficient in some way, she must add simile 2. If even that does not adequately represent the experience, she goes on to simile 3. And if simile 3 doesn't exhaust the problem, she must end the poem in a gesture of incompleteness and incapacity. Since Dickinson was not one to waste words, and was often content to stop a poem after two stanzas, this six-stanza extravaganza (by comparison to her smaller poems) must lead us to think about how each of the two later similes fills in a quality of the experience that has not yet been sufficiently articulated in the preceding figure.

Each simile is a hyperbolic one, and Dickinson's use of the second person, "you," inflicts intimacy on the horror. You are caught in the vortex of a progressively narrowing Maelstrom and will soon drown; you are being held helpless, paralyzed, in the paws of a scientific Goblin (who may be the Devil), in what seems a consignment to hell; you are being led to the Gibbet where you will be executed. These similes, as they are pursued, are alike in only one respect: after a ghastly experience, at the last moment, you are somehow freed. In this, the tales all resemble nightmares that have stopped just short of their dénouement (given Dickinson's aside in the second stanza about something letting you out of a dream, these may well have been nightmares in fact). After all three nightmares—and your sudden unexpected release in each before the expected death—Dickinson poses the question from which the whole poem must have sprung: In such situations, reprieved when you were a hair's-breadth from extinction, "Which Anguish was the utterest - then - / To perish, or to live?"

We must look to what is explained by each simile, suggest why it is not entirely adequate, and go on to the next. The Maelstrom brings to mind the torments of a classical Hell, with its "boiling Wheel" resembling Ixion's "wheel of fire" alluded to by King Lear. It also has elements of slow torture: the Maelstrom, sadistically, tightens its wheel by a notch a day and toys with your terror. It affects the mind, sending you into a delirium in which you drop into the heart of the Maelstrom—and as you sink, nothing is visible to an observer but the hem of your garment. Physical and mental torture, caused by a natural phenomenon, a Maelstrom: Won't that suffice as an illustration of a hideous suffering just past?

Catastrophes caused by the inexorable laws of nature, however, are not deliberate; the sailor lost in a maelstrom merely suffers from bad luck. When torture is deliberately caused, one has more reason to complain. Dickinson's second simile brings in God and the Devil: the "Goblin" turns into a "Fiend" when God enters the picture. This is an absentminded God, who has totally forgotten his creature being tormented by a coolly sadistic inhuman monster (with "Paws" like a beast, not usual in a Goblin), one who likes measuring, second by second, with his gauge, the degree of horror felt by his paralyzed victim. This simile adds malevolence to the picture of suffering, a malevolence permitted by a God who has things more important to think about. Just as you were "let" from a Dream in simile 1, so the Fiend, in simile 2, "Let go" of you, ceding to a greater power. What, we might ask, could be worse than this Goblin?

Humanity could be worse, says Dickinson: Nature and the Devil are greater forces than human beings, and hold us helpless in their grip. But what if the malevolence is wreaked on you by a person like yourself—the judge who, after you had lingered in a Dungeon, finally pronounced your death sentence? Just as you were "lost" in the Maelstrom, and your Sun of sense was "setting" as you became "numb" in the Paws of the Goblin, so you are "frozen" when you know you are to be executed. (Dickinson almost always attaches a sense experience to mental pain.) At least in the Dungeon you had the suspension of final knowledge, could indulge in the "luxury of Doubt." But now? To the physical power of the Maelstrom and the spiritual sadism of the Goblin, we must add the human malevolence—or perhaps error?—of the judge who has condemned an innocent person, yourself, to death. As you close your eyes before the Gibbet lets you drop, a "Film" spreads over the sense of sight. And then, just before you are hanged, you are reprieved from execution. You hardly can take in what has happened: a "Creature" has entered the scene, running to forestall the hangman, and gasping "Reprieve!"— that despaired-of word.

To come back to life—from the Maelstrom, the Fiend, and the Judge— means to come back to an existence where you, now enlightened, know that the future could bring more Maelstroms, more Fiends, and more Gibbets, with their concomitant agonies, torments, and injustices. Would you want to come back to such a life of "Anguish"? Or would it be simpler merely to stop resisting the Maelstrom and its delirium, the Fiend and his paralyzing cruelty, the unreliable system of Gibbets, and leave this life altogether, preferring the (at least limited) "Anguish" of death?

The poem offers Dickinson an opportunity for a triple set of macabre predicaments and a surrounding set of macabre words—"Maelstrom," "boiling," "Agony," "Goblin," "Paws," "Fiend," "Dungeon," "Gibbets," and "Anguish." The dramatic work of the poem is mostly done by these successively grim scenarios. The most imaginative of the poet's inventions is the "Goblin with a Gauge": he resembles the "angry God" in Jonathan Edwards's famous sermon who holds the sinner over the pit of Hell, "as one might hold a loathsome Spider." In thinking up this Goblin-disguise for the Devil, Dickinson resembles medieval painters who drew increasingly grotesque versions of what they imagined the Devil might look like. Some indeed do look like Goblins, but they lack a Gauge—that measure, for this modern and precise poet, of the passage of time observed from Eternity.

[J 414]

# 430

A Charm invests a face
Imperfectly beheld -
The Lady dare not lift her Vail
For fear it be dispelled -

But peers beyond her mesh -
And wishes - and denies -
Lest Interview - annul a want
That Image - satisfies -

In her writing, Dickinson represents erotic desire perplexingly. On the one hand, there are passionate love poems and the piteous "Master letters"; on the other hand, there is a guarded withdrawal from too near an approach. She knew, as Yeats would say, that "Maybe the bride-bed brings despair, / For each an imagined image brings / And finds a real image there" ("Solomon and the Witch"). In "A Charm invests a face," the poet shows the lady fearing that since her lover has been attracted to her by the face he sees only imperfectly behind her fashionable "mesh," he might not want the real image that he would see if she lifted her veil. The argument can be generalized to any revelation of the "real self" that does not fit the demands of coquetry or conventional courtship. Although Dickinson cannot dispute the lady's defensible reasoning, she does not want for herself the sort of relation therein described.

The poem begins with a general axiom, and then specifies its application, not from the (deluded) man's point of view, but from the point of view of the lady who wishes to maintain his estimation of her beauty. If Charm can be "dispelled," it resembles many other things that can attach themselves to that verb: doubt, suspicion, a noxious odor, fears. There is usually something displeasing about that which needs to be "dispelled." Although the verb is derived from the Latin *dis-* and *pellere* (to drive things in different directions), Dickinson must have relished its enclosure, in its past participle, of the word "spell," a word frequently associated with female "charm," which is said to "cast a spell" on the enthralled beholder. The Lady knows that there is something inauthentic about "Charm," and wishes that she could disclose herself utterly, but she is intimidated; she "dare not."

Dickinson often implies "another side"—heaven, Italy, resurrection— that she cannot see because something (death, the Alps, lack of belief) stands in the way. Here an apparently frail bit of lace keeps the lover from seeing the "other side"; and "mesh"—as we can see from "I had not minded - Walls - " (554, J 398)—implies, for Dickinson, a defense. As she tries to reach a lover, she encounters

> A limit like the Vail
> Unto the Lady's face -
> But every Mesh - a Citadel -
> And Dragons - in the Crease -

In "A Charm invests a face," the three verbs ascribed to the Lady—as she first tries to "peer beyond" her own defenses, then "wishes," then "denies"—enact her vacillation between candor and coquetry. And what causes her vacillation? The inability to predict whether the lover will be glad of her candor or repelled by her flesh. Fearing that a face-to-face "Interview" will destroy the lover's desire, which was awakened by the veiled Image, the Lady remains conventional.

Dickinson's interesting substitution here for "destroy" is a word—"annul" —that we associate with contracts and with marriage. A marriage (even one of many years) is ecclesiastically "annulled" when it is decided by a court of canon law that the marriage, when it took place, was "invalid." (There were many reasons for annulment, but here Dickinson probably has in mind the "impediment" of nonconsummation.) The potential union between the lady and her lover would be rendered null and void by the disenchanting truth of the unveiled face. (Such an "impediment" appears allegorized in Nathaniel Hawthorne's tale "The Birthmark," where the husband's attempt to excise the birthmark from his wife's face ends in her death.)

Dickinson takes pains with her rhymes here, as "[Imperfectly] beheld" is made to rhyme with its opposite, "dispelled," and "denies" is made to rhyme with *its* opposite, "satisfies." The meter is the "stopped-short" form of 3-3-4-3, not a restful rhythm. The epigram that closes the poem—

> Lest Interview - annul a want
> That Image - satisfies -

is graphically pleasing, as "Interview" is superimposed (on the page, to the eye) on "Image," and "annul" superimposed on "satisfies." There is a bitter awareness in Dickinson's use of the present indicative for the lover's current pleasure—which the Image "satisfies"—and her use of the subjunctive-of-possibility in the feared "annul." Dickinson does not suggest any possible improvement in the situation. When Otis Lord (a friend of Dickinson's father), courting Dickinson, offered an intensification of erotic closeness, she wrote, "Don't you know you are happiest while I withhold and not confer—don't you know that 'No' is the wildest word we consign to Language?" (562, L II, 617).

[J 421]

# 439

I had been hungry, all the Years -
My Noon had Come - to dine -
I trembling drew the Table near -
And touched the Curious Wine -

'Twas this on Tables I had seen -
When turning, hungry, Home
I looked in Windows, for the Wealth
I could not hope - for Mine -

I did not know the ample Bread -
'Twas so unlike the Crumb
The Birds and I, had often shared
In Nature's - Dining Room -

The Plenty hurt me - 'twas so new -
Myself felt ill - and odd -
As Berry - of a Mountain Bush -
Transplanted - to the Road -

Nor was I hungry - so I found
That Hunger - was a way
Of persons Outside Windows -
The entering - takes away -

This emotionally naked poem of desire and the attrition of desire is founded
on flashbacks. The whole tale is told in the past tense in alternation with the
pluperfect: the speaker has already undergone the experience recounted, and
has learned its lesson. It is thus less dramatic than "'Twas like a Maelstrom"
(ending in a piercing question to the reader) or "The first Day's Night had
come - " (ending in an equally piercing question to the self). "I had been
hungry, all the Years" oscillates between the speaker's early condition, one of
extreme hunger, and her later condition as she at last was enabled to approach

a table bearing "Curious Wine" (she had been subsisting on water) and "ample Bread" (she had been subsisting on crumbs). I arrange the poem below to show its constant oscillation between the then of a recent past and an earlier, pluperfect then:

| Past | Pluperfect (Earlier) Past |
|------|---------------------------|
| | I had been hungry, all the Years |
| | My Noon had Come - to dine - |
| I trembling drew the Table near - | |
| And touched the Curious Wine - | |
| | 'Twas this on Tables I had seen - |
| | When turning, hungry, Home |
| | I looked in Windows, for the Wealth |
| | I could not hope - for Mine - |
| I did not know the ample Bread - | |
| | 'Twas so unlike the Crumb |
| | The Birds and I, had often shared |
| | In Nature's - Dining Room - |
| The Plenty hurt me - 'twas so new - | |
| Myself felt ill - and odd - | |
| As Berry - of a Mountain Bush - | |
| Transplanted - to the Road - | |
| Nor was I hungry - so I found | |
| | That Hunger - was a way |
| | Of persons Outside Windows - |
| The entering - takes away - | |

At the end of this oscillation between the remote past and the nearer past, the speaker reveals the desolate discovery that ends her self-examination: "Nor was I hungry." When at last the object of her desire has been set before her, she does not desire it. She arrives at a new definition of Hunger: it is envy of the plenty of others, rather than a genuine desire for the "Wealth" they seem to possess. (Although the main verbs oscillate between the pluperfect and a nearer past, Dickinson inserts three present participles that make both "pasts" seem notionally present: "trembling," "turning," and "entering.")

The poem allegorizes any and all sorts of mistaken desire: for fame, for marriage, for any dreamed-of satisfaction. When the speaker arrived at the object of her desire, it was unchanged—still a feast of ample bread and curious wine, but one that now "hurt." It was she who had changed. Or perhaps when she saw her contemporaries in possession of fame, or husbands, or any other "Wealth," she eventually realized that she would not change her fate with theirs. But which would she rather be—the earlier intense and starving yearner with only the Birds for company, isolated on her mountain yet full of passion, or the disillusioned later spectator on the common Road who turns aside, empty of desire, from the "Bread" and "Wine" (a secular Communion) which she had longed to take?

The arrangement of tenses by which the speaker constantly turns away from the proffered ample meal to remember her stinted earlier far-off past convinces us that her deprived adult self has now become her only self; she can no longer be the girl she was. The words she uses when she tells us that at the Table of riches she felt "ill - and odd" recall the more dramatic, but comparable use of "odd" at the end of "The first Day's Night had come - " (*423), when she took the measure of the discontinuity of her ego after catastrophe:

> And Something's odd - within -
> The person that I was -
> And this One - do not feel the same -
> Could it be Madness - this?

Although we rely on the continuity of the ego, itself dependent on memory, to construct our self-image, when we find a rupture between our hungry past feelings (feelings long continued that became, over time, the motives and shapers of the self) and our present dismayed repudiation of them—wondering who the person was who ever wanted *that*—we are hard put to it to name the newly repudiating self, since we had been so accustomed to the desiring (and balked) one. That the dramatic vista of satisfaction which opens this poem, "I had been hungry, all the Years - / My Noon had Come - to dine - ", should eventuate in the bleak "Nor was I hungry" illustrates the dour discontinuity between naïveté and knowledge. The only "incomplete" line in this poem (which maintains a steady 4-3-4-3 rhythm throughout) is the penultimate one, which is truncated to three beats: "Of persons Outside Windows." This telling line, like the earlier self, is permanently "missing something."

[J 579]

# 444

It would have starved a Gnat -
To live so small as I -
And yet, I was a living child -
With Food's necessity

Upon me - like a Claw -
I could no more remove
Than I could coax a Leech away -
Or make a Dragon - move -

Nor like the Gnat - had I -
The privilege to fly
And seek a Dinner for myself -
How mightier He - than I!

Nor like Himself - the Art
Upon the Window Pane
To gad my little Being out -
And not begin - again -

When Dickinson, in "'Twas like a Maelstrom" (*425), wondered whether it would not, after Agony, be easier to die than to live, she phrased it peremptorily: "Which Anguish was the utterest - then - / To perish, or to live?" Recounting the frustration of desire, she said, dramatically, "I had been hungry, all the Years" (*439). But she could also pose the question of the starvation of the soul more quietly, and more ironically, in miniature, as she does here. Her opening hyperboles are often entertaining, as this one initially is—it appears playful, even gay. "It would have starved a Gnat - / To live so small as I - ". But the gaiety quickly recedes as we see the "living child" in the grip of a Claw she can no more remove (or move) than a Leech or a Dragon.

The Claw is a pain tearing at her vitals, asserting "Food's necessity." Food was something she, as a living child, had a right to, as she openly says. Who starved her? What was the necessary Food of which she was deprived? There were, then as now, cases of child abuse in which deranged parents did not feed their children, and this is a startling metaphor for Dickinson to adopt. It indicts her parents, her schooling, her contemporaries. And of course she did not know, as a child, what the remedy for this hunger would be; she could not even take action to find the unknown nourishment that would give her peace. In part because the need remained unnamed, it gripped her ever more tightly, in a daily unhappiness from which she found no way to escape.

She thinks first, looking for a simile of her trapped state, of a Claw (of an unspecified beast, but one with a Claw capable of holding a child immobile). Second, she thinks of a Leech (then used by doctors, who considered leeches a way to reduce fever and inflammation by reducing the amount of blood in the body). The Leech of that inner hunger is draining her of her life's blood, but she cannot detach it (that would be impossible), so she tries, without success, to "coax" it away from its prey, as one might coax a rabid dog. Since neither Claw nor Leech seems a bad enough simile to depict the spiritual starvation that attended the poet's childhood, she turns to myth, and finds that she, like Andromeda, is in the clutch of a Dragon. Her attempt to "re-move" and "move" her persecutors (the one rhyme insistently contained within the other) represents her continuing effort at freedom.

She affects to have almost forgotten, in her tale of victimage, her original symbol, the Gnat. Tamping down her giant hyperboles, she returns to irony, becoming once again the Gnat. Her incapacity to redress her own starva-tion—where could she have found another set of parents, or different school-ing, or a church she could respect?—makes her wittily assert that at least a Gnat can independently venture out to look for food. (Her rhymes, internal and external, in stanzas 1 and 3, make her a partner to the Gnat: "I" . . . "I" . . . "fly" . . . "I"). It is, she tells us, a "privilege" to be able to escape and find one's own Dinner. (Has anyone before ever called spiritual nourishment "Din-ner"? Or could anyone else imagine a Gnat eating a Dinner?) The mock-praise of the Gnat ("How mightier He - than I!") rapidly devolves into an image of a different "privilege," a different "Art": that of unwitting suicide. The Gnat, the poet implies with a return to a ghastly playfulness, can, unlike herself, "gad" his "little Being out— / Upon the Window Pane." I have rear-ranged the phrase to examine Dickinson's use of the word "gad." It is an in-transitive verb, of trivial import, as in the noun "gadabout"; but Dickinson makes it into a reflexive verb as the Gnat gads his "little Being out," as if his action were purposive. The little Gnat, ignorant of window panes, intends only to rove out into the air again, but finds himself instantly dead as he crashes into the window impeding his exit. But Dickinson does not (as I have been doing) phrase this tale as one told of the Gnat: "To gad *his* little Being out." Rather, she frames it as a tale of herself: "To gad my little Being out - / And not begin - again - ".

For the Gnat, the Window Pane was the end of the story: he was dead. But the poet is condemned to live; she has not the Art of unintended suicide-by-mistake. She has to "begin - again - " to live her life of starvation. To envy a Gnat its privilege and its Art is to reduce the self to a shrunken entity smaller even than an insignificant Gnat. The poem ends with the poet in the same predicament with which she began: she is a permanent prisoner, trapped as by a monster's Claw, starved of nourishment as by a Leech, and wishing only to die. "It would have starved a Gnat - " is one of Dickinson's best renditions of impotence, conveyed impeccably by this wry irony, this hyperbolic smallness. She may have drawn the gnat from Shakespeare. In *Romeo and Juliet,* Mercutio says of Queen Mab that her "Waggoner" was "a small gray-coated Gnat"; but a more likely Shakespearean Gnat for Dickinson's privation comes from *Cymbeline* (Act 1, scene 3, lines 27–28), in which Imogen, bereft of her husband, says she would have watched his departure "Till he had melted from / The smallness of a Gnat, to ayre."

[J 612]

# 446

This was a Poet -
It is That
Distills amazing sense
From Ordinary Meanings -
And Attar so immense

From the familiar species
That perished by the Door -
We wonder it was not Ourselves
Arrested it - before -

Of Pictures, the Discloser -
The Poet - it is He -
Entitles Us - by Contrast -
To ceaseless Poverty -

Of Portion - so unconscious -
The Robbing - could not harm -
Himself - to Him - a Fortune -
Exterior - to Time -

This poem of definition begins as a past-tense epitaph, "This was a Poet - ";
and then stops, as though before pronouncing this obituary the Poet must
define for herself what she means when she calls someone, dead or alive, a
"Poet." The rest of the poem takes place in the present tense of eternal truth.
The Poet "Distills." And that is all He does for seven lines. The next thing
He does (alliteratively) is to "Disclose." The third thing is to be—to Him-
self—"a Fortune - / Exterior - to Time - ". He is not to look to posterity for
fame, but to rest in His own consciousness of worth. All true Poets do these
three things. (Dickinson here uses a capitalized universalized "He" in refer-
ring to the Poet; I follow her reverent practice. She assumes the ungendered
nature of the Platonic Idea of the Poet. She would not have said that she

meant to exclude, by the pronoun "He," the women Poets whose work she admired: Elizabeth Barrett Browning, George Eliot, and Emily Brontë.)

The Poet does not stand alone; He is attended—by "Us." Although he takes no notice of us, we are affected by Him. Our first response is wonder—at the amazing sense His words make, at the "immense" attar (perfume) He extracts from "familiar species" that we have never paid attention to, and at the pictures He discloses from an imagination far exceeding ours. But if our first response is gratitude, there is a second response that follows: viewing his riches, we feel ourselves diminished—He "Entitles Us" not to a comparable wealth, but to "ceaseless Poverty." The poem, it turns out, concerns not only the Poet, but also our sharp reactions—appreciative *and* painful—to His work. Here, as in the opening of "I would not paint - a picture - " (*348), Dickinson is the audience, not the artist.

The Poet is singled out not because of His extravagance of diction or His musicality of utterance, but rather, first, for His unmatchable cognitive powers. He takes "Ordinary Meanings" (familiar words) and distills from them, by His imaginative arrangement of them, not fiction or fantasy (as others defining poetry might have proposed) but "amazing sense"—a very New England way of putting the achievement of genius. Dickinson is pointing out the importance of recognition in causing "wonder" in an audience: "Heavens, I recognize the place, I know it!" (as Elizabeth Bishop exclaims in "Poem" when she identifies the location represented in the unremarkable painting she has been regarding). "It makes such sense!" we say when we encounter a poem apparently simple but in fact revelatory.

Second, Dickinson points out the degree to which the Poet's capacity to notice, to notice *everything,* and then to disclose His "Pictures," makes *us* notice things too (provoking regret in us that we had let those precious "familiar species" perish like beggars at our door, never perceiving the immense attar we could have "Arrested" in them if we were not too blind or preoccupied to prize their existence). And third, Dickinson points out the indifference of the Poet to us (or to anyone else), an indifference arising not from self-esteem but from His (to him unconscious) Fortune. He is so unaware of the grace bestowed on Him, of the great "Portion" of wealth He has inherited, that no robbing from his worth can harm Him (plagiarism of His work by others does not affect our recognition of the true Poet). He moves in a world (in Dickinson's great phrase) "Exterior - to Time - ", alive in a "radiant and productive atmosphere" (Wallace Stevens, "The Figure of the Youth as Virile Poet"). He is as unaware of Time (and its obverse, Eternity) as He is of us.

Some have found such a description "solipsistic." They wish that Dickinson had emphasized the Poet's desire to communicate, to make a community with readers. Of course she will do just that in "This is my letter to the World" (*519). But there she is speaking *in propria persona,* as a Poet herself, and disclosing her own intentions. Here, she has been speaking of her experience as a reader—often, a reader of dead Poets (such as Shakespeare) who lived long ago and far away, of whom she knew little in personal terms. Yet the "amazing sense" that Shakespeare creates from the most "Ordinary Meanings" (Lear's "Never, never, never, never, never," or Desdemona's "Nobody, I myself")—we recognize and are struck by. If Whitman had not "Arrested" the familiar lilac blooming in the dooryard, would we have felt its "Attar" through the subsequent decades? "Why didn't I think of that?" we say in admiration and jealousy, and often, too, in regret and self-accusation, as we see the dead leaves of our own lilac that wasted its sweetness on us.

There is something about reading Shakespeare that makes one feel, by contrast, not doomed to, but ironically "Entitle[d]" to, a Poverty one would never have had to admit had one never encountered him. The distance between ourselves and the historical Poet—who, remote in time (and now "Exterior - to Time - "), moves to his own tune, never thinking of us—lets us value his Fortune rather than himself. Dickinson aspired (most of the time) to such self-sufficiency; she did not want her art to play to an audience (as she saw the poetry of so many of her contemporaries doing). It is not solipsism that the poem represents. It is a vow, on Dickinson's part, to more closely resemble the dead Poet elegized in the first line—to notice more, to extract more from existence, to wonder at its scenery, to attend especially to things close to home, to be aware of the unlimited cognitive and expressive possibility in "Ordinary Meanings." The Attar the Poet extracts is "immense," but the mind recognizes in it (via the rhyme) the "sense" He makes.

The reason that the first line of the poem is separated from its two-beat rhythmic completion ("It is That") is that Dickinson is here engaging two genres at once, writing a one-line epitaph followed by a sixteen-line eulogy, both genres part of the commemoration of the dead. (It has been suggested that Dickinson intended this poem as a tribute to Elizabeth Barrett Browning, who had died in 1861; but I doubt she would have used, in such a directed elegy-eulogy, the term "He." Dickinson's other poem about Barrett Browning, "Her - last Poems - " (600, J 312), is a clear "tribute" to a female Poet). Although "This was a Poet" may have been occasioned by Barrett Browning's death (we don't know), it is not directly about that Poet's work but about the work that all Poets do, written by one of their readers.

[J 448]

# 448

I died for Beauty - but was scarce
Adjusted in the Tomb
When One who died for Truth, was lain
In an adjoining Room -

He questioned softly "Why I failed"?
"For Beauty", I replied -
"And I - for Truth - Themself are One -
We Bretheren, are", He said -

And so, as Kinsmen, met a Night -
We talked between the Rooms -
Until the Moss had reached our lips -
And covered up - Our names -

This little fable, stemming ultimately from the motto "Beauty is Truth, Truth Beauty" spoken by Keats's Urn, is one of many poetic attempts to reconcile the Good, the True, and the Beautiful (traditionally known as the "Platonic Triad"). Perhaps no poet has been able to give equal weight to all three concerns. Keats himself was in fact beginning to put new emphasis on the Good in his last works, but he had spent most of his short life thinking about the relation of Beauty (aesthetic creation and its product) to Truth (both philosophical and representational). Dickinson resolves the old quarrel between the truth of Beauty and the truth of Reason by letting Reason deny the existence of the quarrel: "'We Bretheren, are,' He said - ". How is it that these "Bretheren," if they are indeed brothers, have never met until the grave unites them? Dickinson allows the person who died for Beauty, who is the "lead speaker" of the poem, to revise the relationship a little: they are "Kinsmen," but have strayed into a shared domain only now. "Truth" is male in this narrative, as the pronouns tell us; it seems probable that Dickinson intended "Beauty" to be female. Each a hemisphere, together they make a whole.

Why have Truth and Beauty died? Truth puts the question first, to

Beauty: "Why did you fail?" (in the sense of "weaken and die"). "For Beauty,"
she replies. "And I - for Truth," he says, but continues with his declaration
of their intimate relationship (as though Beauty would not know, unless he
told her, that Truth is her Brother). Beauty had apparently never thought
about her relation to Truth; she was self-sufficient. But Truth had thought
about his relation to Beauty—he had ascertained what his complement must
be. This interesting asymmetry has separated them until now; but Truth has
convinced Beauty that a near-relation of hers, a Kinsman, lies in the Room
adjoining hers in the Tomb. Dickinson will not attempt a complete fusion. A
wall separates Beauty from Truth, and it does not disappear.

When we use an expression such as "He died for God and Country," we
envisage a battle; when we say, "She died for her faith," we envisage a martyr-
dom. Apparently, Beauty and Truth have died in affirmation of the values
they endorse; society will not permit their continued existence. Yet there is
no recrimination in these two who have been so steadfast, nor any indict-
ment of the values opposed to their own. They were not executed; they
merely "died" or "failed" for Beauty or Truth. The idiom "I died [failed] for
Beauty" substitutes a weak verb of nonaction for a strong verb of action, as in
"I fought for Beauty" or "I spoke for Beauty." In the Tomb, the adversary no
longer matters; to "fail" in the service of a cause places agency within the self,
rather than in the hands of an enemy ("I was martyred for Beauty").

In any case, what seems to be—astonishingly—the *first* mutual recogni-
tion of Truth and Beauty softens the impact of the grave, to which Beauty is
"scarce / Adjusted" (as though it were a new climate). She is "Adjusted"; he is
"adjoining": Dickinson's graphic and phonetic "matches" confirm the rela-
tionship of the two ideals. Beauty's "Tomb" matches Truth's "Room." They
are Kinsmen indeed. Their warm talk continues, until—in one of Dickin-
son's startling flashes of metaphor—they metamorphose into their own
Tombstones.

Eventually, but mercifully only after some time, the moss on the stone
will grow high enough to obliterate the names of these Kinsmen, as, in a sec-
ond flash-forward to the future, the lips that were enabling speech in the
Tomb fall silent when the moss covers their names. It is not the attrition of
time and weather that obliterates the names, as it would be in an ordinary
cemetery; rather, in Dickinson's gentle close, it is the beneficent green of na-

ture that eventually resolves all distinctions. As "Tomb" rhymed with "Room" in the first instance, now "Rooms" rhymes with "names" as even the highest Platonic concepts gradually disappear under the Moss.

The simplicity of both fable and diction has made "I died for Beauty - " one of Dickinson's best-known poems, but under the simplicity lies a real inquiry into the relations of Truth and Beauty. The fact remains that they can never occupy the same room, however much their lips can express kinship in words.

[J 449]

# 450

The Outer - from the Inner
Derives its magnitude -
'Tis Duke, or Dwarf, according
As is the central mood -

The fine - unvarying Axis
That regulates the Wheel -
Though Spokes - spin - more conspicuous
And fling a dust - the while.

The Inner - paints the Outer -
The Brush without the Hand -
Its Picture publishes - precise -
As is the inner Brand -

On fine - Arterial Canvas -
A Cheek - perchance a Brow -
The Star's whole secret - in the Lake -
Eyes were not meant to know.

Convinced of the two truths she is about to articulate, Dickinson puts them in parallel aphoristic form: "The Outer - from the Inner / Derives its magnitude - " and "The Inner paints the Outer - ". These statements neatly divide the poem in two, but the halves differ greatly in spite of their initial declarative resemblance.

In the first half, the authentic Inner is the regulator of the human wheel: it is "The fine - unvarying Axis," or Axle, without which the Wheel could not turn at all. There are other parts of the Wheel that pretend a greater importance: "Spokes - spin - more conspicuous," but Dickinson scorns their show, which merely flings "a [shower of] dust" into the eyes of the beholder. (Dickinson enjoys rhyming "Wheel" with "while": rhyming different parts of speech—here, a noun with an adverb—gives an unexpected luster to a stanza. It is more usual to rhyme similar parts of speech.) The spokes are not, like the Axis, "fine"; they spin all around, while the Axis is "unvarying." This metaphor is a Bunyanesque allegory for the constant man versus the frivolous man, as the Wheel is man's engine of (spiritual) progress. We can see that the magnitude of that progress depends intrinsically on the axle of the Soul remaining fine and unvarying in its constancy to virtue, its "central mood." This is all elevating and rather Christian, but Dickinson's first gesture in this stanza had been a flippant one: you can be either a Duke or a Dwarf, depending on your "mood." Is the inner life merely a court joke? As Dickinson continues her investigation into the relations of Inner and Outer, her tone, so frivolous at the beginning, takes on gravity.

As the poem changes gears, it asks what traces are left on the countenance by the fiery trials that the constant Soul undergoes. There is an inner Painter, and he holds a self-activating paintbrush, which—contour by contour, color by color—creates an outer "Picture" precisely reproducing the inner "Brand." The root of "brand" is "burn," and here, as in Dickinson's Webster, it means "the mark made by burning with a hot iron." Some "Heavenly Hurt" has left an inner scar, an "internal difference" (*320, J 258). The skin is the outer canvas on which the Inner paints—and Dickinson here repeats the Axle-adjective "fine," telling us where we stand. The skin is a "fine - Arterial Canvas," and on "A Cheek - perchance a Brow - " the Brand reproduces itself, until one sees, on a faded cheek or a furrowed brow, what the Soul has paid for its pain. "I measure every Grief I meet," says Dickinson, "With narrow, probing, eyes - " (originally "Analytic eyes," *550). Dickinson's eyes were sharply analytic and probing, and she must have read the faces of her acquaintances very closely. She alone, for instance, seemed to sense that the dead housewife (in *238, "How many times these low feet staggered") had lived a life that had frequently made her falter; she, the scholar of the inner life, could read the cheek and the brow and calibrate the extent of the staggering to an accurate degree.

"Eyes were not meant to know" another's degree of inner agony; people protect their secret inner life of suffering. But looking into the eyes of another, Dickinson can tell—from the reflection of the "Brand" (now a burning Star of glory) in the "Lake" of their gaze—exactly the dimensions of what the inner Painter has revealed in his Picture: "The Star's whole secret." Stars, for Dickinson, were the "Asterisks" of the sky that represented the just (see, for example, 1673, J 1638); she was thinking of Daniel 12:3: "They that turn many to righteousness [shall shine] as the stars for ever and ever." Who would have thought that a poem juggling Duke and Dwarf would have ended in this mingling of commiseration and admiration? Dickinson, seeing inner tears as "The Star's whole secret," demonstrates how to interpret the signs visible on the "fine - Arterial Canvas" of another's face.

[J 451]

# 466

I dwell in Possibility -
A fairer House than Prose -
More numerous of Windows -
Superior - for Doors -

Of Chambers as the Cedars -
Impregnable of eye -
And for an everlasting Roof
The Gambrels of the Sky -

Of Visitors - the fairest -
For Occupation - This -
The spreading wide my narrow Hands
To gather Paradise -

The "normal" opposite of Prose is Poetry. Reflecting on that tired contrast, Dickinson renames poetry "Possibility," a witty gesture that requires her to describe her "dwelling" place. Prose is normally considered to be far more roomy than poetry, able as it is to house many points of view, to have more acreage, even to exhibit more "ways in" to its theme than a poem could offer. A novel may be thought sturdier, more resistant to abuse, than verse. Not so, says Dickinson, and proposes her own view.

Poetry is, in the first place, more beautiful than prose—and hardly anyone will argue that point. She claims for it more vantage points on the world. And since she herself would eventually display almost 1,800 of such windows, what novelist could exceed that number? How is poetry, as a dwelling, superior to prose in terms of "Doors"? I am not entirely sure, but doors are for going out as well as for coming in, and the "possibilities" of poetry seem to Dickinson to allow for her readers much mental passage in and out of the concerns of their lives.[6] Ordinary prose houses are built of pine; her house is

---

6. Domhnall Mitchell suggests (personal communication) that these Doors are "Superior" because they are harder to open. He also proposes that Dickinson's hands—one steadying the page, the other writing—are extending over her (graphically) narrow poem.

built of the everlasting Cedar of Lebanon. Ordinary houses are subject to inspection by others, but Possibilities—those shimmering and ever-changing fantasies—being inner, cannot be seen from outside. And prose—with its expository linearity, even in fiction—is a closed form, whereas the whole hemispherical sky, with its cloudy "Gambrels" and "Roof," is open to Possibility.

So far, Dickinson has instanced—architectural feature by architectural feature—her comparison between Prose and Possibility, using, as we might expect, the comparative degree to organize her statements of superiority. Possibility's House is "fairer"; its Windows are "more numerous"; it is "Superior" in terms of Doors. And the quasi-biblical hyperboles of the next stanza—the everlasting Cedars, the everlasting Roof—imply a comparison with inferior terrestrial Prose. (Those who see Dickinson reflecting her own class privilege in according to herself a "fairer" house, "Superior" in architectural elements, are reading her imagination overliterally, and forgetting the 1,800 poem-windows.)

The pattern of comparison is discarded in the final stanza. Dickinson, at home in Possibility, ceases to consider others' Houses, others' "eyes," others' hostility, against which she has made herself "Impregnable." She has arrived in her own home, and no longer needs the defiant assertiveness with which she began. Whom does she entertain in her home? Her Visitors are not from the land of Prose; they are congenial to her "fairer" house, with their superlatively seraphic "fairest" selves. A great happiness suffuses the House of Possibility, as the "narrow Hands" of its inhabitant are lifted—but not in prayer to a superior being. Seeing around her a fertile space of Creation, with every species available to "Possibility," the poet realizes she has recreated the plenitude of Eden, and has only to open her arms to gather it to herself. It is the sudden turn away from comparison, and the ecstatic entrance into the superlative of Being itself, that distinguishes this poem.

Dickinson seems at first glance to be recommending a wholly idealistic poetics, leaving behind the confining world of Prose. "They shut me up in Prose - " (445, J 613), she says, just as they shut her in a closet when she was a child, to make her be "still." In Possibility, one can spread one's "narrow" self into amplitude. Dickinson ensures that we come away from this exercise in Possibility with a very strong contrastive picture of the House of Prose. It is an unattractive dwelling, with ineffective doors and an insufficient supply of windows (therefore with stinted light and no vistas), with chambers of shoddy materials, easily invaded by others' peering, and with a roof preventing a view of the heavens. This is as "realistic" as one could wish, and Dickinson's aim in leading us into the Paradise of Possibility is precisely to make us realize, by comparison, the limits of our own "prose" shelters. By affixing the verb of habit, "dwell," to the limitless abstraction "Possibility," Dickinson generates a host of particular features constituting her spectacular dwelling place. Through the poet's enumeration of its splendors, Possibility becomes (imaginatively speaking) real to us—so much so that we, now ashamed of our dreary Houses, might begin to construct in our mind a new House for ourselves, with sturdy doors, multiple windows, and an exalted "Roof." Visitors might come to such a House, fairer visitors than we have yet encountered.

[J 657]

# 479

Because I could not stop for Death -
He kindly stopped for me -
The Carriage held but just Ourselves -
And Immortality.

We slowly drove - He knew no haste
And I had put away
My labor and my leisure too,
For His Civility -

We passed the School, where Children strove
At Recess - in the Ring -
We passed the Fields of Gazing Grain -
We passed the Setting Sun -

Or rather - He passed Us -
The Dews grew quivering and Chill -
For only Gossamer, my Gown -
My Tippet - only Tulle -

We paused before a House that seemed
A Swelling of the Ground -
The Roof was scarcely visible -
The Cornice - in the Ground -

Since then - 'tis Centuries - and yet
Feels shorter than the Day
I first surmised the Horses' Heads
Were toward Eternity -

Dickinson's single most striking invention in this poem is the substitution of "Eternity" for "Immortality." The two words occupy the same position in their respective stanzas, with one dramatically opening the poem, the other dramatically closing it. The point of the poem is to describe the moment when the concept of personal "Immortality" was shocked into disappearing from the speaker's consciousness—although, at the outset, it had been comfortably ensconced with her in the Carriage of Death.

When this poem was first published, in 1890, the editors gave it the vaguely archaic and religious title, "The Chariot." They wished to remind readers of the chariot sent from heaven to "translate" Elijah (who did not die) to eternity. Nothing could be more misleading with respect to Dickinson's poem, which is about the apprehension of real death, offering no rescue. The early editors also omitted the fourth stanza. It is the only one which is not arranged as a ballad stanza, 4-3-4-3; the first line has only three beats: "Or rather - He passed Us - ". Yet, like other "mislineated" stanzas, this one could have been regularized:

> Or rather - He passed us - the Dews
> Grew quivering and Chill -
> For only Gossamer, my Gown -
> My Tippet - only Tulle -

It could not have been only the "missing" foot, so easily restored to the first line from its Dickinsonian "misplacement" in the second, that made the editors cut this stanza. Something in it disturbed them, as did other things in the poem. Their most significant change was made in the fifth stanza, where Dickinson sees an ominously sinking tomb, its cornice already out of sight "in the Ground." The editors substituted "Its cornice but a mound," keeping the cornice still reassuringly visible, and removing the suggestion of the gradual subsidence of the body's "House." And yet this bleak poem, even in its restored state, has seemed so harmless that it is regularly found in school anthologies.

What unnerved the editors about stanza 4? It is the first moment in the poem where apprehension sets in. Until that stanza, Dickinson has pretended—in her assumed naïve voice—that she had no objection to her journey in Death's Carriage. Death "kindly stopped," and his passenger had willingly put aside all her occupations—whether of labor or of leisure—for His "Civility." In the fiction of the poem, the naïve speaker had been, till this event, youthfully interested in the concept of Death, without making any personal application of it to her own life. After the first stanza, the separate pronouns "I" and "He" have fused in the untroubled mutuality of "We," the pronoun presumably including the third passenger in the Carriage, "Immortality." Only the shock of the penultimate stanza frightens the speaker out of the comfortably spoken "We" back into an appalled "I."

Before stanza 4, the ride with Death and Immortality had continued placidly. The poet chronicles the journey with a series of parallel clauses: "We passed the School," "We passed the Fields," and then, as the naïve voice continues, "We passed the Setting Sun - ". To pass the setting sun means to pass into darkness—so the speaker then shifts uncomfortably, and by reversing subject and object, keeps the Setting Sun still ahead of her, rather than behind. She tries to shield her sense of safety: "Or rather - He passed Us - ". Her apprehension deepens as she realizes that the "kindly" Carriage owner did not warn her of the length of this journey, did not remind her to take warmer clothing for the evening hours. It is she who begins to quiver, as suddenly (without a dash to be seen within the hurrying phrase) "The Dews drew quivering and Chill - ". Dismayed, she shivers in her summer Gossamer and Tulle, suspecting that her caller has never had her welfare at heart at all.

Dickinson's first editors wished to suggest that her escort was sent by God's will, bringing along "Immortality" as the reward for the journey. An indifferent and even malevolent escort, conducting her into an apprehension ratified by the sunk cornice, did not fit their conception of the poem. Had they dared, they might even have revised Dickinson's grim closing word "Eternity." "Immortality" is glorious; "Eternity" (as Andrew Marvell knew, writing of "deserts of vast Eternity"), chilling.

The Carriage ride replicates the stages of life: first the schoolchildren, then ripening Grain, then the Setting Sun. In Dickinson's formulation, the Children "strove," with all the natural fierceness of young energy (the editors replaced "strove" with "played"). There is nothing particularly remarkable about the Children or the Sun, but any reader is brought up short by the "Gazing Grain." Grain, yes, symbol of ripening fields. But why is the Grain "Gazing"? And on what does it gaze? It has not much more time to gaze before it is cut down; it is gradually incorporating within itself, in its gaze, all it can see of the world. "To gaze" is to fix a long look; the grain knows of its coming slaughter by the scythe. Dickinson spent her whole life "Gazing" like the grain, intent on registering spaces and details before Death should over-take her.

Living is over, as the Dews set in. The speaker trembles, and for the first time the Carriage has not "passed," as it did thrice before; it has ominously "paused." The poet's escort has never spoken, and does not speak now. It was not He who invited Immortality into the Carriage: the poet, indoctrinated in the concept by her whole culture, brought it with her as she entered on her journey. Death simply shows her a grave, and leaves her to her own infer-ences. She conceives of the grave first as a legitimate "House," but then won-ders why the ground is "Swelling." Something underneath it is unnaturally pushing it upward, and the idea is not a peaceful one. As the poet looks at the "House," she can see only its Roof, since the Cornice below the roof, she per-ceives, has already subsided out of sight. The combination of the noxious "Swelling" of the earth and the sinister sinking of the tomb creates a fear that is only heightened when the speaker realizes that she is never again to be driven back home to live in childish ignorance with "Immortality." The jour-ney will continue, but only onward, her escort pointing the Horses' Heads toward the unimaginable: Eternity. With the vanishing of Immortality, Dickinson is alone with Death. And she is forced to inquire: When her body is consigned to its sinking House, making only a "Swelling in the Ground," where will she herself be?

In the penultimate stanza, the realizations of bodily decay are marshaled all at once in Swelling Ground and sunk Cornice, confirming the earlier ap-prehension of "Chill" at sunset. But the poem does not end there. In the last stanza, Dickinson is back home again, reflecting on that "pause" as though the whole episode had been a dream:

> Since then - 'tis Centuries - and yet
> [That length of time] feels shorter than the Day
> I first surmised the Horses' Heads
> Were toward Eternity -

This sustained conclusion, with every line enjambed, is as unstoppable as the unavoidable journey to death. As the journey had "paused" only at the sight of the grave, so the accompanying coda pauses only at the void of Eternity.

"The last kiss is given to the void," Yeats wrote in a letter shortly before he died; and Dickinson, on encountering Eternity in "My period had come for Prayer - " (525, J 564), cries out "Infinitude - Had'st Thou no Face / That I might look on Thee?" At the end of "Because I could not stop - for Death - ", Dickinson, still a living speaker, has lost her lifelong companion Immortality (whom she had significantly rhymed with "me" in the first stanza), and must encounter the *horror vacui* alone. She still prefers to consider an obliterative end a "surmise," but neither the visible grave nor the invisible foreign Eternity contradicts her suspicion. She seems to have no other clothing but her insufficient summer wear (there is no indication that these, as some have fancied, are bridal garments). She has described her clothing in a telling alliterative semantic chiasmus:

Gossamer : Gown :: Tippet : Tulle

That the protective "Gown" and "Tippet" (long scarf)—which might have been made, in winter, of wool and fur—are "walled in" by the lightweight unprotective nouns "Gossamer" and "Tulle" argues that there can be no change for the better in the body's frail defenses. Finally, Dickinson's deliberate rhyming of "Ground" with "Ground" when she sees the grave eliminates any other destination for the body but under the earth. Her early editors did not like that violation of the rules of rhyme (or of Christian hope); in their version, the cornice has not sunk beyond sight—certainly not. They printed "The cornice but a mound." No sepulchral sinking there.

Although this is a journey to realize the fact of the grave, I do not believe (as others have suggested) that the Carriage is a hearse and that Dickinson is being borne within it, already dead, while another part of her (her Soul?) watches the successive events. Such an interpretation vitiates her continued ordinary life at the end of the poem. No: like all "striving" Children, she had taken lightly the concept of "Death," not seeing its personal consequence. As she matured, Death gained a certain relevance, as she "gazed" steadily at life, realizing its brevity—but she still had Immortality in the carriage to console her, and even her "quivering" at sunset leaves her relatively unscathed. It is when the passing becomes a pausing that Immortality suddenly vanishes without a word. As the unmistakable knowledge of her own death grips her, and she asks herself insistently what really lies in wait for her once she has been buried, she can no longer confidently say "Immortality." Conventional doctrine drops entirely away, replaced by a humanly meaningless word: "Eternity." Time will be over. What can such an incomprehensible state mean?

Once possessed by this knowledge, Dickinson cannot (in this poem) return to a belief in personal Immortality. We are not here commiserating at a funeral; on the contrary, the speaker is, in every corporeal sense, alive and well. But the mind is unhinged. Its "surmise" has blanked out all hope of personal survival after death.

[J 712]

# 515

There is a pain - so utter -
It swallows substance up -
Then covers the Abyss with Trance -
So Memory can step
Around - across - upon it -
As One within a Swoon -
Goes safely - where an open eye -
Would drop Him - Bone by Bone -

Resolving, as always, to define the indefinable, Dickinson takes on the limit of pain. She has attempted this a bit earlier, in a poem (508, J 1712) beginning with a dangerous Pit:

A Pit - but Heaven over it -
And Heaven beside, and Heaven abroad;
And yet a Pit -
With Heaven over it.

To stir would be to slip -
To look would be to drop -

That faith-based "Heaven" disappears as she rewrites, in "There is a pain - so utter - ", the poem of the Pit. She is still speaking of emotional pain, but includes, in this poem's two dramatic episodes, its effect on the body.

In episode 1, something "swallows substance up." Usually, when we imagine a force that can swallow substance up, we recall a devastating mythical or natural event: the Deluge, an earthquake—manifestations utterly out of human control that leave behind an unrecognizable landscape. Dickinson had originally written "It swallows Being up," but we usually restrict the word "Being" to living things; she wants to be all-inclusive (as well as, whenever possible, to be alliterative—so Pain "swallows substance up"). That is episode 1: a huge fissure in the earth opens, and everything on its terrain is swallowed up within its depths. (In the corresponding poem "A Pit," Dickinson says explicitly that she thinks about nothing but the fathomless Pit: "The depth is all my thought - ".)

As episode 2 begins, the "utter" pain, having inflicted itself on the victim and ravaged the landscape of the inner life, leaves in its wake a merciful "Trance" blotting out recollection of past agony. The fissure in the earth is still there, of course. Nothing will reverse that tragedy, as Dickinson emphatically knew and said; she opens *861 with a bald truth: "They say that 'Time assuages' - / Time never did assuage - ". In the blank of repressed event, Dickinson sleepwalks through her life. (See "I tie my Hat - I crease my Shawl - " (522, J 443) for a longer description of this process, in which "existence - some way back - / Stopped - struck - my ticking - through - ".) She still has a Memory, but the deletion of trauma from Memory produces a Trance in her mind that enables her to negotiate safely—at least for the time being—the open fissure.

She watches herself from a distance as her Memory cautiously treads, first, "Around" the fissure. So far so good, one remains on safe ground. Then Memory steps "across" the cleft, with a giant step. Ah, it can be traversed! But as Memory approaches the edge of the chasm, Dickinson panics. Can anyone walk "upon" an Abyss? Yet Memory, enabled by the post-traumatic Trance, walks on vacancy as Jesus walked on water—exhibiting a superhuman power. The price of the Trance is blindness to the past; just as a sleepwalker goes safely over gaps into which he would fall if he opened even a single eye, so the sufferer walks on the air over the Abyss, where an open eye would "drop Him - Bone by Bone - ". This imagined death occurs in slow motion. It is not one in which the victim would fall entire to his death, but rather one in which a sadistic Fate would first watch him decompose, and then drop the skeletal residue, Bone by Bone, into the bowels of the earth.

Dickinson's alternative to "drop" was "spill": her thought went probably to a victim shedding drops of blood, and dying piecemeal in that way. Perhaps the implicit "drops" of liquid in "spill" suggested that the victim should be "dropped" Bone by Bone, and die in that drawn-out fashion. By the time Fate here prepares her ultimate sadism, she has a pile of bones at her feet, which she toys with by dispatching them, severally, into the cavernous Abyss. If the sufferer is protected from this Fate by walking like one in a "Swoon"—

a kindly (but temporary) obliteration sent by the failure of the body—then it will not be long before the eye opens. As "Bone" arrives to rhyme with the necessarily diminishing "Swoon," the sufferer perishes.

Although this is by its rhyme a two-quatrain poem, Dickinson runs the two quatrains together without a break, and does something even more rare: she enjambs her quatrains, bridging what would normally be the white space separating two stanzas. She literally steps "across" her Abyss, making the end-word of line 4 "step" and the first word of line 5 "Around," acting out that "Swoon" of which she writes.

[J 599]

# 517

A still - Volcano - Life -
That flickered in the night -
When it was dark enough to do
Without erasing sight -

A quiet - Earthquake style -
Too subtle to suspect
By natures this side Naples -
The North cannot detect

The solemn - Torrid - Symbol -
The lips that never lie -
Whose hissing Corals part - and shut -
And Cities - ooze away -

There exists on the earth, says this poem, a kind of life that Dickinson first described as "Volcanic" in making her fair fascicle copy, but changed at the bottom of the page to "Volcano." I think we should read the first line as speaking about one species of life, a "Volcano - Life," because later in the poem Dickinson contrasts this "Torrid" sort of life to the very different sort lived in the North. The reference, consequently, cannot be to every life as a Volcano, but is rather (in the light of her other "Volcano" poems) to her own life. Those around her, not possessing such a tropical temperament, never suspect—and cannot detect—the "Naples" nature in their midst. If the Volcano let loose all its powers, the result would be an "erasing"—Dickinson's violent choice over the rather less hyperbolic "endangering"—of sight with its blaze; but until now, checking its molten nature in pity for its context, the Volcano has merely "flickered." Similarly, if it exploded in an Earthquake, it would cause death, but, restraining its might, it substitutes for a quake a mere premonitory quiver. Still, on some future night, the Volcano may erupt, as its kinsman Vesuvius did near Naples, destroying all in its vicinity.

Many of those who knew Dickinson remarked on her extraordinary power of language in everyday life. She herself was puzzled by the incomprehension of her neighbors: in August of 1862, she wrote to Thomas Wentworth Higginson, "All men say 'What' to me" (L 271). We can imagine the interchanges. To a cryptic remark issuing from Dickinson's mouth: "What?" To a bizarre metaphor: "What?" To an unorthodox opinion: "What?" No wonder her father invited in a clergyman to discuss her beliefs with her. (The clergyman pronounced her "sound.") She liked thinking of herself as a Volcano, but as one curbing her power to dismiss, to wound, to hurt, to "erase." She had a moral objection to words designed to hurt, an objection spelled out in "She dealt her pretty words like Blades - " (458, J 479):

> She dealt her pretty words like Blades -
> How glittering they shone -
> And every One unbared a Nerve
> Or wantoned with a Bone -

Unwilling to inflict personal harm with her words (no doubt much more "glittering" than the ones she mentions here, and more powerful than "Blades"), she monitored and censored her opinions and their expression, even within the family home. Only in writing her poems could she be the Volcano, flickering at night in her room as she wrote, keeping her "Earthquake" temperament (relatively) quiet during the day, and doing so in such a subtle way that those near her might neither "suspect" its existence nor "detect" its intentions. Such a practice required daily censorship on the poet's part. She had learned in youth to participate in social euphemisms, exhibit impeccable politeness to those for whom she felt contempt, bridle her tongue, suppress the retorts that rose to her lips.

Yet such self-constriction builds up a smoldering resentment. The first two stanzas, occupied in finding metaphors for Dickinson's everyday life of concealment and restraint, exist only to open the path to the third stanza, the poet's description of the Volcano in itself. (We see now why she removed "Volcanic": an adjective cannot be a Symbol, whereas a noun can.) Unlike her neighbors, who live on this side of Naples and have mild natures, she possesses an (alliterating and assonating) "Naples" nature; her restless and dangerous fires were present from birth. She allows herself finally to imagine what it would be like to express herself fully, to give up social "lie[s]" for unswerving and utterable truth, to express the simmering dismissiveness she has so often felt for others. The Volcano takes on monumentality as a "solemn" Symbol, comparable to the ninth Commandment in its injunction not to bear false witness; its unsaid "Verily, verily" issues from "lips that never lie." And when those Coral lips part, hissing in revenge and letting loose their torrents of lava, they shut only when they have voided their magma to their own superb satisfaction.

The last line of the last stanza gave Dickinson the most trouble. What are the consequences (as we know them from Naples) of an eruption of nature's rage? Nature has no enmity with itself or with its indigenous inhabitants, so it will not be "Vineyards" or "Dwellings" that are devastated (these are words the poet considers and crosses out). But nature abhors the unnatural agglomerations of civilization (decides Dickinson). So it will be "Cities" that are laid waste. And what verb best manifests the look of them as they die of the fatal lava? "Slip," "slide," and "melt" are all words that occur to Dickinson: "slip" is the understatement of "slide," as the Cities, pushed by lava, lose their footing and begin their downward motion. "Melt" has the virtue of including the "Torrid" nature of the Cities' destruction; but "melt" is a "soft" word, often used of a "melting glance," or a "melting smile." At last, Dickinson hits on a word sufficiently revolting, one with which she punishes the Cities that choose never to acknowledge the Volcano's truths. Under the Volcano's onslaught, "Cities - ooze away - ". (The root of "ooze" is a noun meaning "sap," "juice.") Slime oozes; mud oozes; and Dickinson may have remembered Keats's Autumn, who watches by a cider press "the last oozings, hours by hours." Whole cities turn liquid, and are liquidated. The slow nature of the process of oozing prolongs the torment. Dickinson's revenge-fantasy on repressive New England is complete.

Dickinson rhymes by opposites here. She pairs "night" and "sight," "suspect" and "detect," and adds the internal rhyme of the eruption as the lethal lips of the Volcano "part" and "shut." Among the end-words, only "Naples" and "Symbol" end in an unaccented syllable, making them "kin" to each other.

[J 601]

# 519

This is my letter to the World
That never wrote to Me -
The simple News that Nature told -
With tender Majesty

Her Message is committed
To Hands I cannot see -
For love of Her - Sweet - countrymen -
Judge tenderly - of Me

This justly famous poem is addressed by the poet to her hoped-for readers, her fellow Americans, her "Sweet - countrymen - ". Nonetheless, she begins grandly with the whole globe by saying, "This is my letter to the World," and there are today many non-American hands that hold her book. Ours are the "Hands [she] cannot see," and the poet's legacy is a sacred trust: "The simple News that Nature told - " is committed to us as a bequest.

We might expect that the poet's injunction to us would be, "Pass Nature's 'Message' on to others, as I have passed it on to you." But having defined herself as the bearer of Nature's News, Dickinson turns her attention not to the Message but to herself, the messenger, hoping only that her countrymen, in their love of Nature, will judge Nature's messenger "tenderly." Dickinson implies here that her verse and her name alone would not be sufficient to elicit a "tender" judgment. Her poetry is precious not in itself but in the Message it bears. She is the Evangelist, bearing the Good News not of Jesus but of Nature, minimizing her personal self, maximizing her message.

Her letter is addressed not to the private receivers of her poetry in her time and place, but to the worldly world, unaware of her existence. Nature's News is "simple" because it is Herself she conveys: like God, she says merely, "I am," and Dickinson pronounces, "She is." On the other hand, she does not say, "This is my [Pauline] epistle to the [specified] Galatians"; her News is preached to all in an informal "letter." As we recognize the allusions implied by her privileged nature—she is the person to whom Nature chose to confide her crucial "Message," charging her to deliver it to the World—we see her as one proclaiming the Word of Nature to all nations.

Yet almost everything about both this Nature and this messenger puts into relief the maleness of God's authoritative messengers, from Moses and the prophets to Jesus and his disciples. Jehovah is masculine, but Nature is feminine (by virtue not only of her Latin gender, but also of her ability to bear fruit). God's "Majesty" is intimidating; Nature's is "tender." God gives a Decalogue; Nature gives "simple News." Only the emphasis on universal dissemination is common to both God and Nature. "By this act [of my life-work], I hereby commit to my heirs Nature's Message." Dickinson's phrase "is committed" characterizes her act as a legal one: she is the executrix of Nature's will.

Dickinson's only repeated word in these two brief stanzas is "tender[ly]," appearing as both adjective and adverb. "Tender" majesty is a paradox. When has any historical majesty approached tenderness? Perhaps the idea of judging "tenderly" is equally paradoxical: pious wishes by judges—"May God have mercy on your soul!"—are scarcely "tender." Dickinson is issuing a new Commandment, in which the tenderness of feminine "Majesty" is matched by the tenderness of Nature's subjects. We are reminded of Jesus' injunction to "tenderness": "A new commandment I give unto you, That ye love one another; as I have loved you, that ye also love one another" (John 13:34).

The rhymes of both stanzas exhibit the same vowel sound, and the first and the last rhyme-words are "Me." Dickinson rhymes "Me" with "Majesty" so that she participates in the majesty of Nature. Although Dickinson cannot "see" the Hands into which she commends her spirit, she is confident enough to rhyme that second-stanza "see" with "Me" as well. Jesus commended his spirit "vertically" into the hands of his Father above; Dickinson commends hers "horizontally" into the hands of her fellow countrymen. Dickinson's boldness in paralleling herself—in this "simple" poem—with the prophets, the disciples, the evangelists, and Jesus, and her equal boldness in paralleling Nature with Jehovah and Jesus, has not been adequately recognized.

[J 441]

# 524

It feels a shame to be Alive -
When Men so brave - are dead -
One envies the Distinguished Dust -
Permitted - such a Head -

The Stone - that tells defending Whom
This Spartan put away
What little of Him we - possessed
In Pawn for Liberty -

The price is great - Sublimely paid -
Do we deserve - a Thing -
That lives - like Dollars - must be piled
Before we may obtain?

Are we that wait - sufficient worth -
That such Enormous Pearl
As life - dissolvèd be - for Us -
In Battle's - horrid Bowl?

It may be - a Renown to live -
I think the Men who die -
Those unsustainèd - Saviors -
Present Divinity -

The Civil War did not elicit many specific poems from Dickinson. Committed as she was to absolute authenticity of expression, she would not have been able to appropriate the voice of an active combatant, as Whitman sometimes did in his war poems. She feared that Thomas Wentworth Higginson would be killed during his military service, but since he was not, she had no duty to mourn any intimate friend. The only authentic voice available to her was that of a citizen ("One" and "I") or of a collective citizenry ("we"). This 1863 poem about the Civil War dead, "It feels a shame to be Alive - ", does not invoke the conventions of elegy; it is, rather, a meditation on justice. Do the citizens at home deserve the sacrifice made by the dead?

In saying, "Greater love hath no man than this, that a man lay down his life for his friends" (John 15:13), Jesus gave later generations a standard for the highest form of love—but he did not stipulate what the "friends" owed in return for that sacrifice. Dickinson's references to the Bible were often mocking, but here there is no mockery: "I am being defended by brave men, who have died for the rest of us. How am I to respond to their deaths?" She puts the question in varying ways, calling up shame and envy in the first stanza, querying our merit in the third and fourth stanzas, and giving up on those ordinary forms of estimation in her last stanza. No payment of ours could exceed, or even equal, the worth of our salvation by the war dead, since nobody, in Jesus' judgment, could possess "greater love" than those who laid down their lives.

Dickinson, reaching into patriotic expression, classical reference, and the New Testament, calls the soldiers by different names, plural and singular: "Men so brave"; "This Spartan"; "lives" (the plural noun); "Enormous Pearl"; "unsustainèd - Saviors." One could say that the phrase "Men so brave" represents the literal base on which the more imaginative appellations of the soldiers are constructed, just as the military grave—with its headstone telling the story of the engagements in which the dead soldier participated—is the literal base from which Dickinson's subsequent metaphors of death spring. The dead soldier is specified, at his grave, as "This Spartan" because the grave pointed to is singular (the Spartans, at Thermopylae, died defending Greece against the Persians); but Dickinson knows herself obliged to regard the wider, horrifying spectacle of mass death, "lives - like Dollars . . . piled." That searing remark about war profiteering is the only sardonic moment in this honoring of the dead. Jesus' parable (Matthew 13:45–46) about the merchant who found a "Pearl of great price" makes its way into Dickinson's "The price is great," and then is crossed in her imagination with the pearl which, according to legend, Cleopatra dissolved in a cup of wine, to show the extent to which she disdained wealth.

The first two stanzas of the poem are declarative—"It feels a shame to be Alive - "; "One envies the Distinguished Dust - "; "This Spartan put away [his life]"—and Dickinson even continues the declarative mode in the first line of stanza 3: "The price is great." But having stated her premises, she allows her "shame" to raise the temperature of the poem by posing two questions: "Do we [citizens] deserve [this sacrifice]?" "Are we that wait - [of] sufficient worth?" The implied answer to each of these questions is "No." The first question turns the heap of bodies into a literal "price" in heaped-up dollars, but the second question turns to the inestimable value of life for each living person. Rather than continuing to speak of the piled "lives" of the war dead, Dickinson—in the best "turn" of the poem—regards them one by one, as singular persons, each with a life, each seeing his "Enormous Pearl"—all that he has—"dissolved" for the sake of his countrymen in "Battle's - horrid Bowl." In representing herself and other civilians as "we that wait," she is probably recalling Milton's Patience, who tells the blind poet that "They also serve who only stand and wait." What will be *her* service?

"Horrid" may strike us today as an inadequate adjective to choose for battle, when many other disyllables—"tragic," "dreadful," "lethal"—were available to Dickinson (all, however, more conventional than "horrid"). As always, the Bible gives us some idea of what the word meant to the poet. "A horror of great darkness" falls on Abraham in Genesis 15, and for Milton, too, "horrid" always has overtones of "horror": the devil falls to Hell together with his "horrid crew" (*Paradise Lost,* Book I, line 51). "Horror," in Dickinson's 1844 Webster, is "terror accompanied with hatred," which must have seemed to her a telling characterization of battle.

In her closing stanza, Dickinson abandons both the declarative sentences of the beginning, and the indicting questions of the middle, in favor of speculation. After all, it is the victors who are normally thought the heroes of battle, gaining Renown in the history books ("Renown" meaning "being named over and over"), and Dickinson concedes to popular valuation: if you survive battle on the winning side, you may gain fame. True enough. But she sets her own opinion against popular "Renown":

> I think the Men who die -
> Those unsustainèd - Saviors -
> Present Divinity -

The "Men so brave" of the opening have become the "Men who die"—and Dickinson, by applying to them the word "Saviors," compares them to Jesus, who died for human salvation. That comparison in itself would not be origi-

nal; but what Dickinson adds to it is. The men who die are "unsustainèd -
Saviors," a phrase placing them with the Jesus who cried out from the Cross
to his Father, "Why hast thou forsaken me?" The soldiers have borne death
"unsustained" by faith, but they have saved the country. If you ask me where I
find Divinity, says Dickinson, it is in the forsaken Jesus and the unsustained
dying soldier. She was not prepared to acknowledge any Divinity, any Savior,
incapable of suffering. Dickinson had referred earlier, in "I should have been
too glad, I see - " (283, J 313), to Jesus' cry on the Cross, speaking of it as "the
Prayer / I knew so perfect - yesterday - / That scalding one - Sabacthini - "
(Aramaic: *sabachthani*, "thou hast forsaken me").

The nouns Dickinson applied to the soldiers—"Men," "Dust," "Spartan,"
"lives," even "Pearl"—climax in "Saviors" and "Divinity." Her references to
Sparta and to Cleopatra dwindle in the light of the biblical references, espe-
cially the allusion to the Crucifixion. The poet presents her concluding state-
ment, against the world's praise of renowned victors, as merely personal
opinion ("[But] *I* think"), while buttressing it with the most powerful nouns
(and myth) of Christianity. Although this war poem is rarely anthologized,
it deserves a place in any selection of Dickinson's poems, not only because of
the rarity of the war in her work, and because of its expression of civilian
shame, but also because it presents Dickinson's valuing of personal patriotic
sacrifice.

[J 444]

# 528

'Tis not that Dying hurts us so -
'Tis Living - hurts us more -
But Dying - is a different way -
A kind behind the Door -

The Southern Custom - of the Bird -
That ere the Frosts are due -
Accepts a better Latitude -
We - are the Birds - that stay.

The shiverers round Farmer's doors -
For whose reluctant Crumb -
We stipulate - till pitying Snows
Persuade our Feathers Home

Like so many of Dickinson's poems, "'Tis not that Dying hurts us so - " begins in generalities, with a dry contrast between Dying and Living as states inflicting hurt. The abstraction lessens a little with a remark about the unexpectedness of losing another person to death when one least suspects it: Death has been unfairly operating "behind the Door." A poem could go almost anywhere from here: it could begin to define the loss more specifically, could address the dead friend, and so on. Many of Dickinson's "axiomatic" poems begin in this open-ended way, leaving us to wonder what will follow. The last thing we expect to be told about "hurt" is that it's what we feel when birds migrate. Death becomes a "Custom" (followed by every human being); in this case the migration is premature, but nonetheless the departing bird "accepts" it. The departure is put as one that is desirable and voluntary: it is the custom of birds to depart, and some depart early, knowing that they are going to a "better" place. This is the Christian view of death, and those left behind are supposed to look forward to a reunion in heaven with their beloved companions. But in addressing the true feelings of the desolate friends who remain behind, Dickinson removes the mask of acceptance.

Suddenly, directly after the departing Bird "Accepts a better Latitude - ", the poem is wrenched into pathos, not even waiting till after the stanza break: "We - are the Birds - that stay." That is the moment of deepest loss. It declares, with its emphatic period, unusual in Dickinson, the total new self-definition of the mourner. The clash of life before and after loss is felt in the absolutely noncoinciding rhymes: "due" (related sonically to "Latitude") and "stay." And what is life like for "the Birds - that stay"? The new personality of the survivors is that of "shiverers," doomed to eternal cold, bargaining for a Crumb from a reluctant Farmer. Dickinson, writing in the collective "We," depicts us as birds begging crumbs from that "Burglar! Banker - Father! [Farmer!]" addressed in "I never lost as much but twice - " (39, J 49), to whom we cry again, "I am poor once more!"

Our shivering life continues until—when? When warmth returns? When new birds join us? When the Farmer becomes more generous with his Crumbs? No, we shiver until we die of the cold, till "pitying Snows," more merciful than the Farmer, "Persuade our Feathers Home." The Birds that stay will die in the painless way experienced (if they do not survive) by the "Freezing persons" of "After great pain" (*372): "First - Chill - then Stupor - then the letting go - ". The kind Snows are persuasive because the death they inflict is gradual; and the weightless feathers melt so inconspicuously into the snow that they join the earth, their "Home," with no clamor. The home of the bereft Birds will never be in the "better Latitudes" of the warm South, because they cannot "accept" the idea that there exists such a better life elsewhere; they observe no "Southern Custom." The world is divided into the Southerners and the Shiverers, the Believers and the Unbelievers.

Dickinson's candor, as she admits that living hurts us more than dying does, shocks us, perhaps even into acquiescence. We are also shocked (whether we imagine an afterlife or not) that the dying are not more grieved at leaving us behind, when we find ourselves so bereft after they are gone. And we are shocked at the stinted rations we are expected to live on, once the marauder Death has robbed us of our essential nourishment. One of the poet's transferred epithets here—"reluctant Crumb"—is easy to accept, because we have just seen the Farmer's reluctance to admit the shivering Birds to shelter. What is more startling is Dickinson's attachment of the word "pitying" to "Snows." To whom is that epithet "pitying" properly ascribed? Snows are not known for "pity." But when Nature reclaims her own from the uncontrollable shivering of loss, she can seem—by contrast to the harsh Farmer—a merciful Being. The initial sounds of "pitying Snows" are repeated in "Persuade," making the predicate fit the subject and convincing us of the truth of the statement. Finally, nouns ascribe essence: creatures who were once "Birds" have no name now but "shiverers," a noun constantly in motion, trembling.

[J 335]

# 533

I reckon - When I count at all -
First - Poets - Then the Sun -
Then Summer - Then the Heaven of God -
And then - the List is done -

But, looking back - the First so seems
To Comprehend the Whole
The Others look a needless Show -
So I write - Poets - All -

Their Summer - lasts a solid Year -
They can afford a Sun
The East - would deem extravagant -
And if the Further Heaven -

Be Beautiful as they prepare
For Those who worship Them -
It is too difficult a Grace -
To justify the Dream -

Dickinson's fascinating estimation of poets has Shakespeare somewhere in mind: "But thy eternal summer shall not fade," says Shakespeare in Sonnet 18, setting the beauty of the Young Man (the addressee of many of his sonnets) above that of a summer's day. "You perhaps exaggerate in using the word 'eternal,'" says Dickinson in reply—but it is certainly true at least, she asserts, that the Poets' "Summer - lasts a solid Year." "And truly not the morning sun of heaven / Better becomes the gray cheeks of the East," says Shakespeare (Sonnet 132). "Well," Dickinson retorts of Poets, "They can afford a Sun / The East - would deem extravagant - ". Sometimes she is mitigating Shakespeare's boasts; sometimes she is going him one better. In any case, she is amusing herself by her witty allusions.

The poem is of course blasphemous, but also philosophical. The "List" is designed to give offense to the pious, putting Poets not only higher than the

Sun and Summer, but also higher than the lowest item on the list, "the Heaven of God." In a moment, "the Heaven of God" becomes "a needless Show," because the category "Poets" includes all other categories: "So I write - Poets - All - ". Dickinson is raising, even if in an ironic way, the question of representation: if we in fact know the world only as it has been mediated to us through language, then we know Summer and the Sun and the Heaven of God only as the Poets have described them in words. (Dickinson always assumes the truth of the proposition that poetic representation exceeds in accuracy and precision all other forms of linguistic expression.) In the pages of the Poets, their Sun, displaying more glory than its lesser counterpart in nature, need never set. Their Summer can displace all other seasons, and last as long as the poems mentioning it—centuries, perhaps.

Dickinson presents herself in the act of making a "reckon[ing]"—that is, drawing up an arithmetical account. Almost as soon as she sets herself to reckoning, she remarks that it is not something she often does: "I reckon - When I count at all - ", and then proceeds to her List. But why does she rarely count her blessings? This reckoning is one listing only blessings. She would be afraid, she implies, to make a reckoning of disasters; that list would be heartbreaking. So she decides to count up only the things she values. She includes among the seasons only Summer, for instance, since in Spring "Rough winds do shake the darling buds of May" (Sonnet 18 again), and Autumn and Winter are melancholy. She lists only the Sun (and not the Moon or the Stars) because the Sun is the most splendid among the celestial lights. Her culture represents "the Heaven of God" as the highest blessing; although Dickinson knows that she should include it in her List, she immediately erases it, together with the Sun and Summer, as she subsumes them all in the higher radiance of the Poets. She has no difficulty praising the Summer and Sun of the Poets, in hyperbolic praise at that. But she ends on a doubter's hypothesis: "If" (a pregnant "if") Heaven is as beautiful as the Poets say it is, it is nonetheless a favor ("Grace") too "difficult" to believe in; inaccessible, it cannot "justify" by visibility the "Dream" of the believer. Heaven floats away, insusceptible of proof.

Dickinson—skeptical of Heaven—did not wish to denigrate the Poets who have described it, from Dante on; but neither did she want to put credence in their descriptions. She found it hard to discover (as the variants of the poem attest) the right words to convey both their belief and her skepticism. What adjective should she attach to "Heaven"? Should she say the "Other" Heaven? But this would imply that besides the Heaven of Poetic Description, there was another eternal Heaven to balance the poetic one, and she did not (here) believe that. The "final" Heaven? Worse and worse: this adjective sets up a teleology by which life ends up in Heaven—and she did not believe that either. She settled for "Further": a "further Heaven" is one imagined as "yonder" (as Hopkins's "Golden Echo" would have it), but "further" merely means "one in the distance," "speculated upon"; the adjective implies no belief in a spiritual realm or in a final destination for the soul.

Dickinson found equal difficulty in deciding how to fix on what Poets actually do when they write about Heaven. Her first impulse was to say that they "disclose" Heaven, but this would imply that it was there to be "disclosed," in a quasi-apocalyptic "uncovering." If there is no Heaven, there is nothing that can be "disclosed," in or out of poetry. She found a more neutral word: "prepare." The Poet's religious descriptions, she thinks, can be said even by an unbeliever to "prepare" us for Heaven, but they offer no guarantee that Heaven is there to reward preparation.

Finally, she juggled her phrases to describe what the attitude of readers to Poets ought to be. "If the Further Heaven - / Be Beautiful as [the Poets] prepare / For Those who"—who do what? She thought of "Trust in"—but if there is no Heaven, the Poets would be duping those who trust in them. She thought of "ask of"—but the readers would be cheated if they asked and did not receive. She found the most blasphemous word in the poem: the Poets prepare a Further Heaven for those who "worship" them. Theologically speaking, "worship" is reserved for God alone; other verbs, such as "venerate," can be used with respect to saints, but never "worship." The Poets have therefore totally replaced God and Heaven, and one does not need to go beyond their words to find both God and Heaven there described, realized as fully as they can be in a world of mediated representation.

This fastidious debate on the precise word that would allow a literary description of Heaven (she knew Herbert, she knew Vaughan) without lending it personal credence is one of Dickinson's most delicate balancing acts. One can read the poem without being conscious of the extent of its blasphemy, because it is full of playful exaggeration during its first three stanzas, coming to ultimate seriousness only in the closing lines. Dickinson spends her first two stanzas on her charming "reckon[ing]," and then drops her counting in favor of the third stanza's witty contest with Shakespeare. Yet the question of Heaven cannot be put off indefinitely. The Dream of Heaven exists in many hearts, but the existence of Heaven cannot be justified on the basis of literary Grace.

[J 569]

# 550

I measure every Grief I meet
With narrow, probing, eyes -
I wonder if It weighs like Mine -
Or has an Easier size -

I wonder if They bore it long -
Or did it just begin -
I could not tell the Date of Mine -
It feels so old a pain -

I wonder if it hurts to live -
And if They have to try -
And whether - could They choose between -
It would not be - to die -

I note that Some - gone patient long -
At length, renew their smile -
An imitation of a Light
That has so little Oil -

I wonder if when Years have piled -
Some Thousands - on the Harm -
That hurt them Early - such a lapse
Could give them any Balm -

Or would They go on aching still
Through Centuries of Nerve -
Enlightened to a larger Pain -
In Contrast with the Love -

The Grieved - are many - I am told -
There is the various Cause -
Death - is but one - and comes but once -
And only nails the Eyes -

There's Grief of Want - and Grief of Cold -
A sort they call "Despair" -
There's Banishment from native Eyes -
In sight of Native Air -

And though I may not guess the kind -
Correctly - yet to me
A piercing Comfort it affords
In passing Calvary -

To note the fashions - of the Cross -
And how they're mostly worn -
Still fascinated to presume
That Some - are like my own -

Dickinson's "narrow, probing, eyes" could, with a psychological penetration trained by her own scrupulous and unforgiving introspection, indeed scrutinize and "measure every Grief" she met. Like the worm of "In Winter in my Room" (*1742), who, she said, "fathomed me," she "fathomed" others. From youth, she had compiled through her writing a taxonomy of grief, and she names (in the least inward part of this poem) her external categories: "There's Grief of Want - and Grief of Cold - / A sort they call "Despair" - / There's Banishment from native Eyes - / In sight of Native Air - ". These categories are too fleetingly named (especially "Despair") to be the substance of "I measure every Grief," and they are recited in singsong fashion as if they were a lesson. Nonetheless, each has an edge of irony.

The categories are very disparate. "Want" is associated with economic poverty—"those in want," of whom Amherst would have provided, in its working class, many examples. "Cold" is associated with poverty as well, in those who lack money for coal; but it is also associated, in Dickinson's mind, with homelessness and death—see, in "'Tis not that Dying hurts us so - " (*528), the homeless Birds perishing in the snow. In Dickinson's list of Griefs, "A sort they call 'Despair'" suggests that the "they" who name it lightly have never known it truly. The plight of the exile banished to an island within sight of the mainland provides the last item of Grief, with a particularly Dickinsonian combination of longing and frustration.

But within the framework of her taxonomy of the Grieved, Dickinson pursues the origin and course of particular Grief in others, in order to be able to compare it with, and foresee the future of, her own. The standards of measurement she mentions are several. She begins with weight: Is another's burden as heavy as hers, or is it "Easier" (it is self-evident to her that nobody's weight of grief could be "harder" than her own, and she makes that judgment implicit in her measuring). The next standard is temporal length: Is the other's Grief recent, or of long standing? Hers is of such long standing that she has forgotten when it began; again, her experience contains the superlative degree of pain. The third standard is that of degree of agony, and once again, Dickinson implies the superlative: to feel that it hurts to live is, one could say, the minimal degree of grief; to have to make an effort to live at all is the comparative degree; to prefer death to life (were the choice offered) is the superlative. And we know she has already posed that question to herself in "'Twas like a Maelstrom" (*425): "Which Anguish was the utterest - then - / To perish, or to live?"

After the invocation of standards of measurement—during which the poet finds no Grief equal to her own—she proceeds to ask how one lives with a chronic Pain that is daily renewed (she may have in mind the plight of Prometheus, whose vitals were consumed daily by a vulture). Does the Pain lessen under protracted patience? Her practice is now to note and wonder, rather than to "measure," but with some of the same precision. Her scrutiny has shown her that some sufferers can smile again, but their smile is a pale shadow of their former one; the lamp of their inner light is burning very low. She wonders about Harm and its hurt: Will it have lessened after the passage of "Thousands" of years? (She returns here to her original standard of weight, but crosses weight with time to speak of years "piled" on years, like the increased weight of stones piled one by one on a martyr pressed to death in the old method of torture.) "The Harm - / That hurt them Early - ": Does it, once it becomes so remote, lessen? "Or"—she wonders in the opposite direction, in her final question (with a diminution of time from "Thousands" of years to mere "Centuries")—would sufferers go on aching forever? She feared becoming "a Light / That has so little Oil - ", but now sees that the Oil is magnified by time: the Lamp is "Enlightened" precisely as Pain illuminates by contrast the Love of the lost object.

The poet's Grief, although named again and again as superlative, has been caused by something not yet revealed. We know there was Love; and then there was intolerable Pain; and as the Pain grew, the Love in all its greatness was made manifest. It is only after this long prelude that Dickinson, acknowledging that the Grieved are "many" and the causes of Grief are "various," comes at last to her own case once again, ascribing her Pain to the single superlative and final Grief, that which follows a loss by Death:

> Death - is but one - and comes but once -
> And only nails the Eyes -

Dickinson's unnerving "only," with its gruesome attached image of vulnerable eyes pierced by metal nails, performs the awful finality of death by violating the gaze with the nails closing the coffin. But the abrogation of the physical body does not quench Love. As is the measure of Love, so is the measure of Pain; as the magnitude of the Love is revealed by Loss, the mourner is "Enlightened to a larger Pain."

If Dickinson's Grief is irremediable (because it stems from a death), and superlative (which makes the subsequent recitation of other kinds of Grief almost perfunctory), where will she find a Grief by which to measure her own? Only on Calvary. I suspect she had read George Herbert's poem "The Sacrifice," in which Jesus, uttering the reproaches to his people formalized in the Good Friday liturgy as the *Improperia,* repeats two versions of the refrain: "Was ever grief like mine?" and "Never was grief like mine." This refrain strongly resembles Dickinson's measuring of other Griefs against her own, and her conclusion that her Grief is greater not only comparatively but superlatively. Only Christ's passion is a Grief on the same order as hers. As she passes Calvary, she finds it a comfort to "note"—repeating the earlier "note" of line 13—"the fashions - of the Cross - / And how they're mostly worn - ". In Dickinson's democratic multiplication of the Crucifixion of Jesus, she perceives many versions of Calvary, and they are various. Like a commentator on worldly "fashion," she notes that the torture of the sufferers may vary in kind, but that each, like Jesus, bears a Cross. Having come to the only place where the equal to her own suffering might be found, she can "measure" the Griefs among those crucified, "Still fascinated to presume / That Some - are like my own - ".

Dickinson structures the first six stanzas of "I measure every Grief I meet" very simply, by their repetitive verbs: "I measure"; "I wonder" (thrice); "I note"; "I wonder." Then, after the brutal crux of the whole poem—the laser-like penetration and sealing of the eyes by Death's coffin nails—she embarks on the rapid inventory of the lesser species of Grief, that cursory inventory which is but a way station to a Grief matching her own. A pro forma acknowledgment of fallibility ("I may not guess the Kind - / Correctly - ") allows the final irreverence: Dickinson's fascinated presuming, as she reaches Calvary, that other Griefs may resemble her own. All the wondering and the noting and the listing are clearings of the ground until Dickinson reaches Calvary—the place she has planned to attain since she conceived the poem.

There is something very eerie about Dickinson's initial emphasis on her own specialized sort of eyes ("narrow, probing") and the fact that Death "nails the Eyes." The eyes represent, of course, the intellectual speculation enabling all the measuring and noting and wondering and presuming that goes on in the analytic brain. And although there are other interesting rhymes ("try" and "die," "Harm" and "Balm"), the most striking one occurs when Dickinson rhymes "Me" and "Calvary," just as she had rhymed "me" and "Majesty" in "This is my letter to the World" (*519).

[J 561]

# 558

A Visitor in Marl -
Who influences Flowers -
Till they are orderly as Busts -
And Elegant - as Glass -

Who visits in the Night -
And just before the Sun -
Concludes his glistening interview -
Caresses - and is gone -

But whom his fingers touched -
And where his feet have run -
And whatsoever Mouth he kissed -
Is as it had not been -

When Dickinson wrote "The Soul has Bandaged moments - " (*360), she imagined the loathsome substitution of the suitor "Fright" for the legitimate lover:

She feels some ghastly Fright come up
And stop to look at her -

Salute her, with long fingers -
Caress her freezing hair -
Sip, Goblin, from the very lips
The Lover - hovered - o'er -

This gothic fantasy of a demonic caress is rendered far more dryly—and more convincingly—in "A Visitor in Marl - ", in which a black-garbed grim Artist, in the person of the first killing Frost, comes to the garden like the biblical "thief in the night." (He wears "Marl" because Dickinson associates him with the Devils in *Paradise Lost*, who walk on a burning floor of "Marl," or clayey soil, in Hell.) From the earlier visit of the Fright, Dickinson now repeats the verb "caress" and the act of kissing (no longer a bee-like "Sip" from the lips but a human kiss on the "Mouth"); she even repeats the "fingers" of the earlier poem. The initial elegance of the Frost is unnerving in light of his lethal ultimate effect. In his unobtrusive (and unobserved) "visit," he resembles the courtly "Death" who appears with his Carriage in "Because I could not stop for Death - " (*479).

The poem is an unstopped sentence fragment, with no main verb, resembling the answer to a riddle: "Who is the Frost?" He is "A Visitor in Marl." The rest of the poem is a series of relative clauses modifying the "Visitor": "Who influences Flowers . . . Who visits in the Night and concludes, caresses, and is gone." The result of his touch is extinction, or rather annihilation: "[whatever] he [influenced] is as it had not been." While the first two stanzas show the activities of the Frost, all in the present tense until he "Concludes . . . / Caresses - and is gone - ", the last stanza shows the ghastly effects of his former (now rephrased) activities: touching, running, and kissing. Why did Dickinson not give the poem a main verb? She could easily have begun (as she often does) with an overt definition: "The Frost is . . ." But then the poem would not have been a riddle, and the deadly artistic Interviewer would have been too tamely introduced.

There is no doubt that the Frost is an artist, who does not approve of Nature as it is, and would rather correct it into something more formed and formal—a Bust, a transparent wineglass. ("Bust" derives from the Latin *bustum*, a funeral monument.) The sinister verb "influences" implies that the Visitor persuades the Flowers that they would really look more beautiful in more formal dress, and indeed they begin to change imperceptibly until—once the night is over—they have become "orderly" and "Elegant." Whose judgments are these? The Frost's, no doubt, in the first place; but also they are the first judgment of the gardener at dawn, seeing an exquisite strictness and poise in the stalks and cups of the flowers which they could not manifest while they swayed to every breeze. All night long the "glistening interview" has "influence[d]" the flowers in a species of seduction; no external force has been applied, it seems (no snow, no hail, no sleet), but by dawn a sheen of frost glistens from the garden. ("Glisten" is one member of that family of verbs beginning with "gl-" to which Dickinson, like Hopkins, paid attention: "glimmer," "glister," "glow," "glare," "glance," "glisten," "glitter," and so on, each with a different connotation for the eye and ear.) Nothing could be more

gentlemanly than a pristine "glistening interview," especially one with a con-
cluding caress.

The equation of the Artist with Satan is close to Hawthorne's view in his
tale "The Birthmark," and reflects the Puritan distrust of any attempt to cor-
rect the handiwork of God. Dickinson, however, is not interested here in the
melodrama of evil versus good; she sees that the flowers are orderly, marmo-
real, transparent, and elegant, as they were not before the advent of their
Visitor. But the price of art (as Keats made explicit with the deserted little
town in the "Ode on a Grecian Urn") is that what has been transformed into
art is erased in Nature. What did the flowers feel as their interview took
place? The past-tense "posthumous" stanza of effect, suspending its "whom"
and "where" and "whatsoever" from its severely just "But," is one of Dickin-
son's most lightly touched imaginings. A flower feels the evanescent touch of
a finger—and is as if it had not been, its lifelong identity annihilated in favor
of a marble replica of itself; an acre feels the swift imprint of a foot—and is as
if it had not been, its terrain taking on the consistency of marl; a Mouth is
kissed—and the buttercup-flower is as if it had not been, having become a
glassy vessel. Each of the three clauses is left incomplete, as the suspense
mounts from "whom" to "where" to the all-inclusive "whatsoever"; each is
completed by the single close, "Is as it had not been." Annihilation of the or-
der of Nature, in the course of an overnight creation of the order of Art, re-
veals that Art is to Nature as Death to Life. Interjecting a "Mouth" where
before there had been only "Flowers" is a surreal slash of substitution, as hu-
man death intrudes on the "innocent" natural process of seasonal change.
Only at the close are we aware that Dickinson's "whom" has already forsaken
Flowers in favor of human beings.

Just as Dickinson had preserved the "ee" sound in all the rhymes of "This
is my letter to the World" (and creates the "un" sound in all the rhymes of
"The things we thought that we should do," *1279), so she allots the same
rhyme-sound ("un," with "been") to the last two stanzas of "A Visitor in
Marl," making them a single conclusive narrative, mutating from present to
past, and counteracting, by the end, the implicit opening depiction of Flow-
ers made "orderly as Busts - / And Elegant - as Glass - ". We see, now, the
corpses of the suddenly dead that lie behind those Flowers.

[J 391]

# 578

The Angle of a Landscape -
That every time I wake -
Between my Curtain and the Wall
Upon an ample Crack -

Like a Venetian - waiting -
Accosts my open eye -
Is just a Bough of Apples -
Held slanting, in the Sky -

The Pattern of a Chimney -
The Forehead of a Hill -
Sometimes - a Vane's Forefinger -
But that's - Occasional -

The Seasons - shift - my Picture -
Upon my Emerald Bough,
I wake - to find no - Emeralds -
Then - Diamonds - which the Snow

From Polar Caskets - fetched me -
The Chimney - and the Hill -
And just the Steeple's finger -
These - never stir at all -

Dickinson here writes three sequential "poems" in one. The first "poem" (occupying three stanzas) offers an enticing picture of a small sliver of landscape that is familiar to Dickinson because she sees it every morning between the edge of her curtain and the wall of her room. In fact, the landscape "Accosts" her, puts itself in her way. The principal item in the landscape is a beautiful living Keatsian autumn object: a "Bough of Apples - / Held slanting, in the Sky - ". The Bough is so opulent that Dickinson transforms it into a visitor from Venice (and it would be Shakespeare's Venetian Desdemona she has in mind as model for this figure of Nature), dressed in the rich robes of that city, waiting for Dickinson to wake up so that she can be accosted. Also in view, surrounding the living Bough, are oddly disconnected things. One is a truncated part of the greater landscape, a hill's summit (anthropomorphized to a "Forehead"); another is a portion of a brick Chimney, interesting for its "Pattern"; and a third, only occasionally visible when the wind blows, is a weathervane's pointed end, anthropomorphized as a "Forefinger." The Apples remind us thematically of the cornucopian plenitude of Keats's ode "To Autumn," with its several scenes of the natural world, and Dickinson mixes (as Keats does) manmade items in the landscape (the Chimney, the Vane) with views of Nature (the Hill). But Dickinson, confining herself to a "Crack" of the outside world, has minimalized almost out of existence the normally broad genre of the landscape poem. Nonetheless, even so small a sketch— small if compared to an oil painting or an ode—delights her eye.

The second "poem" (in a Keatsian move) alters the beloved Picture twice. First, it is set later in autumn, and the ruby-red apples are gone, but the Bough is still beautiful, with its clustering "Emerald" leaves, which went unnoticed in the poem until the disappearance of the Apples. Although the leaves fall, Dickinson suppresses the naked picture of what Stevens would call "the winter branch" ("Sunday Morning"). Instead, she moves to later winter, when the Bough takes on a glittering radiance; the Snow, an inspired handmaiden, has fetched, to interest the poet, Diamonds from polar "Caskets" (like Portia's Venetian "caskets" in Shakespeare). In "Frost at Midnight," Coleridge promised his infant son (brought up not in the inhuman city but in Nature), that "all seasons shall be sweet to thee," even the winter, with its icicles "Quietly shining to the quiet Moon." Dickinson the observer finds all seasons sweet to her, whether they bring Apples, or Emeralds, or Diamonds. And there ends the second "poem," enraptured in the successive gifts of Time.

The third "poem" consists of the last three lines. In them, the Bough vanishes altogether, and, with it, its ravishing temporal treasures. What is left is immovable, static, almost (one could say) dead: "The Chimney - and the Hill - / And just the Steeple's finger - / These - never stir at all - ". Both the aesthetic Pattern of the Chimney and the anthropomorphic Forehead and Forefinger of Hill and Vane have vanished with the disappearance of the Bough. What we took for playful minimalism in the charming scene viewed through a bit of windowpane, what we took for plenitude in the lavish seasons with their Rubies (Apples), Emeralds, and Diamonds, has cruelly paid us back for our illusions of pathetic fallacy (Nature seen as a Venetian visitor, an adorner "fetch[ing]" jewels from Ultima Thule) by deadening the landscape down to what will still be there when the delighted observer no longer occupies her bedroom, and nobody wakes to the Bough. "Oh, Lady, we receive but what we give," says Coleridge, "And in our life alone does Nature live, / Ours is her wedding garment, ours her shroud" ("Dejection: An Ode").

In Dickinson's short five stanzas, we go from wedding garment to shroud, from the lover of Nature alive to the beauty of the world to Nature no longer vivified by a sustained love. To the living senses, even a "Crack" is wide enough to manifest all the wealth that the eye could desire. At the end, the meaningful veering of the Vane is gone, and only the fixed religious Steeple with its inflexible "finger" monitors the world. The denuding of the landscape in the last stanza is an almost invisible process; but we are meant to notice, in the absence of the Bough, how differently the stationary items are mentioned, without affect, as they reappear. Only then do the three poems-within-the-poem coalesce into a heartbreaking picture of a once-enhanced Nature which, with the death of its participatory observer, itself suffers rigor mortis.

[J 375]

# 584

We dream - it is good we are dreaming -
It would hurt us - were we awake -
But since it is playing - kill us,
And we are playing - shriek -

What harm? Men die - Externally -
It is a truth - of Blood -
But we - are dying in Drama -
And Drama - is never dead -

Cautious - We jar each other -
And either - open the eyes -
Lest the Phantasm - prove the mistake -
And the livid Surprise

Cool us to Shafts of Granite -
With just an age - and name -
And perhaps a phrase in Egyptian -
It's prudenter - to dream -

The ghastly game being played in dream by "it" and "us" opens with a dance
lilt in which iambs become anapests, generating more syllables per line of
trimeter than the necessary six. There are, for instance, nine syllables in line 1.
Dickinson's line-endings can also tack on an extra syllable (here italicized) in
what is known as a "feminine" ending:

> We dream - it is good we are dream*ing* -
> It would hurt us - were we awake -
> But since it is playing - kill *us,*

But then the anapests thin down, and, in line 4 of the first stanza, vanish.
The rhythm has begun to alter its lilt in line 3, and has lost it entirely in line 4,

which exhibits only the normal six syllables of a normal iambic trimeter line:

> But since it is playing kill *us,*
> And we are playing - shriek -

Dickinson revives the lilt and the extra end-syllable in the following stanzas, in lines such as "But we - are dying in Dra*ma* - " and "And perhaps a phrase in Egyp*tian* - ". This prevalence of anapests is a rather unusual feature in Dickinson's verse, and it is presumably called into being here as a rhythmic correspondent of the macabre game being described.

Although Dickinson neutralizes the drama of homicidal pursuit by naming it a dream, that defense mechanism is exploded in the third stanza, when we suspect that the "Phantasm"—Death—which is bent on killing us is not part of a nightmare, but real. As the inner "shriek" continues, the hounded prey would like to wake up to end the nightmare, but fear that with open eyes they will see they were mistaken in their belief that they were dreaming. Dickinson has conceded that although men die "Externally," she and her companion are safe, because they are merely "dying in Drama." But what if they are mistaken, and wake to a threat so real that the "Surprise" itself kills them, turning them into their own granite headstones, engraved with their own epitaph? The anapests and iambs of the dream change to the hammer-blows of reality, expressed in the trochees and dactyls of stanza 3, which expire, after line 13, into iambs. But Dickinson leaves a hint of the deadly lilt of the game in the third line of the final stanza, with its anapests and its extra end-syllable in "Egyptian."

> Lest the Phantasm - prove the mistake -
> And the livid Surprise
>
> Cool us to Shafts of Granite -
> With just an age - and name -
> And perhaps a phrase in Egyp*tian* -
> It's prudenter - to dream -

Needless to say, Dickinson was never an advocate of closing one's eyes so as to avoid reality. On the other hand, once you realize that "it" is coming at you in reality with the intent to kill, it would be "prudenter" to choose to think that you are still dreaming.

The difficult lines are "Cautious - We jar each other - / And either - open the eyes - / Lest the Phantasm - prove the mistake - ". It helps to know that Dickinson had originally written "And either - open its eyes - ": the two fleeing persons that make up the "We" are cautious when they "jar" each other, lest either should open its eyes and see that the phantom is real. But since Dickinson had already used the pronoun "it" to signify Death-the-Predator, the same pronoun could not logically signify the hunted creature opening "its" eye. Realizing the confusion, Dickinson substituted "the eyes," keeping the eyes plural so as to accord with the plural subject "We." It also helps to know that line 3 originally read, "But since They [are] playing - kill us - "; in that version, "They" are the social "majority" that always prevails, as Dickinson will say bitterly in "Much Madness is divinest Sense - " (*620). The fear of society expressed in "They are playing - kill us - " hardly suggests a game; but when the predator is "it," a ghost in a dream, the fictive nature of the Phantasm can be maintained. Originally, too, Dickinson had conventionally written that on the "Shafts of Granite" there might be "a latin inscription." As she changes that intelligible Latin epitaph into an exotic and unintelligible "phrase in Egyptian," she ends the "game," its residue being the poetic hieroglyphs she will leave behind after she is dead. The dreadful comedy of "it is playing - kill us, / And we are playing - shriek - " devolves into the silent characters of the poet's "Egyptian" epitaph that nonetheless will one day be interpreted by means of some poetic Rosetta Stone.

[J 531]

# 588

The Heart asks Pleasure - first -
And then - excuse from Pain -
And then - those little Anodynes
That deaden suffering -

And then - to go to sleep -
And then - if it should be
The will of its Inquisitor
The privilege to die -

Dickinson's rack-and-screw narrative depends on a single main clause: "The Heart asks." The list that follows is a narrative beginning with delight and ending with a suicidal wish, going downhill all the way. In this severe poem, a bare skeleton is held together by its inflexible repetitions of "And then," emphasized because they are placed over and over at the beginning of a line (in the figure called *anaphora*).

The arrangement creates a ladder, by which one descends lower and lower into torture. The narrative could be graphed:

*The Heart asks:*
             Pleasure (first)
(And then)      excuse from Pain
(And then)      those little Anodynes that deaden suffering
(And then)      to go to sleep
(And then)      if it should be the will of its
                   Inquisitor the privilege to die

This graph can apply to almost any crucial emotional experience. The opening clause implies no suspicion; but after Pleasure has been denied, and then excuse from Pain has not been granted, and then analgesia (just a little, just to deaden the suffering) has been withheld, we realize that there exists a sadistic Refuser who is the speaker's Interlocutor. He will not even let her close her eyelids and forget the Pain in sleep. Tortured, the creature in agony tries to understand the character and motivation of the Refuser, who is now given his historical persona: he is an Inquisitor. And since simple asking won't move him, the prisoner realizes that she must grovel. "Please, Master, if it be thy will, would'st thou vouchsafe me the privilege (one that lies not in my power but in thy bestowing) to die?"

Dickinson modulates the poem by changing the length of her requests. The Heart asks, in one bold word, "Pleasure"—a positive quality. What follows is a little longer because more complex: Pleasure is now defined negatively as being "excuse from Pain." What follows is longer yet because the beseecher is trying to explain to her naysaying Interlocutor that she is no longer seeking a permanent "excuse" from Pain, but merely, she says propitiatingly and explanatorily (at further length), a temporary relief, just a little something to take away the keen edge of Pain, putting the relief in the diminutive: those "little" Anodynes that "deaden" (not remove) suffering. But the anguish persists until the speaker, her will broken, her appeal for any relief refused, pleads for unconsciousness (in an exhausted four-word request: "to go to sleep")—if just for a little while. When even that is refused, she comes to a full awareness of where she is and with whom she has been speaking. At that point, her will-to-live shattered, she begs—in the longest and most uninterrupted request of the poem, unstopped by any punctuation—not for her life (as prisoners are expected to do), but for something she has no right to, yet prays will be allowed her: "to die."

That Dickinson should have turned to the Spanish Inquisition for her torturer suggests that she was not about to take as her metaphor an American figure nearer home—say, the Salem judges who hanged witches—but rather would choose a model from the lurid "Old World" of absolute power, where church and state were one, and there could be no appeal. The resembling of the last self-abasement to some forms of prayer puts the shadowy figure of God behind that of the Inquisitor. The extremely firm syntax and the relentless turns of the verbal screw "And then"—each repetition stretching the rack further—match the Torturer's inflexibility of will to His inflexibility of means. The final cessation of speech suggests the approach of the unconsciousness eventually brought about by any torture long inflicted.

[J 536]

# 591

I heard a Fly buzz - when I died -
The Stillness in the Room
Was like the Stillness in the Air -
Between the Heaves of Storm -

The Eyes around - had wrung them dry -
And Breaths were gathering firm
For that last Onset - when the King
Be witnessed - in the Room -

I willed my Keepsakes - Signed away
What portion of me be
Assignable - and then it was
There interposed a Fly -

With Blue - uncertain - stumbling Buzz -
Between the light - and me -
And then the Windows failed - and then
I could not see to see -

This famous poem startles from the very first line, because that line is spoken posthumously. Self-presentation as a posthumous voice is not original; it had been done before by George Herbert in "Love" (III), in which the speaker tells in the past tense of his entrance to Heaven: "Love bade me welcome." But Herbert's speaker is newly alive, and Dickinson's is truly dead. And Herbert's narrative is chronologically ordered, while Dickinson's is not. Narrated chronologically, Dickinson's poem would begin with line 2, and the Fly would appear where it belongs (and where it reappears), in line 12. The inconsequentiality (as it seems) of the first line—what difference does it make whether or not the speaker heard the noise of a Fly when she died?—sets the first puzzle of the poem. The second puzzle is the late placement of the making of the will. Surely, in the normal course of things, this action would have well preceded the moment of suspense when the speaker is about to die, as the family awaits "that last Onset," the last gasp, when "the King" will come, "royally reclaiming his own" (as Hopkins says in "The Wreck of the Deutschland"). The King's coming will be "witnessed" by these bystanders.

The first two stanzas (following the first line on the Fly) exist to build up suspense: "Stillness" occurs twice, "Room" occurs twice, and "Room" is made to rhyme with "Storm" as the room is made the eye of the hurricane, its stillness "like the Stillness in the Air - / Between the Heaves of Storm - ". Dickinson creates an enclosed space by making the "Room" the outer bracket of a chiasmus of rhymes:

Room : Storm :: firm : Room

The "Heaves" of Storm are the convulsive last throes of the body in illness, and the corporeal "Stillness" that follows them presages the last sunken breaths of the dying. The Eyes of the family have exhausted their tears; the relatives' Breaths are held in abeyance, almost, as they gather strength for the trial to come. The word "last" enters the poem with the expectation of the King. The family will know his arrival by the death-stillness of the body.

At this solemn moment, the near-corpse breaks in with chatter, and even with dry wit: "I willed my Keepsakes - Signed away / What portion of me be / Assignable." Which "portion" of her is not "Assignable"? Her spiritual self, which awaits the coming of the King. This stanza is the second "lead-up" to his arrival; it presents the expectation of the dying person, as the first two stanzas presented the expectation of the others in the Room. Between the speaker and the expected light of salvation "There interposed a Fly." Not "a Fly interposed itself": the presence of the Fly seems directed from another sphere. The aural uncapitalized verb "buzz" that introduced the Fly now recurs, but at this moment of death it turns into a noun that takes over sight and hearing, a capitalized "Buzz" that (to the dying person's fading sight) amalgamates into itself all its several sense-qualities. The Buzz is "Blue," since it comes from the iridescent blue-black of the Fly; it is enclosed in the Room with no exit, so its passage is "uncertain"; and as the speaker falters, so does the Fly, "stumbling" in assonance with its "Buzz." The synesthesia in the Fly—of the visual, the kinetic, and the aural—is complete.

The Tennysonian word "fail" is applied at first not to the dying person's sight, but to the windows, in a transferred perception. (Dickinson takes "fail" both from *In Memoriam*, where it appears several times—"The wish, that of the living whole / No life may fail beyond the grave"—and from "O That 'Twere Possible," where channel-water "windeth far / Till it fade and fail and die.") When "the Windows failed," the speaker "could not see to see - ". Dickinson italicizes the moment of death with the two successive meanings of "see": the first, intellectual one means "to manage to make out the form of"; the second, physiological one means to have eyes that still function. The double "see" matches the earlier repetitions of "buzz," "Stillness," and "Room," in Dickinson's constriction of means within a narrow space.

The last phase of life takes its shape from the moment-by-moment stylization made possible by the poet's threefold "and then": "*and then* it was . . . a Fly . . . *And then* the Windows failed . . . *and then* I could not see to see." The triple occurrence of "and then" goes the earlier word-doublings one better, a sign of approaching climax. Such incremental moments did not occur in the earlier narrative of the death-watch in the room, where all was held still. When the Fly appears where the King was expected, and blocks the light; when its carrion-haunting presence is imposed on the death-room; when the Fly's stumbling without the possibility of exit matches the impossibility of the exit of any putative soul; when Dickinson deliberately rhymes "me" with "Fly" over the last two stanzas, everything changes. The dying speaker realizes the insignificant Fly is herself. Her death-emblem is no winged Psyche-soul rising like a butterfly from the discarded body, but rather the Fly, a mocking (and songless) sign of mortal dissolution. The rendition of the hopeless "fail[ing]" of the speaker, with the Fly her last object of vision, would not have its conclusive strength if the Fly had not so bizarrely been the thing of utmost importance that the corpse first mentioned to us, her listeners. When the Fly returns at the end, we have been forewarned of its inevitability, its inextricability from the death-moment.

The poem, in its replacement of the King with the Fly, is in one sense entirely blasphemous—but in another sense (as generations of readers have felt) true. Mortality, in the person of the monumentalized and actual Fly, possesses the grandeur of Truth defeating Illusion. Dickinson was committed, as she wrote later, to telling all the truth but telling it "slant" (*1263). In the buzzing Fly she found her most convincing, if unlikely, symbol of the Truth of mortality itself. The voice is speaking posthumously, positioned nowhere.

[J 465]

# 615

God is a distant - stately Lover -
Woos, as He states us - by His Son -
Verily, a Vicarious Courtship -
"Miles", and "Priscilla," were such an One -

But, lest the Soul - like fair "Priscilla"
Choose the Envoy - and spurn the 'Groom -
Vouches, with hyperbolic archness -
"Miles", and "John Alden" are Synonyme -

Dickinson's waltz-rhythm joke on the Incarnation, which she crosses with the courtship of Miles Standish, appeared first, rather incredibly, in the Unitarian weekly, the *Christian Register* (1891), after Dickinson's death. Could the editors have actually read it? Protests followed that publication, and more protest was made after the poem's 1929 inclusion in *Further Poems,* leading to its suppression until, in the 1945 *Ancestors' Brocades,* it finally became part of the canon.

Dickinson may have begun to conceive the poem when reading Longfellow's long poem *The Courtship of Miles Standish* (1858), a legend mixing melodrama with love, war with a wedding. It tells how the rough Pilgrim warrior Miles Standish sent his proposal of marriage to Priscilla Mullins via a proxy, his young aide John Alden (who had long secretly loved Priscilla), and how Priscilla famously replied, "Why don't you speak for yourself, John?" Dickinson (whose mind always brought up religious parallels) was struck by the subversive comedy inherent in treating two persons of the Trinity as, respectively, "Miles" and "John Alden," and treating Jesus' Incarnation as having taken place because Jehovah decided to send a proxy—presumably more appealing than himself—to save men's souls. (She is relying on John 8:16: "My judgment is true; for I am not alone, but I and the Father that sent me.") By yoking together theology and New England "history" (transferring the secular word "woos" to God, and analogizing the religious concept "Soul" to Priscilla), Dickinson hints that divine affairs are not very different from human ones, that similar transactions can be exercised on both planes.

The comic effect of the tetrameter verse is gained by tacking an extra syllable onto the odd-numbered lines: the words "Lover," "Courtship," "Priscilla," and "archness" give to the lines the fillip associated with "feminine" rhymes. (One suspects that the word "Priscilla" may have been the template for Dickinson's "feminine" extra syllables, since in Longfellow's hexameter *Courtship of Miles Standish, every* line ends with an unaccented syllable: "Letters written by Alden and full of the name of Priscilla!" exclaims Longfellow at the end of part I.) Other comic features here include the gloomy remoteness of God, who not only is "stately," but when he talks, "states"; the translation of divine Salvation into common "Woo[ing]" and "Courtship"; the rash familiarity of "Miles" and "John Alden" as applied to Jehovah and Jesus; and the preposterous alliteration and assonance attached to God's sending of Jesus: "Verily, a Vicarious Courtship" (its graphic elements—"V," "ou(s)," and "ou(r)"—reproduced later by the alliterating "Vouches"). Appropriating Jesus' own word of asseveration, "Verily," the poet ascribes to herself a (fanciful) scriptural authority.

The last comic touch is God's "hyperbolic archness." Dickinson had a good deal of hyperbolic archness of her own, and it amused her to transfer her own "style" to God. Also, like herself, God is delighted by semantic resemblances. Priscilla, choosing John Alden, reacted "wrongly" in Jehovah's view. Lest the Soul do the same, taking Jesus rather than Jehovah as Bridegroom, God trumps the potential mistake with semantic mystery: in the Trinity, Father and Son are One. This is the evangelical formulation (John 10:30, "I and my Father are one"), but Dickinson, as usual, will transform her source. By saying that God "vouches" (or guarantees) that "'Miles', and 'John Alden' are Synonyme," Dickinson once again, for ironic purposes, translates Miles and John, Jehovah and Jesus, to yet a third plane—neither a divine plane nor a human one, but rather the linguistic plane of the word "Synonyme." The Soul's neat choice between Envoy and Groom is mirrored in Dickinson's equally neat framing of the dilemma in a single, perfectly balanced left-right line: "Choose the Envoy - and spurn the 'Groom - ." (Lines of equal balance are frequently meaningful in Dickinson's poetry as means of representing contrasting alternatives.)

Does Dickinson's playfully blasphemous appropriation of Longfellow have any wider application? It implicitly argues that God is not transparent in his dealings with us: he pretends we have to make a choice, but then triumphantly tells us he has arranged things all along so that either choice will produce the same result. It is as though the long tradition of the Soul's crucial choice between God and Mammon were suddenly to be made ridiculous by God's declaring that the two words, "God" and "Mammon," are actually synonyms.

[J 357]

# 620

> Much Madness is divinest Sense -
> To a discerning Eye -
> Much Sense - the starkest Madness -
> 'Tis the Majority
> In this, as all, prevail -
> Assent - and you are sane -
> Demur - you're straightway dangerous -
> And handled with a Chain -

Dickinson's common way of leaving out inference, so that the reader may supply the want, appears here. Logical completeness would require something like this to fill out the missing complement:

> Much Madness is divinest Sense -
> To a discerning Eye -
> And to an undiscerning One -
> Divinest Sense a lie -

Similarly, the next bit of the poem, properly "filled out," would read:

> Much Sense - the starkest Madness -
> To that discerning Eye -

But of course Dickinson, with her love of ellipsis, would not repeat something that the reader should be able to infer (and inject). After the splendid paradoxical ring of the first line, its parallel in line 3 makes us, as I have said, expect a fourth line matching line 2 and completing the aphoristic quatrain. Instead, Dickinson begins a new sense-unit, sacrificing to it the white space normally occurring between stanzas. The central remark—"'Tis the Majority / In this, as all, prevail - "—replaces the previous declarative confidence with irrefutable fact. The two lines seem almost an offhand parenthesis (as though everyone knows the perennial social triumph of majority rule) and seem included only pro forma (while in reality they prepare for the savagery to come).

Long before twentieth-century analysts inquired into the social construction of mental illness, inspired "caged" madmen (see Shelley's *Julian and Maddalo*) were a common literary property, and Dickinson's sympathy with the "Mad" here is not unexpected. She has led us to think that those who do not agree with her merely have undiscerning Eyes, even if they will, as the majority, always (in a neutral verb) "prevail." Even the sharp comment "Assent - and you are sane - " does not prepare us for the transformation of the undiscerning Majority into a sadistic mob, imposing chains on one who disagrees with their majority opinion. And what has the offender done to deserve social ostracism and social torture? She has "demur[red]" to something said. "Demur" (in its modern sense) is the mildest word of opposition in the language: it is polite—it is almost demure. But the slightest degree of nonconformity is viciously punished. "All men say 'What' to me," Dickinson wrote Thomas Wentworth Higginson (L 271). Everyone knew instantly, by her merest adjective, that she refused conventionality. The alliteration of "Demur" and "dangerous" suggests society's instant—"straightway"—response to a demurrer.

Human beings are not supposed to handle other human beings by chaining them. The social exclusion and revenge implied in this handling (and future torment) chill the blood. The way of "sanity" is easy; one has only to join the consensus, and in four words you are accepted: "and you are sane - ". If you demur, eight words are necessary to see the dangerous You excluded, "handled," and chained.

To Dickinson's mind, a special gift enables the "discerning" Eye to distinguish the genuine from the false; see "Some - Work for Immortality - " (536, J 406):

> A Beggar - Here and There -
> Is gifted to discern
> Beyond the Broker's insight -

Dickinson is aware that she can't expect the "Majority" to have the discerning gift of the few. Her protest is against the Majority's vehement conviction that a demurral to its views is so dangerous that it must be repressed, censored, or bestially punished. She indicts the intolerance of that Majority. Has one no right to expect at least tolerance for the Minority? The hyperbole (if it is that) in Dickinson's religious superlative—"divinest," used of the "Sense" to be found in "Madness"—brings the Mad under the general category of inspired prophets without honor in their own country. When the demurrers hear the discourse of the "sensible" Majority, the opinions voiced seem to them "starkest Madness." Dickinson, answering "starkest" with "divinest," represents the permanent mutual critique of "solid" citizen and "dangerous" demurrer.

[J 435]

# 633

I saw no Way - The Heavens were stitched -
I felt the Columns close -
The Earth reversed her Hemispheres -
I touched the Universe -

And back it slid - and I alone -
A speck upon a Ball -
Went out upon Circumference -
Beyond the Dip of Bell -

"I am the way," said Jesus ( John 14:6). That path is closed to Dickinson: "I saw no Way - ". Ascension to the Father is equally barred: "The Heavens were stitched - ", as though they were a tent with an upper opening of access to God which has been stitched shut by some unnamed agent. To that metaphor succeeds another: Heaven's door is a portico with stately Columns. But that portal, too, is inaccessible: "I felt the Columns close - ", barring entrance. Giving up on a putatively paternal Heaven, the poet turns to the maternal Earth; but She is too unstable to be trusted, able to "reverse" her Hemispheres at will, turning what was North to South, transvaluing all values. With both Heaven and Earth uninhabitable, the poet extends her uncertainty to the whole Universe as she seeks some universal truth. The Universe evades her grasp, sliding back into its interstellar spaces, leaving her alone on the geographic globe of Earth, that "Ball."

But she has had a revelation (not to be had from the rejecting Father-God, not to be had from the unreliably revolving maternal Earth) of her entire parentlessness, her orphan status in the void of the Universe, her ultimate insignificance. She has gone as far in sight and insight as the human mind can reach, attempting to hold in a single thought the illimitable Universe and her flawed "speck"-like self. The realization of her existential status— that of a solitary self with no parents and no home, whether in the Heavens, the Earth, or the Universe—leaves her (to use Hopkins's term) "a lonely began." Dickinson's state resembles Hopkins's own, as he described it in "To seem the stranger lies my lot." Displaced in Dublin, estranged in belief from his parents, not knowing where to turn, every life-project vitiated, Hopkins exposes his helplessness and his despair of any future:

> Only what word
> Wisest my heart breeds dark heaven's baffling ban
> Bars or hell's spell thwarts. This to hoard unheard,
> Heard unheeded, leaves me a lonely began.

Dickinson, banned from heaven, is marooned on the outer reaches of the mind's circumference, and no Bell can reach that far to call her back to God. She may be thinking of Herbert's "Prayer," in which the poet is confident that God listens to prayer ascending to Him from churches calling the faithful: prayer is "Churchbells beyond the stars heard." In her retort to Herbert, "Prayer is the little implement" (623, J 437), Dickinson describes prayer skeptically, doubting that men's desperate speech, flung to the Heavens, is heard by God's ear:

> Prayer is the little implement
> Through which Men reach
> Where Presence - is denied them -
> They fling their Speech
>
> By means of it - in God's Ear -
> If then He hear -
> This sums the Apparatus
> Comprised in Prayer -

Dickinson finds herself stranded, at the end of "I saw no Way - ", beyond "the Dip" of a Bell as it swings back and forth, exposing its "Tongue," as Dickinson had said in "It was not Death" (*355). In Hopkins, a bell calls souls to salvation: in "The Wreck of the Deutschland," as the "tall nun" calls out to Christ, "a virginal tongue told" (with the homophone "tolled"). As she recalls "lovely-felicitous Providence" to the drowning souls, she could, for them, says Hopkins, "be a bell to, ring of it, and / Startle the poor sheep back!" Dickinson the unbeliever remains beyond the range of the saving Bell.

In the bleak ending, when Dickinson is left solitary, at the edge of the universe, what redeems her lonely status is the fact that she has attained it by her own exploration: she *went out* to where she finds herself. She is not a "castaway" like William Cowper, who thought he was damned (see his poem "The Castaway"); she is the agent of her own enlightenment. "There shall no man," says God in the Bible (Exodus 33:20), "see me, and live" (see 1353, J 1247, "To pile like Thunder to its close"). But one can see Circumference and live—at the cost of remaining alone, unreachable by others.

No one can read this difficult poem without wondering why Dickinson chose the metaphors she did, making the poem hard to follow in its careening in space and metaphor—from stitches to Columns to Hemispheres, to a touchable (and sliding) Universe, to a Ball, to a Bell. The slightly dissonant closing rhyme of "Ball" (where she remains) and "Bell" (which she has gone beyond) leaves her at an angle to the world of human life. When Dickinson is following the convulsions of consciousness very closely, her metaphors tend to create this sort of nearly unintelligible cascade, which, once understood, makes the reader a participant in the sort of vertigo transcribed in the poem.

[J 378]

# 647

> To fill a Gap
> Insert the Thing that caused it -
> Block it up
> With Other - and 'twill yawn the more -
> You cannot solder an Abyss
> With Air -

Otherwise rendered in standard metrical form, this would read:

> To fill a Gap - Insert the Thing
> That caused it - block it up
> With Other - and 'twill yawn the more -

In short, one could imagine a "normal" Dickinsonian quatrain (not that she would have tolerated such a one) getting underway, but the "quatrain" breaks down entirely after "more." One cannot turn the last two lines of "To fill a Gap" into any sort of trimeter to complete the putative "quatrain." When Dickinson allows an expressive distortion of her usual prosody, it is by a felt inner necessity. Here, as elsewhere, the arrangement of the words is mimetic, with the brief "To fill a Gap" in line 1 being matched by the even briefer "Block it up" in line 3. Both recommended ways of dealing with the Gap are impossible. One cannot insert a dead friend back into one's life (to take one figure for the "Gap"), nor can one block up the absence of one indispensable person with the presence of a different person. Balked, the poet finds in her instructions no positive possibility, at least as the difficulty has been stated. Dickinson turns to a different metaphor to express the futility of any attempt to close or obliterate—fill up, block up—the Gap. The idea of using the absence itself—the blank "Air"—to "solder" together the cliffs of the Abyss is also unthinkable. Life is unlivable within that memorial fissure, the grave of the remembered dead.

Dickinson's rejected alternative for "solder an Abyss" was "Plug a Sepulchre"—but this Sepulchre of the dead has (like any Sepulchre) a body already filling it in the mind; the metaphor of inserting a plug into an inhabited Sepulchre is incoherent. The Abyss has no preexisting inhabitant; it is an absence, not a presence. Whenever Dickinson uses the word "solder," she means a permanent seal, a figure for the irrevocability of Death. The lips of the dead can be "soldered" (*238); sod can be "soldered down" on a grave (648). But the absence of the friend is not a thing, like a body; it can't be decently buried, as a body can be; it can't be "solder[ed]" in place forever. It is like a ghost, unattainable to human handling. To use the absence to forget the absence is impossible. The more you attempt to forget, the larger grows the vacancy of the Abyss.

The disorder of Dickinson's prosody here is a sign of trying, and giving up. No neat "solder[ing]" can close the poem—no axiom, no proverb, no wit. Closure is always important to Dickinson; some of her most memorable lines appear at the end of her poems. As "To fill a Gap" staggers to its close, it evanesces into that space of "Air" that the poet cannot fill or block up or use as closure. She remains in the very atmosphere of the Abyss. One feels that no word but "Air" could have been more satisfactory to the poem, or less satisfactory to the soul.

[J 546]

# 664

Rehearsal to Ourselves
Of a Withdrawn Delight -
Affords a Bliss like Murder -
Omnipotent - Acute -

We will not drop the Dirk -
Because We love the Wound
The Dirk Commemorate - Itself
Remind Us that We died -

Who has withdrawn the Delight? At first we might ascribe the act to the Dickinsonian God, that expert "Burglar" (39, J 49). But we soon discover that an act of self-wounding has taken place in the heart through the agency of the self-attacker. The wounding "Dirk," however, remains unjettisoned, as the sole Commemorator of what turns out to be not simply self-wounding but self-murdering: "We died." This is Dickinson as Lady Macbeth, rehearsing over and over the bloody deed of the dagger.

The tricks that such a narrative plays with time are among Dickinson's securest strategies. She begins out of time altogether, in a form of abstract discourse—not, here, a definition or an axiom or a proverb, but rather a psychological observation, making universal (by the first-person plural) a truth that may well be specific to herself: that "We" take morose delectation in harrowing recitals to ourselves of a past Delight now self-withdrawn. ("Rehearsal" derives from the Middle English *herse,* a harrow, the large agricultural rake that breaks up solid ground into clods, whence the use of the word "harrowing" for a painful and disturbing experience.) The shocking word "Murder"—following on "Bliss"—reveals the speaker as someone familiar with the keen feelings of omnipotence experienced (the poet suggests) when one murders; and one cannot murder anyone but a human being. With each "Rehearsal" of its loss, the "Withdrawn Delight" vanishes once again, and our power of renunciation is exalted to the exact degree to which the Delight was valued. To the extent that the Delight was the sole constituent of a former Self, the Withdrawal—each time it is rehearsed in memory—is the murder of that self.

The simile "like Murder," conveniently distanced when perceived as hyperbole, is then violently literalized—with the appearance of the Dirk and the Wound—as a self-stabbing with a dagger. The dagger, after the original murder, could have been dropped in horror, but the speaker clings to it as a relic of the original pang. She keeps the Dirk before her eyes as she rehearses over and over the bliss of self-deprivation, using the Dirk as a fetish to "Commemorate" the beloved Wound. One usually commemorates a momentous occasion: here, the Dirk Commemorates the moment in which the poet recognized, by her repudiation of Delight, that it was essential to remaining alive, and therefore "died." It is that moment she revivifies again and again as her sole remaining possibility of authentic action. Memory's recastigation of the flesh is the only available exaltation. In that act of compulsive repetition ("We will not drop the Dirk - "), and only there, does the Soul feel its power.

As elsewhere, Dickinson uses the unmarked form (one not exhibiting tense or number) of the verb—here, "Commemorate"—to signify a tenseless eternity, further complicating the poem's temporal sequence: from the eternal present of "Affords" to the determined future of "We will," to the eternal present again in "love," and thence to the untensed, unnumbered "Commemorate." If Dickinson had said that the Dirk "commemorates" the Wound, she would have been restricting its activity to the present tense; but the Dirk always did, does now, and forever will "Commemorate" the Wound in every "Rehearsal." Caught up in her fixated "Rehearsal" of the crucial moment of self-murder, the poet has forgotten (temporarily) the past annihilation of the self in that act. It is only when, in the obsession of "Rehearsal," she comes around to the fatal stabbing, that the remaining souvenirs in the flesh—the lethal Dirk in her hand and the fatal Wound in her Heart—remind her that she died. Although Dickinson keeps to the original universal "We" with which she began the poem, both the self-murder, and the forgetting of that act in the rehearsal of the act, are too lurid to be easily predicated universally.

The rhymes of the poem are, as so often, significant. Matching "Delight" with "Acute" makes them proportional to each other; matching "Wound" to "died" identifies cause and effect. The succession of erotic words—"Delight,"

"Bliss," and "love"—suggests that the self-withdrawn Delight was passion. "Rehearsal to Ourselves" belongs with the other renunciatory love poems of Dickinson's "crisis"—but rather than emphasizing the speaker's loneliness and sadness, this one displays the savage pleasure of self-sacrifice.

[J 379]

# 675

What Soft - Cherubic Creatures -
These Gentlewomen are -
One would as soon assault a Plush -
Or violate a Star -

Such Dimity Convictions -
A Horror so refined
Of freckled Human Nature -
Of Deity - Ashamed -

It's such a common - Glory -
A Fisherman's - Degree -
Redemption - Brittle Lady -
Be so - ashamed of Thee -

When Thomas Wentworth Higginson wanted Dickinson to come to a meeting of a Ladies Circle in Boston, she politely declined. She was too impolite for "polite society." She clasped a Bomb to her breast (see "A Pit - but Heaven over it - "; 508, J 1712), and carried it with her wherever she went. As we know from her poems and letters, she loved her women friends; it was not gender she disliked but convention. The upper-class "Gentlewomen" of her society, "Cherubic" in their asexual affectation of innocence, have turned themselves into soft, rounded creatures, "Plush" pillows. They idealize a woman's role beyond human possibility: a Gentlewoman is higher than the clichéd woman "on a pedestal"—she is a "Star." Such a "Lady" does not expose herself to sunlight unprotected by hat or parasol; it might give her freckles. Dickinson would like to drop her Bomb in the midst of these unreal creatures—to "assault" them, to "violate" them, to do anything that would make them sit up and take notice.

Glad as we are that Dickinson left us withering comments on forms of religious hypocrisy (see 1266, J 1207, "He preached upon 'Breadth' till it argued him narrow - "), we wish we had more of Dickinson the social satirist.

Here she brings herself into the very midst of a company of Gentlewomen: they are pointedly "These," not "those." She must often have sat, in her rebellious youth, in such a group, while metaphors deriding them crowded into her head. She detested their "refined" Horror at what Hopkins would have called "pied" human nature—"whatever is fickle, freckled" (see his poem "Pied Beauty"); their coded vocabulary of disdain for the "common" laboring classes; their fluttering "Convictions," no sturdier than the "Dimity" (cotton fabric) of their gowns. If these women had seen Jesus and his fishermen-disciples passing by, they would have dismissed Deity itself as a "common" Glory, no higher on the social ladder of rank ("Degree") than any other attribute of the lower classes, and they would have been "Ashamed" to be seen in Jesus' company. Dickinson is no doubt recalling the criticisms of Jesus by others, relayed by himself, as "a man gluttonous, and a winebibber, a friend of publicans and sinners" (Matthew 11:19).

Dickinson increases the force of her antipathy by phrasing the first two stanzas of the poem in exclamatory syntax: "What Soft - Cherubic Creatures - / These Gentlewomen are - / . . . / Such Dimity Convictions - ". Her mockery of them as "Plush" and "Star," when combined with the hostility in her implicit wish to "assault" and "violate," produces in the stanza both a belittling of their minds and an anger at their pillowed protection from assault. To convict them further, she quotes them as commenting, in high, "Brittle" voices, on Jesus' divinity and the sanctity of his fishermen-disciples: "It's such a common - Glory - / A Fisherman's Degree - ". In an unexpected move, Dickinson speaks harshly back to the women's snobbery: in a damning direct address to a representative "Lady," she prophesies the woman's fate: "[May] Redemption - Brittle Lady - / Be so - ashamed of Thee - ". Just as the "refined" Ladies have been "Ashamed" of Deity, on the Day of Judgment God will be "Ashamed" of them, and they will see themselves repudiated by the God they have scorned.

With the exception of the tetrameter line 3, all the odd-numbered lines of this trimeter poem end in unstressed syllables, which allow, as they bridge the pause to the next line, a more conversational ordering of rhythm than sharp unprolonged trimeters would offer. Besides, what could be more suitable to this poem than "feminine" endings?

It has often (perhaps too often, lately) been pointed out that Dickinson was herself of the upper classes, and exhibited (in her youth) some disdain of the "common" inhabitants of Amherst paralleling that expressed by her "Gentlewomen." In her defense, it might be said that her objections here are directed not only to the Ladies' social insulation from external hardship, but also to their absolute incomprehension of the figure of Jesus. Because they have not suffered (since no one would dare to "assault" or "violate" them), they are incapable of being moved by the figure of Deity as it appears in Jesus, the Man of Sorrows. Dickinson's valedictory "curse"—"May you be among the damned at the Last Day"—although it is lightly phrased, erases the "false" original picture of the ladies as angelically "Cherubic." And the brief, last, exclamation—"May Deity repudiate you!"—superimposes itself on the "tamer" satiric exclamations with which the poem began: the Ladies are not Cherubim, but Bad Angels. In the female verse of Dickinson's era, there is nothing else like this satire on Gentlewomen by one of their "own kind."

[J 401]

# 686

It makes no difference abroad -
The Seasons - fit - the same -
The Mornings blossom into Noons -
And split their Pods of Flame -

Wild flowers - kindle in the Woods -
The Brooks slam - all the Day -
No Black bird bates His Banjo -
For passing Calvary -

Auto da Fe - and Judgment -
Are nothing to the Bee -
His separation from His Rose -
To Him - sums Misery -

Dickinson's vehement refusal of the "pathetic fallacy" (by which a poem shows Nature grieving in sympathy with the grieving speaker) dismisses the entire fiction of a harmonizing Nature, in which the poet can find symbols illuminating her own desolation. There is, for her, no "correspondent breeze" (of the natural sort that Wordsworth found in *The Prelude*) to match the breath of inspiration. On the contrary. At first, Dickinson attempts to be fair to Nature. It is indifferent, that's true, but in the Keatsian "abroad" the day displays its usual beauties, as the Mornings take on a further warm amplitude and "blossom" into Noons; and when the brilliant sunset comes, the Mornings, like plants gone to seed after the Noon flowering, "split their Pods," spilling out not seeds but "Flame." No pallor of loss tinges natural glory; nor does any unwillingness to celebrate permeate the poet's beautiful subsequent announcement of the Spring, "Wild flowers - kindle in the Woods - ," where the progressive verb "kindle" creates an extension of flower-flames over the whole season.

But then the irritation of the grieving speaker at the total lack of Nature's sympathy for her sorrowful state breaks through. "Could I not have a moment of music suitable to my lamenting heart?" she asks. But no: raising the level of noise (the day and the flowers had verbs which, while active, were silent), Dickinson says that the Brooks "slam" (an extraordinary verb for a babbling brook, more violent to the ear than her rejected alternative "brag"). As for the birds, there is only one, and his music is not dulcet. To the mourner's ear, there is only assault in his alliterative clamor: "No Black bird bates His Banjo - ". (This was too much for the early editors, who softened it down to "No Black bird bates his jargoning"—from the French *jargonner,* used of birdsong.) One can hear Dickinson's anger at the bird for its forcible Banjo, which is "slam[ming]," like the Brooks, against her sorrow. (The Banjo, sometimes associated with black musicians, or musicians in blackface, may be making the Black bird into an American Black Banjo-Player, the antithesis of the warbling English nightingale.)

And now Dickinson reveals the immeasurable suffering taking place in three tableaux to which these natural presences are massively indifferent: Calvary, an Auto da Fé, and the Day of Judgment. The Black bird wings his noisy way past Calvary without noticing the Cross; the Bee cares nothing for human torture or human damnation. The absence of social imagination in these "dumb creatures" points up the affliction that social sympathy can create in human onlookers—except in those who, like the Black bird and the Bee, can pass unaffected the worldwide, time-out-of mind sufferings of others. The Bee, it is true, can suffer, but only narcissistically, only in the private realm of eros and satiety: he experiences his full capacity for Misery when the Rose, his source of "Balms" (205, 491, 1552, 1635), goes missing. Dickinson certainly knows what it is to suffer loss. But in her poetry, private Pain is often generalized to a larger Pain, as she identifies psychically with those "Freezing persons [who] recollect the Snow - " (*372).

This brief scan of Nature's indifference, at first allowed and then repined against, can be projected onto a wider canvas. Dickinson rarely betrayed her most intense feelings to her family, within whose daily circle she lived; and around her in the house there were servants as well. In her presence, human Brooks "slam[med]," and human talk, like the insistent plinking of a Banjo, continued unabated. The noise afflicted her ear and her mind. Yet one cannot impose quiet on household chatter, and eventually the desire to silence the exterior exchanges of talk rises to resentment of the innocent "slam[ming]" talkers (while one's sanity says they cannot be expected to recognize an undivulged sorrow). Dickinson summed up her relations to the beloved persons around her in an (unsent) poem addressing her friend Kate Anthon. The poem, "I shall not murmur" (1429, J 1410), uses "murmur" in the biblical sense of "protest":

> I shall not murmur if at last
> The ones I loved below
> Permission have to understand
> For what I shunned them so -
> Divulging it would rest my Heart
> But it would ravage theirs -
> Why, Katie, Treason has a Voice -
> But mine - dispels - in Tears.

> [J 620]

# 696

The Tint I cannot take - is best -
The Color too remote
That I could show it in Bazaar -
A Guinea at a sight -

The fine - impalpable Array -
That swaggers on the eye
Like Cleopatra's Company -
Repeated - in the sky -

The Moments of Dominion
That happen on the Soul
And leave it with a Discontent
Too exquisite - to tell -

The eager look - on Landscapes -
As if they just repressed
Some secret - that was pushing
Like Chariots - in the Vest -

The Pleading of the Summer -
That other Prank - of Snow -
That Cushions Mystery with Tulle,
For fear the Squirrels - know.

Their Graspless manners - mock us -
Until the Cheated Eye
Shuts arrogantly - in the Grave -
Another way - to see -

Dickinson's attempt to grasp the "Graspless" import of Nature begins in delight (as Frost said a poem should) but ends in bitterness. Just as music seems to both elude and solicit formulation in words, so Nature keeps offering tints and arrays to the eye that seem to demand that the poet find their verbal counterpart.

Dickinson links her stanzas together by beginning them all (except for the last) with the definite article "The," specifying each noun: "The Tint," "The Color," "The . . . Array," The Moments," "The . . . look," "The Pleading." The Landscape is eager to be known; the Summer pleads for interpretation; the playful Winter asks for the removal of her obscuring veil of snow. Emerson had asserted, in Chapter 4 of *Nature* (1836), that "every natural fact is a symbol of some spiritual fact," and Dickinson hopes to intuit those spiritual facts lying within natural phenomena. When a moment of "Dominion" happens on the poet, she feels she has conquered Nature's concealment—but with the lapsing of that privileged illusion of mastery, that fleeting "Dominion," she falls into an exquisite (and alliterating) "Discontent." The Mystery has not been revealed, the secret has not been transmitted; all remains ungraspable, "remote," "impalpable." What began as pleasure and challenge— "See if you can take this Tint!" says Nature, sending colors that "swagger" into the sky—ends with a "Cheated Eye."

How is Dickinson to track that decline into frustration and render the steps in her journey credible to the reader—who may not, after all, undergo personally the torment of a writer committed to translating the impalpable into adequate language? Dickinson tethers her allegory of a contest between mind and Nature by providing a running undercurrent of allusion to human transactions, bringing the story into the circuit of a reader's experience.

Dickinson's first statement is one of gratitude for poetic incapacity, rejoicing in Nature's capacity to withhold her best secrets: "The Tint I cannot take - is best - ", she alleges, wanting something to be saved from human exploitation. Just as she would find (in *788) that "Publication - is the Auction / Of the Mind of Man - ", so she finds it repellent that Nature's best tints should be reduced to commercialization, to be shown (and presumably sold) in a "Bazaar" catering to the rich (expensive shops in England used to set their prices by the "Guinea"—a pound plus a shilling—instead of in "common" pounds, shillings, and pence).

Soon enough, however, the poet's competitive instincts rouse themselves, and she engages in a struggle with Nature's withholding, desiring for herself a moment of "Dominion," and even feeling she has experienced one or more.

In this competition with Nature, she finds herself in the same position as Whitman in "Song of Myself," who at sunrise encounters "The heav'd challenge from the east that moment over my head / The mocking taunt, See then whether you shall be master!" Whitman wins Dominion at that point by issuing out of himself a rival sunrise, but Dickinson cannot maintain here such moments of Dominion. She has not been the agent of her triumphal intervals: those moments "happen" not to the Soul but "on" the Soul, lighting on the Soul by chance in their free float across the universe. And in the post-ecstatic interval, as the Moments pass on, Dickinson is, like Keats at the departure of the nightingale, forlorn. Such adieux always have an erotic sadness, an "exquisite" Discontent, which demands redress and a longed-for return to ecstasy. But one cannot will such a return. To excuse her yearning for it, Dickinson claims that Nature as intensely desires a response from her as she longs to fuse with it. She is like a magnet toward whom the seasons hurry like lovers, one feeling a pulsing in the breast, another pleading, another whimsically hiding behind "Tulle." But as she approaches them, they retreat, their seductions merely mockery.

Everyone has known such erotic disappointments; and everyone has known, too, what it is to live on the appetitive side of the encounter, being the "eager" one of the pair, having to "repress" a love-secret "that was pushing / Like Chariots - in the Vest - ." That erotic parallel tallies the poet's perception when she sees Nature's secrets "pushing / Like Chariots - ", wanting to be loosed into a fierce race of words. Readers understand the coyness of courtship, as the woman hides her "Mystery" behind the Tulle of the wedding veil. The "Squirrels" who must not penetrate that Mystery are the nature-spirits held off so that the Bride can wait for the Bridegroom.

Cleopatra's swaggering retinue and its brilliant colors have mutated, in the poet's Discontent of lapsed Dominion, into the blank and unfeeling "Prank" of Snow. Dickinson now perceives not eagerness (as in Landscape) or pleading (as in Summer) but rather a premeditated obscuring of essence on the part of a whimsical Nature. Replacing Dickinson's original relief at incapacity (felt while Nature was being lavish) is her resentment of incapacity (felt when Nature is stinting). In the final stanza—which departs from the constant singular "The" to begin with the plural of summary, "Their"—Nature's manifestations, her already-inventoried "manners," are found wanting in their "Graspless" manifestations; and the Eye has no hope of any alteration in Nature's fickleness. The poet's only remaining defense against a perpetual cycle of elation and discontent within Nature is deliberately to exclude herself from it, to return Nature's arrogance with arrogance, and to shut her "Cheated Eye" in the grave. And after that? Is there "Another way - to see - "? Dickinson manifests only a skeptical prospect—she exhibits no certainty that there is "Another way - to see - ." "Eye hath not seen, nor ear heard, neither have entered into the heart of man, the things which God hath prepared for them that love him" (1 Corinthians 2:9, in which Saint Paul is quoting Isaiah 64:4). Dickinson knew such promises of both Testaments, but could not ratify them.

The stanzas of "The Tint I cannot take - is best - " employ meaningful rhymes. What is "remote" is unavailable to "sight"; the "eye" looks to the auroral "sky"; the "Soul," in frustration, cannot "tell"; what is "repressed" is covered by the "Vest"; because of "Snow," even the squirrels cannot "know"; and the cheated "Eye" cannot "see" on this earth, nor perhaps anywhere else.

[J 627]

# 700

The Way I read a Letter's - this -
'Tis first - I lock the Door -
And push it with my fingers - next -
For transport it be sure -

And then I go the furthest off
To counteract a knock -
Then draw my little Letter forth
And slowly pick the lock -

Then - glancing narrow, at the Wall -
And narrow at the floor
For firm Conviction of a Mouse
Not exorcised before -

Peruse how infinite I am
To no one that You - know -
And sigh for lack of Heaven - but not
The Heaven God bestow -

Dickinson has recourse, in her narrative of pleasure, to the same words of unfolding—"then" and "and then"—used for her narrative of torture in "The Heart asks Pleasure - first - " (*588). This structure is an all-purpose ladder, with rungs upon which any number of successive items can be placed. Just as the last request in "The Heart asks" is (for purposes of suspense) the longest, so here, too, the last step of the poet's actions occupies more space than the others. To read her letter from a secret beloved, she does the shortest thing first—"I lock the Door - ". She follows that with a set of three two-line actions: she secures the Letter for transport; she retreats from the Door; she unseals the Letter. After these three preliminary advances, she bursts into a six-line expansion of action, both comic and ecstatic, the high point of the poem. The ecstatic part is to "Peruse" how "infinite" she is to—and then she addresses the reader ("To no one that You - know - ").

Since the poet had begun the poem by making the reader her confidential friend—who is admitted where even the family is refused entrance, behind the locked Door—this sudden coyness repudiates the original apparently confessional nature of the poem. Withholding even the fact of the Letter from those in the rest of the house, Dickinson nonetheless wants an audience for her drama of erotic triumph—but an impersonal audience, not an intimate one. The coyness is bound to annoy the seduced reader; and it is followed by a further closing coyness, which replicates in two lines the same invitation to, and repudiation of, intimacy that had structured the first fourteen lines of the poem.

As she closes, Dickinson offers the reader a revelation: "When I have read the Letter, I sigh for lack of Heaven." Sighing for the lack of Heaven is a well-known convention of hymns and of religious poetry, and the nineteenth-century audience would have expected the usual conclusion, some evocation of the longed-for Heavenly Jerusalem. With a smile and a turned shoulder, the poet refuses both the expected religious conclusion and the comparable secular one (a paradise with her lover) that would replace it. The refusals of intimacy parallel each other. "I," says the poet,

> Peruse how infinite I am
> To no one that You - know -
> And sigh for lack of Heaven - but not
> The Heaven God bestow -

Such evasion of confession would be irritating if the poet herself did not mock her own secrecy: in the sanctuary of her room she must exorcise all worldly intrusion, even that of a Mouse. Only after a preposterous exercise of caution, prolonged by her surveillance of each part of the surface on which she stands, ensuring a "firm Conviction" that not a Mouse lingers, can she begin to "Peruse" her letter. If she cannot even confide in a mute Mouse, how could she possibly confide in her admitted companion? The extension of surveillance (after she has locked the Door) is mimicked by Dickinson's care in continuing the rhyme-sound of the first stanza into the third: "Door . . . sure"; "floor . . . before."

This little drama has been one of Dickinson's most popular poems. Her successive actions are familiar to everyone who has ever had a secret corre-spondence, as is the guilty joy of keeping it from the eyes of "household spies." Yet such a secret begs to be told, and lacking the "best friend" to whom such secrets are confided in adolescence (but sometimes with a part of the secret withheld), Dickinson puts next to her in the room her invisible reader, a hearer quieter and less obtrusive than a Mouse. She will not, however, act out the last two steps: the revelation of a name, and the disclosing of ultimate desire.

The absurd premise of the poem—that the action of reading a letter is as complicated as that of performing a religious ritual, in which every step is rigorously specified—is carried out by the intensification of difficulty. The Letter has already been tucked into a pocket or a bodice, lest anyone see; yet even after *locking* the Door, the poet has to "push" with her "fingers" (the physicality of reference mimicking the action) to check the security of the Letter so that it will withstand the hazardous length of its "transport" from the Door to the "furthest" corner of the room. Instead of merely unsealing the Letter, she has to pick its lock, as though it were a safe for valuables; and that takes yet more time, since she must pick the lock "slowly." And her scru-tinizing glances at the Wall and at the floor have to be separately specified, and separately adverbially qualified (even if both take the same adverb): be-fore she can unfold her letter she has to glance "narrow, at the Wall - / And narrow at the floor." The comic envisaged consequence—if an infidel and unexorcised Mouse were in the sanctuary, she could not possibly Peruse her Letter—parodies the sacred ritual that she is imitating.

And yet, when all of that has been said, pointing out Dickinson's comedy and self-parody, there is one aspect of the poem that both escapes and denies comedy: the perusal of how "infinite" she is to someone else. Dickinson's emotions ran deep, and her attachments to the men she loved (such as her "tutor" Benjamin Newton and her father's friend Otis Lord, together with others more speculative, such as Charles Wadsworth) were life-long. To her, such beloved men were "infinite." She said to Thomas Wentworth Higgin-son that when her "tutor" died, "Death was as much of a Mob as I could master—then" (L 265); and she continued to write to Wadsworth's family (whom she had never met) long after he died. What one needed most when dying, she thought, was to know with Certainty that for one other person, to whom you have been "infinite," all colors would vanish from the rainbow at your death. He would be feeling not merely a sad "Friend's Regret," but something far more annihilating, as she asserts in "The Dying need but little, Dear" (1037, J 1026):

> The Dying need but little, Dear,
> A Glass of Water's all,
> A Flower's unobtrusive Face
> To punctuate the Wall,
>
> A Fan, perhaps, a Friend's Regret
> And Certainty that one
> No color in the Rainbow
> Perceive, when you are gone -

The first things named by Dickinson as "need[ed]" by the dying are small —a glass of water, a flower, a fan; the next is of more consequence—a Friend's Regret; but the third is infinite—the consciousness that you have been life itself to one other. He is not there at the bedside—that Other—but there is no doubt of his fidelity, nor of his sorrow when, at your death, he can perceive in the Rainbow of the covenant no color at all. Perusing a Letter in which the writer calls you his infinite Other could not be, for Dickinson, a matter of comedy. She had staked her emotional life—and much of her poetry—on the possibility of "infinite" relation. Her unobtrusive management of tone from comic self-mockery to erotic intensity in "The Way I read a Letter's - this - " protects the infinity of love from the domestic, and comic, Mouse.

[J 636]

# 706

I cannot live with You -
It would be Life -
And Life is over there -
Behind the Shelf

The Sexton keeps the key to -
Putting up
Our Life - His Porcelain -
Like a Cup -

Discarded of the Housewife -
Quaint - or Broke -
A newer Sevres pleases -
Old Ones crack -

I could not die - with You -
For One must wait
To shut the Other's Gaze down -
You - could not -

And I - Could I stand by
And see You - freeze -
Without my Right of Frost -
Death's privilege?

Nor could I rise - with You -
Because Your Face
Would put out Jesus' -
That New Grace

Glow plain - and foreign
On my homesick eye -
Except that You than He
Shone closer by -

They'd judge Us - How -
For You - served Heaven - You know,
Or sought to -
I could not -

Because You saturated sight -
And I had no more eyes
For sordid excellence
As Paradise

And were You lost, I would be -
Though my name
Rang loudest
On the Heavenly fame -

And were You - saved -
And I - condemned to be
Where You were not
That self - were Hell to me -

So we must meet apart -
You there - I - here -
With just the Door ajar
That Oceans are - and Prayer -
And that White Sustenance -
Despair -

In this heartbreaking poem, the "Quaint - or Broke - " meter (more scanna-
ble, as we shall see, than it seems) takes its measure from the absolute disjunc-
tion of the first two lines: "I cannot live with You - " (the Hell on the left)
and "It would be Life - " (the Heaven on the right). The disjunction, symbol-
izing the poet's intransigent dilemma, occurs several times, although it can be
differently distributed in size. Examples of the two-line variety, besides the
first one, include "I could not die - with You - / For One must wait," "And
were You - saved - / And I - condemned to be," etc. There are four-line dis-
junctions, too:

And I - Could I stand by
And see You - freeze -
Without my Right of Frost -
Death's privilege?

In its last occurrence, the terrible disjunction occupies only one line: "You there - I - here - " (its three dashes emphasizing the separation).

But if the meter is "Quaint - or Broke - " on the page, it sounds suspiciously familiar if one writes out each four-line quatrain as two lines (I regularize the punctuation and ignore initial capitals of even-numbered lines):

I cannot live with You; it would be Life,
And Life is over there behind the Shelf
The Sexton keeps the key to, putting up
Our Life, His Porcelain, [x] like a cup
Discarded of the Housewife, quaint or broke,
A newer Sevres pleases, old ones crack.

In short, save for a missing syllable in line 4 of my distortion above, we could say that Dickinson is writing iambic pentameter, but breaking it up into a three-beat piece and a two-beat piece. This is true for most of the poem, even for its apparently desperately irregular last stanza, which, rewritten, is three lines of pentameter:

So we must meet apart, You there, I here,
With just the Door ajar that Oceans are,
And Prayer and that White Sustenance, Despair.

It would, of course, ruin the emotional turmoil of the poem to read it as pentameters. But the regularity of its irregularity (3-2-3-2) leads us to see that Dickinson has the pentameter somehow in her mind (the extent to which she throughout her life avoided it—the common coin of most English poets from Chaucer on—is in fact extraordinary). She forces us, by her short lines, to pause in the "middle" of a "pentameter." Regular pentameters can and often do pause at that point, but their "breaks" are indicated merely by midline punctuation rather than by the portentous pause of a line-end. I write out a bit of *Hamlet* in Dickinsonian line-breaks to illustrate what Shakespeare would look like in "Dickinsonian" prosody:

> To sleep—perchance to dream—
> Ay, there's the rub—
> For in that sleep—of death
> What dreams may come—
> When we—have shuffled off
> This mortal coil—
> Must give us pause—

So Dickinson, with some memory of the pentameter in her ear, has invented a disjunctive meter to go with her disjunctive theme; and the meter becomes "rocky" often enough that we cannot fully impose a 3-2-3-2 regularity on it:

| | |
|---|---|
| They'd judge Us - How - | 2 |
| For You - served Heaven - You know, | 3 |
| Or sought to - | 1 |
| I could not - | 1 (or 2) |
| | |
| Because You saturated sight - | 4 |
| And I had no more eyes | 3 |
| For sordid excellence | 3 |
| As Paradise | 2 |

These are the irregular spasms of a voice in perilous disequilibrium.

Dickinson's plot is simple: she is forbidden the union she most desires, because her beloved serves Heaven—or at least attempts to—and she is an unbeliever. She is at her most blasphemous in saying that if she and her lover rose to heaven together, his face would "put out"—extinguish—Jesus' countenance. Jesus said, after all, "I am the light of the world" (John 3:12 and 9:5), but Dickinson is having none of that. The "New Grace" of Heaven would seem plain and foreign to her, "Except that You than He / Shone closer by - ". Any alternative that would separate her from her beloved is anathema to her, and, advancing her narrative by counting off the ways she would react to separation, she rises to her apogee of contrast: she could not serve Heaven

> Because You saturated sight -
> And I had no more eyes
> For sordid excellence
> As Paradise

"Sordid"—in its multiplicity of meanings literal and figurative—is Dickinson's most interesting word in the poem. The range of connotations in the *OED* citations is phenomenal. Dickinson's 1844 Webster, after stating the etymology (from Latin *sordes*, "filth"), offers the following meanings, all of them implied by Dickinson:

> Filthy; foul; dirty; gross.
> Vile; base; mean.
> Meanly avaricious; covetous; niggardly.

By comparison to the shining Face of her beloved, Paradise is foul and filthy; by comparison to his excellence, Paradise is base; and because Paradise wants to keep her beloved away from her, it is meanly covetous. In a later poem, "With Pinions of Disdain" (1448, J 1431), Dickinson used "sordid" of the "Flesh," perhaps in a recollection of Hamlet's "O that this too too solid [sullied] flesh would melt"; and of course denigration of the body as sordid is common in Christian rhetoric. But in "I cannot live with You - ", Dickinson will not adopt the Christian position. It is Paradise, not the flesh, that is gross and vile.

"I cannot live with You - " is, in the Dickinsonian scale, a very long poem —fifty lines, its length ensured by its repeated futile strivings against disjunction. In spite of its broken meter contradicting the idea of consciousness as a flowing stream, the stanzas of the poem are logically and even symmetrically grouped. In Dickinson's three-stanza prologue, the Sexton (a lowered figure for God, lowered still further to a "Housewife" a few lines later) has decided that these two lives, her beloved's and her own, are of no worth. He has given no reasons for having discarded them, leaving the poet to barren speculation (perhaps she and her beloved are out of fashion, or broken, or old). As the poem continues after the prologue, Dickinson uses the first three quatrains to explain "I cannot live with You - "; the next two to explain "I could not die - with You - "; and the next two to explain "Nor could I rise - with You - ". In spite of the disjunctive content and the apparently broken meter, the logic of separation keeps the progress steady. The next two stanzas consider the religious distinction between the lovers; and then twin stanzas ponder "And were You lost" and "And were You - saved - ". Within the rigid Procrustean bed of logical exclusion and forbidden conjecture, Dickinson enlivens her poem with quickened phrases. She claims "my Right of Frost"; the Grace of Heaven would "Glow" (she gives it its due) but in a way "plain - and foreign"; [You] "saturated sight"; Paradise offers only "sordid excellence"; and (with a glance back to Milton's Satan) "That self - were Hell to me - ".

How—having come to the end of her ladder of logic—can Dickinson end her poem of separation? To our surprise, she allows her fatally disjoined lovers to "meet" over the distance, while still separating them: "So we must meet apart - ". She and her beloved (like the "Kinsmen" of "I died for Beauty," *448) exist in two distinct rooms. There is a Door ajar between them (as there was a sound-permeable wall between the Kinsmen) but that door is "Oceans" wide. On two different continents, the lovers are still able to "meet" in their love, though apart. What is left to each, in such individual sequestration?

The last "quatrain," if written out regularly, would amount to six lines (or three of pentameter, as I said above). But all the stern logic and symmetry of the preceding quatrains breaks down here. The first two lines are "regular" in syllable count—six and four—but the dashes in line 2 keep us from reading it as a simple dimeter, "You there I here." It could almost be a tetrameter, with each word having an accent of its own, or a trimeter, with "You there" representing one beat:

$$\text{\textasciiacute}\quad\text{\textasciiacute}\quad\text{\textasciiacute}\quad\text{\textasciiacute}$$
You there - I - here -        (tetrameter)

$$\text{\textasciiacute}\quad\text{\textasciiacute}\quad\text{\textasciiacute}$$
You there - I - here -        (trimeter)

"With just the Door ajar" is, again, a regular trimeter, like "So we must meet apart." But no more than "You there - I - here - " can the line "That Oceans are - and Prayer - " be read as a regular iambic trimeter. "[A]nd Prayer - " is an afterthought, and must be read as such: "What will sustain *him* in our separation? Prayer." Nor can the last two lines be amalgamated into one. Dickinson has assigned "Prayer" to her beloved, and then must ask herself, "And what sort of nourishment have *I* found in my prison?" It is meager; it has no taste nor color; it is ever the same; it is a "White Sustenance." Only after she has described it thus is she able to name her daily portion—in a second afterthought—"Despair - ". The lovers remain spiritually disjoined, even in their paradoxical meeting apart, by his Christian hope and her blasphemous Despair, the very qualities that separated them in life. Like "The Heart asks Pleasure - first - " (*588), "I cannot live with You - " is a poem of torture, as, with each alternative logical dilemma enacted in the verse, the lovers are wrenched further and further away from each other.

[J 640]

# 708

They put Us far apart -
As separate as Sea
And Her unsown Peninsula -
We signified "These see" -

They took away our eyes -
They thwarted Us with Guns -
"I see Thee" Each responded straight
Through Telegraphic Signs -

With Dungeons - They devised -
But through their thickest skill -
And their opaquest Adamant -
Our Souls saw - just as well -

They summoned Us to die -
With sweet alacrity
We stood upon our stapled feet -
Condemned - but just - to see -

Permission to recant -
Permission to forget -
We turned our backs upon the Sun
For perjury of that -

Not Either - noticed Death -
Of Paradise - aware -
Each other's Face - was all the Disc
Each other's setting - saw -

Dickinson continues and varies here the separation narrative of "I cannot live with You - " (*706). In this crisis, the lovers, awaiting their execution, are pent in their separate dungeons under the guard of armed torturers. The distance between the lovers, at the beginning, is like that of the Sea from her nearest land, an uninhabited "unsown Peninsula - ". The Peninsula's longing for the Sea, causing it to extend its promontory as far as it can, is frustrated: land and sea remain distinct domains. Yet over that distance, the lovers have "signified" somehow that they can see each other. The torturers put the lovers' eyes out, and threaten them with Guns; the lovers invent "Telegraphic Signs" (some form of coded telepathy) so that they can still respond to each other, with the help of the spiritual eyes of the Soul. The torturers, with their "thickest skill," devise granite walls ("Adamant") for the dungeons, but the lovers can see each other just as intensely when separated by walls as when together. Finally, the order of execution arrives, and the lovers are joyfully reunited at the place of execution. Standing on their shackled feet, they are "Condemned" in the literal sense, but they go to execution with "sweet alacrity," for they are "Condemned" to the supreme gladness of seeing each other once more. Offered mercy by their jailers if they recant or forget their unspecified crime, they disdain the offered "Permissions," turning away from that sort of perjury, a perjury that it would shame the Sun to behold. As they die, fixing their minds on the "Paradise" of their present union, they do not notice Death. Each is a setting Sun, each watching the other set, each beloved Face now a glowing Disc about to sink out of sight in the dark.

The most beautiful lines in the poem occur at the very end, as the repetition of "Each other" individuates yet twins the lovers in their last act. Each "Disc" mirrors the other as they set (a setting eased by the slipping alliteration in "s" at the close). Until that last stanza, devoted to the lovers' Death, the poem has been structured as a tug-of-war between the savage acts of the torturers ("They") and the steadfast response of the lovers ("We," "Each"). "They put Us," but "We signified"; "They took away our eyes - / [and] thwarted Us," but "Each responded"; "They summoned Us," but "We stood"; [They offered] "Permission" to recant or forget, but "We turned our backs." After this struggle, the torturers merely vanish. The last stanza so wholly returns the lovers to each other that they do not even notice (nor does the poem) the person executing them or the manner of their execution.

Because Dickinson so varies the elements of the tug-of-war, it takes a moment to perceive that she emphasizes seeing—whether of the Eyes or of the Soul—in five of the six stanzas, italicizing immediately the importance of the word "see" by rhyming it exactly with "Sea" in stanza 1. (It also appears as the rhyme-word for stanza 4: "alacrity" / "see.") In stanza 2 it appears as "I see Thee"; in stanza 3, "Our Souls saw - "; in stanza 4, the lovers are "Condemned" to "see - "; and in stanza 6, Dickinson gives it pride of place as the very last word of the poem, "saw - ". The stanza in which the lovers do not "see" is the one in which they turn their backs to the Sun to signify their wish *not* to see the perjury of recantation.

Dickinson's myth of the beloved as the Sun had animated the ecstatic poem in which she most fully celebrates his coming: "To My Small Hearth" (703, J 638). She strives to give a name to his presence—fire, light, Sunrise, Sky, Noon, Day:

> To My Small Hearth His fire came -
> And all My House a'glow
> Did fan and rock, with sudden light -
> 'Twas Sunrise - 'twas the Sky -
>
> Impanelled from no Summer brief -
> With limit of Decay -
> 'Twas Noon - without the News of Night -
> Nay, Nature, it was Day -

Dickinson is remembering—and transvaluing—the promise of everlasting day that is made in Revelation 22:5: "And there shall be no night there; and they need no candle, neither light of the sun; for the Lord God giveth them light." When Dickinson's lover appears, she has no further need of her "Small Hearth" in the fire of eternal Day. In "They put Us far apart," we see the tragic end of this triumphant "Day"—tragic because the lovers die, but triumphant in its own right because they have *both* become Suns, even if setting ones. The "sweet alacrity" with which the lovers hasten to execution—because they will be once again in each other's presence—is the most humanly touching phrase in the poem, but the poem has more to do than imply continuing desire. It wants to register the exalted mutual gaze of those setting Discs, geometrically perfect in their symmetrical Faces, sending forth to each other their last signifying sign, their exchange of radiance.

[J 474]

# 729

The Props assist the House
Until the House is built
And then the Props withdraw
And adequate, erect,
The House support itself
And cease to recollect
The Augur and the Carpenter -
Just such a retrospect
Hath the perfected Life -
A Past of Plank and Nail
And slowness - then the scaffolds drop
Affirming it a Soul -

The first five lines of the poem sketch the most important event in the construction of a House: its completion, when the scaffolding surrounding the structure can be dismantled, and the House can stand on its own. At this glorious moment of first independence, the House can "cease to recollect" the Carpenter and his painful tools, the shapers of its earlier existence. To complete her poem, Dickinson borrows (in her own way, as we'll see) the form of Jesus' parables (abstract X is like concrete Y) as in, for instance, the Parable of the Mustard Seed (Matthew 13:31–32): "Another parable put he forth unto them, saying, *The kingdom of heaven is like to a grain of mustard seed,* which a man took, and sowed in his field: Which indeed is the least of all seeds: but when it is grown, it is the greatest among herbs, and becometh a tree, so that the birds of the air come and lodge in the branches thereof" (italics added). Like Jesus' parable, Dickinson's is one of growth, but whereas Jesus here begins with his "spiritual reality"—the kingdom of heaven—and then points out its emblem—the mustard seed evolving into a tree—Dickinson reverses Jesus' order. She begins with her emblem, the evolving House, and only after the emblem is complete does she make the comparison (in parable form) to spiritual growth: "Just such a retrospect / Hath the perfected Life - ".

Poets earlier than Dickinson, considering what a "perfected Life" might be, affirm the worth of suffering in the slow shaping of spiritual perfection. In "Paradise," George Herbert sees God's pruning knife (with the "pruning" imitated in Herbert's pruned spelling) as the means not only to the spiritual "fruit" of the soul but also to its aesthetic "order":

> I blesse thee, Lord, because I GROW
> Among thy trees, which in a ROW
> To thee both fruit and order OW.
>
> . . . . .
>
> When thou dost greater judgements SPARE,
> And with thy knife but prune and PARE,
> Ev'n fruitful trees more fruitfull ARE.

And Keats, in his inspired journal-letter to the George Keatses (February 14–May 3, 1819), says he would call this world "the Vale of Soul-making" rather than "a vale of tears," but he still, like Herbert, points to suffering as the way by which a "blank Intelligence" is schooled into being a Soul: "I say '*Soul making*[,]' Soul as distinguished from an Intelligence. . . . Do you not see how necessary a World of Pains and troubles is to school an Intelligence and make it a soul?"

Dickinson, inheriting the tradition of chastisement from both Christian and secular predecessors, must make something of her own out of it, just as she had reordered the usual structure of parable. Like Herbert, she takes her emblem for suffering from ordinary life: his emblem is a pruning knife shaping fruit trees, hers the Augur (a two-handed instrument for boring holes) and the Nail, which work on the Planks of the House under construction. But she adds another emblem: the "Props" that first (all by themselves) "assist the House" and then "withdraw" or "drop," once they become unnecessary. (The "Props" receive two different names in the two variants of the poem: in Version A they become both "the Scaffold" (line 7) and "the Stagings" (line 11); Version B does not give an alternate name to "the Props" until line 11 presents "the scaffolds.") Just as the mustard seed evolves from its miniature beginning to its flourishing end, so the House gradually passes from instability to strength.

The first five lines of "The Props assist the House" appear to state a truism, and the rather ordinary metaphors ("assist," "withdraw") seem pro forma, rather than flashes of imagination. We arrive in line 5 at the point at which the House can support itself. Then the poem becomes interesting. At last the House can stop remembering its painful past: the Augur burrowing into its entrails, the Carpenter who hammers at its surfaces, the scaffolding that supports the workmen (Webster's definition). Dickinson is an expert in post-traumatic repression, and the House, she says, can now rejoice in its self-sufficiency as it "cease[s] to recollect" its suffering. The external completion, as the House becomes "erect," noticeably rhymes with its internal counterpart, "cease[s] to recollect." The material emblem now demands its parabolic application to the spiritual life. But whereas the House, desiring to forget its suffering, "cease[s] to recollect," the perfected Life voluntarily engages in continual "retrospect" (made to rhyme, as antonym, with "[cease to] recollect" to show how opposite these two actions are—the one of repression and the other of retrospection). The internal rhyme of "perfect[ed]" with "erect" and "recollect" and "retrospect" reminds us that retrospection and recollection are inherent to "perfecting" a Life.

What does the perfected Life see in its unsparing "retrospect"? A Past composed of Plank and Nail and slowness. The Carpenter has disappeared, but his slow, repetitive work—a violent wounding of the planks with hammered Nails, Plank after Plank, Nail after Nail, throughout the preparation of the House—is remembered by the perfected Soul in every detail, in every plank, in every nailing. Suffering unrecalled has nothing to teach; but suffering internalized and remembered "school[s] the Intelligence and makes it a Soul." Dickinson, in the most wounding of her end-words, rhymes "Soul" with "Nail." Without the latter, no former.

In Dickinson's last review of the Soul's spiritual education, the scaffolds "drop," just as earlier they had "withdraw[n]." The "scaffolds" that drop in Version B were "Stagings" in Version A. How does this matter? Dickinson was content, in the later version, to retain the obscure "Props"—vague in reference—until, at the very end, she would reveal the scaffolds. But her original "Stagings" suggests another meaning for "scaffold," found in her 1844 Webster: the platform on which medieval plays were performed, and on which Dickinson stages her Mystery play of the Soul's dramatic suffering.

And her use of "scaffold" as a place of execution in "I sometimes drop it, for a Quick - " (784, J 708) may also have played a subliminal role in "The Props assist the House," since the perfected Soul presumably finishes its work of retrospective perfection only at death.

Some readers have seen an allusion to Calvary in the Carpenter and the Nail and the scaffold. Dickinson compared herself to Jesus elsewhere (naming herself "Queen of Calvary," for instance, in "I dreaded that first Robin, so"; 347, J 348). But the theme, if it is here, is so lightly touched that the poem can stand on its own without it. After all, Jesus' Soul was always perfect, so it is difficult to see him as a work in progress, like the House.

What exactly is happening when the scaffolds "drop"? While most scaffolds are supported by posts or trestles, some are suspended; the props that assist and withdraw seem more like scaffolds with posts supporting them. But the "scaffolds" that "drop" may suggest the death of the body (in "The shepherd's brow," Hopkins, thinking of the articulation of the vertebrae, called man a "scaffold of score brittle bones"). As the poem's variants reveal, Dickinson had some difficulty in deciding on the closing participle. Should she say "pronouncing" or "affirming"? Does the dropping of the scaffolds/stagings "pronounce" or "affirm" the House to be a Soul? "Pronounce" is a verb of authoritative declaration: someone from the outside (God) would have to pronounce the House a Soul, as the minister says, "I pronounce thee man and wife." In "'Twas like a Maelstrom" (*425), Dickinson says that the "Sentence stood - pronounced - " by the torturer. The word "Affirm," however, requires no outside agent: by the mere ability to do without "Props," the House Affirms itself a Soul. The scaffolds seem to know when the work is finished, and "drop" of their own accord as soon as they perceive the presence of the perfected Soul, its suffering completed.

[J 1142]

# 740

On a Columnar Self -
How ample to rely
In Tumult - or Extremity -
How good the Certainty

That Lever cannot pry -
And Wedge cannot divide
Conviction - That Granitic Base -
Though none be on our side -

Suffice Us - for a Crowd -
Ourself - and Rectitude -
And that Assembly - not far off
From furthest Spirit - God -

Dickinson begins with an image of personal rectitude: the Self as a single strict Column with a Granitic Base. A Column is slim, not "ample" like a portico, yet it is amply reliable in questions of conduct. Columns are found in both classical and Christian architecture, and when they occur in groups, they can support a temple or a church. Dickinson, with her inescapable singularity, her unwillingness to form part of any church, finds a single Column her best emblem for the just Self—perhaps with a glancing allusion to the early church's stylites (from Greek *stylos,* "pillar"), ascetics who lived atop pillars.

Her gratitude for such firmness is expressed in the exclamatory syntax of "How ample . . . / How good." To strengthen her praise, she borrows her syntactic rhythm from Jesus, who said (Matthew 6:20) "Lay up for yourselves treasures in heaven, where *neither moth nor rust doth corrupt, and where thieves do not break through nor steal.*" Dickinson: "How good the certainty that *lever cannot pry, and wedge cannot divide,* conviction." (Both sets of italics added.) The "magic Perpendiculars" that Dickinson—in "The Road was lit with Moon and star - " (*1474)—associated with ethical virtue have here taken on, in the classical form of the Column, their customary vertical shape. Yet her Column's base is carved not from Greek marble but from Granite: it is founded in Conviction and cannot be moved. A Lever cannot pry it loose, nor can a Wedge be driven into it to split it. These tools of vandalism bestow imagery on Dickinson's abstractions "Tumult" and "Extremity." She is perhaps thinking of Shakespeare's Sonnet 55:

> When wasteful war shall statues overturn,
> And broils root out the work of masonry,
> Nor Mars his sword nor war's quick fire shall burn
> The living record of your memory.

Shakespeare's "war" and "broils" (brawls, conflicts) become Dickinson's "Tumult" and "Extremity"; but her Columnar Self with its Granitic Base—itself a "work of masonry"—cannot be "rooted out" by Lever or Wedge.

In extremity, with no one on her side, Dickinson stands alone—or so she thinks, until she realizes that when her Columnar Self is joined by Rectitude and the spiritual "Assembly" of the Just, she is a crowd unto herself. (Although she has been speaking in the first-person plural, her use of the singular "Ourself" shows that she is writing as "I," rather than as "We.") What comes closest to God? A Columnar Self with impregnable Conviction, accompanied by Rectitude and the (invisible) Assembly of the Just. She had first thought of being accompanied by a single "Companion," and had spoken of God as the "furthest Good Man" or (borrowing from Bunyan) the "furthest Faithful," but in the final version of the poem she did not domesticate God into a human ethical form. She left only his name, in the last line, as a beacon to all those Just who, "not far off," approach the furthest realm of "Spirit."

The poem is oddly structured, with new "sentences" starting up in unlikely places. Written out, the sentences would look like this:

How ample to rely in Tumult or Extremity on a Columnar Self. (lines 1–3)
How good the certainty that Lever cannot pry and Wedge cannot divide Conviction, that Granitic Base. (lines 4–7)

Though none be on our side, [let it] suffice Us for a Crowd [to have]
    Ourself and Rectitude and that Assembly [located] not far off from
    furthest Spirit, God. (lines 8–12)

These sentences visibly strive against the quatrain divisions of the poem. Yet Dickinson does not run the quatrains together by eliminating the white space between them (as she does elsewhere). Here, by the "mismatch" of statement and stanza, she evokes the strain of remaining "Columnar" while standing alone (except for her invisible Assembly) with rectilinear Rectitude against a visible Crowd armed with Lever and Wedge. The division of sentences into packets of three, four, and five lines suggests the increasing strength of the virtuous soul. It is not accidental that "rely" rhymes with "Certainty," and "Rectitude" with "God." The idea of virtue here seems a legacy of Protestant individualism: one stands alone with one's Convictions and one's chief virtue, Rectitude—and a sense that one belongs to the Assembly of the Just. Although the theme is strict, it is modified by its emblem. It is in the nature of a Column to be an aesthetic (as well as a functional) object; lofty and beautiful, it rises from its Granitic Base, and its foot cannot be moved.

[J 789]

# 747

It's easy to invent a Life -
God does it - every Day -
Creation - but the Gambol
Of His Authority -

It's easy to efface it -
The thrifty Deity
Could scarce afford Eternity
To Spontaneity -

The Perished Patterns murmur -
But His Perturbless Plan
Proceed - inserting Here - a Sun -
There - leaving out a Man -

This coolly satiric image of God-as-unserious-artist, making and effacing as
He pleases, puts Dickinson in sympathy with the "Perished Patterns" who,
like the rebellious Jews in the desert, "murmur" against God's plan: "And the
whole congregation of the children of Israel murmured against Moses and
Aaron in the wilderness" (Exodus 16:2). God enjoys being a spontaneous art-
ist, inventing new things every day. His *élan vital,* his imagination, would be
impeded if He let all His previous creations remain permanently visible be-
fore Him in Eternity. Every day, when God relaxes the rigidity of His "Au-
thority" and desires to "Gambol" (like a lamb), He invents a Life, like a nov-
elist. As easily as He invents, He effaces (with a pun, perhaps, on "face"),
saving the energies of His Spontaneity for another day, thrifty as He is.
("Thrift, thrift, Horatio," says Hamlet sardonically.)

And that is what goes on in Heaven, in Dickinson's dry observation. The
extinguished Patterns—"so various, so beautiful, so new" (Matthew Arnold,
"Dover Beach")—each incarnating what Hopkins (after Duns Scotus) would
name *haecceitas,* an individual "thisness," are still just alive enough to object
to God's cavalier disposal of them. But God is not interested in their protest;

his plan, like the orbit of a planet, cannot be perturbed by mere human complaint. Dickinson, by alliteration, sets the pathos of the two-word phrase "Perished Patterns" squarely against the authority of God's own two-word phrase, "Perturbless Plan," but then gives God the alliterative victory with an extra "p" as his "Perturbless Plan / Proceed." She mocks God's artistic "Spontaneity" as He carelessly inserts a Sun here and leaves out a Man there, treating a Man as if he were an insensible Sun. The ending, cast into present participles, leaves God still inserting this and leaving out that, with no end in sight, indifferent to the results of His gamboling, surrounded by his perishing Patterns left out to die.

In writing a poem about the religious idea of Providence (God's plan for every living creature), Dickinson makes the recognition of her theme inevitable by labeling God's actions with her "p" words. She was troubled constantly by life's falsification of Hamlet's assertion that "there's a special providence in the fall of a sparrow" (*Hamlet,* Act 5, scene 2), itself stemming from Jesus' words in Matthew 10:29: "Are not two sparrows sold for a farthing? And one of them shall not fall on the ground without your Father." The Providence of Dickinson's narcissistic God does not protect lives, but cruelly sports with them. In a poem such as this, Dickinson pitches her satire of God back at the preachers of her childhood, who, while affirming God's omnipotence and providential care, accepted His absolute capacity to allow evil and catastrophe. And, by showing God-the-artist's careless "Spontaneity" in action, she defines, by opposition, her own idea of the artist as precise, intent, and motivated by a love for those "Patterns" created by imagination that are preserved, not jettisoned, after they have taken shape.

[J 724]

# 760

Pain - has an Element of Blank -
It cannot recollect
When it begun - Or if there were
A time when it was not -

It has no Future - but itself -
Its Infinite contain
Its Past - enlightened to perceive
New Periods - Of Pain.

Dickinson had of course encountered the truism that human beings have no
memory of a time before they were born, nor any memory of their earli-
est years. By declaring that her present Pain "cannot recollect / When it be-
gun - Or if there were / A time when it was not - ", she makes Pain cotermi-
nous with life as she has known it. If Pain is there no matter how far back she
looks into the Past, what of the Future? We are not surprised when she fore-
sees that Pain "has no Future - but itself - ". Once Past, Present, and Future are
assimilated to Pain, the work of the poem can really begin. In one of her
twists of grammar, Dickinson turns the adjective "Infinite" into a noun, cre-
ating the atmosphere in which Pain lives: like God, Pain is an "Infinite" and
lives, as he does, in infinitude. The poem becomes Manichean as soon as it
employs the theological word "Infinite" with reference to Pain: Pain is the
dark God engaged in constant strife with the God of Light. Although else-
where Dickinson has been able to see a spiritual purpose in suffering, here
there is no mitigating excuse for its existence. It simply is.

Once one has perceived Pain's "Infinite," one has become "enlightened."
In Dickinson, the word always appears with searing irony—in, for example,
"I measure every Grief I meet" (*550), where those suffering Grief, after en-
during "Centuries of Nerve," are merely "Enlightened to a larger Pain - "; or
"I play at Riches" (856, J 801), where it is "Want" (lack) which "Enlighten[s]"
the deprived. Her contemporary Herman Melville used the word in the same
grim way in "The March into Virginia," describing how ignorant young
Union soldiers, who went off to war as if to a "berrying-party," "Perish, en-

lightened by the volley's glare." Strictly speaking, one can say nothing of an "Infinite": our minds cannot transcend their own finite limits. But Dickinson imagines a spherical Infinite (not unlike the globe of the earth) which contains a continuous periodic Möbius loop of Pain: "Its Infinite contain[s] / Its Past, enlightened to perceive - / New Periods - Of Pain." As elsewhere, Dickinson substitutes, for the "normal" present tense ("contains"), the "unmarked" form "contain" (lacking tense, mood, and number), a type of verb suited to a temporal continuum without end.

The poem begins and ends (as it must, given its theme) with the word "Pain." Inside the Infinite of Pain, the Past—which naïvely believed when it first became sentient that its Pain would end—undergoes an endless "enlightenment" in which it learns that its hopes were vain. Now it knows, in retrospect, how mistaken it was in its first hope of relief, since whatever the Future held, it would be describable only as "New Periods - of Pain." The "rewriting" of the Past by experience, so that one must now judge a past feeling of hope as foolishness, is itself a painful form of self-adjustment.

I have not yet explained why Dickinson begins the poem as she does, with the statement that Pain has "an Element" of Blank. Its other elements are presumably interpretable, but the Blank element refuses to be interrogated. For Dickinson, this aspect of Pain frustrates poetic completeness: the Infinite should contain *all* of the Past, not merely some of it. She extrapolates, of course, back to her first breath when she sums up Pain as having had a Past. But there remains a nagging uncertainty. What was the nature of the earliest period of life now characterized as a "Blank"? It is indescribable—the writer cannot inscribe experience on that Blank. The Infinite, we realize, has a Blank in it too. The aesthetic sphere that should be completely rounded— with the word "Pain" bracketing and thereby completely encircling Past, Present, and Future—is flawed by the "Blank," which stands for the necessary imperfection of human cognition. The poem attempts to conceal its conceptual flaw by beginning and ending with "Pain," rounding out its Infinite—yet we remember the "Blank." Nonetheless, the curling of all tenses into the Infinite is such a cunning display of language that the Manichean power of the poem survives its intrinsically necessary, and aesthetically essential, "Blank."

[J 650]

# 764

My Life had stood - a Loaded Gun -
In Corners - till a Day
The Owner passed - identified -
And carried Me away -

And now We roam in Sovreign Woods -
And now We hunt the Doe -
And every time I speak for Him
The Mountains straight reply -

And do I smile, such cordial light
Upon the Valley glow -
It is as a Vesuvian face
Had let its pleasure through -

And when at Night - Our good Day done -
I guard My Master's Head -
'Tis better than the Eider Duck's
Deep Pillow - to have shared -

To foe of His - I'm deadly foe -
None stir the second time -
On whom I lay a Yellow Eye -
Or an emphatic Thumb -

Though I than He - may longer live
He longer must - than I -
For I have but the power to kill,
Without - the power to die -

This vividly mysterious poem has received much comment, without any consensus as to its interpretation. This is not the place to give a survey of those comments. In brief—some think that Dickinson approves of the gun's actions; others take the opposite view. The idea that Dickinson could write in the first person as a "Loaded Gun" that not only has the power to kill but actually boasts of that power has seemed unacceptable to a few readers; but Dickinson could indeed imply her capacity for mass destruction, as she does here with her "Vesuvian face."

The relation between the Gun and its "Owner" is also a disputed one. All can agree that the Gun by itself has had (although loaded) no agency until carried away by the Owner; before his coming, the Gun had only stood in "Corners," inactive. The Owner asserted his right to carry the Gun away because he "identified" it as his, and since that day the Gun has been happy in its life with its "Master." The narrative of their joint habitual life occupies most of the poem, which describes the activities of Master and Gun, sometimes roaming the Woods, sometimes hunting the Doe. The Gun is able to "speak for" its Master, but can also "smile" of its own accord; by night the Gun does not share the Master's pillow, but guards his head. So far, the narrative at least is understandable and clear. Its import, however, is not. Some ask whether what the Master and Gun do together (hunt and kill) is morally acceptable and is presented as such by Dickinson. Is Dickinson imagining herself into the role of the Master or the role of the Gun—or a symbiotic role, both-as-one?

The last two stanzas of the poem present the more difficult problems. Suddenly the Gun takes on grammatically independent action: it lays a "Yellow Eye" on the Master's foes; it presses an "emphatic Thumb" on its stock as it shoots. It kills only the Master's foes, granted—but the Gun's triumph in its own expert aim is palpable: "None stir the second time - " if the Gun has shot them.

As for the last stanza, it is phrased as a riddle. The Gun may outlive the Master, in terms of natural life, true; but the Gun cannot kill itself, although it has the power to kill others. The Master must, says the Gun, live longer than I because I could not bear to watch his death and be unable to kill myself to accompany him. As Dickinson says in "If any sink" (616, J 358), "Dying - annuls the power to kill - ". The Master's outliving the Gun can be assured only if the Master has the compassion to kill the Gun before he dies himself. We have seen this sentiment before, in "I cannot live with You - " (*706):

> I could not die - with You -
> For One must wait

To shut the Other's Gaze down -
You - could not -

And I - Could I stand by
And see You - freeze -
Without my Right of Frost -
Death's privilege?

It is imperative that lovers die at the same moment; being left behind is too painful. In "I cannot live with You - " Dickinson claims death as her Right and her privilege, but the Gun is impotent in that respect. It is too late for the Gun to return to its wonted "Corners." In spite of its intrinsically long-lived materials, which in the order of things would make it survive the Master's death, the Gun implores that it be allowed to predecease its Master.

There are at least three basic ways of imagining the relation of Gun to Master. The Gun is a prosthetic: it speaks for him; it belongs to him by its very identity; it kills his foes; and the Master is the only one to activate its "Vesuvian" powers. If Dickinson longs for a Master (as in the "Master letters" —those drafts of piteous pleas to an unknown "Master," letters perhaps never mailed; L 187, 233, 248), then one can read Dickinson as the Gun, glad to have been identified and owned, wishing to die before her Master, and depending on him to ensure that she does, since as a Gun of wood and steel she has no independent power to die.

Another way to read the poem would imagine the Gun to be speaking as the socially repressed Id of the Master, embodying his lust to kill harmless Does and exterminate his enemies. It lives in a symbiotic relationship with the Master's Ego, but sympathizes with the Master only in his moments of dealing out death. Its quasi-demonic "Yellow Eye" and "Vesuvian face" identify the Gun as contained Rage, able at any moment to employ its "emphatic Thumb" or erupt over the unsuspecting Valley, killing all within its range.

Or we could read the Master as a male Muse, and the Gun as the poet. Before she was taken up by the Muse and identified by him as a poet, Dickinson had lived a reclusive life in domestic "Corners." But once she began her joint life with the dominating Muse, her powers of expression became unlimited. She could be animated in pursuit of a fleeing insight; she could speak so loudly that the Mountains echoed in response; she could radiate power with her cratered Fire, "smil[ing]" while she awaits her next eruption. Even at night, she is by her Muse's side, a fate better than sexual companionship; and when the Muse directs her, she can loose a bullet (of focused hatred, of satire) that demolishes the foe of art. She does not want to outlive her Muse. He must outlive her because without him she is as good as dead.

Each of these interpretations has a degree of plausibility. Because I believe the actions of the Gun to be symbolic, I cannot join in deploring the hunting of female deer and the killing of foes, as some women readers have done. The poem is not "realistic," and no assaults on helpless female animals are being made in actuality. It is certainly true, however (as some feminist critics, Adrienne Rich among them, have seen), that the poem is about the sudden empowering (by a male Master) of an impacted inner violence always potential in the Gun, which was already "Loaded" before the Master ever came. Those stored-up bullets inside the Gun are rather like the silver "Bulb[s]" inside the Lark (*905):

> Split the Lark - and you'll find the Music -
> Bulb after Bulb, in Silver rolled -
> Scantily dealt to the Summer Morning
> Saved for your Ear, when Lutes be old -

(The cascading notes dealt out by the Lark for her Master are stopped when the Master suspects her of infidelity and, in a "Scarlet Experiment," kills her.)

It seems to me that the formerly powerless impacted violence in "My Life had stood" was stored up inside Dickinson, and when it was released into poetry she recognized it fully, often with vengeful joy, speaking aloud on the page (in sight of the Holyoke Mountains) and exhibiting the Volcanian smile of "Vesuvius at Home" ("Volcanoes be in Sicily"; 1691, J 1705). She describes a Volcano taking satisfaction in his "projects pink," which will devastate surrounding slopes:

> The reticent volcano keeps
> His never slumbering plan;
> Confided are his projects pink
> To no precarious man.
>
> [1776, J 1748]

The Master in "My Life had stood" does confide his "projects pink" to his faithful Gun, which then acts upon them. Acting as ventriloquist to the Muse is one definition of a poetic calling: if the Muse sometimes smiles, one ventriloquizes the smile; if the Muse rages, one awakens one's "Yellow Eye." The traditional idea of dictation by the Muse (Milton, Milosz) puts the poet in a subordinate position comparable to that of the Gun, which but repeats the thoughts of the Muse/Master. They are lifelong companions, and the poet does not want to survive her Muse's commanding voice.

The first and last stanzas of "My Life had stood" employ perfect rhymes: "Day . . . away" in the first, and "I . . . die" at the close. These "calm" rhymes represent the opening nonaction of the unused Gun and the closing nonaction of the later Gun (hoping to be killed before the Master dies). These are the moments of "peace." In the intervening stanzas of fire (from Volcano or Gun), the rhymes are imperfect, so as to keep us from losing the restless energies of the joint life of Inspirer and Inspired, even during a temporary rest at night.

Perhaps no single allegorical meaning can be made to fit the poem perfectly. But if I had to choose, I would see fiery Dickinson and her eroticized Male Muse as Gun and Master, and think of the poem as the depiction of Dickinson's ecstatic and aggressive release of her firepower into the world of expressive language, stunning herself—and, here, others as well—with (as in *348) "Bolts - of Melody!"

[J 754]

# 772

Essential Oils - are wrung -
The Attar from the Rose
Be not expressed by Suns - alone -
It is the gift of Screws -

The General Rose - decay -
But this - in Lady's Drawer
Make Summer - When the Lady lie
In Ceaseless Rosemary -

"There's rosemary, that's for remembrance; pray, Love, remember" (*Hamlet*, Act 4, scene 5). "Essential Oils - are wrung - " is Dickinson's version of the "eternizing" claim of poetry, drawing on two of Shakespeare's sonnets, 5 and 54. Sonnet 5 laments the coming of winter to nature and to youth, but toward the end finds consolation in the preservation of "Beauty's effect" in perfume. Winter has seen "Beauty o'ersnowed and bareness everywhere," but Shakespeare continues with the compensatory close:

> Then were not summer's distillation left
> A liquid prisoner pent in walls of glass,
> Beauty's effect with beauty were bereft,
> Nor it nor no remembrance what it was.
>   But flowers distilled, though they with winter meet,
>   Leese [lose] but their show; their substance still lives sweet.

Shakespeare's figure for the process by which perfume is obtained from flowers is "distillation," and the perfume is a prisoner, pent in a vial. In Sonnet 54, Shakespeare denigrates the "canker roses" that do not yield perfume, and merely "Die to themselves." He continues,

> Sweet roses do not so,
> Of their sweet deaths are sweetest odours made:

And so of you, beauteous and lovely youth,
When that shall vade [depart], my verse distils your truth.

Dickinson, reading these sonnets, agrees that roses yield perfume, but doubts that the process is distillation, the slow extraction of essence by heating, vaporizing, and condensing. Rather, she says—correcting Shakespeare—the making of Attar of roses, and of verse, is not a distillation but a violent pressing until the Essential Oil is forced out from the crushed petals.

This very brief poem intertwines many words that can be assimilated to the single category of "The Beautiful": the Rose, its Attar, Essential Oils, a gift, Suns, Summer, Rosemary, and a Lady. The words that do not belong— and around which all the other words are arrayed—are "wrung," "Screws," and "decay." All three are forceful words that tonally disrupt the atmosphere of the Beautiful in the poem (as Shakespeare's liquid "distillation" does not). The chronological sequence of the poem is: natural growth and beauty ("Sun," "Summer," "Rose," natural "Attar"); then violent extraction ("wrung" and "Screws") and then the concentrated product of that violence ("Essential Oils"). In life, there is a forked outcome, bad and good—either "decay" (if the Rose dies naturally) or a memorial perfume of "Summer" (if the Rose has been "wrung"); or, literalized, the death of the "Lady" and then the scent of Roses remaining in the Lady's Drawer after her death. The pressing of the Rose happens in the center of the first stanza, and Dickinson brackets that process with the end-words "wrung" in line 1 and "Screws" in line 4. Between the words of torture we have the natural expressing of the Attar by the summer Suns, so that the atmosphere around the rose garden is permeated with the scent of roses. To achieve a posthumous permanence for the Attar, however, expression of scent by natural means must be intensified by the Rose's being "wrung" and compressed between plates tightened by "Screws." Dickinson's gentle touch in allowing for the natural diffusion of the Rose's perfume by the Sun emphasizes the violence of human intervention by mechanical wringing and Screws.

The figure of bracketing or "boxing in" (seen in the first stanza) is employed in the second stanza as well, where death—symbolized both by natural "decay" and by the residual perfume of "ceaseless Rosemary"—compresses, within those two brackets, the memorial Summer of perfume in the Lady's Drawer. The impermanent "General Rose" (line 5) is similarly paired with the dead Lady (line 8), brackets again compressing the "Essential Oils" in the Lady's Drawer. The General Rose (which decays) matches the General Lady (who dies).

Dickinson begins her poem in the present tense of eternal truth: "Essential Oils - are wrung - ." But with "The Attar from the Rose" she changes her marked "are" to the unmarked "Be," aligning it with her later statements, all (except "It is the gift") given unmarked verbs—"decay," "make," and "lie"—creating axioms of universal application, no matter whether we speak of past, present, or future. We may ask why the Lady has to die. Couldn't the memorial Summer, in the form of perfume, exist in the Lady's Drawer while she was still living? As we have seen, one reason for her death was to install, in the second stanza, two brackets comparable to the "wrung" and "Screws" of the first stanza. The other reason was to vitiate the hope that just as the perfume in the Drawer kept Summer alive, so embalming spices in the coffin could preserve the Lady. Dickinson's last lines originally said that the perfume can "Make Summer - When the Lady lie / In Spiceless Sepulchre - ". In that formulation, the poet suggests that perfume and art alike are helpless against mortality: in the Sepulchre, there are no "spices" sweetening decay. This cruelty to a human being—equating her with a decaying Rose—gave Dickinson pause. Yes, the Lady is in her grave, but she is not simply a decaying body. She is also a person held in grieving memory. Ophelia comes to the rescue of the Lady, and the Lady is allowed to lie not in a sepulchre but in the ceaseless Rosemary-remembrance of others. The symbolic herb-of-memory becomes no longer a thing, but rather a "Ceaseless" temporal medium.

Both perfume and art, then, are the gift of Screws; the heart, wrung by suffering, yields an Essential Oil of emotion that would never have come into being through ordinary Suns and the mild fragrance they elicit. And the "Screws" are the exigencies of poetry—the Procrustean bed of the Shakespearean sonnet, for example. The need to make rhythm, meter, figuration, emotion, and intellection coincide in a single pattern works "Screws" of its own on language.

[J 675]

# 778

Four Trees - upon a solitary Acre -
Without Design
Or Order, or Apparent Action -
Maintain -

The Sun - upon a Morning meets them -
The Wind -
No nearer Neighbor - have they -
But God -

The Acre gives them - Place -
They - Him - Attention of Passer by -
Of Shadow, or of Squirrel, haply -
Or Boy -

What Deed is Theirs unto the General Nature -
What Plan
They severally - retard - or further -
Unknown -

This poem on apparent Chance (in the features and random distribution of four trees), and apparent Uselessness (of the trees to the world at large), is a meditation on nature as a permanent withholder of meaning. Dickinson sees a solitary single-acre field; on it are four trees. They were not planted by a human being, since they show no Order; nor is a house nearby which might imply the presence of human beings who could benefit from their shade or enjoy their seasonal change. Dickinson asks: What do the Trees do in the world? They exhibit no describable Action. They merely "Maintain" (a transitive verb used intransitively); they maintain themselves in place. Who are their daily visitors? The Sun and the Wind. Their nearest Neighbor, in this solitary place, is God, who remains invisible and never, unlike the Sun and the Wind, visits them.

The poet, on further reflection, perceives one small usefulness of the

Trees: they establish a reciprocity of place and focus. The Acre gives the Trees a context; the Trees give the Acre a focus. Together, Acre and Trees constitute a composition. And just as painters place a group, or a building, or a tree, as a focus organizing the landscape, so the Acre, if it is to attract attention, needs something for the eye to fix on. Even though the Trees have no "Apparent Action," they do serve as a change from an unplanted terrain, so that the Sun has someone to "meet" in the Morning, as does the Wind—which would otherwise sweep over the passive grassy Acre unmet by any resistance.

Whose attention is drawn to the Acre by the Trees? We are reassured when Dickinson mentions a "Passer by," but no householder, or workman, or schoolteacher—no "grownup"—notices the Acre on account of the Trees. Dickinson's "Passer-by" might, she says, be an insubstantial Shadow (after the Sun "meets" the Trees); or it might be a Squirrel noticing the Acre because of the Trees' potential harboring of nuts; or perhaps the Acre catches the eye of a Boy looking for trees to climb. These unassorted categories of "Passer by"—Shadow, Squirrel, Boy—are all unimportant in the larger world. Despite the mutually beneficial visual symbiosis of Acre and Trees, it is "Unknown" (Dickinson reflects) what the Trees could be said to do that is of general benefit. And their random appearance and placement give no hint of any Plan that they could be thought either to retard or to further.

Because nature had been traditionally read as a book of symbols, which, interpreted, would shed light on God's Providence (his "Plan" for all living beings, beginning with the Creation), Dickinson, seeing no such Plan deducible from her Acre and its Trees, remains skeptical. She refuses to intimate that the Trees have any symbolic function, that they carry a message. Looking for the climax of her first list—that the trees exist "Without Design / Or Order, or . . ."—she first thinks of "signal"; but she has no right to expect a "signal" any more than—her second notion—a "notice." "Signal" and "notice" are words implying meaningful semantic freight. "Action" has no coded message within it, as a signal or a notice would. Since Trees don't "act"—in the normal use of the word, which involves motion or transmission by gesture—the poet's denial of Action to the Trees is baffling at first. What Action could be expected of trees?

Perhaps, if planted by men, they would have, along with Design and Order, an "Action." George Herbert, wishing that God would give him some work to do, laments, in "Affliction" (I), that he is not a tree, which at least does some work in the world:

> I read, and sigh, and wish I were a tree;
>    For sure then I should grow
> To fruit or shade: at least some bird would trust
> Her household to me, and I should be just.

Dickinson is careful not to put a house near her trees. They were not planted for a purpose, such as to give fruit or shade, and no nesting bird is introduced into the poem. It's entirely possible that Dickinson read Herbert's poem, and thought (with her usual habit of interrogating the truth of what she read): "But what if the tree did *not* grow to fruit or shade, and there *were* no tree-nesting birds at hand? Of what use would the tree be then?" She has relented to the extent of giving the Trees their function of visual reciprocity with the Acre. But what of more general good? She first wrote, when thinking of a possible Action for the Trees, that they "Do reign," but that verb would imply that someone had crowned them the kings of the Acre, and she wants no such conferral from a putative Power outside. So she substitutes her neutral "Maintain." All the Trees do is stand. And "Maintain" cannot have an object, because it can't be said that they maintain "Design" or "Order"—or anything but themselves.

If there were a divine "Plan," everything would have some function within that Plan—would either aid it or impede it. Do the Trees do either? Who can say? In deciding on the words she will choose for the opposite concepts "aid" and "impede," Dickinson first writes "promote" and "hinder." But can nonsentient Trees be said to "promote" or "hinder" anything? These are words generally associated with human action. Taking thought, Dickinson comes up with two words that are ostentatiously neutral: the Trees, one by one ("severally"), seem not to "retard" or "further" any visible Plan. Almost anything—money, time, weeds, an institution—can "retard" or "further" an enterprise. The words do not immediately summon up human effort, as "promote" and "hinder" do.

Dickinson's complex of Acre and Trees is not put forward as an aesthetic whole that might attract, and delight, a painter's eye. It is simply a piece of the world. If it disappeared, it would not be missed; Shadow and Squirrel and Boy have other trees to look at. Dickinson austerely refuses to allegorize the site as comparable to a work of art (such as her poetry), or as a place someone might love and be attached to (such as a domestic garden). Unlike the little piece of landscape outside her window that she watches so intently in "The Angle of a Landscape" (*578), this landscape doesn't change with the seasons.

To present the world devoid of any "meaning" but its own self-maintenance is a stubborn undertaking for a poem, and requires a metric suitable to its severity. Dickinson alternates long lines with short ones in each quatrain. The long ones can have five or four or three beats; the short ones have one or two beats. (The exception to this rule arrives in stanza 3, in which the central and important symbiosis of Acre and Trees is enacted syntactically in lines 1 and 2 without respect to meter.) The system of Long/Short/Long/Short is one that brings us up sharply at the short lines, many of which, especially in the close, bear the significant weight of a punch line: "Maintain - "; "But God - "; Or Boy - "; and, in the last stanza, both "What Plan" and its lethal rhyme, "Unknown - ".

The extraordinary thing about this poem of deliberate withholding of significance—physical, moral, religious, erotic, aesthetic—is how unforgettable it is. It is as though readers had been waiting to be told that the physical world is just that—a physical world. In the poem's stern phrases, Dickinson welcomes the absence of transcendental intelligibility.

[ J 742 ]

# 782

Renunciation - is a piercing Virtue -
The letting go
A Presence - for an Expectation -
Not now -
The putting out of Eyes -
Just Sunrise -
Lest Day -
Day's Great Progenitor -
Outvie
Renunciation - is the Choosing
Against itself -
Itself to justify
Unto itself -
When larger function -
Make that appear -
Smaller - that Covered Vision - Here -

"Renunciation" belongs to the group of poems in which Dickinson takes it upon herself to define something—often, as here, an abstraction, and often, as here, a word so much in common use that everybody knows what it means. What Dickinson does to be original here is to write two poems, each beginning "Renunciation - is," and make them into one double poem. The first "poem," "Renunciation - is a piercing Virtue - ", is a poem of generalization: this is what Renunciation is like for everyone. The second, "Renunciation - is the Choosing," is a very painful narration of Renunciation in one particular soul (ungendered as the all-purpose pronoun, "itself").

The poem draws our interest in its draft alterations, because it directly contradicts itself in the last line's crucial modifier for human "Vision." What can we say about our Vision "Here" on earth, and from what vantage point do we say it? Originally, Dickinson had characterized our Vision Here as "flooded"—one so great it overwhelms us. Next she tried "sated," thinking of it as a Vision that has led to total fulfillment ("my cup runneth over"). But she ends by calling our Vision Here a "Covered" one, making a pun on the word "Apocalypse" (which means "the Uncovering"), when all shall be seen in its true appearance. No matter how satisfying our earthly Vision, it must be judged—by comparison to what is imagined of the revelatory Apocalypse—as "Covered." Dickinson's final choice of adjective sets limits to the human mind. Our intellect cannot know whether there is such a thing as the uncovered Vision to which Revelation testifies—but if there is, what we can see on earth, with our partial and limited knowledge, must be described as "Covered." The complete reversal in meaning from "flooded" to "Covered" changes the poem entirely, and offers at least a potential reward at the Last Day for the person's excruciating "Renunciation." (It is interesting that Dickinson wants the *sound* of the new word to approximate as closely as possible to "flooded." In that single respect, the rounder "covered" is preferable to the more angular "sated.")

The double poem is constructed on gerunds (verbal nouns). Renunciation here is "The letting go," "The putting out," "the Choosing." Renunciation is not "to let go" or "letting go." "To let go" could be a single act; so could "letting go." "*The* letting go" creates an overarching untensed Idea that can be chosen over and over again (e.g., "*The electing* of state officials is under perpetual reform"). Renunciation—as expressed by Dickinson's gerunds—may be a single grand act (as it seems to be in the first of the two "poems"), or it may be a daily action (as it seems to be in the second "poem").

In the first "poem," the choice is worded in two ways: Renunciation is the forgoing of a Presence (which one passionately values) for an Expectation (not yet fulfilled). As if we did not understand what that could mean, Dickinson, like a preacher, gives an example—but where a preacher's example would be designedly "reasonable," Dickinson's is shocking: "As if, just when the Sun was about to rise, you put out your eyes." Given the horror of "putting out" one's eyes (with its reminiscence of the torture of Gloucester in *King Lear*), why would one forbid one's eyes the ravishment of Sunrise? Because of the danger that a beautiful human "Day," to one's human eyes, might outshine God, "Day's Great Progenitor." In choosing the human Day over its Creator, you might forfeit your soul. After all, God's first utterance in Genesis is "Let there be light"; the very first thing created, in the universe of which

He was the Great Progenitor, was "Day." You would incur His wrath in preferring his Creation over Him.

This first of Dickinson's two "poems" has recommended—as a virtue—the performance of horrifying violence on oneself in a preemptive propitiation of God's potential wrath. Something about this scenario has not reached far enough into what the poet feels Renunciation to be, and so she begins her poem all over again. This reprise, although it opens in exactly the same way as the first—the phrase "Renunciation - is," followed by a gerund—leaves out God the Creator and one's duty to prefer Him to his Creations. Instead, it focuses on one's duty to one's own values. "Renunciation - is the Choosing / Against itself - ". We have to assume some agent of the Choosing, such as "the Soul's Choosing / Against herself"—but that would be to restrict the meaning of the sentence unduly. As John Henry Newman said of choice, in considering the nature of assent, "The whole man moves." What moves is not some portion of "the man"; rather, his sensibility, mind, soul, and temperament all move together, and Dickinson represents that "whole man" by a single ungendered and undivided "itself."

Why does "it" choose "Against itself"? So as to be able to keep its self-respect, to justify itself "Unto itself." And why does it have to make this self-denying choice, forbidding itself love, or fame, or whatever flooding or satiation is on offer in this life? Because it has perceived some higher ideal of satisfaction to which it has—with its whole self—vowed allegiance. Compared to that higher ideal, which animates the whole self, choices which would satisfy one portion of the self—one's eroticism, or one's vanity, or one's pride—must be refused. Settling for the "Covered Vision - Here - " would shame the self, in view of that "larger function" which it has glimpsed, but to which no earthly choice seems to correspond.

When we have read Dickinson's two "poems," we are almost forced to choose between them. The first version is the Renunciation taught by religion, which measures all values as seen by God. But the second version of Renunciation, correcting the first, is the critical virtue that Dickinson taught herself.

[ J 745]

# 788

Publication - is the Auction
Of the Mind of Man -
Poverty - be justifying
For so foul a thing

Possibly - but We - would rather
From Our Garret go
White - unto the White Creator -
Than invest - Our Snow -

Thought belong to Him who gave it -
Then - to Him Who bear
Its Corporeal illustration - sell
The Royal Air -

In the Parcel - Be the Merchant
Of the Heavenly Grace -
But reduce no Human Spirit
To Disgrace of Price -

Dickinson seems to allow, in this poem, no *tertium quid* between silence and commercial publication—yet her own practice fell between these two poles. There are, she says, two people in whom Thought may be found: in Him who gave it and in Him who bears its "Corporeal illustration." The Giver is unseen and unknown; the one who bears the Corporeal form of thought will (apparently) not publish it. Yet Dickinson characterizes that second person as the one who bears the "illustration" of thought in material form. "Illustration" is not generally thought of as something that remains unspoken and unseen; it is an explanation, a picture. Certainly, Dickinson had every right to conceive of her poetry as bearing "Corporeal illustration" of Thought. As long as she kept its circulation private in letters to friends, the Corporeal illustration would not be auctioned off to the highest bidder in the marketplace.

As she often does, Dickinson anticipates an implied objection: Could not poverty justify the writer in selling his work? "Possibly - ", she answers; but by calling publication "so foul a thing," she contaminates even the necessary selling of work for survival. Opposing her own practice to commercial publication, she makes a virtue of compositional Whiteness: she (wearing White) would rather go to her Creator (White in purity) than "invest" her white Thought (unpolluted Snow) for commercial profit. By introducing financial speculation (investment) into her description of trade publication, she adds—to the sin of accepting a flat price for one's work—the sin of self-interested hope of multiplied dividends.

Better, she sardonically observes, to "sell / The Royal Air - / In the Parcel - " or to "Be the Merchant / Of the Heavenly Grace - " than to reduce the "Human Spirit / To Disgrace of Price - ". Nature gives Air freely away to all; God bestows Grace freely on every penitent; so the Thought of the Human Spirit should be offered free to others. Grace, not Dis-grace, should be the mode of diffusion of Thought. It should flow from Him who gave it to Him who bears its illustration and from Him to others.

Dickinson's choice of words becomes symbolic chiefly in her emphasis on "White": she seems to equate it with virginity, sinlessness, and a blank page. A woman might be thought to invest her "Snow" in committing herself to marriage, but in that sense Dickinson, secluded in her artist's "Garret," is still "White"; the Creator, incapable of sin, is "White"; and the unpublished page is "White"—unblemished by mechanically produced print. The pristine nature of the entire passage of Thought from Creator to Poet, from Poet to others, is a species of *marriage blanc,* unconsummated in any earthly sense, managed in the pure sphere of Thought given, received, and distributed.

The thought of the poem is conspicuously managed so that it spills over the white space between stanzas 1 and 2, and again over the white space between stanzas 3 and 4. In stanza 1 Dickinson seems to say, "Poverty [may] justify so foul a thing"—but she then ironizes that statement with the spillover "Possibly - ". Again, in the third stanza, the description of the nonpublishing writer is suddenly cut off partway through line 3, where Dickinson begins a series of mock commands with "sell." Sell "The Royal Air - " would do very well to end the stanza, but in a spillover resembling that of line 5, Dickinson adds, after the white space, "In the Parcel - " to insist on the mercantile nature of the transaction. Although she does not say so explicitly, the "Merchant" of "the Heavenly Grace" is the preacher who extorts money from his congregation. The Seller of the Air is a swindler; the Merchant of Grace is a huckster. "Be a swindler, be a huckster, sell air, sell grace, but do not set a price on the Human Spirit." There is perhaps a Shakespearean cadence hiding here: "Banish Bardolph, banish Poins, but for sweet Jack Falstaff . . . banish not him" (*Henry IV, Part I,* Act 2, scene 4). The purpose of the spillovers is to mimic impulsivity: the second thought jumps to mind as Dickinson inserts line 5's "Possibly - ", and the sardonic critique leaps to the lips in lines 11–13. The rhyming of "Heavenly Grace" with "Disgrace of Price" sets the antitheses of the poem in sharp relief.

Dickinson did write, in her second letter to Thomas Wentworth Higginson, "If Fame belonged to me, I could not escape her" (a remark presuming eventual publication), but she ultimately gave up hope of an audience among the public, trusting to her form of private dissemination. Publication (as she somewhat misleadingly told Higginson) was as foreign to her "as Firmament to Fin" (L 265). Nonetheless, when she first wrote to Higginson, her letter was stimulated by an *Atlantic Monthly* article of his addressed to a "Young Contributor"—and she perhaps saw a future version of herself in that phrase.

[J 709]

# 790

Growth of Man - like Growth of Nature -
Gravitates within -
Atmosphere, and Sun endorse it -
But it stir - alone -

Each - its difficult Ideal
Must achieve - Itself -
Through the solitary prowess
Of a Silent Life -

Effort - is the sole condition -
Patience of Itself -
Patience of opposing forces -
And intact Belief -

Looking on - is the Department
Of its Audience -
But Transaction - is assisted
By no Countenance -

"Lord, lift thou up the light of thy countenance upon us," implores the Psalm-
ist (4:6). "Transaction - is assisted / By no Countenance - ", retorts Dickinson
in this poem about inner growth, unassisted by God but directed toward a
"difficult Ideal." Just as a fruit gradually swells because of the biological prin-
ciple of growth acting within, so inner growth, its "stir," its self-enlargement,
although "endorse[d]" (looked on benignly and vouched for) by air and Sun,
gravitates inward, and is accomplished by the self alone. Having begun with
the concept of "Man" to tell us she is referring to human beings, Dickinson
resolutely shifts to her ungendered pronoun "it," asserting that spiritual
growth is equally open to both sexes. The two qualities required for that
growth seem contradictory: "prowess" is a quality of active heroes, "Patience"
(twice) a quality of sufferers. (Dickinson makes "prowess" and "Patience" al-
literate to show us that they are linked.) In this alliance, she is both agreeing

with and contradicting Milton, who explains, in *Paradise Lost* (Book IX, lines 29–33), that hitherto the only undertaking considered appropriate for heroic verse was "to dissect / With long and tedious havoc fabled knights / In battles feigned; the better fortitude / Of patience and heroic martyrdom / Unsung." Dickinson will not relinquish "prowess" in her account of the soul's struggle, but she adopts as well Milton's "better fortitude" of Patience.

We are prompted to ask: What sort of "prowess"? What sort of "Patience"? "Prowess" is etymologically related to "pride," and implies honor and valor in combat. In the ascent toward its "difficult Ideal," the soul must summon up courage sufficient to face discouragement and hostility. To each soul belongs its own Ideal; and having discerned that aim, the soul needs valor in pursuing the Ideal all by itself, in solitude and silence. Why is the Life of growth silent? The examples in Christian spiritual history of a "Silent Life" of growth were the anchorites living alone in the desert, and Dickinson here aligns herself with them (rather than with the evangelists, preachers, and hagiographers who diffuse popular versions of spirituality).

To the bravery and splendor of "prowess" Dickinson adds Patience, with its attendant "Effort" and "intact Belief." The first thing that human Patience has to be patient about (Dickinson says with insight and correctness) is the human self; "Effort" is marked always by failure and slippage. And it is not only "prowess" that is needed against "opposing forces" (left unspecified, as was the difficult Ideal, since these will vary in each life). One needs patience to endure those forces' untiring determination to undermine the spiritual life by attrition. If one has acquired prowess and Patience, and has maintained the ascent toward the Ideal, one still needs Belief as motivation for the Effort (again, the Belief is unspecified, because different sorts of Belief are required for different difficult Ideals). But the Belief must still be "intact"— not shattered, crippled, or weak. After all the reiterated assaults of the opposing forces, one's Belief might well be in shreds. But as if Belief were a *sine qua non* that had to be protected from all vicissitudes, Dickinson places it in the climactic position in her instructions for the pursuit of a spiritual life.

Dickinson has emphasized the solitude, silence, and difficulty of the spiritual life to such an extent that in almost every line she has placed a word of inner loneliness and trial: "within," "alone," "Each," "difficult," "Itself," "solitary," "Silent," "Effort," "Patience." The Ideal is never reached; growth is never complete. We are surprised to discover that there are onlookers to this spiritual progress, an "Audience" to its drama—but the Dickinsonian script allows no help from anyone in that audience. The "Transaction" of growth is carried out alone, "assisted / By no Countenance." Even Jesus was "assisted" in his Passion by Simon of Cyrene and Veronica; but in this New England version of the Passion, the soul must walk alone, as others stand by (even if in admiration). By "Transaction" with the Ideal, Dickinson means what a Christian poem would name "Salvation." But by repudiating the help of God's Countenance, Dickinson creates a resolutely secular picture of the self's struggle toward perfection.

This poem is a didactic account, from the "outside," so to speak, of how spiritual growth takes place. As in so many cases (for example, *782, "Renunciation - is"), Dickinson matches the didactic definition with the same process as seen from the inside, by the spiritual pilgrim in the act of rising toward an ideal. "Growth of Man" is paralleled in this way by "The Road was lit with Moon and star - " (*1474). Although in "Growth of Man," only Sun and Atmosphere "endorse" the spiritual growth, in "The Road," a more inward poem, the poet descries, if not direct "assistance," a fellow seeker who "endorses" the Ideal. On the road she sees:

> A traveller on a Hill -
> To magic Perpendiculars
> Ascending, though terrene -
> Unknown his shimmering ultimate -
> But he indorsed the sheen -

Here, the visual perception of a "shimmering ultimate" and its exalted "sheen" replaces the abstract "difficult Ideal" of "Growth of Man - ", as we see a traveler intent on his vertical ascent to an ethical absolute—one not divine, but "magic."

[J 750]

# 796

The Wind begun to rock the Grass
With threatening Tunes and low -
He threw a Menace at the Earth -
Another, at the Sky -
The Leaves unhooked themselves from Trees
And started all abroad -
The Dust did scoop itself like Hands
And throw away the Road -
The Wagons quickened on the street
The Thunder hurried slow -
The Lightning showed a yellow Beak
And then a livid Claw -
The Birds put up the Bars to Nests -
The Cattle clung to Barns -
Then came one Drop of Giant Rain
And then as if the Hands
That held the Dams, had parted hold,
The Waters wrecked the Sky,
But overlooked My Father's House -
Just quartering a Tree -

Franklin's three-volume edition spends five pages on the five variant drafts of this storm-song. I will mention a few of Dickinson's brilliant revisions below, but I begin with some elementary facts about this ballad. It is built on the definite article—"The"—followed by a host of nouns making up a list of actors. The Wind began to do this, The Leaves did that, and then, in turn, The Dust, The Wagons, The Thunder, The Lightning, The Birds, The Cattle, The Hands, and The Waters added their contributions to the scene. Each "The" is a pointing device, a "deictic." The alternatives for the poet would have been plurals (Wagons quickened), or a general reference (Thunder threatened), but those choices would have eliminated the gestural element—

"Look! The Wind is doing this, the Birds are doing that!"—which Dickinson uses so successfully. The attached unusual verbs personify the actors, generating a series of active and excited motions. A clause such as "The Wind begun to rock the Grass / With . . . Tunes" is (aside from the poet's common use of "begun" for "began") already deviant, with "rock" suggesting a cradle, and "Tunes" a lullaby, but this lullaby is "threatening": the Wind is not a reassuring mother, but an unnatural father ("He" in line 3).

Most of the following verbs are also linguistically deviant in some fashion. "He threw a Menace" links a physical act to an abstract assault; the reflexive verb in "The Leaves unhooked themselves" (in lieu of "the Leaves fell") shows them as active in their own displacement (whereas the Wind is the true agent); "The Dust did scoop itself like Hands" makes the same reflexive move (although the Wind is really what is disturbing the Road); and just as the Wind "threw" a Menace, so the Dust can "throw away" the Road (the verb linking it visibly to the Wind); "The Wagons quickened" displaces to the Wagons the act of their drivers; "The Thunder hurried slow" matches a verb and adverb rarely joined before (but see "Deliberate speed, majestic instancy" in Francis Thompson's "The Hound of Heaven"); "The Birds put up the Bars" is an impossible act for birds; Cattle do not "cling" to Barns; Hands have never "held" Dams; Waters do not "wreck" the Sky. Each of these metaphorical phrasings needs to be investigated.

Since Dickinson's figures of speech turn all of these entities, from the Wind on, into human beings, her whole account could be read as an example of human disaster—as an epoch when rulers menace or threaten, when fleeing inhabitants quicken their pace, when people tear themselves away (like the leaves) from their domiciles, when a bomb wrecks a house. When Nature begins to act like Man, and scoops up and throws away the very roadways (as happens in battle, or in scorched-earth policies); when Hands that previously held back catastrophe let go and allow the flood of disaster; when Menace approaches with slow hurry, or hurried slowness (in either case not less horrible)—then Chaos is come again.

Dickinson had originally begun the poem far more tamely: "The Wind begun to knead the Grass - / As Women do a Dough - ". Kneading Dough would not terrify; and it is imaginatively inconsistent to imagine the Wind as Women and, four words later, refer to it with the masculine pronoun "He."

An even more significant revision occurs in the most lurid moment of the storm, first phrased as:

> The Lightning showed a yellow Head -
> And then a livid Toe -

Since neither Head nor Toe is an instrument of attack, Dickinson revises them into the instruments of a savage and giant predator:

> The Lightning showed a yellow Beak
> And then a livid Claw -

A bird does not have claws; it has talons. But Dickinson may be remembering *In Memoriam*, with Tennyson's grim view of Nature as "red in tooth and claw."

At our first reading, Dickinson's list of storm-actors may seem almost random, but as the picture it stimulates creates itself, we see that the poet's language leaps back and forth from sky to earth and back again, becoming itself the livid forked lightning reaching from the thunder above to the plain below. The alternating sequence of low to high, high to low, is heralded in the verbally parallel lines 3–4 (third version), as the Wind "threw a Menace at the Earth - / A Menace at the Sky - " (line 4 was finally revised to "Another, at the Sky - "). The Wind (which is intermediate between earth and sky) first rocks Grass (earth), then menaces Earth and Sky equally; Leaves (high) fall and Dust (low) disturbs the Road; Wagons (earth) quicken and Thunder (sky) hurries; Lightning (sky) shows its power, and Birds (on earth, here) bar their Nests; Cattle (earth) cling to Barns, and Rain (sky) drops; Hands (in the sky) let go of Dams (earth); and Waters (sky) make wreckage in Amherst (earth). The rapid "rock[ing]" back and forth, high and low, is responsible for the constant disturbing of our attempt to visualize Dickinson's scenes. Our eyes, flashing up and down as they follow hers, become uneasy.

The poet announces that the storm miraculously "overlooked," in its fury, the family house—phrased not as "my" house or "our" house, but as a patriarchal possession ("My Father's House"). The storm then departed, after

"Just"—Just!—"quartering a Tree." Not merely "striking" or even "halving," but "quartering." And Dickinson, after writing a whole poem in the past tense, leaves us with a present participle: not "But overlooked My Father's House - / [And quartered - just] a Tree - ", but "quartering" a Tree. The storm thus remains active to the end. Just as other aspects of the storm had been anthropologized into forms of destructive human behavior, so "quartering" has overtones of execution by hanging, drawing, and "quartering," in which a human being, after being hanged, but while still alive, was torn apart by having his limbs attached to four different horses, all of which then pulled in different directions.

Inner storms, for Dickinson, matched outer ones, so we may wonder at the oddness of the prosodically regular iambic meter here. Dickinson keeps the meter constant not only to remind us of the poem's origin in the narrative ballad, but also to clear the floor for her principal actors—the natural agents and their unnaturally human verbs. The human actions (war or massacre) contributing symbols for this storm are correlatives to fear, rage, savagery, and menace. The poem can be read as a narrative of a storm, of societal mayhem, or of psychic terror. As Wordsworth, creating "lyrical" ballads, changed the nature of the ballad by emphasizing (over plot) the psychology of its characters, so Dickinson changes the nature of this weather-ballad by making it fiercely symbolic on several planes at once.

[J 824]

# 800

I never saw a Moor.
I never saw the Sea -
Yet know I how the Heather looks
And what a Billow be -

I never spoke with God
Nor visited in Heaven -
Yet certain am I of the spot
As if the Checks were given -

When as an adult I read this poem in Johnson's edition of 1955, I was shocked. The poem I had memorized as a girl (in the version rewritten by Dickinson's 1890 editors) had been much tamer: line 4 had read "And what a wave must be," and line 8 had read "As if the chart were given." The felt lift and buoyancy of "And what a Billow be - " revealed to me Dickinson's ebullient sonic daring. Rides on trolley cars in my childhood were paid for by "Checks" (I later learned that Dickinson's "Checks" were railway tickets), so I would have understood that noun, had the editors left it alone. Reading finally what Dickinson had actually written, I could see that you were far more likely to arrive at a destination if you had tickets than if someone had merely given you a "chart" or map. The first editors were willing to sacrifice the blithe alliteration of "Billow be" in order to regularize the poet's grammar, and had decided to eliminate the common word "Checks" (which implies that one can buy a railway ticket to Paradise) in favor of the more literary "chart."

At first glance, both stanzas of "I never saw a Moor" seem constructed on the same base: a statement of inexperience ("I never saw X"), followed by a statement of the unnecessariness of experience ("Yet I know X"). In the syntactic sense, that is true; but this fact does not tell us why Dickinson did not end her poem after stanza 1. Moor and Sea are unknown to her, she says, but she knows "how the Heather looks" and "what a Billow be - ". She had learned such things from books—perhaps from Emily Brontë's *Wuthering Heights* and Byron's *Childe Harold*. No credulity is required in a response to literary description of the world's heather and billows. But—asks Dickinson in her second stanza, representing a second thought—what of literary evocations of invisible things, God and Heaven? Are they equally convincing?

She knew the powerful religious lyrics of George Herbert and Henry Vaughan, in which both Heaven and God are represented. She cannot, however, convey spiritual concepts by the sensuous delight of "what a Billow be - ". How, then, is she to make them credible? Dickinson persuades herself of their credibility by imagining such experiences as part of familiar Amherst custom, in which one speaks with someone, visits someone in (say) Northampton, and buys "Checks" to ride on the train. If she can imagine a Heaven that is only a few train-stops away, and think of God as a next-door neighbor, she can make these nouns at least familiar, if not visible. The Heaven of scriptural Revelation, with its jeweled décor, is not the Heaven she wants to visit here. In perceiving, and showing, how human beings tend to project Heaven as a version of their everyday lives of visiting, conversation, and travel, Dickinson raises an eyebrow at the palatial imaginings of the Book of Revelation.

[J 1052]

# 830

The Admirations - and Contempts - of time -
Show justest - through an Open Tomb -
The Dying - as it were a Hight
Reorganizes Estimate
And what We saw not
We distinguish clear -
And mostly - see not
What We saw before -

'Tis Compound Vision -
Light - enabling Light -
The Finite - furnished
With the Infinite -
Convex - and Concave Witness -
Back - toward Time -
And forward -
Toward the God of Him -

Although Dickinson never mentions the Resurrection of Jesus in this exalted poem, that story of an "Open Tomb" animates the whole. Yet her story is not divine but human, saying that only at someone's death do we understand the true value of that person. "The Admirations and Contempts of Time" is a phrase of dignified eighteenth-century abstraction, such as might be found in an essay or sermon. It implies that one can look with the eyes of Time itself at the vista of history, which alone reveals such final verities as the admirable worth of saints (which is hidden during their lifetime) or the contemptible cruelty of emperors (who are flattered during their reign). The homely Gospel image of sheep and goats representing the blessed and the damned (Matthew 25:32–33) is rewritten with the distance of an Edward Gibbon and with the conscious superiority of judgment bestowed by Time, when even "Contempts" are warranted. The elaborate diction (from the author, remarkably, of "I'm Nobody! Who are you?"), and the broad pentameter with which the poem opens, are so uncharacteristic of Dickinson that they warn us of something serious to come.

In fact, as we read the poem, we hear not only its short lines but also the long lines compounded of the short ones. If one were to print the poem as if it continued with its initial premise of pentameters, it appears that after line 4 Dickinson is "really" writing heroic couplets. The poem, as she left it, begins with two couplets (lines 1–4, unchanged in my revision below), the first consisting of a pentameter followed by a tetrameter, the second entirely in tetrameter. She was writing in rhyming couplets, then, in lines 1–4. (I insert, below, a space after line 4 to alert the reader to the change in rhythm.) After line 4, in the poem as she left it, the poem rhymes in quatrains alternating lines of two beats and three beats, which can be combined to construct a series of "pentameters." We have seen this Dickinsonian practice before, in "I cannot live with You - " (*706), but there the "pentameters" were far more jagged. Among Dickinson's "couplets" here, the last matches the poet's opening couplet, pairing a pentameter with a tetrameter. The close of the poem is thus left "open" for the ascension of the beloved dead as they approach the God of Time:

| | |
|---|---|
| The Admirations - and Contempts - of time - | 5 |
| Show justest - through an Open Tomb - | 4 |
| The Dying - as it were a Hight | 4 |
| Reorganizes Estimate | 4 |
| | |
| And what We saw not We distinguish clear - | 5 |
| And mostly - see not What We saw before - | 5 |
| 'Tis Compound Vision - Light - enabling Light - | 5 |
| The Finite - furnished With the Infinite - | 5 |
| Convex - and Concave Witness - Back - toward Time - | 5 |
| And forward - Toward the God of Him - | 4 |

The "knot" of the poem occurs in lines 5–8, epigrammatically elegant in formulating the cognitive results of a death. Death reveals the hitherto hidden nobility of the humble, and we no longer (more or less) take note of the social "commonness" of the morally worthy. Such a reversal of worldly judgment forces those left behind to recognize their former moral blindness. But having engaged in reproach, Dickinson leaves it behind, and begins a grand description of the new cognition after former "Estimate" has been "Reorganize[d]." (It is reorganized rather than repudiated; we "mostly" see not what we saw before, but the less welcome aspects of the dead are not entirely erased; some respect for our earlier adverse judgments is maintained.)

Once she leaves the errors of the past behind, Dickinson soars to the highest praise for the supreme sight enabled through loss. Death's illumination bestows "Compound Vision" (the ultimate version of our normal left-right-combining stereoscopic vision, since it affords, as she later says, "Convex" and "Concave" Witness). Death's "Light" confers more power on the Light of earlier ordinary seeing; the Finite human being we have lost is ennobled by the furnishings of "the Infinite." What can "the Infinite" mean in this nonreligious version of Resurrection? To what degree does a beloved person become, in our eyes, furnished "With the Infinite" after death? The concept of that person becomes "Infinite" because it has no conceivable future limit. It becomes like a Platonic Idea, complete in its "circumference," with no beginning and no end—a hieroglyph, X.

To see backward and forward at once is to have godlike power. Convex [ ) ] looks to the left, backward toward Time; Concave [ ( ] looks to the right, forward, to the God of Time. The beloved dead do not ascend vertically; they advance "forward," still on the human horizontal plane, to the God of Time. Time's "God" must be that timeless "Infinite" of memory which has already come into view enlarging the beloved dead. Enlightened by the disappearance of a person one loved, one possesses a new Star (as Dickinson said elsewhere). A poet of print, she translates the new Star into an Asterisk, as in "Go thy great way!" (1673, J 1638):

> Go thy great way!
> The Stars thou meetst
> Are even as Thyself -
> For what are Stars but Asterisks
> To point a human Life?

In "The Admirations - and Contempts - of Time," Dickinson composes, in terms of rhyme, high elegiac "pentameters," while also composing, in her lineation, short quanta-bursts of new perception ("Light - enabling Light - ", "Convex - and Concave Witness - "), permitting herself to be a mourner and a visionary at once.

[J 906]

# 836

Color - Caste - Denomination -
These - are Time's Affair -
Death's diviner Classifying
Does not know they are -

As in sleep - all Hue forgotten -
Tenets - put behind -
Death's large - Democratic fingers
Rub away the Brand -

If Circassian - He is careless -
If He put away
Chrysalis of Blonde - or Umber -
Equal Butterfly -

They emerge from His Obscuring -
What Death - knows so well -
Our minuter intuitions -
Deem unplausible

Dickinson's calm manifesto against discrimination by color, class, or sect is not well known, but it deserves wider dissemination, if only because Dickinson's (early) class attitudes, and her accompanying youthful wit, have been thought to indicate in her a permanent insensitivity to the sufferings of others. Here, "Color" stands for racial discrimination, "Caste" for class discrimination, and "Denomination" for religious discrimination. Dickinson is not arguing that they can be eliminated in modern social life; she sees them, as "Time's Affair," arising in every society, and remediated, if at all, only by the passing of Time. But Death has no knowledge of such prejudicial bars to equality: in His "diviner Classifying" they simply do not exist. Using the old literary parallel between sleep and death, Dickinson remarks that when we are asleep, skin color and ideology alike are forgotten, and that the same oblivion occurs in death. She puts the European past behind her, and claims for Death "large - Democratic fingers" that erase the "Brand"—a word particularly associated with branded slaves. She then shows Death in specific action. If an exotic beauty (a "Circassian") dies, He takes no special care in dealing with her; and He knows that from every chrysalis (whether pale or dark) there will emerge, after the dark of death, a Butterfly that is the equal of any other. This synopsis takes us through line 13, which is a spillover from line 12, suggesting the emergence of the Butterfly after the white space separating it from its Chrysalis.

The last three lines have to be read backward, so to speak: "Our minuter intuitions - / Deem unplausible / What Death - knows so well - ". Death's *large* "intuitions" (like his large fingers) know that the dead are indistinguishable by skin color; our "minuter" intuitions, so fixated on visible difference, think it "unplausible" that there could ever be a place where real democracy would obtain, where "Tenets" did not separate Congregationalist from Presbyterian, and where "Hue" would not divide "Blonde" Circassians from "Umber" Africans.

The poet here throws down a gauntlet before prejudice. In the United States in 1864, slaves were still being "Brand[ed]" and sold; the "Tenets" of doctrine divided the churches from each other; racial and class pretensions discriminated "Blonde" from "Umber." The only true Democrat in the United States is Death, treating everyone equally, practicing what others preach. Why, in a Democratic country, are our "intuitions" so "minute"? What has happened to the larger intuitions of the Founding Fathers, who wrote down among their "self-evident" truths (despite the remaining inequality of blacks) that "All men are created equal"? What has happened to the American self to make this truth no longer self-evident?

Martha Dickinson Bianchi, publishing the poem in 1929 in *The Nation*, changed line 5. The assertion that in Death "As in sleep - all Hue [is] forgotten - " must have seemed to her too radical for a gentlewoman. Was Dickinson endorsing miscegenation? To what degree did she imagine that in the United States Hue—let alone "all" Hue—could be forgotten? Falling back on Christian cliché, Bianchi changed the line to read "As in sleep - all here forgotten." Once the earthly world was left behind, one could forget (the pious editor says) everything, including the sins of one's prejudiced countrymen. I believe Dickinson's language in her mockery of "Tenets" echoes Saint

Paul (1 Corinthians 13:11): "When I became a man, I put away childish things." In death, sectarian tenets, childish things, are "put behind," Dickinson's temporal equivalent of the Pauline spatial "put away" (which she reserves for Death's handling of the chrysalis).

The structure of stanza 2 parallels that of stanza 1: two lines for worldly life, two lines for Death. But this structure of symmetry changes when Death is given center stage for the next five lines, the climax of the poem. Written out as prose, those lines would read: "Death is careless [i.e., does not take particular care] even if the dead person is a Circassian beauty; if he puts away a Blonde Chrysalis or an Umber Chrysalis, equally as Butterflies they emerge from his obscuring." It is only in the last three lines, after Death's "diviner Classifying," that the poem diverges into the first-person plural, and the human response to this didactic poem is imagined: we Americans find implausible any proposal asserting that Color, Caste, and Denomination could ever cease to matter in society. Someone reads out, "All men are created equal," and "we" respond, "But that's so implausible!" ("Unplausible" was editorially replaced in 1929 by Dickinson's rejected variant "incredible.") Dickinson's scorn is not hidden, but she mitigates it by including herself in the undemocratic American "we" who have not adopted the principles of the Declaration of Independence, however we affect to honor it. Dickinson avoids mention here of the Christian "Soul" which survives death. She prefers the natural symbol of the Butterfly, which is also the mythological symbol of Psyche, the classical Soul.

[J 970]

# 857

She rose to His Requirement - dropt
The Playthings of Her Life
To take the honorable Work
Of Woman, and of Wife -

If aught She missed in Her new Day,
Of Amplitude, or Awe -
Or first Prospective - or the Gold
In using, wear away,

It lay unmentioned - as the Sea
Develope Pearl, and Weed,
But only to Himself - be known
The Fathoms they abide -

Year after year, Dickinson watched her girlhood friends marry, herself "the only Kangaroo among the Beauty" (as she said to Thomas Wentworth Higginson in her letter of July 1862, L 268, but not on this subject). From watching the marriages of others (not least that of her brother), she knew that much in marriage remains hidden, the good as well as the bad, and that the social pretense of marital happiness may cover misery and bitter disillusion. Nonetheless, she admires the marital loyalty that does not confess dissatisfaction.

"She rose to His Requirement - " is a psychological study of three stages in the life of a married woman: first, her consent to marriage and the result of that consent; second, her disappointment both physical and metaphysical; and third, the hidden later life of the married woman's soul. Given its economy, the poem is remarkable in its changing "colors" of diction as time passes. The first stanza begins promptly and energetically in its very first line with two active verbs, "She rose [and] dropt." But what did she rise to? "His Requirement"—an eerie formulation of the proposal of marriage. The Requirement seems to be that she should drop the "Playthings" of her Life (everything in which she had reveled) and take on the opposite of play, "Work." It is as though the words of the marriage ceremony, in lieu of saying "to love and to cherish," were to say "to work as woman and as wife." Yes, it is an "honorable" estate—but does it have to be all work and no play? The "Requirement," at least in this poem, does not seem to include sexuality or motherhood. Her Work as Woman is to keep house and regulate servants; her Work as Wife is to serve and please her husband. To the extent that love and sexuality consort ill with the idea of "Work," they are suppressed. I think we are to see this stanza through the eyes of the new wife, eager to assume the responsibilities required of her by her husband, but knowing them as yet only vaguely.

In the following stanza, that of disillusion, Dickinson enumerates what the wife might miss in her new station in life. The first two things she misses are those, we suspect, that Dickinson thinks she herself would miss if she were to devote herself to married domesticity: she would miss "Amplitude" —a wider sphere; she would miss "Awe"—the sublime. And the Wife would miss the joyous "Prospective," described in the first stanza, that animated the assumption of her "honorable" role as matron. But the next disillusion is more profound; what happens to the joy of marriage, symbolized by the gold wedding ring? If it should "wear away," what Prospective then? The gold ring is meant to last a lifetime—but if it should become thinner and thinner with the years, will it not eventually disappear altogether, as the wife is left unloved and unloving?

The real suspense in the poem concerns what happens in the Wife's mind after marital disillusion. What will be the Wife's response to a life that seems increasingly narrow, stinted, and declining in joy? Will the poem end in bitterness, cynicism, petulance, self-elegy? In a ravishing moment of inspiration to truth, Dickinson sees that the Wife's response to joy and sorrow alike— because of the need to preserve the secrets of marriage—must be silence and self-scrutiny. All of the attrition of stanza 2 will lie unmentioned—to others, including her husband. This silence would be an anticlimax, were it not for Dickinson's deep-drawn simile for the Wife's mind: it is a Sea (as always, in Dickinson, masculine), one unfathomable by any but itself. The unseen underwater realms that hide oyster and algae, pearl and seaweed, are unknown to the terrestrial world.

The crucial word in the stanza is "develope." During the first stage of marriage, the Wife may be developing Pearl; in the second stage, Weed; but in the third, reflective stage, she fathoms the depths of what she has developed. We may think, concerning this stage, of Keats's picture of human development in "The Human Seasons." After a "lusty" spring and a summer of dreaming, the mind of man comes to its autumn:

> Quiet coves
> His soul has in its Autumn, when his wings
> He furleth close; contented so to look
> On mists in idleness.

The autumnal mists, like the unfathomed sea, preclude, in their depiction of contemplation, any energetic activity. The prompt young girl who "rose to His Requirement" owns now a realm of deeps in which "abide" the joys and griefs of her soul's long formation.

[J 732]

# 861

> They say that "Time assuages" -
> Time never did assuage -
> An actual suffering strengthens
> As Sinews do, with Age -
>
> Time is a Test of Trouble -
> But not a Remedy -
> If such it prove, it prove too
> There was no Malady -

This is the crisp and truthful Dickinson that readers prize. How many people must have been glad to read the first two lines of this volley against cliché! Dickinson's boldest statements—and this is one of them—are said with a certainty that is enviable. What Time is usually said to "assuage" is the grief of death. Since the root of "assuage" (as Dickinson would have known) is the Latin *suavis,* "sweet," she is within her rights in saying that nothing about corporeal dissolution can be made "sweet." When Dickinson is issuing one of her fiery rebuttals, she does not even hesitate to say dubious things. Do Sinews actually strengthen with Age? In Olympic athletes, perhaps. But she furiously writes "Age" (already present in "assu-age") to counteract that consoling verb. Age can't be "assuage[d]" any more than death.

Having demolished "assuage," Dickinson goes on to demolish "Time" as Consoler. With three alliterating "t's"—"Time is a Test of Trouble"—she "guarantees" the truth of the statement, creating three strata. First you lay down the word "Trouble," and on top of it you lay "Test," and on top of that you lay "Time." Then, reading from top to bottom of your pile, you see "Time," "Test," and "Trouble," in that order—a perfect piece of logic. The "Test," or Ordeal, was a medieval way of determining the reliability of a witness's testimony: survival proved truthfulness. So here: surviving the Test of Trouble is good for the soul, but it is less a remedying of the Trouble than a strengthening of the soul.

Dickinson said (in *550) that she measured every Grief she met "with narrow, probing, eyes - ". She perceives here that a grief she had imagined to resemble her own disappeared from its owner's face. The irreversible grief attending on death is an incurable "Malady," with no known "Remedy." By antithetically rhyming "Remedy" and "Malady," Dickinson makes her point. As "They" recite their banalities of reassurance, she stands rigid with her strengthened suffering, denying, with all her power, that any assuaging is possible. And Malady, committed to the page, never dies, as she says in "A Word dropped careless on a Page" (*1268):

> Infection in the sentence breeds
> We may inhale Despair
> At distances of Centuries
> From the Malaria -

When Dickinson lost her only "playmate," her dog Carlo, Higginson expressed sympathy. She wrote back (L 319), saying, "Thank you, I wish for Carlo," and continuing with the second stanza of "They say that 'Time assuages' - ". But she added, "Still I have the Hill, my Gibraltar remnant. Nature, seems it to myself, plays without a friend." She never acquired another dog.

It is astonishing that the editor of the *Independent,* in which this uncompromising poem posthumously appeared, dared to entitle it "Time's Healing."

[J 686]

# 867

I felt a Cleaving in my Mind -
As if my Brain had split -
I tried to match it - Seam by Seam -
But could not make them fit -

The thought behind, I strove to join
Unto the thought before -
But Sequence ravelled out of Sound -
Like Balls - upon a Floor -

A "Cleaving" is etymologically done by a Cleaver, one of the more horrible human instruments, always wielded with force. In "We met as Sparks - Diverging Flints" (918, J 958), Dickinson compares the parting of herself and a beloved to a Flint "cloven with an Adze - ". (Elsewhere—in "After all Birds," 1383, J 1395—she also uses "cleave" as a reflexive verb to mean that something separates itself into two parts. We cannot perhaps be certain which usage she intends here, but it seems to me that the violence in "split" suggests the first.) In any case, such "Cleaving" does not happen by itself in the healthy brain; some agent has caused it, and here the agent seems internal. The poet feels as if her Brain "had split"—like an overripe fruit, forced to contain more than it can bear. She does not attempt to isolate a cause; the poem looks not backward but forward, to the poet's attempt to repair the split. Unsure whether the cleaving had taken place only virtually (in her "Mind") or physiologically (in her "Brain"), she does not stop to inquire, but desperately turns to action. Before she can sew the bicameral brain together, she has to match one half with the other—not too hard a task, one might think, given the symmetry of the brain's two hemispheres. The fact that she cannot match them suggests that the problem is more mental than physiological (as she has already implied by first locating the split in the Mind before co-opting the Brain into a simile). The failure of the attempt to match the two halves—to establish a common "Seam"—fails with the tumble of the singular "it" (which had been reinforced by "split" and "fit") into the plural "them."

In another (futile) attempt at mending the split, Dickinson thinks to distinguish the two halves of her thought from each other, calling one "The thought behind" (in the past) and the other "the thought before" (the prospective, next thought). These almost identical phrases, differing only in their respective adverbial modifiers "behind" and "before," suggest the ease with which the articulation of one to the other "ought" to be accomplished. How hard can it be to connect thought A with thought B? The very fact that what ought to be easy is insuperably difficult represents the finality of the cleaving. The gash is irreparable.

The inability to join the present to the past is so disturbing that Dickinson presses toward clarification by metaphor. What was it like, she asks herself, when she tried to reestablish sequential thought? She thinks of balls of yarn, unraveling the owner's knitting as the balls fall and roll across the floor. "Ravel" is a rich word: besides the literal meaning—"to unweave, to unknit"—Dickinson's 1844 Webster defines the intransitive use of the word as "To fall into perplexity and confusion." The example offered is a quotation from Milton: "Till by their own perplexities involv'd, They ravel more, still less resolv'd" (*Samson Agonistes,* 305, in which the Chorus speaks of men who question God's justice). The second definition in Webster is also apt: "To work in perplexities; to busy oneself with intricacies."

In her first rendering of the balls on the floor, Dickinson used the literal word "reach," creating a perfectly intelligible metaphor:

> But Sequence ravelled out of reach -
> Like Balls - upon a Floor -

In revising, though, Dickinson drops "reach" for "Sound." Why? It is the "Sequence" of past and present that is undoing itself; this tells us that Dickinson perceived "Sequence" (from the Latin *sequor,* "to follow") as a kind of "Sound," as in music. Dickinson's "strings" are "snapt" here as conclusively as in "The first Day's Night had come - " (*423). There she had represented the Brain as unhinged by the catastrophe it had undergone ("My Brain keeps giggling - still."), but she also said, "That person that I was - / And this One - do not feel the same - ," a literal way of saying that sequence had frighteningly turned into difference. In "I felt a Cleaving in my Mind - ", when Sequence becomes Sound, the "Balls - upon a Floor" resemble the notes of a musical score which are disarticulating themselves and forming a dissonant heap.

Dickinson attempted a further, more powerful metaphor in a version sent to her sister-in-law Susan Dickinson:

> The Dust behind I strove to join
> Unto the Disk before -
> But Sequence ravelled out of Sound
> Like Balls upon a Floor -

The new metaphor remakes "The thought behind" and "the thought before," the past and future, by borrowing emblems from nature. The past is "Dust" (like all mortal things). But what is the Disk? It is the Sun of sunrise—always a sign of a new beginning. In the four-line poem "The pattern of the sun" (1580, J 1550), Dickinson argues that radiance alone is not enough to constitute the sun's appearance. Many creatures may have "sheen," but only one is a sun, unique because he has been shaped to a pattern, a Disk:

> The pattern of the sun
> Can fit but him alone
> For sheen must have a Disk
> To be a sun -

The inability to join "Dust" and "Disk" is all the more painful to the poet because in some ways they so resemble each other: each (like "Dickinson") begins with "D," each has four letters, and the middle sounds—"us" and "is"—are very much alike. It should not be hard to join two words already joined so closely by sound and appearance. But as the poet reaches for the past, it crumbles to dust; as she reaches for the dawn, it will not come. "Disk" is one of Dickinson's talismanic words (occurring fifteen times under its two spellings, "Disc" and "Disk," in the *Emily Dickinson Lexicon*); she uses it always with high seriousness, in one or the other of the multiple connotations outlined in her Webster. We see her here with a disarticulated sequence of past moments, each originally a golden Disk, but now a heap of dust. And then we see the total tragedy of the mind to which no articulation of a future Disk is possible.

[J 937 and J 992]

# 895

Further in Summer than the Birds -
Pathetic from the Grass -
A minor Nation celebrates
Its unobtrusive Mass.

No Ordinance be seen -
So gradual the Grace
A gentle Custom it becomes -
Enlarging Loneliness -

Antiquest felt at Noon -
When August burning low
Arise this spectral Canticle
Repose to typify -

Remit as yet no Grace -
No furrow on the Glow,
But a Druidic Difference
Enhances Nature now -

Dickinson made a fair copy of this poem, enclosing it in an envelope addressed to Mabel Todd (the lover of Emily's brother, Austin), but the envelope "was never stamped or postmarked," Ralph Franklin notes. "Also enclosed," he continues, "was a cricket, wrapped in a piece of paper." The literal base of Dickinson's nature poetry is brought forcibly home to us when we contemplate the dead cricket, but the imaginative transformations she performs on her base become even more visible. Real things were, one could say, already metaphorical for her. "Further in Summer" originally closed with a hierarchical remark on elegy: "The Cricket is [Nature's] utmost / Of Elegy, to Me - ": she was more pleased by the Cricket's "unobtrusive" elegy than by a more rhetorical one. Given the preeminence in English lyric of educated elegy, Dickinson, in preferring a minor music, expresses her own more reticent (and more "natural") poetics through the medium of the cricket song. Because this poem has been so often praised as one of Dickinson's finest achievements, her artistry in it asks for special attention.

That artistry was one of ruthless excision, as she cut five entire stanzas from her first seven-stanza version. Initially, she found the last two stanzas of the first version worthy of retention. (They were once thought to be a separate poem, because they were found on a detached leaf of paper, but it was matched by Franklin with its counterpart.) Here are those last exquisite stanzas from the first version (not found, of course, in Franklin's *Reading Edition,* given his choice of the last fair copy as his copy-text):

> The Earth has many keys -
> Where Melody is not
> Is the Unknown Peninsula -
> Beauty - is Nature's Fact -
>
> But Witness for Her Land -
> And Witness for her Sea -
> The Cricket is Her utmost
> Of Elegy, to Me -

The sheer assertive confidence in these lines—the praise of all musical keys; the declaration that there is no part of Nature devoid of Melody; the aphoristic assertion that what Fact is to us, Beauty is to Nature (i.e., the undeniable substratum); and the closing hyperbole setting the Cricket highest in the ranks of Elegy—is very Dickinsonian, but the élan of the lines does not replicate the "minor" elegiac tone ascribed to the cricket's Canticle. In writing the beautiful lines of these two stanzas, Dickinson is doing one of the things she is best at—writing in the voice of certainty, a technique reassuring to a reader, who trusts such an authoritative voice. Declarative force is what draws many of us to Dickinson: "There is no Frigate like a Book"; "Pain - expands the Time - "; "I dwell in Possibility - ". It must have cost Dickinson a good deal to give up the splendor of the asseverations in these two cut stanzas. But with the ruthlessness of the exacting artist, Dickinson rejects, in her final version, her memorable closing stanzas and their ringing certainty.

As the poet revises other parts of her first draft (always in the direction of a subtler expression), she arrives at her final four-stanza version, in which, as I have mentioned, only two of the original seven stanzas remain. Some of the changes are startling. At first the cricket song is "Audiblest, at Dusk." How did that perception ever metamorphose into "Antiquest felt at Noon"? (Dickinson began with "Antiquer" but graduated rapidly to her wonted superlative.) Franklin spends more than four pages examining the variant drafts of this irreproachable poem, but in the restricted space here, it would be useful, I think, to begin by rewriting in prose the four sentences of the final version:

> A minor Nation celebrates, [in a time] further [along] in Summer than the Birds, its unobtrusive Mass.
> No Ordinance [ceremony] can be seen; the Grace is so gradual that it becomes a gentle Custom enlarging Loneliness.
> It is at Noon that the song is felt to be most ancient; as August burns low, there arises this spectral Canticle to typify Repose.
> No Grace is as yet remitted; nor is there any furrow marring the Glow, but a Druidic Difference enhances Nature Now.

The topic of the poem is gradualness; autumn steals upon us before we are aware. How is the poet to represent such an imperceptible yet perceptible change? By what senses—given that "Grace" has not been lessened, that the "Glow" of the season remains unmarred—do we perceive the incremental difference as summer wanes and autumn approaches? "Further in Summer" represents gradualness in many ways. It is still summer—the Birds are still singing—but a new (and Keatsian) sound has been added to the chorus: it is that of the crickets. Like Keats, who allowed, in "To Autumn," the remaining "treble soft" of the redbreast to be heard along with the hedge-crickets' song, Dickinson does not replace birdsong with cricket chant but rather allows the two musics to coexist; yet the Crickets come "Further [along] in Summer" than the Birds. Among "Nature's People" (see *1096, "A narrow Fellow"), the Crickets are "A minor Nation" (with a pun, perhaps, on the minor key of their Canticle); yet they announce the great change from flourishing to decline.

Dickinson's timekeeping is by season and phenomenon: in Summer, first Birds and then Crickets. The "Grace" of the Crickets' Mass is so gradual that it (almost) becomes "Custom"—a habitual unchanging phenomenon. The poet has already been in some sense lonely, she implies, earlier in the Summer, but the Crickets' song has the gradual effect of "enlarging Loneliness." "Loneliness," as an abstract noun, is tenseless; but as a continuing seasonal feeling it can be enlarged into a more encompassing phenomenon. (The verb "enlarge" is one of the powerful "progressive" verbs in English that keep on going. Because such verbs as "to become," "to redden," "to spread," "to brighten," "to enlarge," and so on, when used intransitively, have no intrinsic terminus, "enlarge" can take part in the habitual gradualness of the phenomenon of the imperceptible. Just when is it that one can say that one's Loneliness today is strangely "larger" than it was yesterday?) The "Custom" of the Crickets' song has persisted so long in Western culture that it is not merely "Antique" or "Antiquer," but "Antiquest"; its mythological origin lies in the Greek myth of Tithonus, who, granted eternal existence—but not eternal youth—by the gods, withers gradually over time as his lover, the goddess of the Dawn, remains perpetually young.

One might have felt that the proper time for the Crickets' song would be dusk, and in fact Dickinson first wrote, as I have mentioned, "'Tis Audiblest, at Dusk." Yet, just as John Donne observed of love that "his first minute, after noon, is night" ("A Lecture upon the Shadow"), so Dickinson observes that it is at Noon that one notices how low in the sky, now that it is August, the sun has begun to burn. At noon, the Crickets' unvarying song in the grasses —as though sung by invisible fellow specters of our coming spectral selves— speaks of the undisturbed Repose of the grave. (In the draft, Dickinson explains why the Crickets' song typifies Repose. It does so because it is unvarying: "Nor difference it knows / Of Cadence, or of Pause - "). Dickinson's words for the Crickets' ritual ("Mass," "Ordinance," "gradual," "Grace," "gentle Custom," "Antiquest," "spectral Canticle," "Repose," "typify," and "Remit") are conclusively Latinate, suited to a "Mass," but eventually they are replaced by something far more primitive. Like the Catholic Mass and its ordinance of ritual, like its gradual Grace, the religious word "Canticle" (internally rhyming with "spectral") suggests that this intermediate "sacrament"—like the "sacrament of summer days" in "These are the days" (*122)—offers a "Last Communion in the Haze." But that earlier poem (in its resentment—"Oh fraud that cannot cheat the Bee") still expressed a bitterness in experiencing the mimicry of true Summer by an Indian Summer. By the end of "Further in

Summer than the Birds" (as we shall see), no resentment remains: the hallowing is more genuine than that predicated of the closing haze-surrounded "sacrament" in "These are the days," a sacrament that one had to be a "child" to receive believingly. Now Dickinson no longer needs to pretend to be a child, nor does she veil the reality with a Keatsian "mist" or the coming of dusk. She allows at high Noon a complete awareness of decline, while determined, at the same time, to represent its imperceptibility. Except for the first full rhyme—placing a Mass in the Grass—the rhymes are slant, themselves separating from each other by less or more: "Grace . . . Loneliness," "low . . . typify," and finally the graphically identical but aurally distinct "Glow . . . now," with "Glow" echoing the earlier "low."

Insisting on the imperceptibility of change, Dickinson reiterates the word "Grace." Although Grace be "gradual," it is as yet not visibly remitting (sending back) any part of itself. The verb "Remit" is an unmarked version of "remits," of which the subject is "Grace": "No Grace remits as yet—[there is] no furrow on the Glow." The "furrow" is Shakespeare's metaphor for wrinkles on the fair brow; in Sonnet 22 ("My glass shall not persuade me I am old"), he grieves that "in thee time's furrows I behold." In Dickinson, the "furrow" will arrive when the glowing fields of Summer hay are ploughed under after harvest.

How will Dickinson end her adagio on gradualness? Not with the superlative of the draft version ("The Cricket is Her utmost / Of Elegy, to Me - "), which would sound bombastic with respect to this "minor Nation," but with the praise of the fragile moment in which the year insensibly passes from flourish to decline: "a Druidic Difference / Enhances Nature now - ". With a single "pagan" word—"Druidic"—Dickinson overturns her Latinate (requiem) Mass of Grace and Canticle, and reverts to a pagan tradition of more remote antiquity, that uninterpretable religion of those Druid-poets imagined by Wordsworth in the 1850 *Prelude* (XIII, 345–349). In his reverie near Stonehenge on Salisbury Plain, he beheld them—

> Beheld long-bearded teachers, with white wands
> Uplifted, pointing to the starry sky,
> Alternately, and plain below, while breath
> Of music swayed their motions, and the waste
> Rejoiced with them and me in those sweet sounds.

Dickinson, who sometimes in her poems also pointed to the starry sky, here imitates the Druids' other motion as she points her "white wand" of language to the grassy "plain" and hears—in the "sweet sounds" made by the Druids' "breath of music"—an analogue to the Crickets' music accompanied by her own song.

Wordsworth's blessing of a veneration of Sky and Earth among the Druids enables Dickinson's gratitude toward Nature's processes. No longer mourning the turn of the year, she can end her poem not in an elegy but in an enhancing: "a Druidic Difference / Enhances Nature now - ". The positive verb "enhance" (derived from the Latin *inaltare,* "to raise," "to exalt"), which looks back via its prefix to her earlier sad verb "enlarge," "corrects" (without erasing) the poet's first interpretation of the Crickets' ceremonial as one of pathos, her melancholy perception that Loneliness enlarges as the season turns. Now, precisely because she has intuited the almost-invisible approach of Autumn, she sees the "Glow" more keenly, hears the "unobtrusive" sound of the Crickets more intently. As Wordsworth says of poets and prophets, each one has "a sense that fits him to perceive / Objects unseen before" (1850 *Prelude,* XIII, 304–305). A reader of Dickinson can hardly hear invisible crickets now without thinking of how Dickinson's sense of the world fitted her to perceive this sound of late Summer in New England, transforming Keats's English Autumn into a New World "object unseen before."

[ J 1068 and J 1775 ]

# 905

Split the Lark - and you'll find the Music -
Bulb after Bulb, in Silver rolled -
Scantily dealt to the Summer Morning
Saved for your Ear, when Lutes be old -

Loose the Flood - you shall find it patent -
Gush after Gush, reserved for you -
Scarlet Experiment! Sceptic Thomas!
Now, do you doubt that your Bird was true?

The poet-speaker, accused by her lover of some kind of infidelity, and wounded by his lack of trust, finds a violent metaphor for her pain at his assault. Remembering how, at the Crucifixion, "one of the soldiers with a spear pierced his side, and forthwith came there out blood and water" (John 19:34), she turns her own case into that of Jesus. Remembering, too, the subsequent account (John 20:24–29) of Jesus' appearance to his disciples after the Resurrection, she puts her lover into the role of "doubting Thomas," that disciple who, not having been present at the Resurrection and not believing that Jesus had risen from the dead, said: "Except I shall see in his hands the print of the nails, and put my finger into the print of the nails, and thrust my hand into his side, I will not believe." Eight days later, Jesus came again to his disciples and spoke to Thomas: "'Reach hither thy finger, and behold my hands; and reach hither thy hand, and thrust it into my side: and be not faithless, but believing.' And Thomas answered and said unto him, 'My Lord and my God.' Jesus saith unto him, 'Thomas, because thou has seen me, thou hast believed: blessed are they that have not seen, and yet have believed.'"

The poet now has one analogy, that between her suspicious lover and doubting Thomas. But what will be her figure for herself? At this query, she invents her self-metaphor: she is the Shakespearean lark of Sonnet 29, who, "at break of day arising," would "sing hymns at heaven's gate"—but she can no longer sing, because her lover has dealt her a fatal wound. Dickinson amazes us with her image of the potential poetry in herself. Like eggs in the ovary, all

*Selected Poems and Commentaries* · 367

of her future notes are already packaged within, but she replaces human eggs with flower bulbs, ready to unfold at the coming of every Spring. Her notes are flutelike, "in Silver rolled," but the poet's (female) song so far has been "Scantily dealt" at break of day. She is withholding much of her music so as to have a sufficient supply for her lover-courtier's ear, even after the court Lutes have, like him, grown old.

Dickinson's fierce opening downbeat, "Split the Lark," finds its later rhythmic counterpart in "Loose the Flood." Under each four-beat line runs an implicit dactylic meter: "*one* two three." It is a waltz rhythm, in which a trochaic foot can replace a dactylic foot, but the meter is not the bald eight-syllable trochaic one we hear in "Tiger, tiger, burning bright." A trochee in this poem is like a dotted note in music followed by another note: "*one* [x] three." Dickinson chooses her meter from her governing metaphor of a "Gush" of blood. The dactylic downbeat represents the first pulse of the Gush; the two light syllables following represent its dwindling until the next dying heartbeat pushes the next Gush out.

We don't come upon this "meaning" of the meter until the second stanza, when Dickinson speaks *in propria persona;* something "Scantily dealt" (as are the notes, or drops of blood) begins to "Gush" only when a wrong exit (the wound rather than the throat) has been created. The exclamatory rhetoric of the second stanza begins with Dickinson's hypothesis: if you "Loose the Flood" ("Flood" where we expected its rhyme-word "Blood"), you will find the supply "patent"—open to the eye, rolled in its Silver—and then the first "Gush" erupts, "Gush after Gush" as the lover sees all the music reserved for him alone pouring forth from the Lark's side.

There are two final alliterating "Gush[es]" of blood in the Lark's rebuke to the skeptical lover who, like Othello, would not believe without "ocular proof": "Scarlet Experiment! Sceptic Thomas!" These last dactylic and tro-chaic "Gush[es]" are followed by the "dying fall" of the expiring Lark, gasping, "Now, do you doubt that your Bird was true?" "True" rhymes ironically with "You," the faithless lover. And "old," the second rhyme in the first stanza, is neatly contained in "rolled," imitating those bulbs rolled in Silver.

Dickinson's first editors unaccountably gave to this poem, with its scarlet gushes of accusation, the title "Loyalty."

[J 861]

# 926

> I stepped from Plank to Plank
> A slow and cautious way
> The Stars about my Head I felt
> About my Feet the Sea -
>
> I knew not but the next
> Would be my final inch -
> This gave me that precarious Gait
> Some call Experience -

Here, Dickinson employs one of her frequent practices, that of beginning very literally: she steps from Plank to Plank, slowly and cautiously (an experience others may have had on the floor of a half-finished house or on a decaying bridge). She continues with a scene that could almost be conceived of as literal—a view of a person at the shore, with Stars overhead and the Sea underfoot. Even the fourth and fifth lines—until the words "final inch"—could seem almost factual: "I knew not but the next / Would be my final [step until I reached safe ground]." But as soon as Dickinson substitutes the word *"inch"* for the expected "step," we know we are in allegory. We are therefore not surprised when she appends, in the last two lines of the poem, the meaning of the allegorical narrative: an explanation of what "Experience" does to the self. Carefree and impulsive, the self runs ahead in youth—and then the setbacks, mistakes, and sufferings begin the long attrition of that first impulsive and thoughtless foray, until one gains, inch by inch, that unwished-for "Experience."

The poem probably began with the choice of the fundamental metaphor for Experience: a "precarious" Gait. But since this is a riddle-poem, Dickinson wants to reserve the solution to the riddle—posed in the first six lines—for the end, so that she can conclude the poem with the word "Experience." If so, a rhyme has to be found for "Experience" that will embody a "precarious Gait," and the poet, thus challenged, provides one of her characteristic superlatives. We speak in real life of "the last mile" or "the final step," but only in proverbs do we normally find forward movement measured in inches: "Give him an inch and he'll take an ell" (an ell was a measure used in England, a unit of forty-five inches). Advancing by inches, plank by plank, over a Sea, calls to mind "walking the plank," the capital punishment inflicted on sailors. (For a poem about walking the plank beyond the final inch, see "This is the place they hoped before," 1284, J 1264.) "I stepped from Plank to Plank" shows no visible landscape—only the illimitable extent of the starry sky above and the unfathomed Sea below. To walk with the Sea about one's feet and *feel* (Dickinson's extraordinary verb in the circumstances) the Stars above one's Head is to envisage no possible salvation in any human being, any civilization, or any ship. Only a spiritual body could "feel" at the same moment the Stars and the Sea.

The vastness surrounding the unstable Planks suggests the many connotations of "precarious." Originally meaning "dependent on the will of another," it comes from the Latin for "prayer" (*prex, preces*) and has since taken on such meanings as (I reduce the *OED*'s list) "liable to fail," "hazardous," "fraught with physical danger," "at risk of falling or other accident." A "precarious" situation makes one feel the need to implore authority to provide a less hazardous environment. But in Dickinson's poem, there is no such authority: one will walk with a "precarious Gait" until death. "Experience"—itself also from Latin (*experientia,* the act of trying)—means "to put to the test." Like any "experiment," this trial should have a result. But walking slowly and cautiously, step by step, over and under a void, produces no visible outcome here, except the escape, for a temporary inch, from fatality. The poem begins in everyday Anglo-Saxon language, to emphasize the literality of "I stepped from Plank to Plank"—but by the end, to represent gained Wisdom, Dickinson moves to the polysyllabic Latinate "precarious" and "Experience." The physical word "Gait," however (coming from the same Teutonic root as "go"), confirms the "literal" side of the allegory.

[J 875]

# 930

The Poets light but Lamps -
Themselves - go out -
The Wicks they stimulate
If vital Light

Inhere as do the Suns -
Each Age a Lens
Disseminating their
Circumference -

In nineteenth-century lamps, a wick floats in a liquid medium such as oil or kerosene; the lamplighter ignites the wick, which continues to give light indefinitely if the fuel is regularly replenished. God was the original provider of light, with his *Fiat Lux*. He, being eternal, could not "go out," but poets, being mortal, do. Their stimulating effect on other Wicks, however, continues after their death—if the Light the Wicks produce be "vital." If the Light is vital, the poetry-Wicks "inhere" (stick, cling) Age after Age, as Suns do. Each Age becomes a Lens, which, both focusing and diffusing the Light, goes on, "disseminating" (aggrandizing) its total breadth out to light's Circumference (potentially, the whole world).

Why do some poems last? asks Dickinson. Any Age has a great number of Poets, and each one creates a Lamp emitting the Light of a certain spectrum of sensibility. All of these Poets, as physical beings, perish; and, in the case of most, their poems perish too, as the era of their creation expires. Daringly, Dickinson begins her poem with the Poet's end: she will "go out." What will make her Light "vital" instead of mortal? The great example of agelessly vital light is that of the Sun: "For as the sun is daily new and old, / So is my love still telling what is told" (Shakespeare, Sonnet 76). But since "vital" Poets are many, poetic "Suns" are many, too.

Does the Light keep on burning, invariant, Age after Age? That was Shakespeare's hope in his "eternizing" sonnets. Dickinson goes him one better, explaining that "vital" poetry survives because each era produces an individual historical "Lens" of its own that serves, like the lens of a lighthouse, to focus and spread light. If the Lens of each era finds something on which to focus in the poetry of earlier ages, then once again the Light is revitalized and disseminated. To "disseminate" means to scatter seeds; and the enlarging of the circumference of a light by its projection through a lens enables the light to function once again as a Sun functions, producing from seeds both growth and fruit.

The poem's language—which speaks of a lamp, a wick, a medium, ignition, light, and the dissemination of light by means of a lens—belongs to an illustration in optics. What saves the poet's precision from being chilly is the second, epitaphic, line, "Themselves - go out - ". The poem is written at a great distance from that mortal fate; it sees, as God sees, a panorama of Age succeeding Age. Dickinson allows for the appeal of different poems to different Ages (the lens of one Age may fix more rarely here, more frequently there) and also for the difference between eras (as between convex and concave lenses), but the affirmation that every Age is a new Lens for old Light is a reassuring one: somewhere, at some time, the vital poem will find its audience. If the mortal poets go "out," Dickinson will rhyme the word of their death with "Light," the word of their survival. And the small circle of the "Lens" rhymes with (as it resembles and disseminates) the Poet's "Circumference." The Circumference widens as each era adds a new Lens, until finally no limit can be placed on the influence of poetic radiance.

[J 883]

# 935

As imperceptibly as Grief
The Summer lapsed away -
Too imperceptible at last
To seem like Perfidy -
A Quietness distilled
As Twilight long begun,
Or Nature spending with herself
Sequestered Afternoon -
The Dusk drew earlier in -
The Morning foreign shone -
A courteous, yet harrowing Grace,
As Guest, that would be gone -
And thus, without a Wing
Or service of a Keel
Our Summer made her light escape
Into the Beautiful -

Once again, as in "Further in Summer than the Birds - " (*895), Dickinson writes of the invisible turn of the year from Summer to Autumn. "As imperceptibly as Grief" was originally an eight-stanza poem. In cutting her poem to half its draft size, reducing it to four stanzas, Dickinson demonstrates, as in "Further in Summer," the sternness she exercised against her own charm. The first two and last two stanzas were kept; the middle four were excised (and consequently do not appear in Ralph Franklin's *Reading Edition*). Here are the four cut stanzas concerning autumn, reprinted from Version A, with my right-column list of their essential noticings:

| | |
|---|---|
| Sobriety inhered | Sobriety |
| Though gaudy influence | Gaudiness (redness) |
| The Maple lent unto the Road | |
| And graphic Consequence | Fallen leaves |

| | |
|---|---|
| Invested sombre place - | Sombreness |
| As suddenly be worn | Sudden change |
| By sober Individual | Sobriety |
| A Homogeneous Gown - | A single-color, unpatterned cloth |
| | |
| Departed was the Bird - | Absence of Birds |
| And scarcely had the Hill | |
| A flower to help His straightened face | Absence of Flowers, stress |
| In stress of Burial - | Burial |
| | |
| The Winds came closer up - | Sound of Wind |
| The Cricket spoke so clear | Sound of Crickets |
| Presumption was - His Ancestors | |
| Inherited the Floor - | Right of Possession |

Dickinson's observations of both presence and absence are always cogent. In the part of this scan denoting *presence,* only the gaudy Maple counters the general passage down to sobriety and somberness, brownness and bareness. In the part of the scan denoting *absence,* the departure of birds gives pain, and hardly a flower can be found to soothe the Hill's face, contracted in hardship and sorrow. As Dickinson closes this portion of her original draft, she returns to presence, yet (borrowing from Keats's "To Autumn") she creates a presence not to the eye but to the ear. Nature's voice, once birdsong has lapsed, can be heard in the proximity of Winds and in the Cricket's elegiac claim to immemorial ownership of the ground of Being.

Why, then, would Dickinson repudiate these four stanzas, representing, in logical sequence, the presence of the (altered) visible, the absence of the formerly visible, and the sound-presence of the invisible? The stanzas do not lack powerful images—of which the most powerful is the abstract rendering of how presence brings about "Consequence," as we see the gaudy Maple stripped of its leaves as "graphic Consequence // Invested sombre place - ". We feel Dickinson's eye passing from the Maple tree to its context, missing the birds and the flowers, and feeling the minatory approach of Winds and the Cricket's requiem, as it possesses, as it always has, the ground which is now a scene of "Burial." The trouble with these stanzas, we realize (as we compare them to those that Dickinson retained) is that they do not represent the "imperceptible"—which is, after all, the theme of the poem. It can hardly be said that the lapse of Summer is "imperceptible" when the poet's eye is noting the perceptible change from scarlet gaudiness to sobriety. Nothing imperceptible can be said to happen "suddenly." The absence of birdsong and flowers is stated too boldly to seem "imperceptible," and to remark that the Winds are "closer" than before is to perceive the perceptible rather than—Dickinson's topic—to be deceived by the "imperceptible."

Having seen the inconsistency between her original claim of imperceptibility and her only-too-perceptible inventory of Nature's graphic changes, Dickinson daringly decides to return to the imperceptible (far harder to illustrate, needless to say, than the perceptible). Her human abstractions are at first Grief and Perfidy, suggesting that behind the poem lies an experience of betrayal, the (voluntary) departure of a friend or lover. But she is now far removed from that original shock of Grief; she has known what it is for Grief to "lapse" (fall away) little by little, until one realizes one is grieving less than before. And if the breaking of the relationship also took place little by little, as in "Now I knew I lost her - ", where "Remoteness travelled / On her Face and Tongue" (*1274), there did not occur the melodramatic break that might be labeled "Perfidy." What would it be to sense (in another, as in Nature) a Quietness, and then to feel it becoming more concentratedly so, "A Quietness distilled"? What would it be to say "It is Twilight," and then much later, "It is still Twilight"? Concentration and prolongation are changes, but ones so gradual that they may not be remarked. Nature, no longer the generous and copious goddess of early summer, withdraws to her own company, but nothing has yet acted upon her. It is she who has sequestered herself, in keeping with the Quietness of oncoming Twilight.

Finally, Dickinson allows a comparative remark: Dusk comes earlier than before. But it is the same "Dusk" in quality as it was yesterday; and just as prolongation forward did not change "Twilight," so retrospective prolongation does not change Dusk. No new noun has appeared to mark a perceptible change in kind. At the end of the day, as Dusk draws in earlier, we speculate that morning may bring, at last, a perceptible change, as it in fact does: "The

Morning foreign shone - ". But no name arises as proper to this foreign quality. It is still Morning, and the Morning is still shining, shining as before, if with an unnerving but unnamable difference. The human analogies of lapse and Perfidy and consequent Grief seem momentarily to have gone into abeyance, but they are resuscitated in the person of the "Guest, that would be gone - ". Now Dickinson's Grief and Loss are given another interpretation: they side with the Season, rather than with herself, in their readiness for voluntary departure. Yet they show their wish to depart only in their "courteous . . . Grace." Not a word escapes them, but the poet's sense that they are withdrawing from view makes that very courtesy and grace, Nature's kindness to her, harrowingly painful.

The poem formally ends at this point, with the last stanza summarizing what has gone before. One can see certain departures by their material signs: birds depart as their Wings lift them into flight; a ship departs as its Keel deepens in the water. Summer's departure is signless; she employs no visible Wing, uses no moving Keel, as she consigns herself to "the Beautiful." "The Beautiful" is one of Dickinson's permanent mental categories. Although the current Summer may go, yet the category to which it belongs is Platonically retained.

The most startling word in the poem is "escape." One escapes from servitude, or from a prison. What Dickinson has been seeing as Perfidy on the part of Summer, is—as she now recognizes—not infidelity but ethereal "escape" from human bondage. Time has its own obligations: "The sacred seasons might not be disturbed" (Keats, *Hyperion,* 293). In the "escape," the imperceptible has been preserved even into the act of departure. The poem takes place in Autumn—after all, it is narrated in the past tense: "Our Summer *made* . . . her . . . escape." It is a retrospective poem, in which the poet examines her feelings in sequence, from her first perception of Summer's alteration to her late understanding of why Summer must depart.

Dickinson will not say that Summer died; no, it escaped into its ethereal essence. Although the poet began by speaking impersonally of "The Summer," she ends with the intimate "Our Summer." There was no perfidy; there must be no grief. It is simply that our memorial category of "the Beautiful" has gained one more familial species, "Our" Summer. Only rarely has the imperceptible been so scrupulously described. And Dickinson's acute sense of the seasonal cusps of the year, one of the great bequests of her work, created a subsequent cluster of such poems in Wallace Stevens, whose debt to Dickinson is profound.

[J 1540]

# 962

A Light exists in Spring
Not present on the Year
At any other period -
When March is scarcely here
A Color stands abroad
On Solitary Fields
That Science cannot overtake
But Human Nature feels.

It waits upon the Lawn,
It shows the furthest Tree
Upon the furthest Slope you know
It almost speaks to you.

Then as Horizons step
Or Noons report away
Without the Formula of sound
It passes and we stay -

A quality of loss
Affecting our Content
As Trade had suddenly encroached
Upon a Sacrament -

"Trade," we might recall, encroached upon the Sacrament of Penance when Chaucer's Pardoner hawked indulgences—which granted a reduction of the soul's time in Purgatory, for a fee—without attaching to them the requisite sacramental repentance for sins committed. Dickinson's sudden recourse to a religious simile to end her poem requires some thought. In what sense is the light we have been witnessing a sacrament? In what sense is the victorious light of later Spring blasphemous? It has encroached illegally on a territory not properly its own (the word "encroach" comes from the French *croc*, "hook," the implication being that one is reaching out to ensnare the property of another). But if the world of March "Light" was originally the property of another, someone who did not commercialize it, who was that owner? The religious vocabulary of the close suggests that early March light resembles the light of the original Eden—and that after recreating innocent Nature before the Fall in the greater part of the poem, Dickinson enacts a version of the Fall in the coming of "Trade," which takes venal possession of the gift-realm of Paradise.

How, then, to describe what Marianne Moore characterized as "the days of prismatic color"? Her adjective "prismatic" suggests not merely light in general, but the pristine quality that Dickinson perceives in the light of early March. When we look for adjectival words in Dickinson, our search is defeated: we meet only nouns—"A Light," "A Color." These are defined solely by their activities, which gradually become more intimate: the Light "exists"; the Color "stands abroad"; but when "Human Nature" enters the equation, bringing feeling along with it, the Light "waits" for its human observer and enters into a display of its own great extent as it "shows the furthest Tree." The Light's symbolic essence then focuses exclusively on its human observer: "It almost speaks to you." With her "almost," Dickinson repudiates the religious belief that the voice of God can speak from Nature (as from Abraham's burning bush). Yet the poet cannot help hearing "tongues in trees, sermons in stones, books in the running brooks" (*As You Like It,* Act 2, scene 2). And in fact it may have been Dickinson's recollection of this speech by Shakespeare's Duke that led her to thoughts of Eden: the Duke says that, in the forest of Arden, he and his company feel "the penalty of Adam, / The seasons' difference."

At the very moment when the Light "speaks to you," it recedes—or rather the world recedes from it in space or time: Horizons "step," or Noons "report away" like soldiers called to another regiment. Such a moment, in the military, would be a ceremonial one, marked by "the Formula of sound," but Nature makes no such bugled announcement of her changes. The simplest moment in the poem comes in Dickinson's plangent summary: "It passes and we stay - ". We are not without Contentment—Summer, too, is beautiful. But it is not paradisal, and so we feel "A quality of loss / Affecting our Content"—one of those nameless mixed states of human feeling that Dickinson is so adept at evoking. We are Adam and Eve expelled from the Garden. Not all

Contentment is gone: the Miltonic couple are hand-in-hand in the world which lies all before them, and through which, as through Dickinson's "Solitary Fields," they take "their solitary way" at the conclusion of *Paradise Lost*. But the quality of loss remains. Life in proximity to the divine has been lost.

When we return to contemplate the poem, we see that the Light prompts Dickinson to assert that Science "cannot overtake" emotional consciousness, that perception cannot be quantified. The metaphor of overtaking betrays Dickinson's awareness that little by little, and always more rapidly, science in the nineteenth century was overtaking natural mysteries and turning them into intelligible phenomena. That admission forces her into singling out the phenomena of consciousness that outrun scientific analysis. One reason for the necessity of art is that these inner phenomena do not otherwise enter the world of representation. What "Human Nature feels" is as worthy of exposition as anything else on earth. That is the argument of Wordsworth's "Elegiac Stanzas," which concern a painting showing a castle in a turbulent storm. Wordsworth says that in his youth, had he been a painter, he would have pictured the castle in "the light that never was on sea or land, / The consecration and the poet's dream." But now the death of his brother at sea has changed his emotional life, and he praises the painter who could depict "this rueful sky, this pageantry of fear." Without the painting, the poet's inner turbulence would not have an external correlative. In similar fashion, Dickinson conveys her feeling of paradisal innocence in the landscape of early March via her "painting" of its elusive Light. The Light casts itself "on" the Year, as if the Year itself is an ever-changing landscape, illuminated by a succession of temporary seasonal Lights, of which the most beautiful is the earliest.

"A Light exists in Spring" is inconsistently voiced, and Dickinson was aware of the inconsistency, without remedying it. The gorgeous opening eight-line double-stanza is impersonally related. But the second stanza admits the second-person pronoun, "you." Dickinson marked the "you" of line 11 for an alternative, but apparently never found one. In the third and fourth stanzas, "you" is replaced by "we" and its adjectival form, "our." The transition from the "no one" of impersonal statement to the "we" of common experience via the "you" of singular intimacy is original, representing as it does an exquisite moment of natural being which occurs not only independently ("A Light exists") but also intimately ("It almost speaks to you") and collectively ("It passes and we stay - "). How could any instruments of Science quantify such delicate registers of feeling? Yet if Science cannot do it, poetry can, the poet insists.

Dickinson's rhymes repeat the essence of the moment. When the "Year" is newly "here," the poet "feels" the "Fields"; when time reports "away," we "stay"; and our "Content" at this moment of inception comes from this natural "Sacrament" of Light. The rhyme that does not enter into this field of play is that of the second stanza, in which "Tree" rhymes with "you" (or, rather, does not rhyme with "you"). Dickinson could have found any number of easy rhymes for "Tree." But she was too deeply attached to her "you" to sacrifice it, even though she gave that solution some thought. Working backward, could she find a noun-rhyme for "you" with which to replace "Tree"? "Dew"? No, one cannot see "Dew" upon "the furthest Slope." "Blue"? No, blue is not the color of the earth's slope. She lets "you" remain, and we see through her eyes "the furthest Tree / Upon the furthest Slope you know"— the horizon's limit of visual perception. The Light, like God, is everywhere— but it is not, like Him, eternal. Its transience makes keener our perception of its paradisal intimacy.

[J 812]

# 983

Bee! I'm expecting you!
Was saying Yesterday
To Somebody you know
That you were due -

The Frogs got Home last Week -
Are settled, and at work -
Birds mostly back -
The Clover warm and thick -

You'll get my Letter by
The Seventeenth; Reply
Or better, be with me -
Yours, Fly.

In this winsomely playful scherzo, Dickinson-Homebody-Fly composes a "Letter" to her wandering companion the absent Bee. She imitates a seasonal Farmer's Almanac voiced with demotic Yankee taciturnity: "Was saying Yesterday / To Somebody you know / That you were due - ". The Frogs "got Home"—where she is—"last Week - "; and within a week were settled and, even more, "at work - ". (Knowing the Bee to be a worker too, Fly is issuing an implicit reproach for tardiness.) What the Frogs do for "work" we need not be told, since they are invoked only as a moral exemplum to the Bee. Fly even concedes that Bee may not really be tardy, because the birds, whose migratory habits are predictable, are only "mostly" back. Abandoning reproach as a form of invitation, Fly turns to sensual incentive: the "warm and thick" Clover awaits the Bee's plundering.

I have been writing as though we knew the "secret" of the poem from the beginning—but it is only in the last line of the last stanza that we are made aware of Dickinson's impersonation. She makes "Fly" into a proper name by signing her Letter "Yours, Fly." "Bee" therefore becomes retroactively a proper name, too: "Bee! I'm expecting you!" This is the Aesopian world of

Bee and Fly (cousins to the Grasshopper and Ant) enlivened by New England tartness. It is only in the last stanza, in Fly's last utterance, that Fly's loneliness is glimpsed: she wants another creature like herself on the scene. Frogs and Birds and Clover are no companions for a Fly. But Bee is a fellow winged insect, and Fly's life will not be complete till he returns. She retains her peremptory quality at the beginning of the final stanza—"You'll get my Letter by / The Seventeenth; Reply." But then, softening her imperative, she longingly woos the Bee: "Or better, be with me - " ("be Bee with me," as Dickinson makes "be" a combination of verb and noun).

The Dickinsonian "secret" jumps out at the close: we have been reading not—as we thought—the words of a human being wishing for the Bee's return, but rather the Letter of an insect-person named "Fly." "Several of Nature's People / I know and they know me / I feel for them a transport / Of Cordiality": this poem makes good Dickinson's own claim of friendship with creatures (see *1096, "A narrow Fellow in the Grass"). Even among "Nature's People" there are tribes, and Bee belongs to the tribe of Fly. Under the poem's mischievous play, there lies the yearning of the unique Dickinson for a natural companion resembling herself.

[J 1035]

# 994

> He scanned it - Staggered -
> Dropped the Loop
> To Past or Period -
> Caught helpless at a sense as if
> His Mind were going blind -
>
> Groped up, to see if God were there -
> Groped backward at Himself
> Caressed a Trigger absently
> And wandered out of Life -

Eight verbs make up this past-tense obituary, tracking its protagonist's course from a new awareness, through disorientation, to suicide. A catastrophic realization has occurred, named simply "it." Whatever "it" is, it is massively destructive. Once "He" has scanned it (perhaps a letter?), he is undone, and staggers, as if felled by a blow. What will be the results in his mind after the initial assault? First, he loses all sense of time: everything preceding the blow vanishes, as a new view of life obliterates the past; and second, he loses all connection to the "Period" in which he lives. Dickinson imagines that all human beings are oriented by "Loop[s]" to Past, Present, and Future, each a "Period." Her protagonist is now untethered to his Past and from any idea that such "Period[s]" constitute life. He lives in the single and eternal Present of "it." The seeing of the Mind ("in the mind's eye, Horatio"), with which he had "scanned" his undoing, has been put out; in his blindness he catches at any sense that will reorient him, but none appears. Deprived of the world of mind and the world of sense, this blind man gropes first toward the vague "up" where God may be found, but he finds nothing. Next, turning away from the unresponding heavens, he gropes "backward" to see whether any past form of security may be found for his blind staggering Self; but just as God is not at home to him, he is not at home to himself.

There is in fact no home for him anywhere in the universe; and so he seeks obliteration of consciousness, in successive steps, like the prisoner of the Inquisitor in "The Heart asks Pleasure - first - " (*588). Unlike the prisoner of that poem, he can be his own deliverer, and the only thing left for him to love is the means of his self-destruction, the "Trigger" of the saving gun, which he gratefully caresses as he ends his broken existence. We normally categorize a death by self-inflicted gunshot wound under the rubric Violence; but Dickinson sees the act as gentle, even consolatory, enabling her protagonist—forsaken by the one who has caused "it," forsaken alike by his sense of time and place, forsaken even by God (analogizing him to the crucified Jesus), and left with no resources in himself—to "wander," in his disintegrated state, out of life.

Conscious of the descending trajectory of her eight successive verbs, and of the importance of the recognition that begins her protagonist's undoing, Dickinson splits her first four beats into two lines, rather than containing them in one. Rhythmically speaking, the first stanza might have read as follows:

> He scanned it - Staggered - Dropped the Loop
> To Past or Period -

Expressively speaking, it might have been shown as a descending series:

> He scanned it -
> Staggered -
> Dropped the Loop
> To Past or Period -

Dickinson's compromise between regularity and expressivity foregrounds the succession of verbs without utterly destroying the underlying rhythm of the stanza. This poem exhibits one of her more "blasphemous" adaptations of the hymn-stanza, as she appropriates it for the suicidal psychic dissociation following unbearable trauma.

[J 1062]

# 1010

Crumbling is not an instant's Act
A fundamental pause
Dilapidation's processes
Are organized Decays -

'Tis first a Cobweb on the Soul
A Cuticle of dust
A Borer in the Axis
An Elemental Rust -

Ruin is formal - Devil's work
Consecutive and slow -
Fail in an instant, no man did
Slipping - is Crashe's law -

We too casually use violent nouns—a "crash," a "collapse"—which obscure
the slowness of the temporal and emotional process by which the violence
(of break or breakdown) often comes about. Dickinson, a sedulous observer
of minute processes both in the sphere of nature and in the sphere of the
soul, unites the two spheres in sinister metaphors of hidden progressive
devastation.

   She begins with utter confidence in the truth of her initial proposition:
"Crumbling is not an instant's Act." It is not a "pause" but a motion. She reit-
erates her argument with the same firmness, resorting first, in the word "Di-
lapidation," to the inorganic crumbling of stone from stone as a wall dis-
integrates. But that is too random a process to serve as illustration: the
"Crumbling" of which she speaks is not random, but rather an "organized"
form of organic "Decay." She has in mind crumbling human beings, not
crumbling walls. But if the ruins of time are canonically seen in fallen stone,
she will translate those dilapidations (Latin: the undoing of a wall of stone,
*lapis,* stone by stone) into fallen Souls.

   Her successive approximations to the process of spiritual ruin make up one of her best runs of metaphor. The Soul (in the form of the brain) is the body's attic; neglected, it becomes abandoned to spiders, of whom the first sign is a single Cobweb. What could be less threatening? The Soul is a house; it grows an unsightly "Cuticle" (from Latin *cuticula,* "little skin") of dust when the housewife does not keep it scrubbed. The Soul is an apple; it has been invaded by an invisible worm, a "Borer in the Axis," the serpent that will guarantee its ultimate undoing. For her last metaphor, Dickinson finds the richest word, "Rust." Literally, it is the oxidized form of the element iron; figuratively, it represents decay or corruption. But it is also a fungal blight of wheat and corn. Either way, the Soul is an untended or unprotected object which is slowly destroyed or corrupted. Dickinson has in mind, of course, Jesus' injunction, "Lay not up for yourselves treasures upon earth, where moth and rust doth corrupt, and where thieves break through and steal: but lay up for yourselves treasures in heaven, where neither moth nor rust doth corrupt, and where thieves do not break through nor steal" (Matthew 6:19–20). The dangers to which human beings are exposed in worldly life (moth in wool, rust in metal, thieves in households) are external and material, but in Dickinson the agent of corruption is seen to be a spiritual one.

The poet's gnomic metaphors enable her, in her final stanza, to repeat her earlier firmness in statement. But while her first declarations of the nature of Crumbling were material ones (Dilapidation and Decay), her third-stanza declaration is spiritual: "Ruin is . . . Devil's work." Such an assertion is conventional in religious discourse, but Dickinson puts her own correction on it: "Ruin is formal - ". What can this mean except that the Devil has an "organized" process that he follows, step by step, in ruining a soul? Cruelly, his process is "Consecutive and slow - ": the Cobwebs proliferate, the Cuticle becomes a Layer, the Borer becomes the Destroyer, the Rust spreads from one element to all, and Eden becomes Hell.

Dickinson has been speaking in the abstract about the diseases of the Soul, but suddenly she reverts to a common experience: a man slipping until he crashes in a Fall. "Crumbling is not an instant's Act" mutates into "Fail in an instant, no man did." We read "Fall" for "Fail," in an instance of our tendency to optic slippage. And, forsaking the Devil and his works, Dickinson ends with a scientific "law of nature": if there is to be a Crash, it will have been preceded by Slipping, instant by instant, slowly and invisibly, till the

Ruin is manifest. Where "Pause" may hide "Decays," where slow "Dust" and "Rust" rhyme, Crash is sudden and inevitable, if only by the nature of the physical universe.

Why, then, does Dickinson bring in the Devil at all? He is not a familiar presence in her work. In fact, he appears in only one other poem ("The Devil - had he fidelity"; 1510, J 1479), in which he may be a personification of someone whom Dickinson had extravagantly admired, but whose moral character she came to find inadequate, not to say repellent. In "Crumbling is not an instant's Act," Dickinson may have been tracking her own gradual but extreme disillusion with a former friend. The relationship declined slowly but irremediably, and only in retrospect could Dickinson see its earliest cobwebs and dust, which were to grow into irreversible dilapidations and decays causing the ultimate "Crashe." Yet with her customary reticence, Dickinson never identifies her "Devil," and the poem remains less a personal account than an exposition of the formal incremental pattern of the law of human ruin.

[J 997]

# 1038

Bloom - is Result - to meet a Flower
And casually glance
Would cause one scarcely to suspect
The minor Circumstance

Assisting in the Bright Affair
So intricately done
Then offered as a Butterfly
To the Meridian -

To pack the Bud - oppose the Worm -
Obtain its right of Dew -
Adjust the Heat - elude the Wind -
Escape the prowling Bee -

Great Nature not to disappoint
Awaiting Her that Day -
To be a Flower, is profound
Responsibility -

Keats's determined conception of the world, in an 1819 letter to George and Georgiana Keats, as a "Vale of Soul-making" (by contrast to the Christian conception of it as a "Vale of Tears") occurs to Dickinson, too, but she plays the drama out on a miniature stage. We are in the Vale of Flower-making now; and although passers-by take the blooming of a Flower for granted, Dickinson wants to reveal the long and effortful process by which the Flower draws Herself into being and protects Herself from predators.

The poet begins by calling this process, with understatement, a "minor Circumstance," but soon enough reveals how "intricately" it is accomplished. The Flower is responsible to its Maker (Nature, not God) for accomplishing its full potential (as in Jesus' parable of the talents in Matthew 25:15–30), so as not to "disappoint" Nature, who is awaiting its Spring appearance. Dickinson significantly does not ascribe gender to the flower until the end of the poem, when "it" (as in "obtain *its* right of Dew") becomes feminine, greeted as a fulfilled species by Nature (who is "Awaiting *Her*"). Although Dickinson's floral parable parallels the continuous spiritual development necessary if a Soul is not to "disappoint" her Great Judge on "that Day" of "Bloom" (Dickinson's witty revision of the Day of Doom), the poet infuses humor into her tale.

Dickinson would have known George Herbert's poem "The Flower," in which Herbert-as-Flower indeed disappoints his Maker through his presumption, encountering God's wrath because he is "Still upwards bent, *as if Heaven were mine own*" (italics added). Dickinson was, then, borrowing a traditional image for her Soul-as-Flower; however, for Herbert's earnest longing for Heaven ("Thou hast a Garden for us, where to bide") she substitutes a brisk gardening guide, didactically enumerating the Flower's obligations, which are "To pack the Bud - oppose the Worm - / Obtain its right of Dew - / Adjust the Heat - elude the Wind - / Escape the prowling Bee - ". Since Bees do not harm flowers, Dickinson's "prowling Bee" adds a last flourish of comedy to the otherwise reasonable list of activities necessary for the emergence of a Flower.

After "pack," which starts the process off with a strong phonetic monosyllable, Dickinson produces a set of strictly parallel two-syllable iambic verbs: "oppose," "Obtain," "Adjust, "elude," and "Escape." She creates a similar symmetry in her disposition of the verb series within her lines: the tetrameter line containing two verbs ("pack" and "oppose) is followed by a trimeter line containing only one verb ("Obtain"), and then the whole form is repeated: the two-verb tetrameter line ("Adjust," "elude") is followed by a single-verb trimeter line ("Escape"). The extreme regularity of the disyllabic series of verbs, matching the extreme regularity of the parallel distribution of those verbs (2, 1, 2, 1) in alignment with the meter, makes the universal process of becoming a Flower ("the" Bud, "the" Worm," etc.) appear as foreknown as the instructions for the assembling of a mechanical engine. Compare the following nonsymmetrical account (my apologies to Dickinson):

> To pack the Bud, defeating Worms,
> Soliciting the Dew,
> To find a shade against the Heat,
> Repel the Fly and Bee -

Such a revision demonstrates, by contrast, how carefully the poet adjusts her forms to represent a diagrammable abstracted process, a Law of Bloom, repeatable every spring by any Flower.

Dickinson might have structured this poem as a narrative beginning with Seed, progressing to Bud, and climaxing in the Flower. And such a narrative is partially "got up" in the third stanza of instruction (although it is accompanied by a catalogue of dangers—Worm, Heat, Wind, Bee—that would not occur in a simple account of biological growth, and that imaginatively enliven the garden awakening). But the poet does not simply recapitulate growth; rather, she begins with a two-stanza remark on the impercipience of the casual glance that does not suspect what goes into the "Bright Affair" of Bloom; the uninquisitive passer-by sees only the opening petals offered to the noon sun, which he likens to "a Butterfly," another pleasing inhabitant of the harmony of Spring.

In one sense, the poem could end here: the Result has been obtained. But impercipience has to be roundly corrected, and Dickinson is at her satiric best in pointing out to the passer-by, in the following two stanzas, all that he has missed. If we draw the spiritual parallel, we see that to a passing glance the evolved Soul is of course found pleasing, but the incurious onlooker remains unaware of all the diligent preparation enabling the emergence of such a Soul. By contrasting the stolid observer of the first two stanzas to a more intuitive person who understands the intricacy of spiritual evolution, Dickinson writes a didactic poem; by lightening her verse with the Butterfly and the prowling Bee, she writes a witty poem. Like George Herbert, she fuses wit and witness.

[J 1058]

# 1064

As the Starved Maelstrom laps the Navies
As the Vulture teased
Forces the Broods in lonely Valleys
As the Tiger eased

By but a Crumb of Blood, fasts Scarlet
Till he meet a Man
Dainty adorned with Veins and Tissues
And partakes - his Tongue

Cooled by the Morsel for a moment
Grows a fiercer thing
Till he esteem his Dates and Cocoa
A Nutrition mean

I, of a finer Famine
Deem my Supper dry
For but a Berry of Domingo
And a Torrid Eye -

"As the Starved Maelstrom . . . / As the Vulture . . . / As the Tiger," so "I," says Dickinson in a long simile-oriented periodic sentence about Famine. The Maelstrom and the Vulture are only pretexts by which to reach the Tiger, whose narrative is fully extended. "I like to see it lap the Miles - ", Dickinson had said of her Iron Horse the Train (*383)—but it is quite another thing to have a Starved Maelstrom "lap" whole human Navies. The equally starved Vulture devours whole unprotected young "Broods" of lesser birds in their lonely Valleys. But the Tiger—ah, the Tiger! Dickinson's relish is palpable.

The Tiger's unnatural hunger has been awakened by finding "a Crumb of Blood" (Dickinson's sadistic substitute for "a Crumb of Bread"), but that preliminary taste will not suffice: he needs a whole human body on which to feast. With the arousing savor of Blood lingering in his mouth, the Tiger "fasts Scarlet," obsessed by his blood-desire, until he encounters his doomed prey—"a Man / Dainty [daintily] adorned with Veins and Tissues" (or so this "Morsel" seems to the Tiger, as impersonated by Dickinson). The Tiger "partakes" of his meal (a "Dainty" word for tearing his victim limb from limb—but Tigers have their etiquette too). Then, in a parody of human addiction, the Tiger's hot Tongue, eased for a moment by its savage supper, grows fiercer, till he scorns his former food (the vegetarian Dates and Cocoa of the tropics) as a mean and stinted form of Nutrition. Henceforth he will be out for raw flesh alone.

Her similes of satiation finished, Dickinson draws her application: so she herself, having been "spoiled" for ordinary food by having partaken of "a Berry of Domingo / And a Torrid Eye - ", finds only famine in her normal "Supper dry." "Domingo" and "Torrid" were descriptions Dickinson would later apply to her sister-in-law Susan in a letter addressed to her:

> To be Susan is Imagination,
> To have been Susan, a Dream -
> What depths of Domingo in that torrid Spirit!
> 
> [L 855]

The relation between the two women had begun with adoration on the part of Dickinson, who found with Susan a form of brilliant conversation she had not known before, and this poem suggests how thoroughly the acquaintance with Susan spoiled her for milder fare. Susan's tropic lips and torrid eyes —with the exoticism Dickinson attributes to Santo Domingo—have transformed Dickinson into a Tiger who, having tasted Blood, wants no more of the insipid Cocoa and Dates of the desert (for Dickinson, the desert of Amherst society). In reflecting on what she has become in the wake of this desire, Dickinson first isolates the turbulence of spirit that has made her a Maelstrom; then the predatory avidity that has made her a Vulture; and only then the blood-hunger that has made her a Tiger. No wonder she found the Amherst ladies "Soft - Cherubic Creatures - " (*675) by comparison to herself, a Vulture/Tiger in their sitting-rooms.

There is a sudden subsidence in the final stanza, as Dickinson ascribes to herself a "finer" Famine than that of her starved counterparts: what bleeding flesh was to the carnivorous Tiger, a tropical Berry has been to her. She retains rational judgment, being able to "Deem" (that word of careful consideration) her New England Supper unpalatable. Even the rhythm of down-beats changes for a moment into the iambs of "For but a Berry of Domingo." The change in decorum makes us conscious of the preceding hammering rhythms of appetite—those dactyls and trochees, with their sharp initial pulse—that have so far governed the poem. And we become aware, as well, that in the first line of this final stanza Dickinson trims down her earlier first-line model (a nine-syllable tetrameter such as "Cooled by the Morsel for a moment") into a seven-syllable trimeter: "I, of a finer Famine." Until this moment, the narrative of ravenous appetite, with its several line-end enjambments, has even roved over the white space between stanzas: "the Tiger eased // By but a Crumb"; "his Tongue // Cooled by the Morsel." A subject can emerge in mid-line ("his Tongue") and find its verb ("grows") only by traversing the stanza break. The subsidence into "Supper" at the end cools the poem to some extent, but the Torrid remains dominant.

The theme of the unsubduable appetite for flesh prompts some of Dickinson's best imaginative efforts. What is it to be "eased // By but a Crumb of Blood"? How does one "fast Scarlet"? Best of all is her evocation of the Tiger's refined aesthetics: what he finds most appealing is a man "Dainty adorned with Veins and Tissues." The relativism of taste is frequently mentioned by Dickinson, as in "The Robin's my Criterion for Tune - " (*256); in that poem, it is conceded that the poet sees "New Englandly," but it is argued that even the Queen can see only "Provincially." Each person's taste is limited by context. Had one the constitution of a Tiger, one might well see "Veins" and "Tissues" as "dainty adornments," while the same words ("dainty," "adornment") in Amherst parlors might be applied to necklaces and cameos. Were one a Cat, a Mouse might be a "Morsel" (from Latin *mordere,* to bite); but when one is a grand Tiger, a suitable "Morsel" is a Man.

The poem is laden with a multitude of two-syllable trochaic nouns and adjectives: "Maelstrom," "Navies," "Vulture," "Valleys," "Tiger," "Scarlet," "Dainty," "Tissues," "Morsel," "moment," "fiercer," "finer," "Famine," "Supper," "Berry," "Torrid." Among all these, Dickinson's two tri-syllabic words, each with the accent in the middle, stand out, "matching" each other not only accentually but also thematically as objects of consumption: the dismissive "Nutrition" (for the Tiger) and the exalted "Domingo" (for the poet). And of course the prolongation of starvation is imitated in the long postponement of the personal correlative ("I") to Maelstrom, Vulture, and Tiger.

The main clause (or kernel) of the whole periodic sentence is "I Deem": it stands festooned with the three similes ("as the . . . Maelstrom laps," "as the Vulture . . . Forces," and "as the Tiger . . . partakes"), together with all their dependent and coordinate "dainty" adornments. The identification of poet and Tiger is made by the thematically allied, and phonetically rhymed, closing verbs—for the Tiger, "esteem," for herself, the echoing "Deem"—both of them the dismissive (and deranged) judgments of passion masquerading as evaluative connoisseurship.

[J 872]

# 1096

A narrow Fellow in the Grass
Occasionally rides -
You may have met him? Did you not
His notice instant is -

The Grass divides as with a Comb -
A spotted Shaft is seen,
And then it closes at your Feet
And opens further on -

He likes a Boggy Acre -
A Floor too cool for Corn -
But when a Boy and Barefoot
I more than once at Noon

Have passed I thought a Whip Lash
Unbraiding in the Sun
When stooping to secure it
It wrinkled And was gone -

Several of Nature's People
I know and they know me
I feel for them a transport
Of Cordiality

But never met this Fellow
Attended or alone
Without a tighter Breathing
And Zero at the Bone.

This is one of several poems in which Dickinson represents herself as a Boy (see also 231, 271, 284, 456, 547, 1271, 1538, and 1577). Such poems tend to envy the freedom granted to boys and denied to girls. This speaker was "a Boy and Barefoot" when he encountered the snake; it's unlikely that a well-brought-up Amherst girl, although she might go barefoot in her own garden, would be allowed to wander barefoot further afield. The boy, with enough outdoor experience to know that snakes prefer a cool bog to a warm field, has been unnerved more than once in his barefoot forays by unexpectedly encountering a snake. (He, and the poet, were aware that New England harbors poisonous snakes, such as the copperhead.) The "boyish" part of the poem vanishes in the last two stanzas, which sound "Dickinsonian" rather than Huck-Finn-like.

In Dickinson's cunning two-part construction, a general view of the snake occupies the first ten lines (in which the speaker addresses a general audience as "You"), while the retrospective boyhood narrative occasions the next six lines. In the opening ten-line description of the "narrow Fellow" and his passage through the Grass, he is referred to for the most part with the personal pronoun "he": "You may have met him? . . . / His notice instant is - . . . / He likes a Boggy Acre." But in the second stanza "he" becomes "A spotted Shaft," as Dickinson defamiliarizes the masculine pronoun into a visual object. In the boyhood retrospect, the deceptive snake / Whip Lash turns into an "it" that undergoes a lightning metamorphosis from inanimate to animate between its two immediately successive occurrences: as the boy stoops to secure "it" (as Whip Lash), "It" (as snake) "wrinkled And was gone - ". At this point, the threatening has routed the familiar: the colloquial "You" vanishes, never to return. The last eight lines, written in an adult first person (rather than the assumed male voice of the previous boyhood tale), distinguish the rest of "Nature's People" from the snake—who has changed from "A . . . Fellow" to "this Fellow" as the pointing finger stops at him. The boyhood shudder has been replaced by an adult awareness of the snake's poisonous power, so that one meets him not with surprise but with physiological terror: one's body temperature, deep in the marrow of one's bones, plummets to Zero, a death-chill.

Some have wanted to see Satan in the snake. Rather, as in "One need not be a Chamber - to be Haunted - " (*407), Dickinson says that one doesn't need a supernatural serpent to envenom a scene; an ordinary (poisonous) snake will do just as well to cause "Zero at the Bone." Dickinson may have intended her "snake in the grass" as an allegorical representation of a person, but hardly of Satan.

"A narrow Fellow" is deservedly famous, and bears investigation at almost any point. Snakes are not "narrow"; spaces are "narrow." This snake is a space-taker; as he smoothly "rides," the Grass "divides" (the rhyme enforcing the causal relation, and explaining the poet's choice of "rides" for the snake's initiating action). The snake's invisible motion causes the grass to "divide" and then "close" and then "open further on"—one can track him only by his effect. In an eerie fusion of empathy between poet and grass, the grass becomes human hair, and the snake is the comb making a part; but this too-domestic analogy is supplemented by the appearance—at the "part" in the grass—of "a spotted Shaft." A "Shaft" (Dickinson's 1844 Webster offers as the first definition "an arrow or a missile weapon") has the potential for destruction. On the other hand, real shafts are not naturally "spotted"; a leopard is spotted, or a page can be spotted with tears. Or the word can turn up in Dickinson as a transferred epithet—see her moral remark on the "spotted World" ("When we stand on the tops of Things - "; 343, J 242).

The "spotted Shaft" prepares us for the divagations to come in the description of the snake. The early easy colloquiality of "You may have met him?" (as though one were mentioning a neighbor) is continued in "He likes a Boggy Acre - ", but with that assertion the speaker is prompted to remember his boyish awareness of the unnaturalness of the snake's invasion of a warm field of grass. The continued unnaturalness of an inert Whip Lash (of braided leather) suddenly "Unbraiding" its strands is followed by the extraordinary verb "wrinkled" for the action of the snake consolidating itself to move forward. We are far more likely to use the word "wrinkled" as a past participle ("the dress was wrinkled") than as an active tensed verb; and the resemblance of "wrinkled" to "wriggled" tells us where Dickinson found her unsettling verb.

The boyhood story is over, and we think at first that the speaker has recovered cheerfulness, given the genial remark about his fellow feeling for his fellow creatures. Just as he is one of Nature's people, so are they; they are of the same tribe, knowing and known, and his heart warms to them (in Dickinson's etymological metaphor of "Cordiality," from *cor,* the Latin for "heart"). But we are mistaken: the impression left by the Snake was too deep, and all the Cordiality in the world can't shut out "this Fellow" (and the death he can bring). The fear he causes is not mitigated by the presence of human companions; the speaker, whether "attended or alone" remains (in memory) terrified, the breath constricted, the cordial warmth annihilated to Zero.

Dickinson was (understandably) annoyed when the *Springfield Daily Republican* "corrected" her punctuation when printing the poem, thereby altering her meaning. She intends to have her speaker say, "You may have met him," "*but if you haven't met him, permit me to tell you* that he arrives instantly, without prior notice." Her own fair copy reads:

> You may have met Him - did you not
> His notice sudden is -

But in the *Republican* it read:

> You may have met him - did you not?
> His notice instant is,

In a letter to Thomas Wentworth Higginson (to whom she had said she did not publish), Dickinson wrote that the poem had been "robbed" from her and that her third line had been mispunctuated: "Lest you meet my Snake and suppose I deceive [in having told you that I did not publish] it was robbed of me - defeated too of the third line by the punctuation. The third and fourth were one - ". Dickinson would have flinched at the incorrect grammatical formulation of the statement as printed. It should have read (to say what the *Republican* thought it meant): "You may have met him - *have* you not?" (italics added), so that the first phrase would match the second. She had said, correctly, "You may have met him. Did you not [meet him in the past], this is what he does." Later, in copying the poem for her sister-in-law Susan, she inserted the question mark in the middle of line 3 to avoid further misrepresentation.

[J 986]

# 1097

Ashes denote that Fire was -
Revere the Grayest Pile
For the Departed Creature's sake
That hovered there awhile -

Fire exists the first in light
And then consolidates
Only the Chemist can disclose
Into what Carbonates -

Dickinson's editors gave the title "Fire" to this poem. Of course it is in part about Fire, but it is also about many other things—Ashes, mostly, but also light and "Carbonates" and a Chemist, not to speak of a corpse, the "Departed Creature." "Ashes denote that Fire was - " helps us to understand how Dickinson saw her poems: she saw them as the cryptic residue of her incandescent emotional and intellectual fires. Her reader had to become a forensic Chemist, who, studying the residue of a fire, can perform the tests determining what materials are present in the ashes, and then deduce, from these, the nature of the original substance that would have produced these particular "Carbonates." This formulation explains why most of Dickinson's poems are so short: they are an intense reduction of life to the embers of verse, a metaphor the poet used later in "The smouldering embers blush - " (1143, J 1132) and in "Long Years apart - " (*1405). The miraculous resurrection of a body from a grave (its archetype Jesus' raising of Lazarus) is a familiar topic in literature. "But even Jesus," Dickinson murmurs *sotto voce,* "did not reanimate Ashes." To know (and revere) this "Departed Creature," one needs a backward-tracking Chemist.

One of Amherst's most eminent figures in Dickinson's lifetime was the Reverend Edward Hitchcock, a professor of chemistry and eventually president (1845–1854) of Amherst College. His fusion of religion and science in his many writings was, according to Dickinson's biographer Richard Sewall, influential in Dickinson's schooling; his volume *The Religion of Geology*

(1851), says Sewall, was read by Austin Dickinson and "almost certainly by Emily." In it, Hitchcock argues that although Christians have tended to believe that eventually "the whole material universe will be utterly consumed or annihilated by fire," this opinion is based on the "common belief that such is the effect of combustion." But nothing at all, Hitchcock argues, is annihilated in the process of combustion. The following passage from the opening pages of *The Religion of Geology* (quoted by Sewall with respect to Dickinson's slightly earlier poem "The Chemical conviction"; 1070, J 954), furnishes an equally relevant context here for "Ashes denote that Fire was - ": "But chemistry informs us, that no case of combustion, how fiercely soever the fire may rage, annihilates the least particle of matter; and that fire only changes the form of substances. Nay, there is no reason whatever to suppose that one particle of matter has been annihilated since the world began." Dickinson agrees with Hitchcock concerning the conservation of matter, but in her second stanza postpones the appearance of her Chemist and his Carbonates until after she has given a brief didactic account of the course of Fire.

The only scientific word in the opening stanza of "Ashes denote that Fire was - " is "denote" ("to signify by a visible sign," says the 1844 Webster); Dickinson uses it here as she does in "My Garden - like the Beach - / Denotes there be - a Sea - " (469, J 484). But the rest of the first stanza is full of ordinary words: "Ashes," "Fire," "Revere," "Grayest," "Pile," "Departed," "Creature," "hovered." We could say that Dickinson originally offers a "humanist" point of view: a departed loved one (now only an anonymous departed "Creature," its identity gone with its body) is signified by the (agèd) gray Pile of Ashes remaining after death. One should "Revere" these relics, while recalling the spirit of the dead person, which, between Death and burial (according to superstitious belief), continues to hover where its body lived. Adjuring her reader to "Revere" this Pile is Dickinson's mutation of the conventional address to passers-by, *Siste, viator* ("Stop, traveler") inscribed on the tombstone. The Pile, in itself unrevealing, offers nothing worthy of reverence; we are to revere it for the sake of the "Creature" now dead. The tremulous intermittency of "hovered" even suggests that the passer-by might still catch the glimmer of the fading ghost. But there are deficiencies in this humanistic account. We know that a dead "Creature" has been reduced to

Ashes by some past "Fire"—but so far as we yet know, the fire could have been simply the conventional fire of cremation (a ritual present in human history from prehistoric times). And the "Creature" is altogether unknowable in its present form of Ashes. So much for the imperfect discernment of the humanist approach to Ashes, Dickinson implies with some scorn.

All changes with the second stanza. There is not another word about the Departed Creature itself, or about its lingering spirit; no exhortation of any sort to the passer-by, nor any elegiac phrase corresponding to the pathetic superlative of "the Grayest Pile." In its chilly scientific words—"consolidates," "Chemist," "Carbonates"—the second stanza exhibits denotation rather than connotation. While the first stanza is one of product—Ashes from the Fire—the second is one of process, a process taken through three steps. First, the "Departed Creature" encounters Light; then it encounters Fire; then the Fire (as it consumes the body in death) "consolidates" the matter of the body into Ashes. "Consolidates" is the verb representing the aggregation of the calcined remnants of the body into solid residue. Scientifically speaking, Fire consolidates the body into "Carbonates"—the third of Dickinson's "scientific" words. In between, mediating between past Creature and present "consolidate[d]" Carbonates, stands the Chemist. It is no accident that these four important words alliterate. In that sound-link, Dickinson binds together the steps of her second-stanza process.

If we take this process as an allegory for Dickinson's view of the passage of life into art, then the poet is implying that a poem, when we first regard it, seems something dry, condensed, almost unrecognizable as something once aflame. The personal has been extracted from it, leaving not—as Dickinson said in "Essential Oils - are wrung - " (*772)—an "Attar" of roses (perfumed, permanent), but the desiccated reductions of a life. Who can interpret these? Who can even imagine that the essence of a Soul lies here? "If I am Ash," says the generic Dickinson poem to its reader, "you must deduce the components of that person I was from what is preserved in this 'Grayest Pile.'" A "Pile" —like a "heap"—denotes an undifferentiated mass not distinguishable into parts. If we had no Chemists, we could never deduce the organic elements— changed by their oxidation into Carbonates, but still identifiable as their past selves—that made up the Departed Creature. That broad word "Creature"— applicable to anything from a caterpillar to a giraffe—provokes us to want to discover and disclose its former species in life. We are all Chemists in search of identifying clues.

Dickinson's vocabulary becomes arid in stanza two because she wants to assert that her poems *are* available to a science—one of measurement and naming—that is as precise as chemistry. Wordsworth, after all, said (in his famous Note to "The Thorn" in the 1800 *Lyrical Ballads*) that "Poetry is passion: it is the history *or science of feelings*" (italics added). Poems are not things which aim merely at the solicitation of sympathetic emotion; they cry out for a "scientific" interpreter of their nature as the residue of feeling, a Chemist/Critic who can discern and disclose their raw materials no matter how arcane or hidden these may be. This material view of poetry generates the terse "consolidate[d]" lines of Dickinson's testimonies in verse. They are the residue of a severe trial of the flesh by the flame of those "passions" whose full "history" would be too long to narrate in lyric form.

Before the consuming Fire, however, there was light. Encountering passion and suffering is at first an enlightening experience, enlarging the mind and soul. "E'en in our ashes live their wonted fires," says Gray's *Elegy,* in a sentiment resembling that of Dickinson; but Gray leaves out the brilliance of the preceding light emanating in life from our "wonted fires." The connection between light and Fire (present in the sun) is an elemental one. Dickinson does not say, "Fire exists at first as light," but "Fire exists the first in light"—a cryptic statement, but one implying that light is the beginning of Fire. Art, too, in revealing our "wonted fires," exists first in light, as our passions are revealed to us by the sentiments offered by poetry. As Dickinson contemplates the massively consolidated, entirely condensed verbal residue of her feelings, she trusts us, as Chemists, to become analysts of the "Departed Creature" that she once was, to become the reverent travelers stopping at her memorial page.

[J 1063]

# 1100

The last Night that She lived
It was a Common Night
Except the Dying - this to Us
Made Nature different

We noticed smallest things -
Things overlooked before
By this great light upon our minds
Italicized - as 'twere.

As We went out and in
Between Her final Room
And Rooms where Those to be alive
Tomorrow, were, a Blame

That others could exist
While She must finish quite
A Jealousy for Her arose
So nearly infinite -

We waited while She passed -
It was a narrow time -
Too jostled were Our Souls to speak
At length the notice came.

She mentioned, and forgot -
Then lightly as a Reed
Bent to the Water, struggled scarce -
Consented, and was dead -

And We - We placed the Hair -
And drew the Head erect -
And then an awful leisure was
Belief to regulate -

This famous and beautiful poem is so seemingly transparent, and so open to us as readers, that at first we can hardly see the art in it. There does exist obvious art, however, in one stanza, the one describing the moment of death, and it was there that Dickinson made two crucial revisions. Originally the stanza read:

> She mentioned, and forgot -
> Then softly as a Reed
> Bent to the Water, shivered - scarce -
> Consented, and was dead -

Since this stanza is the only one in which we see the dying woman—and the only one from which the onlookers are absent—we depend on its deathbed scene for our idea of the dying woman's nature and character. In both versions, she utters a tentative phrase, and then fails to complete it (she doesn't even "say"—she merely unobtrusively "mentioned"). To render the actual death, Dickinson turns the woman, by simile, into a Reed—a slender plant growing out of water, bending with the wind, frail among sturdier growths of shrubs or trees. It is understandable that a Reed might bend to the Water—its medium, its origin—but in what manner does a Reed bend? Dickinson's first choice—"softly"—operates in the realm of sound or touch: the moment of death is unprotesting, almost soundless, smooth. The word Dickinson substituted for "softly," by contrast, operates in the realm of kinesis, bodily motion: the Reed bends "lightly," gracefully, like a dancer—the moment of death is accomplished with physical grace, conducted as the woman conducted herself in life. The other instance of revision originates in the need to choose a word for the ultimate convulsion of the body in death. Dickinson's first choice—"shivered"—represents, like the earlier "forgot," an involuntary action; it has the chill of death about it, and suggests the quivering of the body. The substituted word—"struggled"—is voluntary (like "mentioned" and "Consented") and retains the woman's spiritual status as a free agent, returning her, from her metamorphosed state as a Reed (like the nymph Syrinx in Greek myth), to a human plane.

We learn from this stanza that the woman was gracious, graceful, unobtrusive in speech, and unwilling to disturb those at her bedside by exhibiting an unseemly resistance to death. She dies a "virtuous" death of the sort described by John Donne in "A Valediction: Forbidding Mourning":

> ... Virtuous men pass mildly away,
>     And whisper to their souls to go,
>   Whilst some of their sad friends do say,
>     "The breath goes now," and some say "No."

The "happy death" envisaged by Donne exists, in the Christian mind, against the contrastive backdrop of those who die in sin, who pass away not mildly but horribly, who protest (like Marlowe's Faustus) with their dying breath. With her last breath, Dickinson's dying woman takes possession of the moment of death by consenting voluntarily to it, after her brief and unobtrusive struggle.

Around this woman, the family onlookers gather in vigil. Their presence (as witnesses) organizes the first five stanzas; then the woman dies; and their presence (as mourners) takes custody of the final stanza. "We" onlookers vary, in Dickinson's structure, between being agents and being acted upon, between being "We" (who watch and wait) and being "Us" (to whom things happen). This back-and-forth (from nominative to accusative forms of the pronoun) parallels the going "out and in" of the "final Room." I have italicized the pronouns (and the pronominal adjectives) in the following paraphrase:

| | |
|---|---|
| This *to Us* made Nature different | (us) |
| *We noticed* smallest things | (we) |
| Things were italicized *upon our minds* | (our) |
| *We went* out and in | (we) |
| A Blame, a Jealousy for Her arose [*in us*] | [us] |
| *We waited* | (we) |
| Too jostled *were Our Souls* | (our) |
| [The woman dies] | |
| We placed and drew | (we) |
| There was leisure [ *for us*] to regulate Belief | [us] |

The alternate rhythms of activity and its suspension enclose the psychological reactions of the woman's family. Her relatives feel the "great light" of the momentousness of death—a light italicizing everything that happens as they wait out this otherwise "Common Night" that bounds the time between the woman's living and her dying. The world, for the watchers, is organized between the death room and the household spaces of those who will still be alive tomorrow (themselves among them). They feel a futile protest against irrevocable mortality (expressed by the modal "*must*" of natural law)—that "She *must finish quite*"—while others live. The watchers blame others for existing; they want to be jealous, on her behalf, of those still living. The irony is that the gracious dying woman feels none of these things. She does not blame the living; she expresses no "infinite" jealousy. The souls of the watchers are "jostled" by Death in the narrow moment of the "strait Gate": "Enter ye in at the strait gate: . . . strait is the gate, and narrow is the way, which leadeth unto life" (Matthew 7:13–14). But the dying woman is not "jostled" by a superior force; she has simply consented, after her brief struggle. The poem is not chiefly about her dying. It is about "our" surviving.

This account of the dying hours of a woman beloved by her family is famous chiefly for its laconic but arresting opening: "The last Night that She lived / It was a Common Night / Except the Dying - ", immediately followed by the quintessential understatement: "this to Us / Made Nature different." Life goes on outside in its usual manner; only those inside the house know that they will never forget this "Italicized" date. But Dickinson has ways of making that Night "different" for readers too. The whole poem is related in the past tense, yet signs of the moment as a *present* one are everywhere. We see it in the pronoun "this," the proximal deictic (a "pointing pronoun" for something at hand; the distal deictic is "that"). "This" is a sign of something close by in the present: "*this* to Us," "*this* great light." A present moment is also implied in the mention of "tomorrow" (a narrative of the past would conventionally say "the following day"). We see the ongoing present also in the suspended grammar of the middle sentence that cannot finish—as it could if it were actually relating a past narrative: "As We went out and in / . . . a Blame . . . // . . . A Jealousy . . . arose / So nearly infinite - ". The syntax breaks off there, without a completion of the phrase: "So nearly infinite [that what?]" And finally, the poem ends in a prospective infinitive stretching out into the future, as the mourners have "an awful leisure" (in which) *to regulate* their Belief—which may never achieve "regulation" at all, since the narrative never reveals the outcome of the future to which it looks. The past Night is ever-present to the mourner who speaks, and she cannot yet speak of a successful "regulation" of her belief in order that it should conform to the Christian doctrine of the immortality of the soul. At the end, we stand in "*this great light*" of the past-present, as well as in the yesterday of "*The last Night*" and the tomorrow of "*to regulate.*" Dickinson's expertise shows us the mind of the mourner who will never recover from a past that is ever-present and that undermines her faith now and perhaps into the future.

After Dickinson's lightly touched rendition of the "virtuous" death in that succession of tender verbs—"mentioned," "forgot," "Bent," "struggled" (scarce), and "Consented"—we shudder at the lifeless verbs denoting action on an unresponsive body (its posthumous condition voiced in the definite articles—in lieu of an adjectival "her"—that precede "Hair" and "Head"): "We *placed* the Hair - / And *drew* the Head erect - ". The coldness of the laying out of the corpse generates the mechanical word "regulate." After the regulation of the body comes the "awful leisure" of reckoning with doctrine. (Has "leisure" ever before been termed "awful"?)

When the poem was first published in *Poems* (1890), the editors omitted stanza 3, with its "Blame" of others for existing, a sentiment presumably not considered suitable for religious mourners. The censored poem passed straight from "Italicized - as 'twere" to "That others could exist." Seeing such active worry on the part of the poet's editors produces in us a keener sense of how coercive the force of "respectability" was in Dickinson's day, and how indifferent she was to such "Dimity Convictions" (*675).

[J 1100]

# 1121

The Sky is low - the Clouds are mean.
A Travelling Flake of Snow
Across a Barn or through a Rut
Debates if it will go -
A Narrow Wind complains all Day
How some one treated him
Nature, like Us is sometimes caught
Without her Diadem -

Four items: the Sky, the Clouds, a Flake of Snow, a Wind, each an exemplum of human behavior when the soul forgets its regality. Both Dickinson's susceptibility to rapture before natural beauty, and her reverence of Nature as a queenly presence, experience shock when she encounters a day that does not permit a grateful aesthetic response. As the poet steps outdoors, the first thing she sees is that the Sky is "low"—a word that could of course merely imply low-lying clouds; but when she follows it by naming the Clouds as "mean," it is certain that human qualities are being remarked on. What can make a poet call clouds "mean"? They are stinting of their riches; they are lumps rather than architectures. "Low" and "mean" are words often used to make class distinctions, and the poem might seem to be pitting Amherst gentility against an Amherst underclass. But as we see, even royal Nature, when without her "Diadem," is "low" and "mean" too; so behavior, not class, is the issue here.

The first two items, Sky and Clouds, are barely indicated. Can we hope for a better definition of lowness and meanness as the poem continues? Dickinson's third example seems baffling: an indecisive Snowflake. Presumably a diademed Snowflake would proceed royally through the sky, not remain undecided whether it will take its course near a "Barn" or in a "Rut." It has fallen from its original celestial grace to a mean earthly estate. And finally, the lowest human behavior is exemplified in the querulous Wind. The Wind has not even the force of a wide blast: it is a "Narrow" Wind. Its complaint is unceasing, and wearing on the nerves in its persistence "all Day." There are no sins as such in these exempla—but by citing these falls from grace, Dickinson intimates that there are ways other than sin by which human nature fails.

Since the poem is a list (of Diademless features), Dickinson has to find a way to vary the rhythms of the members of the list. This is how they look:

The Sky is low -
The Clouds are mean.
A Travelling Flake of Snow Across a Barn or through a Rut Debates if it
    will go -
A Narrow Wind complains all Day How some one treated him.

The first two items, at four words apiece, are static and uninformative. Perhaps if the eye followed some phenomenon for a little while, the day might seem more alive? No—the Flake of Snow seems equally uninformative, hardly knowing its own trajectory, even though it takes up seventeen words. The eye gains no appreciable pleasure from the Snowflake's debate with itself. Perhaps if one opened one's ears instead of one's eyes? No—what enters the ear is merely a reiterated whine lasting for eleven words ("all Day," in fact). The poem, until now, has seemed merely a condemnation of a fallen Nature. But in a flick of the Dickinsonian wrist—"like Us"—the epigram becomes reproach. Dickinson is remembering human beings' less-than-beautiful moments, putting them up against the radiant ancient Greek word "Diadem," which represents their potential nobility.

Dickinson enclosed the poem in a letter, preceded by a sentence putting its concept more baldly: "Today is very homely and awkward as the homely are who have not mental beauty" (L 321). (She was interested in homely people, such as George Eliot, who nonetheless charm by their "mental beauty.") Her editors called this piece of social lament "Beclouded"—a title which gives absolutely no idea of Dickinson's analogy of natural to human behavior.

[J 1075]

# 1142

The murmuring of Bees, has ceased
But murmuring of some
Posterior, prophetic,
Has simultaneous come.
The lower metres of the Year
When Nature's laugh is done
The Revelations of the Book
Whose Genesis was June.
Appropriate Creatures to her change
The Typic Mother sends
As Accent fades to interval
With separating Friends
Till what we speculate, has been
And thoughts we will not show
More intimate with us become
Than Persons, that we know.

Dickinson begins riddlingly here, as in "Further in Summer than the Birds - "
(\*895), with the (unnamed) crickets of late summer. But this version of that
cusp of the year does not remain within the meditation of a "Druidic Differ-
ence" in the landscape. Instead, it becomes an allegory of "separating Friends."
They were—some would perhaps say that they still are—"Friends," but by
the end of this short season of Revelations, they will have separated beyond
the power of speech to remedy. What was daily "Accent" between them be-
comes, with their gradual estrangement, "interval," like a departing voice
heard only in fragments as it "fades" further and further into the distance.
The august presider over this melancholy decline is Nature herself, the
"Typic" Mother. It is she who is changing, as "Type" (a prophetic biblical
foreshadowing) encounters its predicted final fulfillment. (The early Chris-
tian church established many such Old Testament "types" prophesying a
New Testament Messiah: Isaac was a "type" of Jesus willing to be sacrificed

for mankind; Samson, his strength restored, pulling down the Temple of the Philistines, was a type of the risen Jesus defeating Sin; Aaron, as High Priest, was not only a type of the sacerdotal Jesus instituting the Eucharist, but also a type of the contemporary Christian priest, as George Herbert assumes in his poem "Aaron.") The "Typic Mother," like all archetypal goddesses, has a retinue and a legend. She sends "Appropriate Creatures" to accompany her change toward her Last Day, as her sacred book of natural legends, with its "Genesis" in June, is encountering its final "Revelations" in Autumn.

It is only after the ten-line prologue that Dickinson arrives at the two-line central comment on the fading Accent between separating Friends. And after that comes, as the third structural part of the poem, a post-facto commentary. The prologue, then, is more important allegorically than we perceive it to be at our first reading (when we have only natural change in mind). The narrative of the prologue relates four main events.

In the first two, the Bees leave off their murmuring as a simultaneous murmuring from some other source arises (the use of the identical word "murmuring" to characterize each of the two different sounds enacts the simultaneity of the two events and the presence of two sets of "Creatures"). The Bees were the "Appropriate Creatures" for Nature's Genesis, but they have been supplanted by—whom? All we are told is that the newcomers are both "Posterior" (post-Summer) and "prophetic" (predicting the end of this year? this world?). Dickinson's deliberate collocation—almost superposition—of these two "p-" adjectives applied to the same company makes us hear the Latin paradox: they are at once "post-" (after) and "pro-" (before). These earlier and later murmurs bracket the whole experience of Autumn.

The third main event of the prologue is the measuring (by poetic "metres") of the moment in which Nature's Comedy is replaced by her Tragedy. In the opening books of her Bible, laughing Nature was Primavera, Flora, and later Pomona. Now, in lower mood and graver aura, her "laugh" conclusively "done," her two testaments exhausted, she approaches her book's apocalyptic Revelations. The fourth event of the prologue is the announcement—by her summoned choral retinue—of the Mother's "change."

If we ask what the allegorical prelude tells us about the tragic separation of Friends to which it leads, we can answer with a scenario derived from the poem. At the very moment when honeyed phrases are still being uttered, a tone that gradually becomes identifiable as something other than the affectionate one of friendship enters the discourse. It even betrays a post-friendship "Posterior" overtone, and is therefore apparently prophetic of—of what? To the grief of the speaker, mutual laughter between the Friends has ceased entirely. The temperature of the friendship has lowered; its pace has slowed. Something is lurking. What unwanted revelation is about to come? The very inhabitants of the grass sense it, as the Bees' genial hums vanish and the cricket's elegy—the analogue to Dickinson's whole poem—begins. Finally, the daily "Accent" of the Friend "fades" from hearing as she fades from sight, and intercourse becomes interval.

With that, the story is complete. But Dickinson attaches a coda representing her posture after the separation has become final, and the prophetic has been proved true. The apprehensions earlier felt as merely speculative have now been confirmed; and the reticent speaker, unwilling to show her sadness to others, hides, within her own heart, the thoughts of betrayal and relegation that are now "More intimate" to her even than the Persons with whom she lives. We perceive that the point of the poem is not only to mourn the separation of Friends, but even more to mourn the subsequent concealment it enforces on us as a way of life. The "Persons, that we know" no longer "know" us; we live behind that scrim of Mirth which is "the mail of Anguish" ("A *wounded* Deer - leaps highest - "; *181, J 165). We exist henceforth in a double consciousness that forever destroys simplicity of response toward other persons, including any other potential Friend.

Dickinson had treated this theme earlier, in "The Crickets sang" (1104, J 1104), where the word "low" is applied not to meters but to "The low Grass"; the bees have not merely "ceased" to murmur, but have "perished from the Scene"; and the Crickets are accompanied by a host of human or humanized figures: Twilight is a Stranger uncertain whether to go or stay, Vastness becomes a Neighbor, and there are "Workmen" who are stitching up the last gap in daylight. (I have been citing the longest version of the poem, Franklin's Version B.) Dickinson's diffusion of attention in "The Crickets sang" into melody, various personages, and the coming of Night points up, by contrast, the beautiful coherence of "The murmuring of Bees," with its strict allegory tallying its events.

The poem gave Dickinson no trouble until she came to describe the post-traumatic state of the soul in the first two lines of the last quatrain, the core of the poem's experience. Here are those lines in earlier versions with her first and second and third and fourth and fifth choice of verbs about how she (disguised as "we") reacted to the elusive waning of a friendship:

Till what we could not {
*prove* (it is hard to prove a waning of friendship)
*choose* (breaking off the friendship ourselves)
*see* (we were oblivious in our lack of insight)
*name* (the change was too tenuous to be characterized)
*face* (we knew what was happening, but were in denial)
} has come

Although Dickinson changes "has come" to "has been," making the separation definitively complete and past, she settles on the infinitely expandable word "speculate," because the basic anguish of the soul is its uncertainty. We can "speculate" on all the matters represented by the five alternative verbs above: on whether what we suspect can be proven; or on our weakness in not choosing to make the break ourselves; or on why others could see what we could not; or on why we could not name what was happening; or on why we were refusing to face the fact of the cooling of the friendship. The word "speculate" shows us a mind constantly nervous, anxiously wondering, always suspecting, relentlessly doubting, covertly denying. It is a superb word, fully ironic in its (optimistic) root meaning "to see" (Latin: *specio*). In this poem, the mirror *(speculum)* held up to Nature gives no constant image to the agitated mind.

The poem begins in beauty and in elegy for the Typic Mother (and the lost Friend); but it ends in a stoic concealment, regretted but maintained, making us no longer the person that the Persons we know once knew.

[J 1115]

# 1150

> These are the Nights that Beetles love -
> From Eminence remote
> Drives ponderous perpendicular
> His figure intimate -
> The terror of the Children
> The merriment of men
> Depositing his Thunder
> He hoists abroad again -
> A Bomb upon the Ceiling
> Is an improving thing -
> It keeps the nerves progressive
> Conjecture flourishing -
> Too dear the Summer evening
> Without discreet alarm -
> Supplied by Entomology
> With its remaining charm

Understanding the opening of this exhilarating poem is helped if we render it into ordinary syntax. Lightning bursts upon the evening: a "ponderous perpendicular" drives itself into the earth from a remote Eminence whose "figure intimate" is the lightning bolt—the attribute of Jove. After that, the poem is on its way. What are the effects of lightning? Here Dickinson ponders; her draft effort says that lightning is "the transport of the Children / The jeopardy of men." The phrases are not untrue: children are delighted by the melodramatic effect of lightning, and men know its danger. Dickinson judges these sentiments too banal, and dramatically reverses them, so that the lightning becomes "The terror of the Children / The merriment of men." No glee in the Children, who crouch in fear; but a source of entertainment to men, safely indoors and enjoying the storm. The Eminence has more than one weapon: having driven his shaft of electricity, he "deposits" his Thunder, a weighty load he is glad to "put down" (the English version of the Latin *de* plus *ponere*). Having done that, the Eminence "hoists" himself back to his kingdom in the sky—as one would "hoist" a sail, in the original nautical sense of the word. And that is the end of the external storm.

As so often, Dickinson then moves inward, and we might expect a serious allegorical assertion that there are storms of the mind as well, causing alternately terror and glee. No—we find instead one of her most outrageous statements about human psychology: "A Bomb upon the Ceiling / Is an improving thing." It could explode in the skull's "Ceiling" at any minute (as lightning and thunder can appear at any time), and it therefore prevents any laxity of the mind. Rather, "It keeps the nerves progressive" in a constant glittering: the "glittering Retinue of nerves" was one aspect of Dickinson's consciousness in "Severer Service of myself" (887, J 786). And the Bomb keeps Conjecture constantly on the go, flourishing like a particularly energetic mental oscillation. The Bomb in the mind, an ever-imminent hysteria, makes even the most boring passages of life interesting.

After this gleeful cartoon of the Bomb on the Ceiling, Dickinson comes back to ordinary life, wishing, just briefly, that she could have a beautiful Summer evening, a time free from anxiety, in which the Night would be neither transport nor jeopardy, neither terror nor merriment, but simply peaceful. That, however, would be Eden before the Fall; the Summer evening would be too idyllic, too "dear," were there not the "discreet alarm" of a Bolt in the sky, a Bomb on the ceiling, and a Beetle on the lawn. The Beetles (the name stems from Old English *bitan,* meaning "bite") are, one could say, the terrestrial version of the alarm in the sky and on the Ceiling, and the poet has announced them as heralds of their alliterating Bomb by allotting to them the very first line of her poem, in which she ascribes to them a "love" for this sort of Night.

Because the "ponderous perpendicular" of lightning disappears from the sky, and the Ceiling-Bomb remains inside, something alarming has to remain outside, in nature—and that is the tribe of Beetles, supplying the evening with its "remaining charm" after Jove has hoisted himself, with his bolt and Thunder, away. Dickinson's dry merriment as she inventories god's Bolts, the domesticated Bomb, and the evening's Beetles is helped by some of the antithetical rhymes: what is "remote" becomes "intimate"; an "alarm" can also be a "charm." And Dickinson, by running all the quatrains into one sixteen-line poem, allows no letup of the multiple effects of the storm on children, men, and the poet herself, as she watches, with the Beetles, the anxiety-provoking elements of conjecture. All the sentimental nature poetry of New England is satirized in this little "idyll" of the glittering nerves of Conjecture under the aegis of the "ponderous perpendicular," the Ceiling-Bomb, and nature's Beetles.

[J 1128]

# 1163

A Spider sewed at Night
Without a Light
Upon an Arc of White -

If Ruff it was of Dame
Or Shroud of Gnome
Himself himself inform -

Of Immortality
His strategy
Was physiognomy -

This bizarre morsel of verse, with its self-rhyming tercets *(aaa),* each a self-contained sentence, moves to a peculiar 3-2-3 rhythm. In its rhyme, stanza-length, and rhythm, it is unique in Dickinson's work. Its spider, however, is not unique; this spider reminds us of the later one (1373, J 1275) for whom Dickinson felt such an affinity:

The Spider as an Artist
Has never been employed -
Though his surpassing Merit
Is freely certified

By every Broom and Bridget
Throughout a Christian Land -
Neglected Son of Genius
I take thee by the Hand -

The Spider arouses fellow-feeling in Dickinson because she too is "Neglected." In emphasizing his "Merit" (he resolutely returns to his art, in spite of housemaids wielding brooms) and his descent from the Spirit of Invention ("Genius" comes from the same Latin root as "generate"), she commends a Creature like herself, anthropomorphizing him to such a degree that she can take him "by the Hand" with that "transport / Of Cordiality" she expressed in "A narrow Fellow in the Grass" (*1096).

The earlier Spider of "A Spider sewed at Night" is not a Son of Genius or an Artist of Merit. He needs no certification by anyone, nor is he concerned with others' neglect; he feels no apprehension about a future oncoming "Broom" manned by an Irish servant girl. He is sufficient to himself; only he knows what garment he is constructing, and it is enough for him to inform only himself. He has laid out the main "Arc of White" that is the circumference of his web, and now he is patiently sewing together the radii which will support it. He needs no light for this work (the web will be discovered in the morning to have been done overnight; it was not there yesterday). The garment he works at so busily might be the Ruff (a lace collar) of a man or a woman; on the other hand, it could just as easily turn out to be the Shroud of a Gnome; we won't know until he has finished. He has the invisible template for the garment in his mind, and is reproducing it perfectly.

The complete autonomy of the Spider is envied by Dickinson—who did care (at least at first) what her sister-in-law Susan or her friend Thomas Wentworth Higginson or others thought of her work. Immortality was one of her favorite subjects, even though she was unable to believe in it as doctrine or describe it as experience; it always remained for her, if anywhere, on the other side of the veil dividing us from the unknown. But the Spider has no doubts (nor does he have any beliefs). He merely adopts the "strategy" upon which his Immortality will depend: to create, in his web, an unforgettable "physiognomy" or outward appearance.

Admission to Immortality has been thought by Christians to be dependent, at least in part, on inward virtue: the prepared heart is offered sufficient grace for eternal life. Reversing doctrine, the poet lodges the Spider's strategy for Immortality in outward virtue: the countenance of his web. The mind of the Spider is inscrutable; he will not confide his template to us. "Behold my web!" (his version of "Fiat Lux!") is his only, and final, gesture. The web (from Anglo-Saxon *wefan*, "to weave") is an old symbol for a text (from Latin *texere*, "to weave"); and although Dickinson never mentions the word "web," it necessarily comes to mind here, and with it the notion of weaving.

Why does Dickinson use the unlikely verb "sewed," instead of saying "A Spider wove at Night" or (using the common Spider-verb) "A Spider spun at

Night"? And why not "Upon a Web of White"? Perhaps she prefers, in representing the act of aesthetic creation, sewing to weaving—not only because it requires no loom (the Spider needs nothing but himself for his art), but also, perhaps, because once she had created a poem, it was destined to be sewn into one of her manuscript fascicles. And why is the Spider male? (Conventionally, the spider is female, the mythical Arachne metamorphosed by an angry Athena into a spider because of her woven portrayal of the infidelities of the gods.) And sewing, too, as well as weaving, is normally ascribed to women—so why not a female seamstress? Since this is a poem of undiluted praise, and since the archetypal Artist (from Michelangelo to Shakespeare to Rembrandt) has always been male, Dickinson made her Spider representatively male. But she is also prompted to maleness by the Christian Trinity.

Dickinson's triple rhymes begin as full ones—"Night," "Light," "White"; then decline to slant rhymes—"Dame," "Gnome," "inform"; and end in a paradoxical weakness (with words rhyming solely on a vowel without congruent consonants preceding it): "Immortality," "strategy," "physiognomy." Refusing the common nineteenth-century conventions of basing the claims of art on the noble character of the Artist, the truth of the ideas of the Artist, or an announcement by the Artist of his sacred intent, Dickinson ascribes to the Artist only the power to create a "physiognomy"—a surface—that is sufficient for his fame. Her poems—the ten that were published in her lifetime, always anonymously—offered only their physiognomy to the reader. (Like the self-sufficient Spider, Dickinson would be known to Higginson for eight years, 1862 to 1870, only through her poems and her letters, where the signature evolved from "E - Dickinson" in 1862 to a single strong word—"Dickinson" —by 1866. From 1875 on, her letters to him were signed "Your scholar.")

The Trinity of stanzas, the Trinitarian rhymes, the quasi-theological loop of "Himself himself inform," and the inscrutability of this Creator of physiognomy all suggest a backdrop of the Creation behind this small crystalline exercise. "Himself himself inform - " bears an intense resemblance to Dickinson's parodic rendering of two Persons of the Trinity, Father and Son, in "Behind Me - dips Eternity - " (743, J 721):

> 'Tis Kingdoms - afterward - they say -
> In perfect - pauseless Monarchy -

Whose Prince - is Son of none -
Himself - His Dateless Dynasty -
Himself - Himself diversify
In Duplicate divine -

In both cases, the same reflexive pronoun ("himself - himself") indicates absolute autonomy.

Reading the poem, one feels acutely the difference between the first two stanzas and the last. After composing two successive stanzas of crisp monosyllables and matching disyllables ("Himself himself inform"), Dickinson creates a third stanza ostentatiously classical ("Immortality" from Latin; "strategy" and "physiognomy" from Greek). She also makes it conspicuously polysyllabic (its three important rhyme-words have five syllables, three syllables, and five syllables). We are in the realm of artifact in stanzas 1 and 2, but have passed to some Platonic plane when we arrive at stanza 3. It is a "second-order" stanza, no longer narrating the facts of the case but speculating on the reason for their existence. Why does the Spider do what he does? Not to make a particular line of goods—ruffs, shrouds—but to achieve Immortality. And by what means does the Artist achieve Immortality? That is the query of the third, "metaphysical" stanza, with its answer: the face, the surface, of his product.

What are we to make of the meter? We notice, as we read this economical thirty-two-word poem, that the first two lines of each stanza make up a pentameter. It could be written,

> A Spider sewed at Night without a Light
> Upon an Arc of White -
>
> If Ruff it was of Dame or Shroud of Gnome
> Himself himself inform -
>
> Of Immortality his strategy
> Was physiognomy -

Reading the poem as transcribed above conveys how strongly the first two lines of each stanza serve as a "run-up" to the third. It is far less important that the Spider sew at night without a light than that he is creating "an Arc of White"—the work of geometrical genius that will make him immortal. It is far less important what the sewing will produce and for whom (Ruff or Shroud, Dame or Gnome) than that its template is known only within and to the Spider: "Himself himself inform - ". It is far less important that he have a strategy by which to obtain Immortality than that he has decided for "physiognomy"—for surface rather than depth, countenance rather than soul. (Of course it was popularly believed that one could intuit the soul from the countenance.) Dickinson arranged her poem so that each stanza would have this "run-up" before the crucial climax.

But we must return to the actual meter of the poem: trimeter, dimeter, trimeter. The two trimeters fore and aft bracket the smaller dimeter in the middle. It is as if the dimeters were throwaway lines, as if the argument of the poem could almost do without them. If the Spider is sewing at Night, it is obvious that he is without a Light. If he can make a Ruff for a Dame, he certainly could also make a Shroud for a Gnome. And if he is to attain Immortality, it is understood that he must have a "strategy." How else? But "strategy" is less easily dispensed with than the other dimeters. We could read (and get the poet's gist) by reading only lines 1 and 3 of the first two stanzas (literally jettisoning the dimeters):

> A Spider sewed at Night
> Upon an Arc of White -
>
> If Ruff it was of Dame
> Himself himself inform -

But this "strategy" breaks down in the third stanza. We cannot read:

> Of Immortality
> Was physiognomy -

But it would not take much tinkering to change this formulation to:

> His Immortality
> Was physiognomy -

Of course the real question is not what his Immortality was, but whether the Spider is gifted enough to win Immortality, and what line he must take to gain it. Artists seeking Immortality have opted for stridency, for up-to-dateness, for critical approval, for patronage; but all of these are audience-directed strategies. Consciousness of audience makes for what Yeats names "rhetoric," an oratorical posture unsuited for lyric; but out of our quarrel with ourselves, he says, we make poetry. Out of his inward supply of potential threads, the Spider, regarding no one and regarded by no one, spins a Face, by which he will live. Here Dickinson is quarreling with Shakespeare's King Duncan, who says, appalled at learning of the treachery of the Thane of Cawdor, "There's no art / To find the mind's construction in the face" (*Macbeth,* Act 1, scene 4). Just as, in music or painting, we find the mind's construction in the score or on the canvas, so also in poetry: the surface offers the "visible core" (John Ashbery, "Self-Portrait") of the mind that made it.

[J 1138]

# 1218

The Bone that has no Marrow,
What Ultimate for that?
It is not fit for Table
For Beggar or for Cat -

A Bone has obligations -
A Being has the same -
A Marrowless Assembly
Is culpabler than shame -

But how shall finished Creatures
A function fresh obtain?
Old Nicodemus' Phantom
Confronting us again!

The best—because most unforeseeable—line in this poem is "A Bone has ob-ligations - ," enunciated in a reproving tone, as one would say, "A Student has obligations." Dickinson's parodies of didactic diction are always witty; here, the "Sinner" is a bone with no marrow, and the "Teacher" asks what possi-ble ultimate end such a dried-out Being can expect. Denigrating the Bone as without useful function, and declaring that to be Marrowless is "culpa-bler than shame," the scolding Teacher/Preacher—if following convention—should next urge repentance and change of life. Dickinson's stunning third stanza turns the poem from parody to plea, from mock-reproach to heart-breaking query, with the famous passage from the gospel of John (to which we shall come shortly) acting as warranty for her anguished question: How can despairing "finished Creatures" be brought back to life and to a useful function? The turn in tone from irony to sincerity is one of Dickinson's most characteristic strategies. At first we are amused by the conceit of a defective Bone, but then we are stricken when the poem turns serious, as Dickinson asks how she can resuscitate her own "finished" emotional life.

Halfway through stanza 2, we see that the Bone is part of a whole "Assembly" of Marrowless Bones, in fact a human skeleton, its life-substance all dried up and gone. Other "shame" is partial, but this deficiency, being total, is "culpabler than shame - ". Coupling blame (culpability) with shame, the Reprover leaves the culprit blamed by others and shamed to himself, destroyed socially and psychologically. We at first take the poem parodically. After all, it begins with the ridiculous first stanza, which (after establishing full vowels with the "Bone," as well as with the "Marrow" it should possess) constructs Marrowlessness in a sequence of thin vowels (except for the long "a" in "Table") accompanied by a spasm of ten mock-irritated "t's" in initial, medial, and final positions, that I print in bold capitals below. The stanza even has three more "t's" (in "The," "that," and "that," which I reproduce in italic capitals) to litter the graphic field, if not the phonetic one:

> *T*he Bone *T*ha*T* has no Marrow,
> Wha**T** Ul**T**ima**T**e for *T*ha**T**?
> I**T** is no**T** fi**T** for **T**able
> For Beggar or for Ca**T** -

The sound "t" is noticeably missing is stanza 2, which exhibits not a single phonetic "t" (although it has two graphic ones, in "obligations" and "than"), setting even more in relief, by its sudden absence, the comic repudiatory effect of the "t"-sound in stanza 1.

What is a human being to do who has lost all Marrow from her inner life and is slowly drying into the skeleton of death? Other poets have written of the dark night of the soul, of spiritual dryness, but none before Dickinson would have begun such a poem with a Bone unworthy of the human Table, too unappetizing for the Beggar, profitless even for the Cat. Suddenly Dickinson becomes deadly serious, as in her hopelessness she recalls the visit of Nicodemus to Jesus (John 3:1–5):

There was a man of the Pharisees, named Nicodemus, a ruler of the Jews. The same came to Jesus by night, and said unto him, Rabbi, we know that thou art a teacher come from God: for no man can do these miracles that thou doest, except God be with him. Jesus answered and said unto him, Verily, verily, I say unto thee, Except a man be born again, he cannot see the kingdom of God. Nicodemus saith unto him, How can a man be born when he is old? can he enter the second time into his mother's womb, and be born? Jesus answered, Verily, verily, I say unto thee, Except a man be born of water and of the Spirit, he cannot enter into the kingdom of God.

The sacramental solution of baptism will not do for the already-baptized and skeptical Dickinson, and Nicodemus' question is one to which she can find no secular answer.

Just as she played with "t's" in stanza 1, so in stanza 3 Dickinson plays with "f's." "Finished," "function fresh," "Phantom," and "Confronting" make up the narrative of the poem. She is finished. Is there a function fresh? Phantom Confronting her! Nicodemus rises in her mind like a ghost, his question hers—but her hope to be renewed is ungranted, and no Savior is present to redeem the "shame" of her inner desolation.

[J 1274]

# 1243

Shall I take thee, the Poet said
To the propounded word?
Be stationed with the Candidates
Till I have finer tried -

The Poet searched Philology
And was about to ring
For the suspended Candidate
There came unsummoned in -
That portion of the Vision
The Word applied to fill
Not unto nomination
The Cherubim reveal -

Dickinson's division into two unequal stanzas of this exalted (if also ironic) narrative mirrors its dramatic division into two scenes. (Her editors Mabel Loomis Todd and Millicent Todd Bingham, in 1945, when the poem first saw publication, split the poem by rhyme into three quatrains.)

In the first scene, the Poet, after poring over all the words she knows, thinks she has found the *mot juste* to fill a space in her poem, and indeed summons the word that has occurred to her. But upon seeing it, she remains dissatisfied, and orders the word to join the already-numerous group of possible "Candidates" for the occupancy of that space, bidding the word wait until she tries again. The word "Candidates" is derived from the white (Latin, *candidus*) robes worn by those seeking office in Rome; each of Dickinson's "Candidates" is seeking to attain some function in the poem.

The second scene shows that the Poet's hard work searching the lexicon of "Philology" (Greek: "the love of words") is not enough to create a viable poem. When the Poet is about to give up her diligent search and compromise by ringing for the "suspended" Candidate/servant/word to fill the vacant place, there appears, without any effort from her, not a suitable new *word* but a reconceived *concept*, a *gestalt* to which she gives the name "Vision." The Vision of a better *contour* of the imagination enables the poem to reorient itself and proceed, presumably, to a successful search for the right *word*. She had thought she was looking for a *word*: but really, she was looking for the completion of her inner *Vision* (which she had not even known to be incomplete). Dickinson utters a final terse comment: the Angelic Messengers at the throne of God—the Cherubim—are not to be "summoned" like servants for whom one rings. Although a worldly Candidate can be nominated for a position, a mere mortal can't nominate Cherubim to the position of Inspirers. The spirit (as Jesus said to Nicodemus) "bloweth where it listeth": one cannot compel the spirit (see *1218, "The Bone that has no Marrow").

The simplicity of Dickinson's first scene is complicated by the word "finer" in "Till I have finer tried - ." The Poet has been trying, and trying hard: she has a whole group of possible Candidates waiting in the wings. She has not merely looked at a few words, she has "searched Philology." Where can she go next in her dissatisfaction, with the empty space still blankly returning her gaze? She says (in one alternative) that she tried "further," meaning "I must seek further." But there is no "further" place than Philology to go looking for a missing *word*. In another alternative, she says she tried "vainer" (meaning not "with more vanity" but "more in vain"), but she rejects the word because it would telegraph prematurely the ultimate unsuccess of her painstaking lexical search. In the end, jettisoning both "further" and "vainer," she arrives at "finer": trying "finer" is like trying "harder," and this choice embodies an aesthetic and moral self-critique. "I have been looking too coarsely, been too willing to settle for what I've found (that 'suspended Candidate'), even though I know it is not the truly 'right' word. I must reform my character, and be faithful to my standard of what Poetry is."

The Poet is admirably commanding in the first scene, evaluating the "propounded word" and then issuing a peremptory imperial order: "Be stationed with the Candidates." The grammar of stanza 2 puzzles by its incompleteness. Originally it had read as a complete sentence with a dependent clause in "when," and this version was adopted in the first printing of the poem in 1945 in *Bolts of Melody* (italics added here):

> The Poet searched Philology
> And *when* about to ring

For the suspended Candidate
There came unsummoned in -
That portion of the Vision]

Dickinson knowingly sacrificed the acceptable grammar of an adverbial
clause in "when" so as not to have the "unsummoned" portion of the inde-
pendent Vision depend in some temporal way ("when") on the Poet's action.
Interestingly, Dickinson sees the whole conceptual "Vision" of the poem as
divisible during composition. The Poet has gotten part of the poem right,
but a "portion of the Vision"—as yet not clarified in her own mind—is re-
sponsible for that annoying and persisting space in the manuscript. She must
retrace her steps, go back to her originating experience of the poem, and try
again. Of course as soon as she realizes that what is blocking the completion
of the poem is not a missing *word* but a missing *part of her Vision,* the *gestalt*
of the whole Vision occurs as if by magic; and we know that in its wake the
right word will soon be applying (as a successful Candidate) to fill the blank
space.

Cherubim, represented in beaten gold on either side of the "mercy seat"
of God (Exodus 25), are at the beck and call of God, not of the Poet. As God
"nominates" them for one function or another, they obey Him; but the Poet
has not God's power to command. However, if the Poet is true to what she
has already seen of her Vision, God will send down—in Dickinson's anal-
ogy—an angelic messenger to reveal the missing portion. Dickinson's happi-
ness when the Vision is complete exhibits itself when she rhymes "fill" with
"reveal," but the sentiment closing the poem is a warning to other poets: do
not think you can compel Poetry into existence; revelation cannot be forced.
The patience required to wait and meditate on the amount of the Vision al-
ready known, in the hope that more will be revealed, is a quality of character.
Self-interest may press a poet to complete a poem hastily with an approxi-
mate word, settling for the best that "Philology" seems at that moment to
offer. But fidelity to Poetry counsels patience in awaiting the completion of
the inner imaginative Vision of the poem before completion of its diction.

"Shall I take thee" is a poem conspicuously unornamental in terms of al-
literation and assonance. Its depth comes from its twenty instances of solemn
Latin-, Greek-, and Hebrew-derived words:

"Poet" (twice) from *poetes* (Greek);
"propound" from *pro* + *ponere;*
"word" (twice) from *verbum;*
"stationed" from *stare;*
"Candidates" (twice) from *candidus;*
"finer" from *finus;*
"tried" from *triare;*
"searched" from *circus;*
"Philology" from *philo* + *logos* (Greek);
"suspended" from *sub* + *ponere;*
"unsummoned" from *sub* + *monere;*
"portion" from *portio;*
"Vision" from *videre;*
"applied" from *ad* + *plicare;*
"nomination" from *nominare;*
"Cherubim" from the Hebrew equivalent;
"reveal" from *re* + *velum.*

The only major words of "Shall I take thee?" that are not derived from classical languages are "take," "ring," and "fill." For all its ironic picture of the earnestly striving (and humanly tempted) Poet, and its final warning to other poets, the poem takes as its governing metaphor the Puritan religious narrative of election and grace. Dickinson reconceives that narrative in secular terms of authorship and vision, and phrases it in a classical vocabulary to suit the immemorial nature of the Poet's character and undertaking.

[J 1126]

# 1263

> Tell all the truth but tell it slant -
> Success in Circuit lies
> Too bright for our infirm Delight
> The Truth's superb surprise
> As Lightning to the Children eased
> With explanation kind
> The Truth must dazzle gradually
> Or every man be blind -

Dickinson defends "slant" telling just as Jesus defended parable: some truths must be told allegorically. But Jesus' motive is esoteric, while Dickinson's is charitable. Jesus says to his disciples, in a mysterious passage (Mark 4:12), that he speaks in parables so that those disposed to convert will understand, but resistant sinners will not (however acute their bodily senses of seeing and hearing may be). He utters his truths in parables "That seeing they [resistant sinners] may see, and not perceive; and hearing they may hear, and not understand; lest at any time they should be converted, and their sins should be forgiven them."

Dickinson, so given to symbolic statement herself, must have pondered Jesus' statement. Perhaps she here decides to make a counter-statement of her own reason for slanting the truth. Her purpose is not to hide it from those preferring untruth, but rather to mediate it, out of kindness, to those as yet too weak to bear its glare. The stunning light that strikes us when we recognize a hitherto-unknown truth is too difficult to gaze at unless it makes a "gradual" approach to us through symbolic statement. Just as adults "ease" the passage of Lightning into the minds of Children who are (understandably) frightened by it, by not immediately revealing its lethal potential, so Dickinson will "ease" the lightning-stroke of truth into her readers' souls by an "explanation kind": her parables.

Dickinson's adjuration to tell "all" the truth implies that a poet can be tempted to tell only part—the part that will be acceptable to her audience.

(She frequently resisted the temptation of popular accessibility, willing to pay the cost of the lesser immediate intelligibility of some poems.) This poem is a "kind" one that even Children can read, and one made instantly appealing by its phonetic and graphic play—first on the letter "t" in both initial and final position ("*Tell* all the *Truth* but *tell* i*t* slan*t*), and then on the letter and sound "s": "*s*lant," "*s*uccess," "*C*ircuit," "lie*s*," "Truth'*s* *s*uperb *s*urprise," "A*s*," "ea*s*ed," "mu*s*t dazzle." This alliteration, along with the inner rhyme in "bright" and "Delight," gives a lilt of frivolity to a didactic poem—which this is, as it recommends its "slant" poetics. We might have expected, after "The Truth's superb . . . ," a noun such as "revelation" or "doctrine"—but when we see "surprise," we recognize that Delight, as well as Lightning, accompanies the discovery of Truth.

Dickinson invents a paradoxical Truth that will dazzle "gradually"—paradoxical, because "dazzle" is one of the brightest, most kinetic, and most immediate words in English for light-illumination. In "The Night," Henry Vaughan writes: "There is in God (some say) a deep but dazzling darkness." Dickinson had originally thought to "dazzle moderately," but corrected the adjective to "gradually," a word closer phonetically to "dazzle" and familiar to us from the gradual brightening of the sun from dawn to noon. "Moderately" is too tepid an adverb to be associated with "surprise," and "gradually," from the Latin *gradus,* "stair-step," implies a steady upward motion, as in the *gradus ad Parnassum,* the poets' ascent to Mount Parnassus (whereas "moderately" implies nothing progressive at all).

Dickinson's boldest revisions are those that assert exactly the *opposite* of what she has just written. "Too bright," she had written; and chasing down another alliteration, she writes "bold" as the modifier of "Delight": "Too bright for our bold Delight." But if we are like "Children" needing truths to be "eased" into our understanding, our Delight that cannot bear the full white dazzle of unmediated Truth can hardly be called "bold." And besides, "bold" yields only one syllable, and Dickinson needs two to fill out the line, so she gives up her alliteration of "bright" and "bold," and substitutes "infirm." With a stroke of the pen admitting human incapacity and limit, she speeds from "bold" Delight to "infirm" Delight.

"Lightning" is a natural phenomenon, with no deleterious physical effect on the eye; but Truth's penetrating ray would blind "every man"—a serious hyperbole—were it not moderated in some way. We all begin as children knowing practically none of the truths of body or selfhood. Little by little, "the facts of life" (emotional and intellectual, as well as physical) are conveyed to us; but even so, we only half-formulate many of them. It takes a poem to make our eyes gradually accept the brilliant light of the Truth hitherto shaded. Dickinson's little vortex of darkening words assonating in "i"— "bright," "Delight," "Lightning," "blind"—gives a condensed scenario of what our fate would be if Truth were too prematurely, and too fully, revealed to us. But as these words also tell us, Lightning is a cousin of Delight.

[J 1129]

# 1268

A Word dropped careless on a Page
May consecrate an Eye
When folded in perpetual seam
The Wrinkled Author lie

Infection in the sentence breeds
We may inhale Despair
At distances of Centuries
From the Malaria -

The conventional feeling in the West about books (other than purely factual ones) was that they could either help the soul (Scripture) or endanger it (until 1966, the Index of Forbidden Books was maintained by the Roman Catholic Church). As Dickinson first drafts this poem, she falls into the scriptural diction associated with religious assistance: "A Word . . . / May *consecrate* an Eye" (italics added). She then violently secularizes the poem, speaking of the Word's now-dead "*Wrinkled* Author." Originally she had had a secular predicate: "A Word . . . / May stimulate an Eye"—and had had a religious "Maker." Secularizing "Maker" to "Author" enables her to use the reverent "consecrate."

Now we have the poem. And we see that Dickinson is not interested, here, in the religious or moral notions of the ethically helpful or the ethically noxious. She is thinking about books that were emotionally infected and are now emotionally infecting. This is not a religious version of forbidden writings; it is a medicalized one. The power of books resides not in their congruence with religious or ethical doctrine, but in their ungovernable transmission of thought and feeling (a view indicating, needless to say, Dickinson's ambition for her own work). Words are permanent; or, as she said in an 1872 letter introducing the first stanza of the poem to her Norcross cousins, "We must be careful what we say. No bird resumes its egg" (*Variorum Edition,* accompanying the poem).

The poem's first, impersonal stanza concerns the longevity of writing: years after its "Wrinkled Author/Maker" lies in his grave, a word "dropped careless" by him on a page may catch someone's Eye ("*an* Eye") and assist it. The second stanza, approaching closer to us in its first-person "we," turns the stimulation into something suddenly sinister. The emotion is now generated not by a Word but by a sentence, and a sentence (as children are taught) expresses "a whole thought." Within a single sentence of his poem—not merely a "careless" Word—the catastrophic emotional worldview of the long-dead Author, expressing Despair, is on display. Reading, Dickinson asserts, is a form of mental breathing; consequently, we "inhale" that Despair, the infection that was quietly "breed[ing]" in the sentence until we transmuted it, by our attention, into active and emotionally destructive form. The page we read can have originated far back in time, at "distances of Centuries"; yet its "Malaria" is still infectious, and we may acquire, as a result of reading, the permanent and perhaps fatal illness of Despair.

Dickinson, as we have seen, often begins her poems with the literal before advancing to the symbolic. Here she reverses the process, beginning with the abstract, general, and religious word "consecrate." Only in the second stanza does she reveal her literalizing metaphor, as the dead Author's "Malaria"— "evil air," in Italian—rises from the page and encompasses us in spiritual hopelessness. "There's a certain Slant of light" (*320) informs us of the finality ("Seal") of giving up hope: "'Tis the Seal Despair - ".

"A Word dropped careless on a Page" begins initially in the abstract, I think, because of the moves Dickinson intends to make as she secularizes the eternal Maker of Scripture into a "Wrinkled Author." The "Wrinkled Author" is curiously disposed of: he lies "folded in perpetual seam." Yes, in his grave. But why this metaphor? Are we to think, "folded in his shroud, sewn up in a perpetual seam of linen"? Perhaps—but I hear as well, in "folded in perpetual seam," a deliberately added suggestion of the folded and sewed "signatures" (grouped pages) of the Author's book as the "folded . . . perpetual seam" in which the Author is enclosed. (Dickinson may have been recalling *Areopagitica,* where Milton says that books are "not absolutely dead things, but do contain a *potency of life* in them to be as active as that soul was whose progeny they are. . . . A good book is the precious life-blood of a master spirit, *embalmed* and treasured up on purpose to a life beyond life"; italics added.) Infection was thought to remain in corpses, even buried ones; just so, says Dickinson, it can emanate from authors "embalmed" in books. ("This open book . . . my open coffin," reflects Robert Lowell in "Reading Myself.") Dickinson's own poems were being preserved in pages that had been folded in half and sewed into fascicles. She may lie "folded [inside her own] perpetual seam."

Dickinson conjoins the words "In-fection" and "in-hale" to connect the result to the action. And she takes pains to make the dactylic trisyllable "Centuries" echo the equally dactylic trisyllable "distances," giving them, in addition to a phonetic resemblance, letters in common that create a graphic mirroring as well: they share the letters *c, e, n, t, i,* and *s*. Whom did Dickinson have in mind, we wonder, as the Author from whose infected book she had inhaled Despair? Shakespeare, perhaps, from whom Keats had inhaled it earlier (see "On Sitting Down to Read *King Lear* Once Again").

[J 1261]

# 1274

Now I knew I lost her -
Not that she was gone -
But Remoteness travelled
On her Face and Tongue.

Alien, though adjoining
As a Foreign Race -
Traversed she though pausing
Latitudeless Place.

Elements Unaltered -
Universe the same
But Love's transmigration -
Somehow this had come -

Henceforth to remember
Nature took the Day
I had paid so much for -
His is Penury
Not who toils for Freedom
Or for Family
But the Restitution
Of Idolatry.

Dickinson reproduces the events of an unadmitted estrangement. The speaker and her friend still see each other, live in "adjoining" places, in the same Universe, among Unaltered Elements—yet they are no longer friends. The narrative, with its bleak opening line, "Now I knew I lost her - ", finishes its plot in that very line. It finishes a more extended version of the plot at the end of the third stanza: "But Love's transmigration - / Somehow this had come - ". The fourth and final stanza (composed of two rhymed quatrains, but inscribed as a single stanza) is written in retrospect, following the end of the narrative of this desolating loss-within-continued-presence. Here, as in

"September's Baccalaureate" (1313, J 1271) Retrospect is "An Innuendo sear / That makes the Heart put up its Fun - / And turn Philosopher."

It is usually thought (see Sewall, 212) that the poem refers to Dickinson's gradual estrangement from her sister-in-law Susan, who (with her husband, Dickinson's brother Austin) lived in the house ("The Evergreens") "adjoining" the Dickinson Mansion, and whom Dickinson had, on early acquaintance, idolized with a turbulent passion. Eventually Dickinson apparently had no face-to-face contact with Susan at all. (Austin Dickinson and Mabel Todd, the young wife of an Amherst professor, had become lovers, and sometimes met in Emily Dickinson's house. Notes still went back and forth between Dickinson and Susan, but the two did not converse. Austin visited his sisters daily in their house, and sometimes met Mabel Todd there; knowing this, Susan would not, and did not, set foot in the Mansion.)

The retrospective close of "Now I knew I lost her - " departs from the original personal narrative in favor of a generalization: what the poet has lost is no longer a particular woman, but "the Day / I had paid so much for - ". The fundamental tragedy is less the loss of the friend than the impossibility, even with toil, of restoring an obsessive "Idolatry" that had for a period consumed a soul. Considering that the First Commandment puts Idolatry at the head of the forbidden sins ("Thou shalt have no other gods before me," Exodus 20:3), Dickinson, toiling for the "Restitution / Of Idolatry," is blaspheming. Her erotic despair puts her, hopeless of "Restitution," into emotional Penury. (The word "Destitution" is, I think, lurking behind Dickinson's use of "Restitution." Semantically, she could just as well have said "Restoration.")

I have summarized the narrative of loss that occupies the first three stanzas, but have not yet mentioned the evolution of the narrative. In the first twelve lines, Dickinson oscillates back and forth between the fact of physical presence and the truth of emotional absence, a rocking which lands, eventually, at a *tertium quid,* the existence of "Latitudeless Place," neither here nor there, to which the former friend has removed herself.

*Emotional absence*                                    *Physical presence*

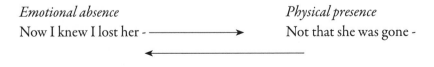

Now I knew I lost her -                                    Not that she was gone -

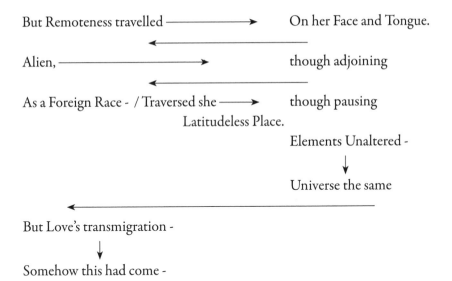

But Remoteness travelled ⟶ On her Face and Tongue.

⟵

Alien, ⟶ though adjoining

⟵

As a Foreign Race - / Traversed she ⟶ though pausing
                    Latitudeless Place.

                    Elements Unaltered -
                         ↓
                    Universe the same

⟵

But Love's transmigration -
      ↓
Somehow this had come -

The oscillation is also marked by Dickinson's unbroken rhythmic alternation between "feminine" end-words in the odd-numbered lines, and "masculine" end-words in the even-numbered, rhyming lines. (In "masculine" end-words, the last syllable in the line bears the beat; in "feminine" end-words, the beat falls on the penultimate syllable.) The rocking from Absence to Presence can take place within a single line ("Alien, though adjoining") or over four lines (lines 9–12), but the oscillation between opposites is the basic nerve of the narrative. Inner remoteness freezes the relationship; although the speaker knows just where her friend really is—across the lawn—the actual "Place" inhabited by the friend is in fact "Latitudeless": no coordinates can give it physical location on the real plane of the earth. It creates its own virtual plane, traversed by the remote friend in her inaccessibility. Every so often the friend descends from her virtual plane, "pausing" for a moment on the physical plane; but then she once again disappears into her own nonlatitudes. A Face that manifests "Remoteness" (during one of those moments of "pausing," perhaps) is conceivable. But how does Remoteness travel on a Tongue? In tone? In words? In irony where there was once sincerity?

There is a great deal of traveling in the first three stanzas. Not physical traveling: the friend is not "gone." But Remoteness "travel[s]," the chilly Friend "traverse[s]" her chilly nonplaces; and—in a surprising turn away from those wounding travelings—Dickinson adds that Love has undergone a "transmigration." Like the startling "Latitudeless," the word "transmigration" demands explanation. Love has migrated, yes. But whose Love, and what does it mean that Love has transmigrated? The word emphasizes "acrossness" in its "trans-"; it resembles such words as "transhumance" (moving livestock from one pasture location to another). But "transmigration" still carries echoes of its now obsolete meaning in the doctrine of "the transmigration of souls"—the movement of a soul away from the body it had once inhabited. The friend's physical body is present, with Face and Tongue visible. But the Love that had crossed from the friend's soul to the poet's has "transmigrated" into an unknown Latitudeless darkness.

The loss is unforgettable; it will be remembered perpetually "Henceforth," with no terminus suggested. In Dickinson's view here, there are only two phases experienced by human beings: the Day and the Night, life and death. Because Nature has taken away her "Day," Dickinson writes from a spiritually posthumous state. In what coin had she delivered the extravagant payment ("so much") for her "Day," before she was robbed of it? In the coin of worship, in the offerings made to an Idol. The poet's whole impulse in her present destitution is toward Restitution: she cannot *not* labor for it. Both the revolutionary who toils for "Freedom" and the laborer who toils for "Family" can hope to see their efforts bear fruit, however small. But true Penury is reserved for the one whose toil is fruitless, as she tries (impossibly) to bend her worship back toward the Idol in whom it had once been lodged. (Dickinson only once used the word "Idolator" of herself, in a letter containing the phrase "Susan's Idolator Keeps a Shrine for Susan"; L 325).

Dickinson designedly links the former "paid" to the present "Penury," just as she links the similarly alliterating "Freedom" and "Family" as comparable objects of toil. The ironic rhyming of "Family" (the domestic circle) with "Idolatry" (worshiping a "strange" "Foreign" god) points up the "wrong" choice of the poet in the original "transmigration" of her own Love, when her most intense affection had been extended to an idolized outsider in a house "across" the lawn.

[J 1219]

# 1279

The things we thought that we should do
We other things have done
But those peculiar industries
Have never been begun.

The Lands we thought that we should seek
When large enough to run
By Speculation ceded
To Speculation's Son -

The Heaven, in which we hoped to pause
When Discipline was done
Untenable to Logic
But possibly the one -

Dickinson's stimulus here is Paul's self-accusation in Romans 7:19: "For the good that I would, I do not: but the evil which I would not, that I do." She rewrites Paul in the first stanza (borrowing his "do," and adding its past participle "done," but pluralizing his "I" into her generalizing, but almost inevitably personal, "we"). She then invents parallels to his verb-template: in stanza 2, the verbs paralleling "do" are "seek" and "run"; in stanza 3, she begins with the parallel verb "hoped to pause," but reverts to the Pauline "do" in the form of "done." She puns on the "done" (an active verb) of stanza 1 and the "done" (predicate adjective meaning "finished") of stanza 3.

Paul is repelled by his inaction: "the good that I would, I do not." His action repels him equally: "the evil which I would not, that I do." As the reader's eye first scans Dickinson's poem, it may miss the most insistent stylistic feature here—Dickinson's monotone serial rhyme in *-un*, which denies the possibility of change: "done," "begun," "run," "Son," "done," "one." Each stanza undoes its initial positive past intention ("we thought ... we thought ... we hoped") by inaction, vitiating the optimistic life-narrative the poet wishes she could have told (concerning *doing, seeking,* and *hoping to pause* *in Heaven*). The whole becomes a parody of the Christian pilgrimage to Heaven. In this poem, in which not-doing is the "plot," not-doing is seen as *un*-doing, and nothing envisaged has been accomplished.

Yes, the poet tells us, she did do some things in life, but "those peculiar industries" to which she was urged by virtue of her talents "have never been begun." The poet's use of the present-perfect ("have been begun"), links the past to the current moment, enabling the faint hope that those industries perhaps could still be begun. Yet if she has not yet begun the work to which she was best suited ("peculiar" in the sense of "belonging to a single person alone"), it is unlikely that her disposition will change. The "other things" do not count if one is neglecting one's personal vocation to do them.

After the general ethical self-reproach of stanza 1, the poet recalls the impulses of youth. She thought to seek out distant Lands; she would run there once she was "large enough" (a child's phrasing: not "old enough," but "as big as the big people"). She speculated on what she might find there; but the charter to explore, because of her hesitation, has been "ceded" to her successor in the dynasty of speculators. The poem moves to adulthood, when she had hopes of a Heaven in which to "pause," gaining a reward for the painful Discipline of earthly life. But those hopes have faded, because that Heaven has proved "Untenable to Logic," to the reasoning mind. At the last moment, the poet snatches back a thread of her former fabric of hope: that Heaven of the Bible may be "possibly the one" she has yearned for.

The three-part poem, so common in Dickinson, is—by contrast to the two-stanza poem of brief comparison or contrast—well suited to the convention that a story must have a beginning, a middle, and an end. But the tolling "*un-*" refuses to differentiate among these phases: the story comes to the same thing, over and over. Industry, Speculation, and Discipline have all come to naught.

Dickinson's revisions are noteworthy. Seeking a word in an earlier version of the poem to fill the place where she finally put "Discipline," she hovered over "Chivalry," "Discipline," and "Tyranny." Each represents a summary view of what her life had been: "Chivalry," her first idea (with herself as knight-errant) was canceled; she then debated the rival claims of "Discipline" and "Tyranny." Saying that her life had exposed her chiefly to "Tyranny" would indeed imply how often she had found herself crushed by institutional or familial opposition; but the word "Tyranny" (she must have felt) offered too partial a view of her life, omitting her considerable independence of mind and spirit. In settling for "Discipline," she was able to include not only the punitive sense of the word (in which one's soul is disciplined by sorrow, trial, loss, and other adversities), but also the idealistic sense of the word, in which self-discipline improves one's work and character. That discipline, outer and inner, will no longer be necessary in Heaven.

Searching in the same, earlier version of the poem for the right adjective to attach to "Heaven" in the penultimate line, Dickinson began with "Impassable to Logic," mixing, in her metaphor, a blocked road and the path of Logic. "Impassable" implies a physical blockage (as a mountain pass is made impassable by snow). She canceled "Impassable" and went on to "Impervious"; but Logic is not rain, or cold, something that would seek a way through (*per* + *via*) to Heaven. Does Heaven block Logic? Does Heaven resist Logic? Neither image satisfied the poet. One can imagine the delight with which Dickinson, on the way to completing her "*un-*" poem, hit on the word "Untenable": the word is actually used in Logic (as in "an untenable proposition"); and the concept of Heaven is at intellectual odds ("untenable") with Logic, rather than at physical odds with it ("impervious"). Dickinson's punning choice of the adjective "*Un*-tenable" to characterize Heaven (another "*un-*" syllable smuggled in), and her placing "one" (the nearest English *word* to "*un-*") as the last sound in the poem, leaves us with the sound "*un-*" beating in our mind, as life's hopes are undone, "*un-dun,*" the unspoken but universalizing word that tolls within the remorse of each stanza.

"The things we thought that we should do" gives us an opportunity to take up recent claims that we should reproduce Dickinson's poems as they occur in her handwriting, in which many single verse-lines take up two successive lines on the page. Because Ralph Franklin's facsimile edition of Dickinson's "fascicles" and "sets" enables us to see how she ran her large script into turnovers, we can be tempted to consider the divisions at the turnovers significant. Domhnall Mitchell, who has examined the manuscripts minutely, argues against such a theory being broadly applied, showing it to be inconsistent with Dickinson's varying practice. Nonetheless, it is sometimes illuminating to see how Dickinson spaced her poems; and I reproduce below Mitchell's transcription, in his *Emily Dickinson: Monarch of Perception,* of

Dickinson's handwritten transmission of this poem (which occurs in a letter to Thomas Wentworth Higginson, L 459):

The things
we thought
that we
should do
We other
things have
done
But those
peculiar
industries
Have never [page break]
been begun.

The Lands
we thought
that we
should seek
When large
enough to
run
By Speculation
ceded
To Speculation's
Son

The Heaven,
in which we [page break]
hoped to pause
When Discipline
was done
Untenable to
Logic
But possibly
the one -

It seems at first, in this reproduction of her handwriting, as though Dickinson is counting by feet in the first four of her lines (one iambic foot per line); but she departs from this norm at "We other," which has one and a half iambic feet. Then we think perhaps Dickinson is counting words: two words per line. That theory holds until "done" creates a line all by itself, soon to be followed by "peculiar" and "industries," each taking up a whole line. The following two stanzas offer examples of all three previous models (one foot per line, two words per line, and one word per line), but they also depart from such models, as in the three-word, one-and-a-half-foot line "in which we," or the two-word, two-and-a-half-foot line "Untenable to." There is no embracing metrical theory that will cover all of Dickinson's decisions to break her handwritten line at one place or another. It is undeniable, however, that one sometimes gleans a different sense of the stanza when remarking her divisions of a single line (some interesting, some not). Therefore, Franklin decided to report them in his edition.

[J 1293]

# 1311

Art thou the thing I wanted?
Begone - my Tooth has grown -
Affront a minor palate
Thou could'st not goad so long -

I tell thee while I waited -

The mystery of Food
Increased till I abjured it
Subsisting now like God -

This must be the most haughty of Dickinson's poems. She at last has the courage to refuse the love she had once desired beyond measure. (I take the addressee to be a woman; Dickinson's tones to male love-objects are not often defiant.) That person who refused to invite an adoring Dickinson to her table, who goaded her sadistically for so long, is now available for worship. (A "goad" is a stick with a spike at the end used to prod and drive cattle. The figurative meaning that most closely approximates Dickinson's use of the verb here is "to drive by continued irritation *into* . . . some . . . uncontrolled state of mind"; *OED*, s.v. 2.) The taunting beloved—scorned now as a "thing" —is no longer to the poet's taste. In saying, unidiomatically, "my Tooth has grown - ," Dickinson is thinking of the word "Toothsome," meaning "attractive to the palate." And the poet even suggests that the woman whom she is banishing should seek out some "minor palate" to "Affront"—implying that even a less refined person than Dickinson would find the woman unpalatable, would feel affronted by her proffered availability.

Such total emotional repudiation did not exist in the first version, in which the woman was to "Supply the minor Palate / That has not starved so long." The earlier version assumes that the "minor Palate" could actually be satisfied by the woman's self, and does not put the blame for Dickinson's starvation on the woman (in the way that "goad" does). Dickinson, searching for the right word in this earlier version, allows—before deciding on "Affront"—

the woman to "Supply" (or "Endow") another with her presence, or "invite" another to her table. Those actions—supplying, endowing, inviting—would be voluntary ones; but no lover would knowingly "Affront" the Palate of a potential beloved. By replacing the voluntary alternatives with "Affront," Dickinson makes the woman unpalatable to all palates, even "minor" ones, while claiming major status for her own connoisseurship.

Has the woman still the power to "goad" her famished friend? No—it is not merely that the poet's "Tooth" has "grown" in discrimination. What has happened is (says the second stanza) that the poet has no "Tooth," no appetite, at all; her long bodily starvation has led her to transform herself into pure spirit. Like God, she needs no sustenance. She is not simply a major "palate"—she is a divine nonpalate. "I tell thee," she says (in imitation of Jesus' frequent "Verily, verily, I say unto thee"), "while I waited - " (leaving after those words an open line-space, reproduced by Ralph Franklin, to signify, perhaps unconsciously, her period of tortured waiting), "The mystery of Food / Increased till I abjured it." This superb literal formulation of the loved person as Food, and the sadistic goading creating the "mystery" of masochistic passion, puts Dickinson's conundrum in plain view: "The mystery of Food." She has been inexplicably maintaining an appetite for someone maliciously withholding herself. Love becomes, as Food, a physical necessity; human beings cannot refuse to eat, or they die. If Love is as necessary to us as Food, how can we "abjure" it—"swear off it," as current idiom would have it? ("Abjure" in its original sense meant "to renounce on oath," from *ab* "away from" and *iurare,* "to swear an oath.")

The longer the poet maintained this masochistic appetite, the longer she was compelled to meditate on why she continued her obsession with a person who denied her emotional access. She has finally enabled herself to break away only by denying (on oath) that she has any appetite left at all. The absurdity of this announcement is mitigated only by the poet's admission that desire (wanting Food) is a Mystery: she has been unable to arrive at an understanding of the tenacity of her own frustrated love. As desire became more and more troubling, the insoluble Mystery of Food (why its attraction? why her subjection?) increased.

As the poet now rises above desire entirely, she has to find a verb for her present condition. At first she wrote that she "dine[s] without [Food], like

God." But does God dine at all? No. So she grandly declares that she *subsists* now, "like God." The verb "to subsist" (literally, "to stand under," from *sub* + *sistere,* "to stand," "to support") has a precise meaning in its theological sense: "God is being itself subsisting by itself" (*OED, s.v.* 1, quoting from a 1701 work by John Norris of Bemerton, a minister and philosopher). God supports himself, maintains himself, is dependent on no one. The poet has moved into a new mode of divine being: she no longer merely *exists*—she *subsists.* Dickinson insists on the absolute either/or of desire by rhyming "Food" and "God." While one is human, one needs Food; abjuring bodily desire, one becomes pure spirit, "like God."

The ever-dramatic speech acts of the poem change audibly (and quickly), varying the poet's tone. The initial dismissive *Question,* "Art thou the thing I wanted?" announces incredulity as the poet scorns—from the position of pure spirit—the insignificant object on which she has expended years of passion. The imperious *Commands* that follow—"Begone" and "Affront"— proclaim the clear hierarchical rank of the superior speaker and inferior (former) beloved. "I tell thee" is a *Declaration* of implacable infallibility. The statement that "The mystery of Food / Increased" is a *Revelation* (from the metaphysical realm of Mystery) of an event that is, humanly speaking, incomprehensible. "Increased" (like other verbs in the same family: "wax," "wane," "redden," "brighten") is a progressive verb that goes on forever, making an asymptotic approach to a never-reached point of termination. Here, the endpoint would be the poet's actually becoming God, who understands all mysteries and needs no nourishment at all.

[J 1282]

# 1325

I never hear that one is dead
Without the chance of Life
Afresh annihilating me
That mightiest Belief,

Too mighty for the Daily mind
That tilling its abyss,
Had Madness, had it once or, Twice
The yawning Consciousness,

Beliefs are Bandaged, like the Tongue
When Terror were it told
In any Tone commensurate
Would strike us instant Dead -

I do not know the man so bold
He dare in lonely Place
That awful stranger - Consciousness
Deliberately face -

I rephrase this condensed poem:

I never hear that one is dead without the unpredictability (the "chance") of Life annihilating me afresh—exposing me to that mightiest Belief (that everyone is eventually annihilated, reduced to nothing, utterly dead)—a Belief too mighty for the Daily mind that, tilling its [own] abyss, underwent Madness, had Madness once or twice, [because of seeing] in the abyss of the mind (during Madness), the yawning Consciousness [of the open grave]. We blindfold—Bandage—our eyes so as not to see (as we would with open eyes) our perishing mortal flesh, so as not to encounter Beliefs (e.g., that we are annihilated at Death) insupportable to the Daily mind. In the same way, we Bandage (bind) the Tongue from speaking of Death. If that worst

Terror were told in any commensurate Tone, it would strike us dead instantly. I do not know any man so bold as to dare, in a lonely place, to face deliberately that awful stranger, Consciousness.

For Dickinson, at least in this poem, truly facing Consciousness compels the admission of final personal annihilation. Melville's relation to religion in many ways parallels that of Dickinson; like her, not believing in a personal afterlife, he had (as Hawthorne reports in an 1856 entry in his *English Notebooks*) "made up his mind to be annihilated":

Melville, as he always does, began to reason of Providence and futurity, and of everything that lies beyond human ken, and informed me that he had "pretty much made up his mind to be annihilated"; but still he does not seem to rest in that anticipation; and, I think, will never rest until he gets hold of a definite belief. . . . He can neither believe, nor be comfortable in his unbelief; and he is too honest and courageous not to try to do one or the other.

One phrase from Dickinson's poem has become common coin for all-purpose citation: the mixed-diction epigram, "Beliefs are Bandaged." The poet insists that terrifying Beliefs are covered over, because they are too painful for the everyday mind to admit. Like Dickinson, Melville was suspicious of the anodyne soothing of religion. As he said in a June 1851 letter to Hawthorne, "Let any clergyman try to preach the Truth from its very stronghold, the pulpit, and they would ride him out of his church on his own pulpit bannister." Melville's derisive image—of the uproar that would ensue if ordinary Consciousness were made to face Truth—supports Dickinson's observation that the other sort of Consciousness, the awe-inducing unbandaged one, is a stranger to most people: that hardly a man would dare to come face to face with it in solitude.

What sort of poem does Dickinson construct around the reality of personal annihilation, the terrors that appear even in the Daily mind, let alone the worse horrors of full Consciousness? Even "tilling" the "abyss" of the ordinary Daily mind led her twice to Madness, her most extreme anguish. What then would it be to contemplate the revelations of a Consciousness that went beyond the quotidian? She creates her poem as an example of the "Bandage[s]" we impose on Truth, phrasing thought in a covered or "Bandaged" way, obstructing her intended sense in almost every line. What is "the chance of Life"? In what way does hearing of a death annihilate her "Afresh"? What is the "Daily mind," and what is its opposite? The eternal mind? The mad mind? The transcendent mind? How does the Daily mind resemble an "abyss"? How can one "till" an abyss? (Answer: one cannot, yet the action is said to be constantly performed by the Daily mind.) What is the result of this tilling of a bottomless space? With what implement does the mind perform its daily tilling? Does that action bear fruit, as earthly tilling does? Is *having* "Madness" the same as *going* Mad? How can Consciousness be described as "yawning" open, like a fissure in the earth, like a grave? With what Bandages does one Bandage a Belief? And what does the Terror under the Bandage look like? What would be a Tone commensurate with Terror? And what Terror is meant? Death? Or Consciousness? Or are they inseparable, since the Consciousness of Death would strike us dead? The "*yaw*ning" Consciousness is also "*aw*ful"—as though the open-mouthed "*aw*" of an abyss is its specifying sound. And finally, since the word "Belief" implies (in religion) a positive truth (one believes in Immortality, or in Salvation), what made Dickinson decide to apply the word to a negative truth? The truth referred to is that of personal annihilation—which is the annulling of creation, the undoing of God's creation *ex nihilo,* his *fiat*—"Let there be this human being."

Answers to all these questions can be ventured, and Dickinson's images and words can be traced back to sources of various sorts. Some are biblical (seeing God face to face, elements of Belief), others etymological (*nihil*—nothing—in "annihilate"; *mensurare*—to measure—in "commensurate"). Some are paradoxical (the transmutation of the positive connotations of "Belief" in the context of Death), or remote in meaning (e.g., "yawning" predicated of a chasm or abyss: Keats, *Hyperion,* "all the yawn of hell"). But until the last, explicit stanza of the poem, Dickinson's deliberately difficult verbal surface is a "Bandage" for the complicated relationships not only of thematic elements—life and death, Consciousness and Madness, labor and fruitlessness—but also of words, syntactic elements, images, and events. Dickinson reveals only gradually that all these relationships, as maintained in life, are "Bandages" covering the inexpressible terror of full Consciousness.

[J 1323]

# 1332

Abraham to kill him
Was distinctly told -
Isaac was an Urchin -
Abraham was old -

Not a hesitation -
Abraham complied -
Flattered by Obeisance
Tyranny demurred -

Isaac - to his Children
Lived to tell the tale -
Moral - with a Mastiff
Manners may prevail.

This brisk little piece of blasphemy, voiced in impertinent colloquiality, is Dickinson's condensation of one of the most famous stories of the Bible, Abraham's sacrifice of Isaac (Genesis 22:1–13). Other such Dickinsonian cartoon-condensations of Bible stories can be found in "The Bible is an antique Volume - " (*1577). In Genesis, God decides to test Abraham, and commands him to take his only son Isaac (whom he loves), and offer him as a burnt offering on a mountain in the land of Moriah. Abraham obeys. Isaac, who is carrying the wood for the fire, understandably asks his father, "Where is the lamb for a burnt offering?" In reply, Abraham says, "My son, God will provide himself a lamb for a burnt offering." There follows the cruel kernel of the story: "And they came to the place which God had told him of; and Abraham built an altar there, and laid the wood in order, and bound Isaac his son, and laid him on the altar upon the wood. And Abraham stretched forth his hand, and took the knife to slay his son." An angel then appears telling Abraham not to slay Isaac, because the Lord now knows that Abraham fears him, "seeing thou has not withheld thy son, thine only son, from me." God provides a ram "caught in a thicket by his horns" (and therefore easily captured); "and Abraham went and took the ram, and offered him up for a burnt offering in the stead of his son."

Needless to say, commentary on this dark episode has been constant, with objectors seeing it as an example of God at his worst, approvers seeing it as a tale rewarding Abraham's faith (expressed to Isaac) that God would provide a burnt offering. The story has a baffling silence at its center: although Isaac speaks to ask his question about the missing lamb, he says nothing at all while his father binds him to the wood and takes out a knife with which to kill him before setting fire to his corpse. (The story has often been taken as a prefiguring of the sacrifice of Jesus, the son of God, on the Cross, and has been reproduced countless times in art.)

Dickinson chooses to be the cheeky secular reteller of this violent story (which she would have read, of course, but also may have heard preached in her youth; we can imagine her, in her pew, concocting her rival version). Her tale, starring God as Tyrant, is so luridly told that any reader of her era would be aware that it was a parodic reduction of the biblical version, but it would still shock. Dickinson omits Abraham's faith that God will provide; she brings in extraneous material on Abraham's age and Isaac's youth; and most of all, she omits God's providing an alternate victim in the ram, ascribing God's final relenting to his despotic pleasure at being flattered by such instant obedience. Her editing of the original story brings it down to three quick episodes: Abraham is told by God to kill Isaac; God-the-Tyrant relents, flattered by Abraham's compliance; Isaac lives to tell the tale to his Children.

Although the style becomes telegraphic—a set of parallel sentences with no subordination and with considerable suppression of explanatory matter —Dickinson keeps the tale lively by varying the grammatical look of each unit, via tenses (imperfect, preterit, present), or action (passive or active), or mood (indicative, subjunctive), or by altering the function of "to be" (from an auxiliary to a copulative verb), or by employing different forms of naming (real and allegorical). I am not arguing, of course, that Dickinson made all such choices deliberately; I mean only to demonstrate that she knew what a springy line should sound like, just as a composer knows by instinct (gained from a lifelong internalizing of much music) how to produce a vivid run of orchestration.

Behind all this variation, Dickinson kept, of course, some invariant syntactic and metrical aspects, such as the short subject-predicate units ("Abraham complied," "Tyranny demurred") and the impeccable repetition of the hard-hitting downbeats of her trochaic trimeters. Like "Now I knew I lost her - " (*1274) and "Art thou the thing I wanted?" (*1311), this poem "Abraham to kill him," alternates feminine and masculine end-words, bringing us up short at each even-numbered line. The poem's staccato is further emphasized by the rhyme, preventing a smooth narrative. The two following poems here (*1347 and *1369) employ the same alternation.

As in other allegories or parables, a Moral concludes Dickinson's story, offering a general application: using "Manners" with a "Mastiff" (a large and powerful dog, often employed as a guard dog), one may win him over. Dickinson might have known, from her lexical explorations, that the word "Mastiff"—which had by her time taken on threatening connotations—derives from the Latin *mansuetus,* "mild," meaning that the dog has been domesticated. The Mastiff, having been taught "Manners" himself, may reciprocate with his "mild" side, if he is not challenged. The preposterousness of using a guard dog as a metaphor for God ends the poem with a sub-surface pun: "dog" is "God" spelled backward.

[J 1317]

# 1347

Wonder - is not precisely knowing
And not precisely knowing not -
A beautiful but bleak condition
He has not lived who has not felt -

Suspense - is his maturer Sister -
Whether Adult Delight is Pain
Or of itself a new misgiving -
This is the Gnat that mangles men -

A poem such as this gives us a glimpse into the way Dickinson arranged categories of experience in her mind: she grouped them in family clusters and gave them gender and age. "Wonder" is a young male; "Suspense" is his more adult Sister. As soon as we enter into such a form of classification, we can imagine more possible categories arising. Who were the Parents of Wonder and Suspense? Does Wonder live in a region different from Suspense? We see as well that Dickinson has constructed a spectrum of Experience, labeling one end "knowing" and the other end "knowing not." Somewhere in the middle of this spectrum lies "Wonder." But there are doubtless other mediating colors in this spectrum of knowing—perhaps Apprehension that a thing might be so, and perhaps Doubt that it could be so. All her life, Dickinson must have been playing games of this sort with Abstractions, yielding her such lines as "Presentiment - is that long shadow - on the Lawn - " (487, J 764). Like "Wonder," "Presentiment" is not exactly knowing, but not exactly knowing not. It connotes, however, with its "Pre-," an anticipation of knowing. Compiling Dickinson's families of Abstract Relations would shed light on how she arrived at a complex and extensive taxonomy of experience.

We expect, after the phrase "Wonder is," a single predicate noun of definition, such as we find elsewhere in Dickinson's frequent definition-poems: "Presentiment - is . . . that . . . shadow - " or "Renunciation - is a . . . virtue - ". But here we receive instead not the satisfying confirming noun, but rather two gerunds confessing their imprecision: "knowing" and "knowing not."

This is an unusual move—refusing exact definition (in which the noun to be defined is almost immediately matched with a predicate complement, such as "shadow" or "virtue") and offering instead two denied gerunds (not *x,* not *y*). Dickinson thereby draws the mind of the reader into perplexity. The paradox in the following line, in which Wonder is said to be "beautiful but bleak," continues the uncertainty of definition, and implies another spectrum, with "bleak" close to one end and "beautiful" close to the other. The alliteration of the two adjectives suggests that they too lie on a continuum rather than compose a disjunction. How would the spectrum go? *Beautiful, blissful, blessed, balmy, blanched, blank, bleak?*

"Wonder" is, according to the poet, essential to emotional existence, since he who has not felt it has not lived. But because it is a "bleak" condition (if also "beautiful") it always prompts a yearning to "know"—a fundamental human desire. By "Wonder" in this poem, Dickinson means something akin to mild Speculation (as in "I wonder whether he will come"). We realize, when we come to the second stanza, that Dickinson has placed "Wonder" in the poem purely to enable a more precise characterization of "Suspense," her real interest here.

"Suspense" says that "Adult Delight is Pain." Either it is Pain *tout court,* or Adult Delight is a foretaste of Pain, a "new misgiving" that Pain will shortly follow. In either case, Adult Delight is fatally compromised; it can never be pure Delight. It is always either identical to Pain or else a forecast of Pain. In *All's Well That Ends Well* (Act 4, scene 3), the First Lord characterizes life as a "mingled yarn, good and ill together," implying the existence of two different colors of yarn which have been wound together ("mingled") into a single string. But Dickinson does not give us an adult life of two separate experiences, Delight and Pain, wound together with their different colors showing; rather, she presents a life in which Pain *is* the same yarn as Delight, since Delight always is Pain or contains a misgiving of future Pain. Hanging (because "Suspense" derives from *sub + pendere,* "to hang") between these two undesirable descriptions of "Adult Delight," we experience that "Suspense" which is the "maturer Sister" of "Wonder." We do not know in which way we will encounter Pain this time—directly during Delight (by instant consciousness of betrayal) or indirectly during Delight (by the merest flicker of suspicion).

Dickinson's conclusion is shocking in its conjunction of the tiny and ephemeral (but painfully biting) "Gnat" with the savage word "mangle" ("to reduce a body, limb, etc., by violence to a more or less unrecognizable condition"—*OED*, s.v. 1a). Suspense during Delight, even in the Gnat-like form of mute misgiving, infiltrates the pleasure and introduces Pain. A fugitive breath of mistrust is enough to break the heart as surely as if the heart had been mauled by a tiger.

The plot of the poem is summed up in the run of alliteration saying "maturer . . . misgiving . . . mangles . . . men." Either "*Gnat*" summoned up its graphic relative "m*ang*le" or vice versa, accounting for the glorious combination of two such unlikely words. And rhyming "Pain" with "men," Dickinson assigns human beings to their intrinsic fate.

[J 1331]

# 1369

The Rat is the concisest Tenant.
He pays no Rent.
Repudiates the Obligation -
On Schemes intent

Balking our Wit
To sound or circumvent -
Hate cannot harm
A Foe so reticent -

Neither Decree prohibit him -
Lawful as Equilibrium.

Sometimes Dickinson herself was not sure how she should divide her poem. Once (if we trust the accuracy of Susan Dickinson's transcription of a lost manuscript) she ran all the lines of "The Rat" together, with no white space at all (Version A). She sent a copy to Susan in which she presented the poem in two pieces (a quatrain and a six-line stanza), with a single white space between the parts (Version B). When she sent it to Thomas Wentworth Higginson, she made it into a three-stanza poem (two quatrains and a couplet), with two white spaces, one after line 4, the other after line 8 (Version C). Ralph Franklin prints the Higginson three-stanza variant in his *Reading Edition,* but we really need to go back to his *Variorum Edition* to understand Dickinson's deliberation about the shape into which her poem should be cast.

There is no problem with the one-piece Version A of no spaces, except that it is unusual (if one notes the rhyme) to see a poem rhyming identically for its first eight lines yet choosing to end, in truncated form, with a rhyming *couplet.* The single-stanza Version A doesn't emphasize, but rather conceals, that rhyme-discrepancy between octave and couplet. However, the two-stanza Version B does call attention to the discrepancy, because it presents a shape-riddle: the eye quickly sees that the six-line stanza 2 does not match the previous four-line stanza 1, and this makes us query Dickinson's intent in creating such an asymmetrical shape. As for the three-stanza Version C, printed in Franklin's *Reading Edition,* it openly displays the peculiarity of the closing couplet by separating it utterly from the two quatrains that precede it. What was Dickinson uncertain about as she hesitated among these shapes?

As we look at the syntax, we begin to understand. The first two sentences of the poem are short and unequivocal, each coterminous with its line:

> The Rat is the concisest Tenant.
> He pays no Rent.

The third sentence (lines 3–6), begins halfway through quatrain 1, and "illegitimately" straddles the subsequent white space, going on to begin quatrain 2. The end of quatrain 1 is marked in the example below with a double slash:

> [He] Repudiates the Obligation, on Schemes intent // Balking our
>     Wit to sound or circumvent.

The fourth sentence (lines 7–10), which also begins halfway through *its* quatrain, also straddles transgressively the subsequent white space between quatrain and final couplet:

> Hate cannot harm a Foe so reticent // Neither [can a] Decree prohibit
>     him, [because he is] Lawful as Equilibrium.

So much for dividing the poem up by *sentences.* Earlier, dividing it up by *rhyme,* starting at the beginning, we had arrived at the shape of an octave and a couplet. But as we now see, dividing the poem up by sentences gives us a syntactic shape in which sentences straddle the white space separating the stanzas. In short, the shape of the quatrain rhyme-units is at odds with the shape of the sentences. This is a feature unusual in Dickinson, who so loves neat epigrammatic quatrain-sentences, where rhyme and syntax fit perfectly into the same four-line package. If we "packaged" the sentences here so that they fit "correctly" into rhyme-quatrains, the poem would read as follows:

> The Rat is the concisest Tenant.
> He pays no Rent.

Repudiates the Obligation -
On Schemes intent
Balking our Wit
To sound or circumvent -

Hate cannot harm
A Foe so reticent -
Neither Decree prohibit him -
Lawful as Equilibrium.

One argument for splitting off the couplet (as Dickinson did in sending Version C to Higginson) is that the final rhyme-feature, a couplet, not elsewhere present in the poem, serves by its uniqueness to indicate closure. But splitting off the couplet into graphic independence shoves the two lines that begin the couplet's sentence ("Hate cannot harm" etc.) upward into the preceding stanza, which in turn shoves into the first quatrain the two lines beginning with the word "Repudiates."

In short, "The Rat" exhibits a strangely uneasy overlap of rhyme and syntax, so that one cannot feel either of the two quatrains to be self-standing in the usual Dickinsonian way. In the version she sent to Higginson (Franklin's *Reading Version*), Dickinson wanted to exhibit that peculiar non-coincidence of stanza and sentence-unit by making the latter half of the sentence "Hate . . . Equilibrium" into a free-standing couplet, thereby dislocating sentence and quatrain from line 4 on. In a moment, we shall see why she did this.

The poem is about the relation of Landlord and Tenant (i.e., Dickinson and her house-Parasite). The Rat is "concise" (from Latin *concidere*, "to cut in pieces") because he is usually invisible; he is not the inhabitant of a fixed space. "You'd hardly know he was there," as a landlord might say of an unobtrusive tenant. He is also "concise" because he nowhere appears in the landlord's ledger. Nonetheless, because he lives in the house, the Rat (thinks the landlord) should pay rent (which would formalize a lawful relation between himself and the landlord). But the Rat is not lawful; he spends his whole day intent on schemes that balk our intelligence (our "Wit"). We can neither sound the depths of his schemes nor get around them, and they are always— when he comes out in the night and raids the larder—successful. (Dickinson

makes the poem personal by progressing from the impersonal third person—
"The Rat . . . pays no rent"—to the first-person plural—he balks "our" Wit—
before returning to the impersonal in the closing lines.)

This is not a poem about an inoffensive mouse; it concerns a hated Rat.
But he will not engage with us; as he is invisible, so is he "reticent." He will
neither pay rent nor talk to us. So far, we have taken the side of the affronted
landlord, who would like a Decree to be issued that would prohibit the Rat's
existence. Is he not unlawful, with his defaults in rent and his thieving
schemes? But Dickinson-as-householder takes thought, and it occurs to her
that one of the fundamental laws of the universe is that of equilibrium: if a
force is exerted, an equal and opposite force is always generated in return.
Who is she to dispute the universe? If there are, in the house, human food-
eaters depleting the foodstuffs, then, to restore a scientific balance, there
ought to be an equal force of animal food-eaters raiding the supplies. By end-
ing the poem with the resonant (and capitalized) Latin word "Equilibrium,"
bearing with it all the weight of scientific Law, Dickinson humorously grants
her Tenant equal rights with herself.

I return to the peculiar dis-alignment of syntax and rhyme-unit. I think it
is Dickinson's fanciful way of enacting in linguistic shape the two-sided Equi-
librium named in the last line: the rhyme pulls one way, the syntax the other.
The neat tetrameter couplet at the end represents things returning to "Equi-
librium"—a proper balance of weight and counterweight.

[J 1356]

# 1393

Those Cattle smaller than a Bee
That herd upon the Eye -
Whose tillage is the passing Crumb -
Those Cattle are the Fly -
Of Barns for Winter - blameless -
Extemporaneous stalls
They found to our objection -
On Eligible Walls -
Reserving the presumption
To suddenly descend
And gallop on the Furniture
Or odiouser offend -
Of their peculiar calling
Unqualified to judge
To Nature we remand them
To justify or scourge -

This very witty poem, with its comic invasion of the poet's house by flies, is
Dickinson's eccentric replica of a famous passage in the Gospel of Matthew:
"Judge not, that ye be not judged," says Jesus. As the poet says that she is
"Unqualified to judge" the "peculiar calling" of houseflies, she is recalling
this verse and its continuation, which speaks of motes (small bits of dust or
grit) and eyes. The small black houseflies "herd upon the eye," and the word
"mote" is etymologically associated with "moth," a winged insect not too dis-
similar to a fly: "Judge not, that ye be not judged. For with what judgment ye
judge, ye shall be judged: and with what measure ye mete, it shall be mea-
sured to you again. And why beholdest thou the mote that is in thy brother's
eye, but considerest not the beam that is in thine own eye? Or how wilt thou
say to thy brother, Let me pull out the mote of thine eye, and, behold a beam
is in thine own eye?" (Matthew 7:1–4).

For most of "Nature's People," Dickinson felt "a transport / Of Cordiality" (*1096, "A narrow Fellow"). But for some—the Snake, the Rat—she feels fear, or hatred. The Flies are to her (in her hyperbolical narrative) odious and offensive, but she will not press her feeling all the way to intellectual repudiation, because as creatures of Nature, the Flies are perhaps, like the Rat, "Lawful" (see *1396, "The Rat is the concisest Tenant"). Jesus reproaches those who notice a mote in the eye of another without having noticed the much larger piece of wood impeding their own sight. Rushing to judgment of Flies in ignorance of Nature's larger purpose of "Equilibrium" would be unworthy of the poet. Only Nature can judge them.

We begin with the repugnant fact that as winter comes on, many houseflies find refuge indoors. In spite of her revulsion, Dickinson watches them like a naturalist. What are their habits? Their habitats? Their actions? In a Swiftian leap of comic imagination, she magnifies the Lilliputian flies into a herd of Brobdingnagian Cattle, and then carries this preposterous metaphor (conceived in householder's outrage) into various nooks and crannies. At first, like living motes, the Flies take possession of the poet's eye, but soon they take over her whole house. After they "herd upon the Eye," they begin somewhat meekly, merely furrowing a bit of bread they come across, as yoked Cattle might turn over the soil while plowing a field. Ending her first quatrain, Dickinson literalizes her metaphor: "Those Cattle are the Fly - ". Not "Those Cattle are these Flies": the poet arouses a slight shock by her insertion of the Platonic/Linnaean Idea of "the Fly." By imposing the Platonic singular noun on the plural verb "are," Dickinson makes her poem as much definition as description.

The Flies land on her walls. She objects—but then, in fairness, she remembers that they are blameless in entering the house. Unlike real Cattle who have stalls in barns for winter shelter, the refugee Flies have not been provided Barns. They have consequently, like human beings, sought protection until they found her "Eligible Walls," which they extemporize into their *pro tem* stalls. The poet tries to find a new ground for accusation: the Flies (like bulls in a china shop) have the presumption to swoop down "and gallop on the Furniture," coming perilously near the human beings sitting on that very settee. That is an odious offense, but the Flies have worse in reserve: they may "odiouser offend"—in Dickinson's intensifying and funny comparative—by extruding fecal matter onto a household surface, an act that Dickinson is too delicate (in her role here as affronted gentlewoman) to make explicit.

The calling of the Fly is "peculiar" (proper to it alone) because it is so nefarious—the call to be an invader spreading disease wherever it goes. To name such a function a "calling" (a vocation, or sacred summoning) is to dignify it beyond its deserts; yet Nature gave the Fly its function, peculiar or not. Dickinson wants to "remand" the Flies—send them back as prisoners—to the custody of Nature (as the supreme Judge). Let Nature be the one to scrutinize their behavior and decide to acquit ("justify") or condemn them (in the latter case, assigning scourging as a punishment).

Dickinson designedly rhymes the Flies' extemporaneous "stalls" with her own "Walls" to show the fated nature of the conjunction. Looking for stalls, what would the Flies choose but walls? In the same way, she links, by her initial capitals, the Flies "Extemporaneous" construction to what they find in the way of "Eligible" walls. The final seriousness of this satiric poem is at first glance surprising, since the Flies behave like marauding children, appropriating the bread, galloping on the Furniture, or offending in some more odious way. As "Cattle" (or children) they do not invite judgments apportioned to adults, so the word "scourge" seems unexpectedly harsh. It may come to Dickinson's mind as one of the punishments inflicted on Jesus by Pilate: trying to decide whether to justify or punish the man before him, Pilate washes his hands of the whole affair and remands Jesus to be scourged. The flaws in human judgment are at their historically most conspicuous in the unjustifiable condemnation of Jesus, and Dickinson, losing confidence in the role of judge, washes her hands of the obligation to ascertain blame, turning the responsibility over to Nature.

Dickinson's wry magnification of the Flies into Cattle carries the poem imaginatively, but the final turn to seriousness, with its allusion to Jesus' own speech in Matthew, casts a backward illumination on all human judgments of people unlike ourselves whom we regard with "abhorrence" (Dickinson's earlier alternative for "objection"). They immigrate into our territory, they behave in unseemly ways, they thieve from us, and some of their behavior is offensive to the point of *odium* (Latin, "hatred"). Should we judge? Or should we "remand" them beyond our fallible judgment?

[J 1388]

# 1405

Long Years apart - can make no
Breach a second cannot fill -
The absence of the Witch does not
Invalidate the spell -

The embers of a Thousand Years
Uncovered by the Hand
That fondled them when they were Fire
Will stir and understand

Dickinson's statements of unquenchable love come in many varieties, often in a tragic context (see *706, "I cannot live with You - "). But here no tragedy obtrudes: the topic is restricted to an involuntary absence by the beloved over an extended time.

In her first stanza, Dickinson opposes the "Long Years" apart from the beloved to the hyperbolic single "second" of his restored presence; in stanza 2, she raises "Long Years" to the hyperbole of "a Thousand Years," and repeats her prophecy of fidelity. In the "topic sentence" of the first two lines, line 1 should, rhythmically speaking, end with "Breach," to obey the 4-3-4-3 pattern of the poem. The abruptness of ending the first line with "no" suspended in air creates the Breach itself—and then the hurried rhythm of "Breach a second cannot fill - " does "fill up" the Breach in a second, justifying its own assertion. Having offered her assertion, Dickinson has to prove it. She tries one metaphor—that of the Witch's spell—in stanza 1, and then supersedes it with her second (and more successful) metaphor, that of the awakened embers.

The Witch was, in a rejected alternative, male. Male witches were not unknown in ancient usage, but Dickinson's 1844 Webster defines the noun as female. Defying convention, Dickinson wrote:

Who says the Absence of a Witch
Invalidates his spell?

A male Witch was perhaps too specific for Dickinson's purpose in this poem, in which a Hand had "fondled" the embers in the past, when they were "Fire." (Dickinson may be remembering Shakespeare's Sonnet 73, "That time of year," and its "glowing of such fire / That on the ashes of his youth doth lie.") The poem is more explicitly erotic with "his," but the reference to the fondling establishes it in any case as a love poem. What, we ask—since the poem does not end after "spell"—is "wrong" with the metaphor of the Witch? It is insufficient because it leaves the enchanted one bound in the original spell, paralyzed within it.

Following on the Witch, the poet's second metaphor—of embers that still preserve heat from their original Fire of a Thousand Years ago—allows two responsive motions on the part of the Embers when their beloved reappears and they recall having earlier been "fondled." Uncovered, the embers "stir" with volition under the remembered touch; what is more, even in their expiring state, they "understand" with their cognitive faculties who it is that has returned and uncovered them. (Originally, Dickinson had written "gleam" before replacing it with "stir." To "gleam" is more static and less human than to "stir," with its implication of sexual arousal.) The embers have mind and will; their past "Fire" is a state impossible in literal terms, but is one of the oldest metaphors for a heart burning with love. The words "fondled" and "Fire" belong together, as the troth of lovers is enacted by alliteration. The sight of Dickinson moving to rework her metaphor in order to bring her poem into the world of human touch (rather than leaving it in the world of an immobilizing "spell") brings the reader closer to the essential stirring that is the motion of the quickened embers.

[J 1383]

# 1408

The Bat is dun, with wrinkled Wings -
Like fallow Article -
And not a song pervade his Lips -
Or none perceptible.

His small Umbrella quaintly halved
Describing in the Air
An Arc alike inscrutable
Elate Philosopher.

Deputed from what Firmament -
Of what Astute Abode -
Empowered with what malignity
Auspiciously withheld -

To his adroit Creator
Ascribe no less the praise -
Beneficent, believe me,
His eccentricities -

Dickinson's scrutiny of this eccentric among creatures, a flying mammal, serves as a defense of eccentricity in general. What is this object which flies, but is not a bird? Its erratic motions in flight, its strangely "wrinkled" Wings, its absence of song define it as something that ought not to exist. Its "Wings" are not really wings in the avian sense; they are homologous to the human hand and arm, with elongated finger-bones connected by a membrane. They can be folded, when the bat is at rest on a cave-ceiling, into something resembling a folded umbrella—or rather, each "Wing" is one half of his quaint Umbrella. The Creator has not made the Bat beautiful, like the Birds. Rather, he is dun-colored, a peculiar "Article" of the yellowish-brown color called "fallow." Dickinson says he is *like* a "fallow Article" because she affects not to know where he might belong in earth's taxonomy. We would say "Thing" where she says "Article," reminding us that "Article" is a commercial word:

"We have some very warm articles here in our Men's Clothing department." "Article" exemplifies, too, the poet's brief attempt to find some descriptive category to which the Bat can be assigned, that of "jointed" things ("Article" is a relative of "articulation").

Dickinson's opening and apparently negative description of the Bat—as an unclassifiable brown "Article," with no song, no proper wings—demands a complementary positive definition, to which the poet now moves: the Bat is amusing, with his "quaintly halved" Umbrella. And because his unpredictable darting motions through the air are "inscrutable" (unlike goal-directed bird flight), he qualifies as a Philosopher, but one who is uncommonly "Elate" (high-spirited), with his rapid swoops through the night air. The curved "Arc" of his Umbrella Wings creates in the sky a matching, equally inscrutable, and geometric but transient Arc. Scrutiny does not further the interpretation of the Bat's purposes.

Dickinson's first two stanzas initiate the run on words beginning with "A" that courses through the poem: "Article," "Air," "Arc," "alike," "Astute," "Abode," "Auspiciously," "adroit," and "Ascribe." "An Article in the Air making an Arc, Coming from an Astute Abode and Auspiciously withholding his potential malignity" sums up the Bat. And the only other two A-words belong to his unknown Maker: in a Dickinsonian *Te Deum,* still in the key of A, we are to Ascribe praise not only to this diverting creature but also to his "adroit" Creator. We are grateful for the Beneficence ("B" as in "Bat") of the Creator in replicating Himself in eccentricity as well as in normality. This odd Bat-creature, like human beings, is "made in the image and likeness of God," as the Christian formula (based on Genesis) puts it. I am not sure of the reason for the A's, but I am certain they are not accidental. Perhaps in order to get to the Bat's "B," one has to proceed through the "A's"?

The unknown Creator launched this Ambassador—"Deputed" him to our world, and "Empowered" him with a malignity (Bats are associated with Witches), which the Bat graciously withholds. From the Bat-Ambassador we are to learn something about the Creator whom in part he replicates. So, with emphatic gratitude, Dickinson thanks the Creator, as we have seen, for having included among his works an archetype for her own "Eccentricities." She has often allied herself, in an idealistic way, with birds: "We - are the birds - that stay" (*528). But, she reflects, in the world of human beings, she is perhaps too eccentric to be symbolized by a bird—and so she comes upon the happy simile of the Bat. After first denying him a song ("Publication," after all, "is the Auction / Of the Mind of Man - "; *788), she relents, and allows him a song that exists but is not perceived. (She seems to have been scientifically aware of the high-pitched call of the bat, inaudible to human ears.) Her own song is not yet "perceptible" to the world, either. Yet, like her Spider who "sewed at Night . . . / Upon an Arc of White - " (*1163), the Bat is shaped in an organic Arc and creates an uninterpretable Arc in the air. These elements of pattern (related to the poet's essential concept of "Circumference," the closed Arc; see, among many others, 669, 858, 1067, and 1636) give her a fellow feeling for Bat and Spider. She too can be seen—with her wit, and her love of aphorism and axiom—as an "Elate" Philosopher, and has often been found, at first glance, "inscrutable."

Since the poem has a formal principle (the "A's") threaded through it to entertain us, it does not need remarkable rhymes. But it does mutate strikingly from description to exhortation—from "The Bat is dun" to "believe me." Why does Dickinson suddenly become didactic? Probably because we have been lulled into thinking that this is a charming and tender picture of an unlikely natural being, the unclassifiable Bat. The leap into a lesson is a Dickinsonian self-defense: "Believe me, the Creator's more eccentric productions, such as the Bat, are proof of his Beneficence, because they reveal to us an aspect of the Creator we might not otherwise have deduced—that he is an Eccentric, too." The Creator is generally praised for the harmony and beauty of the natural world. Dickinson wants to insist that all of nature, even the classification-denying Bat, reflects its Maker. This is in part a joke; but it is a serious joke in insisting on the value, to the more ordinary world, of its animate eccentrics, from Bat to Poet. It is also a serious joke in borrowing an ancient genre—the *Te Deum* of praising God—for an unlikely purpose.

[J 1575]

# 1428

Lay this Laurel on the one
Triumphed and remained unknown -
Laurel - fell your futile Tree -
Such a Victor could not be -
Lay this Laurel on the one
Too intrinsic for Renown -
Laurel - vail your deathless Tree -
Him you chasten - that is he -

Until the publication of Ralph Franklin's *Reading Edition* in 1999, some readers might have thought that this poem-epitaph had only four lines—for so it appeared in *Poems* (1891) and in Thomas Johnson's one-volume edition of 1960:

Lay this Laurel on the One
Too intrinsic for Renown -
Laurel - vail your deathless tree -
Him you chasten, that is he!

Although the longer version, chosen as copy-text by Franklin, was known to Johnson, he kept, as *his* copy-text for his one-volume *Complete Poems,* the short one (while of course printing all versions in his 1955 three-volume variorum edition). Perhaps Johnson thought that the one-stanza version was Dickinson's own preference. The single quatrain was the version that Dickinson sent to Thomas Wentworth Higginson on the third anniversary of her father's death, commenting that she had been rereading Higginson's poem "Decoration" (which Franklin reproduces in his 1998 *Variorum*). In "Decoration," which is situated in a cemetery, Higginson compares the soldiers lying there, whose decorated graves bear wreaths of honor, with the dead woman whom he comes to mourn. Her grave "Bears no roses, wears no wreath." But Higginson, laying lilies on her grave, calls her "the bravest of the brave," who has never flinched before "wrongs and woes."

The tradition of the "Unknown Soldier" is extended by Higginson—as earlier by Dickinson and Hopkins—to civilians, those "who charge within the bosom / The Cavalry of Wo - " ("To fight aloud, is very brave - "; *138). But despite the evidence of the letter to Higginson, Dickinson did leave behind a fair copy of the eight-line poem, which is Franklin's copy-text. Dickinson never left a single-quatrain version as her personal fair copy. She may have decided that the single quatrain sufficiently suggested her memory of "Decoration." The existence of a fair copy of the eight-line poem suggests that in this instance, to Higginson as to other correspondents, Dickinson sent only part of a poem. The free-standing single quatrain, one of the poet's most commented-on works, has such a firm place in the canon that if it is to be dislodged by the eight-line version, we must know why.

Although the eight-line poem, at first glance, seems to repeat itself, the rhyme scheme tells us that Dickinson needed all eight lines:

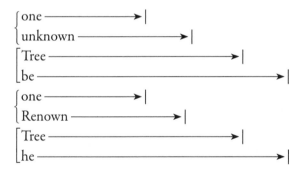

This strikes the eye at first as the simplest of rhyme schemes, couplets: *aabb-aabb*. But some of the rhyming words in the second "quatrain" are identical to those of the first, and those that differ do so to make a point. "Renown" is made to rhyme with its anterior opposite, "unknown," and the pointed-to "[that is] he" is made to rhyme with, and refute, its antithesis "[could not] be." The congruence of the two quatrains—in sentiment and (in some cases) statement—means that they are to be mentally superimposed, the latter on the former, so that the first quatrain becomes a statement corrected, as it were, by the second: Dickinson tells us that "Renown" (rather than "unknown") would have been the correct word, and that specificity ("he") rather than denial of existence ("[could not] be") is the correct conclusion. The poem, although it seems to say the same thing twice, changes its mind about how best to formulate its unchanging conviction of the valor of unknown heroes.

"Lay this Laurel on the one"—the exhortation to reward a dead victor with a laurel wreath laid on his grave—is the only line that remains unchanged as quatrain two succeeds quatrain one: the ritual gesture of honor remains completely unopposed. In line 2, the victor originally was one who "triumphed" (a "victorious" word) while remaining unknown. As corrected in line 6, the statement bears no triumphal verb; the person honored is said to be "Too intrinsic" for fame. Dickinson, in her use of "intrinsic," implies the common meaning "genuine" or (from the Latin root of "intrinsic," *intrinsecus*) "beginning and ending within itself." Dickinson's father, to whom the epitaph is thought to refer, was a person whose triumphs over life's woes began and remained strictly contained within his own breast; he did not speak of them to others, and therefore could in no public sense gain "Renown." (In this he resembled his daughter, who in her lifetime was also "too intrinsic for Renown - ".)

In the third line of the poem, the Tree of Laurel is commanded to cut itself down, since it is "futile" to appropriate a public symbol for hidden virtue. If the Tree obeyed and exterminated itself, there could of course be no Laurellaying at all. Line 7 indeed corrects line 3; rather than exhorting the Tree to self-murder, it commands it to bow down (as army flags are lowered when passing a presidential box). This reverence is perfectly in order, as the tree's killing itself would not have been. Besides, Laurel is a symbol of immortality rather than merely victory; the Tree is not at all "futile," but rather "deathless."

Finally, line 4—denying the possibility that a "Victor" could remain unknown after his triumph—is corrected in line 8 by a definition appropriate to an "intrinsic" personality. "Whom the Lord loveth, he chasteneth," says Paul (Hebrews 12:6–11), adding that God chastens us "that we might be partakers of his holiness," and concluding that "afterward it yieldeth the peaceable fruit of righteousness." In Version A of Franklin's three versions, Dickinson used "thou" to the Laurel Tree ("Him thou chastenest")—evidence of her debt to Paul. But in revising Version A, she altered the archaic "thou" to "you," and changed Paul's present tense to the past tense suitable for one dead: "Him you chastened that was he!" But since that tense speaks of a specific life, now over, she decides, in another step, against the past tense, and reverts to the axiomatic present tense of Paul: "Him thou chastenest - That is he - ". She also has in mind Paul's second letter to Timothy (4:7–8), which gives Paul's words concerning his own posthumous reward. His metaphor is that of victory in "a good fight," for which the Lord will crown him, not with a classical Laurel wreath, but with a crown of righteousness:

> I have fought a good fight, I have finished my course, I have
>     kept the faith:
> Henceforth there is laid up for me a crown of righteousness,
>     which the Lord, the righteous judge, shall give me at that
>     day: and not to me only, but unto all them also that love
>     his appearing.

In telling her "deathless" Laurel to bow down to the chastened one, Dickinson imagines the "intrinsic" one rewarded in death with a crown superior to any the Laurel can offer. But in her fair copy, by substituting the Laurel for the Lord—"Him *you* chasten—that is he - " (italics added)—she boldly conflates all spiritual victories, classical and Christian. She said mistakenly in line 4 that "Such a Victor could not be - ", only to discover, as she corrects the error, that there are so many such "victors" that one can speak about them in her quasi-proverb adapted from Paul: He is victor who is chastened (and nonetheless keeps the faith).

The most "intrinsic" formal gesture of the poem is the correction of quatrain 1 by quatrain 2, conveyed above all by the repetition not only of the same rhyme scheme but of crucial end-words; quatrain 2, in a sense, conquers quatrain 1. The most unusual word Dickinson employs in quatrain 2 is the archaic "vail," meaning "to lower" (used of a battle-standard or a weapon, and deriving from the Latin *ad vallem,* "to the valley"). Dickinson, in exhorting the Laurel to bend in homage, does not demand self-felling by the tree of honor, as in quatrain 1, but asks only for its acknowledgment of the presence of a victor beyond its own powers to crown adequately. Beginning with the laying-on of Laurel—and never abrogating that original gesture of reverence —Dickinson imagines, through Paul, a better crown for her father's ultimate "righteousness" than the Laurel crown of earthly Fame.

The poem gains its energy from the single rapid mutation, in the second half, of its former exhortation. Dickinson twice turns from the quasi-liturgical elegiac instruction to "Lay" the Laurel "on" the grave of a victor, to a startling direct command to the Laurel Tree itself, the command mutating from "fell" to "vail" (repeating almost the same phoneme). The poet's authority asserts itself in declaring (finally) the correct action for the Laurel Tree to perform, as worldly fame bows to a superior value, that of intrinsic and chastened righteousness.

[J 1393]

# 1474

The Road was lit with Moon and star -
The Trees were bright and still -
Descried I - by - the gaining Light
A traveller on a Hill -
To magic Perpendiculars
Ascending, though terrene -
Unknown his shimmering ultimate -
But he indorsed the sheen -

Dickinson here rewrites in miniature the Christian metaphor of the earthly pilgrimage, which has generated works extending from the medieval *Pèlerinage de la Vie Humaine* to Bunyan's *Pilgrim's Progress* to Herbert's "Pilgrimage" to Eliot's "Little Gidding." These works presume a religious intention and a hope for an ultimate gaining of heaven. Sometimes they end in the happy realization of that hope, as in Part II of *Pilgrim's Progress*, when Mr. Valiant-for-truth attains the heavenly city, and "all the trumpets sounded for him on the other side." At other times, the pilgrim can encounter disappointment: George Herbert, reaching the top of what he thought would be "the gladsome hill," finds only "a lake of brackish waters," and cries out "Can both the way and end be tears?" Dickinson of course knew these variant plots, just as she knew the radiant description in Revelation of their destiny, the Heavenly Jerusalem.

How could she retain the idealism of the pilgrimage-plot, the journey up the "gladsome hill" of Zion, and the glowing gems of the Heavenly City—while not submitting them to any of the constraints of doctrine? She invents her own double-pilgrim, herself and the "traveller" she (with some difficulty) "Descried" preceding her on the way. The archetypal "Road" of pilgrimage lies before her, and her quest is so much in earnest that she, like her companion ahead, continues her journey even by night.

The poet begins with an artless simplicity. The Road and the Trees are bright in the moonlight and starlight; by the "gaining" Light of the rising Moon, she sees "A traveller on a Hill - ". In diction, imagery, and syntax, this ballad quatrain would fit into Wordsworth's *Lyrical Ballads,* in which Wordsworth often places persons on the public road and characterizes them in similarly "artless" ways. But in her second quatrain, Dickinson introduces an entirely different level of perception as she describes that other traveller who, although as "terrene" (earthly) as herself, is ascending the taxing hill that symbolizes spiritual progress. He ascends not to a biblical heaven but to (miraculous phrase) "magic Perpendiculars." Dickinson's love for geometric figures serves her well: the "Perpendiculars," idealistic projections of the man's own "Columnar Self" (*740), are therefore "magic," spectral. Just as (in the old definition) a sacrament is the "outward sign of an inward grace," so the imagined magic Perpendiculars are the spiritual sign (to the onlooker bound on the same journey) of the traveler's "inward grace," uprightness.

I pause here for a moment to bring up another poem, but a far darker one, about following one's ideals: Coleridge's "Constancy to an Ideal Object." Coleridge, like Dickinson, presents two travelers: the poet himself and an "enamoured rustic" who pursues (thinking it real) an illusory phantom, which in fact—says the poet with somber irony—is merely a projection of his own shadow in the "snow-mist." Addressing the Ideal Object, Coleridge cries in disillusion:

> And art thou nothing? Such thou art, as when
> The woodman winding westward up the glen
> At wintry dawn, where o'er the sheep-track's maze
> The viewless snow-mist weaves a glist'ning haze,
> Sees full before him, gliding without tread,
> An image with a glory round its head;
> The enamoured rustic worships its fair hues,
> Nor knows he makes the shadow, he pursues!

To Dickinson, by contrast, the pursuit of an Ideal is not a narcissistic illusion, but rather an ascent to our own potential height, projected from our best concept of ourselves. To express this complex idea, she employs, after her ingenuous first two lines, a more complicated syntax mirroring the life spent striving toward a mental Ideal. Rephrased, her sentence would read, "I descried, by the gaining Light, a traveller on a Hill, ascending, though terrene, to magic Perpendiculars; [although] his shimmering ultimate remained unknown, he indorsed the sheen." The spiritual pilgrimage is an unending one: in our last sight of the traveler, he is still "ascending" with no visible "ultimate." To embrace a spiritual journey is to ascend, and to keep on ascending, and to be seen by others as ascending, with no certain end in sight.

The "ultimate" has to be congruent with the "magic Perpendiculars." How is the poet to describe the goal at which the climbing traveler aims? As Dickinson seeks the right adjective for the ultimate, she tries "giddy"—but that implies a purely physical Alpine light-headedness. Then—better—she arrives at "dazzling," a word that, unlike "giddy," has a history of devotional usage (as in Henry Vaughan's "The Night": "There is in God, some say, / A deep but dazzling darkness"). But "dazzling" implies a visible source—"I was dazzled by the sun"—and that is precisely what, in the spiritual ascent, one does not have; the goal remains "Unknown." So Dickinson devises an "ultimate" with the "shimmering" aura of a celestial aurora. By employing the present participle, the poet keeps the traveler's "ultimate" active rather than inert; the elusiveness of "shimmering" suits an invisible ultimate far better than "dazzling." "To shimmer," from the Anglo-Saxon as far back as 1100, means "to shine with a tremulous or flickering light."

The "shimmering ultimate" may exist in the spiritual hope of the traveler, but of what use is that to the follower who speaks the poem? The "sheen" (or shining) of that shimmering ultimate is "indorsed" for her by that traveler ahead of her on the road: if he is ardently ascending the hill, his ardor attests to his vision. Dickinson's employment of a hardheaded, pragmatic, even commercial word—"indorse"—suggests that we all need a predecessor who, by his behavior, vouches for the worth of the arduous spiritual pilgrimage. That predecessor's heart and mind, prompting his ascent, testify to his inner vision of "magic Perpendiculars." He is one of those "Saints" (in Puritan usage, a title for the Elect) whose inner quality is recognizable to all. As Dickinson says in "No matter where the Saints abide" (1576, J 1541):

> No matter where the Saints abide,
> They make their Circuit fair
> Behold how great a Firmament
> Accompanies a Star.

In this brief epigram on the "Saints," Dickinson recalls another biblical text on righteousness (Daniel 12:3), from which she drew her "Firmament" and her "Star": "And they that be wise shall shine as the brightness of the firmament; and they that turn many to righteousness as the stars for ever and ever." In such poems as "The Road was lit" and "No matter where the Saints abide," Dickinson's "natural supernaturalism" (to use the term applied to such work by Meyer Abrams) does not repudiate the ideals of the Bible. It recasts them anew in earthly terms such as "indorse," or in the astronomical language of Daniel. The secularized Saints, rather like planets, "make their Circuit" in the realm of the Ideal, each a Star, each accompanied by the vastness of an attendant "Firmament" illuminated by the Star's radiating influence.

[J 1450]

# 1489

A Route of Evanescence,
With a revolving Wheel -
A Resonance of Emerald
A Rush of Cochineal -
And every Blossom on the Bush
Adjusts its tumbled Head -
The Mail from Tunis - probably,
An easy Morning's Ride -

When sending this poem to her Norcross cousins, Dickinson affixed, as her signature, "Humming bird," confirming our intuition that many of her nature poems embody in their subjects allegories of herself as an artist. The clearest sign of that intention here is the poet's creating of a chimera—a creature combining two species. The Humming Bird (as she referred to it, with two initial capitals, to Thomas Wentworth Higginson and other correspondents) combines the natural with the mechanical: the winged bird gets from place to place on a "Wheel." But what sort of Wheel? The image gave Dickinson trouble when, composing the poem, she looked for an adjective to characterize the "Wheel" of art. To what extent is art—the mechanism that brings nature to the page—reliable? Her (temporarily) final version of the Wheel in Version A was "a delusive wheel": Nature is real, art but a copy—such an accurate copy that the deluded reader believes it to be real. But before settling (temporarily) on "a delusive wheel," Dickinson had considered other possibilities: "a dissolving Wheel" (art is evanescent); "a dissembling Wheel" (art is deliberately misleading); and "a renewing Wheel" (art refreshes life). The Humming Bird reverses the old proverb *Ars longa, vita brevis*—"Life is short, but art is long"—to *Ars brevis, vita longa*. "Delusive"— the poet's "first final" choice—carries no implication that the artist wishes to delude, as does "dissembling"; it means only that the observer is deluded, because the appearance of the bird on the page is so realistic. Sending two poems—one on the Oriole and a version of this one with "revolving" instead of "delusive"—to the writer Helen Hunt Jackson, Dickinson wrote of her aspiration to accuracy, "[I] hope they are not untrue - ".

All Dickinson's early-chosen Wheel-adjectives, reviewed above, embody issues of truth and permanence. If art, even though not "dissembling," is "delusive"; if art, even if it is "renewing," is ultimately "dissolving"—what can Dickinson truthfully say about her art (and herself as artist)? Ceasing to characterize the Wheel with an "intrinsic" epistemological adjective of the sort she had been meditating, she moves to a "mechanical" adjective more suitable to a Wheel, setting it in motion. "Revolving" becomes her permanent final choice, in part because it continues—as the previously listed adjectives in "d" do not—the run of alliteration in "R," which, beginning with "Route," continues immediately with "Resonance" and "Rush" before terminating in "Ride." Is Dickinson's choice of "revolving" an evasion of the moral and metaphysical problems raised by the earlier run of adjectives of cognition—"renewing," "dissembling," "dissolving," and "delusive"? It is truer perhaps to say that the poet, examining her own practice of her art, decided that art is above all the continued activity of moving its object from one region to another: the revolving Wheel of art conducts the whirling Humming Bird of nature to the symbolic region of the page.

The rest of the poem remained unchanged as Dickinson sent it out to other correspondents. With her own revolving Wheel of language moving as fast as the Humming Bird, Dickinson speeds to the metaphors suggested to her by the tiny bird's sound and color as he sips nectar from the Blossoms on a nearby Bush. Her sensitive ear picks up his whirr and rush, and synthesizes them with the Humming Bird's colors—for which the names "green" and "red" would be, she implies, far too common. Whoever "painted" the bird dipped his brush first in paint of such a dazzling green as to deserve the name Emerald, and then in a scarlet paint as vivid as Cochineal, a brilliant red dye made out of the dried bodies of insects, *Coccus cacti*. (Dickinson liked "Cochineal" and used it again, teaming it with "Mazarin," a dark blue paint-color, in "I found the words to every thought" (436, J 581).

No sooner has he come than the Humming Bird is gone, leaving the Bush in a state of agitation. Like a gentleman who briefly passes through a room of young girls, leaving them in a flutter, the bird has unsettled every Blossom on the Bush, and each must readjust her "tumbled" curls. The Humming Bird is so inapprehensible in his "Evanescence" that the brief visible effect on the Blossoms is the only way to track his kinetic speed. It would be too mundane, however, to imagine that such an exotic creature has no purpose but to sip nectar. Such is the urgency of his visit that the poet speculates that he has a "Route," like a postal carrier, and is bringing Mail from a faraway place. "This is my letter to the World," Dickinson once wrote longingly (*519); and the Humming Bird delivers such letters. Why from "Tunis"? Perhaps (it has been suggested) because Tunis, in faraway Africa, is mentioned in *The Tempest* as the very figure of a remote place, where Claribel can have "no note [from her father Alonso], unless the sun were post" (*The Tempest,* Act 2, scene 1).

After the tumbling of "R's"—"Route," "revolving," "Resonance," "Rush" (and later, "Ride")—Dickinson links Blossom to Bush by their corresponding "b's" (a letter which reappears inside "tum-b-led"); and then, starting with the "m" in "tumbled," the "Mail" comes—when else?—in the alliterating "Morning." The indefinite article introducing all the qualities of the bird —"A" Route, "a" Wheel, "A" Resonance, "A" Rush, "An" [easy Morning's] Ride—is the indicator of bewilderment that Yeats used to represent Leda's sudden apprehension of the Jove-Swan: "A sudden blow," the feeling of a "white rush," "a shudder in the loins." These gestures toward indefinable meaning confess an inner tumult in synchrony with the outward disturbance.

This is one of the few poems given a title by Dickinson herself. When she sent it to Higginson (explaining that it was an intended contribution to a sale conducted by a local charity), she purveyed it with a title, "A Humming Bird." Since she nowhere in the poem names the bird, this glittering but colloquial little lyric falls into the ancient genre of the riddle: "Can you guess my name?" "Yes, 'Humming Bird.'" But an alternative answer would be "Yes, 'Dickinson,'" a poet who arrives, like the bird, quickly, vividly, and disturbingly, as she delivers, in her glittering linguistic plumage, her own exotic Mail.

[J 1463]

# 1511

The fascinating chill that Music leaves
Is Earth's corroboration
Of Ecstasy's impediment -
'Tis Rapture's germination
In timid and tumultuous soil
A fine - estranging creature -
To something upper wooing us
But not to our Creator -

With the exception of the first line, this poem exhibits the characteristics of the ballad stanza—and this is especially clear in the second half, with its regular 4-3-4-3 rhythm. According to the demands of the form, the first line "should" have four beats, and it is possible to so compress it: "The FAScinating CHILL that MUsic LEAVES." But because we don't yet know the basic ballad scansion to come, we read it, the first time through, as a pentameter: "The FAScinAting CHILL that MUsic LEAVES." After all, Dickinson does write poems that (legitimately) begin with a pentameter.

In short, the first line—as soon as we see it followed by the next three establishing the normative ballad rhythm—is unnerving, bequeathing to us (by its "extra" foot) a "fascinating chill" akin to that communicated by Music. I don't think Dickinson means that the Chill comes after the Music "leaves" permanently; rather, Music, as it goes on, leaves behind it a continuous wake of signification, causing in its listeners a fascinating chill. "Fascinating" (from the Latin *fascinare,* "to cast a spell") speaks of an enhanced, enchanted, hyperbolic state of sensation in the listener, while "chill" reveals the unearthliness of our sudden invitation into a hitherto-unknown climate, a climate chillier than the human one. ("Chill" is a word that is both nominal and verbal; derived from a verb, it is both a sensation and a result of sensation.) The effect of the first line, in its undue length, is to induce a "strangeness" of aftermath-within-continuity, just as Music does. We know that Dickinson had debated whether or not to extend the line to that extra length, because she had first written a regular four-beat line—"The fascinating chill of music"—only to produce, in a revision, the unduly long line that now prefaces, with its "chill," the rest of the poem.

As we come to the metrically regular second quatrain, we understand what Dickinson means by saying that Music is "Rapture's germination"—that it inserts itself into the "timid and tumultuous" soul/soil as an active ecstatic principle (a seed) that will continue to grow all by itself. But what does she mean by saying that Music is a "corroboration" on Earth of the "impediment" to Ecstasy? What impedes Ecstasy is not only its brevity but the invisibility of its ultimate "upper" goal (in religious doctrine, the Vision of God in Heaven). As with Ecstasy, so with Music: it ends, leaving its Goal indefinable, unknown.

Music is a "creature" (therefore something created), but—unlike the natural creatures described in Genesis—it does not figure in that primal parable of things coming to be; it is not mentioned in the Creator's six days of "work" before he "rested." Who, then, created it? Because it does not issue from Nature, it is an "estranging" creature, however "fine." (Dickinson's "fine" is not without irony.) What do we gain in a permanent sense from Music that estranges us from Nature, besides its "fascinating chill"?

In her last two lines, devastatingly rhyming "creature" and "Creator," Dickinson tells us what we gain from allowing Music to grow within us. We are wooed by it to "something upper." The poet cannot define that realm any further, but it is a competitor to that transcendent upper realm where God used to be imagined (as in Christian painting, where he is enthroned on high). Music has left us no Commandments, no Gospel; it speaks a language universally comprehensible yet lacking the vocabulary and grammar of ordinary language. This "creature" does not woo us to "*our* Creator" but to *its own* Creator—the Principle of aesthetic invention. And its ecstatic "upper" realm is one we inhabit while listening and for a time afterward. After all the elaborate "impediment" of the Latin diction in the rest of the poem, what is dramatically striking, by contrast, is Dickinson's choosing an exclusively Teutonic diction for Music's alternative heaven: the three components of "some-thing" and "up[per]" come from Old English for "sum" and "up," and Old Frisian for "thing"; and "woo[ing]" derives from late Anglo-Saxon. (Because Dickinson is using the word "something" contrastively, it has to receive ironic intonational emphasis: "To *something* upper wooing us / But not to our Creator - ".)

Dickinson is accurately characterizing her own soul/soil in calling it (binding the contrastive words with alliteration) "timid" with respect to the larger world, but "tumultuous" in its inner life. Music offered her soul the Ecstasy to be as tumultuous as it pleased. We must recall, reading this poem, that there was no recorded music in Dickinson's day. Although in her earlier, nonsequestered days she heard music (hymns, organ, Jenny Lind, Anton Rubinstein, brass bands) and also played the piano with frequent improvisation (at home and at her brother's house), eventually she had to rely, to hear music, on herself and her own inner instrument, playing music more rarely as her improvisation became principally a verbal one (see Sewall, 406–409). She sensed in the individuality of both words and music a parallel to her own estrangement from the ordinary.

[J 1480]

# 1513

'Tis whiter than an Indian Pipe
'Tis dimmer than a Lace -
No stature has it, like a Fog
When you approach the place -
Not any voice imply it here -
Or intimate it there -
A spirit - how doth it accost -
What function hath the Air?
This limitless Hyperbole
Each one of us shall be -
'Tis Drama - if Hypothesis
It be not Tragedy -

In writing "Of all the Souls that stand create - " (*279), Dickinson first defined life as "This brief Tragedy of Flesh"; then, reflecting that she was staging the poem in the life hereafter, she revised the phrase to read "this brief Drama in the flesh." While rising above life's "Tragedy" is possible for the resurrected, it is hardly feasible in one still subject to bodily events. If we have an immortal soul that continues to live after the death of the body, how are we to think of that spirit? And if we have not such a soul, and bodily death means annihilation, how are we to think of our fictions of the "spirit" within our body? Is death a "Drama" leading us to a glorious afterlife? Or is death the "Tragedy" of our annihilation? Reviving her earlier debate between "Drama" and "Tragedy," Dickinson attempts to describe a "spirit" in this riddle-poem.

Her first, comparative attempt is a positive one, resting securely on a sense-quality we know, namely color: the unidentified "it" is "whiter" than an Indian Pipe. But the white-flowered Indian Pipe makes a sinister companion; its other common name is "Corpse Plant," and it is (as Dickinson, who had studied botany, would have known) a saprophyte, a plant that feeds on decay. This is not a promising beginning. She looks for another object that is white and delicate, and decides on Lace—but because even the finest Lace is easily seen, this second comparative effort turns out to be unsuccessful: the "it" is "dimmer" than a Lace. There is really no material object, natural or manmade, Indian Pipe or Lace, to which "it" can be visibly compared. The poet's third attempt places a human being, "you," in an unidentified place already fogged in: one cannot estimate the "stature" (moral or material) of the surrounding Fog—and in fact a Fog obscures vision, rather than clarifying it.

Abandoning inquiries directed toward Nature, Dickinson, as is her wont, approaches authority. What do the books say of "it"? They are silent—and that fact pitches Dickinson into a wholly negative statement: no voice arises to imply that "it" is "here," or to intimate that it might be "there." Dickinson chooses pregnant verbs; "imply" means (literally) to enclose something within a fold. If only one could enfold "it"! And "intimate" (as a verb) means "to announce something of which one has inmost knowledge." Because the subtle action of the verb "to intimate" exhibits graphic and etymological identity with the reassuring adjective "intimate" (both coming from the Latin *intus*, "within"), Dickinson's irony is doubly felt. If only there were someone who would be "intimate" with spirit, and could "intimate," from certain knowledge, its location! Literature is full of psychopomps—guiding spirits or deities who lead human beings to invisible realms, as Virgil leads Dante in the *Divina Commedia*. But Dickinson has found, whether in Nature or in books, no such reliable guide. Dickinson's own earlier verbs (before she revised them to "imply" and "intimate") were "denote" and "designate," both pleading for explicit definition.

Dickinson, announcing the object hitherto only riddlingly presented, has desperate resort to the metaphysical realm: "A spirit - how doth it accost - "? ("To accost" means literally "to approach the side of," "come near to"—from Latin *costa*, "rib" or "side.") The poet has read *Hamlet*, in which Hamlet's murdered father accosts him, uttering his "Remember me"; and of course there are Christian legends of angels accosting human beings, as the angel Gabriel accosts Mary. But since Dickinson has never been so accosted, her hope of personal exposure to "it" does not solve the mystery of spirit. And finally, helpless, she asks an unanswerable question: "What function hath the Air?" The Air has only one function for us: it keeps us alive as we breathe it. The classical words for "breath," the Greek *pneuma* and (among the Latin choices) *spiritus*, have been used with religious overtones, as when God breathes life into man, or when the Holy Spirit descends on Jesus' apostles in the form of a rush of air. But Dickinson forcibly repudiates those religious overtones by phrasing her final question around a word ("function") associated with mechanical or material activity. (Her superseded alternative was ethnological: "What customs - hath the Air?")

In her first quatrain, Dickinson uses the modern third-person singular form of "to have": "has." But in her later questions about the materialization of spirit, as she recalls past legends, secular and religious, of such accosting, she diverges to the archaic forms "hath" and "doth." In asking, "What function hath the Air?" she may be recalling God's unanswerable questions to Job (using the same archaic verb forms). In Job 38:19 we find, for example, "Where is the way where light dwelleth? And as for darkness, where is the place thereof?"

There is no further place to go for Dickinson's questioning, once she has alighted on "What function hath the Air?" Giving up on the nature and location of the spirit, she turns from the realm of the epistemological to the realm of the rhetorical, where she is most at home, venturing that after death, when we are pure Spirit, we become (to use earthly terms) a "limitless Hyperbole." Eternity and infinity are by definition "limitless," and the highest possible exaggeration in rhetoric is the figure called Hyperbole. (Because its name derived from the Greek words meaning "to throw" and "over," it was called by the Renaissance rhetorician Puttenham "the Overreacher.") Certainly the concept of the spirit overreaches anything the earth could provide. Dickinson chose her designation for the spirit carefully. At first she had been tempted by denotation and religious diction ("And this - this unsurmisèd thing - "; "And this - Apocalyptic thing - "), but, discarding conventional and religious language, she boldly found her way to her cool "Hyperbole."

How can one describe passing from bodily existence to existence-as-pure-spirit? Nothing could be more theatrical:

> This limitless Hyperbole
> Each one of us shall be -
> 'Tis Drama -

Yes, resurrection surely is Drama—unless religion has deceived us, and on our deathbed we discover that the play in which we have been actors is a tragedy, not the Divine Comedy of ascent to Paradise, but the Mortal Tragedy of extinction. The entirely worldly diction of Dickinson's last quatrain tells us that she considers life a Tragedy.

One of the ways of perceiving how Dickinson makes a poem evolve is to track its nouns, and to ask whether the ending resembles the beginning. Here, this procedure gives us a list that begins in Nature and Culture with Indian Pipe and Lace, and—passing through invisible Fog, silent voice, and immaterial spirit—finds two endpoints: a materialistic one in "function" and "Air," and a literary one that clusters together, in neat antitheses, Hyperbole, Drama, Hypothesis, and Tragedy. The realms Dickinson investigates are Nature, Invisibility, Science, and Verbal Art—and she ends in the one to which she gives most credence. As she concluded elsewhere (1532, J 1503):

> More than the Grave is closed to me -
> The Grave and that Eternity
> To which the Grave adheres -
> I cling to nowhere till I fall -
> The Crash of nothing, yet of all -
> How similar appears -

We notice, prompted by the rhyme *(aab, ccb)* and meter (4-4-3, 4-4-3), that the first tercet embodies the religious view of death (which Dickinson denies, while still being trapped in its vocabulary), while the second tercet—linked to the first by the repeated *b* rhyme—speaks in purely material terms, as the poet liberates herself from a lexicon no longer her own.

[J 1482]

# 1539

Mine Enemy is growing old -
I have at last Revenge -
The Palate of the Hate departs -
If any would avenge

Let him be quick -
The Viand flits -
It is a faded Meat -
Anger as soon as fed - is dead -
'Tis Starving makes it fat -

This drama-in-little accomplishes its first act with a gloating two lines: "Mine Enemy is growing old - / I have at last Revenge - ." The link between the "growing old" of the Enemy and the poet's "Revenge" is not specified; we know only that in age the Enemy has lost what she (or he) most valued. Beauty? Friends? The respect of others? Nor is it specified what event in the past had made the poet feel "Anger" toward the Enemy. In any case, the poet tastes the "Revenge" she has so long and so fiercely desired. The one-line conclusion of the personal drama—"The Palate of the Hate departs - "—presents the poet's desolate realization that she feels none of the expected gloating and satisfaction.

Thus ends the little personal story. As she often does, Dickinson writes the poem over again, keeping her metaphor of taste and Palate, but this time offering an impersonal warning to anyone following in her footsteps. He should not wait for any "at last," but take his Revenge quickly, because "the Viand flits" (like other earthly things) and the Meat of the Viand that "flits" becomes (alliteratively) "faded," like everything that has grown old. Thus ends the applied lesson.

To conclude (or so we think), Dickinson, as she often does, invents a proverb, one made resonant by its significant internal rhyme equating "fed" and "dead": "Anger as soon as fed - is dead - ". She could have ended here, rhetorically speaking. Doesn't the proverb sum up both her personal story and its impersonal retelling? Why does she append a further explanatory line looking back to the time when Anger was "fat"? The closing line surges up to break through the tidy summary proverb, because that starving period when Anger was "fat" is what the poet remembers most acutely of her past emotions at estrangement. Before the poem began, the poet and the other person were Friends; then the Friend became an Enemy; then the poet experienced Anger and desired Revenge. As the taking of Revenge was postponed longer and longer, the poet herself became less and less likely to think only of Revenge, while her Revenge-seeking Anger, fat when she was first starving, diminished as time passed. The grotesque image of Anger swelling with rage recalls medieval depictions of the seven deadly sins; it is Gluttony who is "fat" in those, but in Dickinson's system Anger is the gross emotion. Any emotion, aggrandizing itself, can so obsess the self that it extirpates all others, as Anger first did here. And it is that paradoxical Anger, fattening on starvation, that was, and remains in the last line, the underlying motive of the poem.

[J 1509]

# 1577

The Bible is an antique Volume -
Written by faded Men
At the suggestion of Holy Spectres -
Subjects - Bethlehem -
Eden - the ancient Homestead -
Satan - the Brigadier -
Judas - the Great Defaulter -
David - the Troubadour -
Sin - a distinguished Precipice
Others must resist -
Boys that "believe" are very lonesome -
Other Boys are "lost" -
Had but the Tale a warbling Teller -
All the Boys would come -
Orpheus' Sermon captivated -
It did not condemn -

Dickinson's mock-labeling of famous Bible stories seems at first merely a
send-up. It follows, after all, on a comically blasphemous description of the
Bible as not "ancient" but "antique," the prophets and evangelists as "faded
Men," and the Holy Spirit as a collection of "Holy Spectres." An earlier ver-
sion of this clever parody was considerably less blasphemous in its adjectives:

The Bible is an untold volume,
Written by unknown men
At the request of hallowed spectres -

In all three variants of the poem, Dickinson launches into a list, in car-
toon form, of the subjects of Bible stories. All variants list "Subjects" begin-
ning with "Bethlehem - " and go on to Genesis, Satan, Judas, and David.
("Genesis - Bethlehem's Ancestor - " proved too reverential and stately in its

use of "Ancestor," and was briskly and "Americanly" revised into "Eden - the ancient Homestead - ", while the other subjects remained unaltered.)

Dickinson could not indefinitely postpone—by an entertaining retitling of biblical legend—the dark biblical message transmitted by preachers in the pulpit: that of the danger of Sin. It is a "distinguished Precipice" given grandeur by the fall of the chiefest of the angels, Lucifer. On the other hand, it is to be resisted by "Others" (how can they be expected to resist, if Lucifer could not?). And Belief in the verity of the Bible is essential, says Dickinson's parodied preacher, with a pastoral warning attached: Boys that do not believe are "lost." In one of her finer subterfuges (line 11), Dickinson unobtrusively slips in something that the preacher would not have said, but that she believes: "Boys that 'believe' are very lonesome." Adolescent boys would tend to exclude from their rowdy company a boy who was professing active belief and striving to remain virtuous. Most of the boys are indifferent (as the final quatrain tells us) to what the preacher has to say.

"The Bible is an antique Volume" has become famous because of the pains Dickinson took in the first version with her final quatrain. She asks herself why the boys do not flock to hear the preacher, and she decides that it is his manner, not his matter, that puts them off. Remembering that when Orpheus sang, all the animals and trees came to listen, the poet declares that Orpheus drew an audience because he offered not condemnation but captivation. What sort of a "Teller" of the biblical "Tale" would the preacher have to be, if he were to become as persuasive to his congregation of "Boys" as Orpheus was to the creatures surrounding him?

Pondering how to describe the nature of the Teller, and dissatisfied with her first, conventional choice of adjective ("thrilling"), Dickinson launches into a verbal extravaganza of thirteen different alternative adjectives, each a possible characterization of the Teller:

> Had but the Tale a . . . Teller,
> All the Boys would come -

To fill the blank, try choosing (as Dickinson told herself to do) from the following:

typic
hearty
bonnie
breathless
spacious
tropic
warbling
ardent
friendly
magic
pungent
winning
mellow

As we glance down Dickinson's list of alternatives, we see that they can be roughly grouped into adjectives of personality (hearty, friendly, winning, mellow), adjectives of manner (breathless, ardent, pungent) and a few others that are less subject to categorization (typic, bonnie, spacious, tropic, warbling, and magic). What would make "All the Boys" come? Would it be the Teller's scoutmaster personality—hearty, friendly, mellow, and winning—as he reached out to the Boys? Or would it be his own inner excitement at the matter of his Tale, rendering him breathless (with the suspenseful story of Eden) or pungent (as he related the story of the defeat of the Fallen Angels) or ardent (as he retold the Nativity of Jesus)? Or would it be his own personal beauty—would a "bonnie" Teller be more successful than a plain one? Dickinson decides that it is not personality nor individual excitement nor physical beauty that wins audiences permanently (permanent attention from the "Boys" to religion is the preacher's hoped-for result). What aspect would attract an audience not temporarily but permanently?

There remain as yet unexamined the adjectives "typic," "tropic," "magic," "spacious," and "warbling." Dickinson called Nature "the Typic" ("archetypal") mother in "The murmuring of Bees" (*1142); and she knew that "typic" could mean "prophetic"—characterizing a Teller able to show the connection between Old Testament "types" and their New Testament fulfillments. "Tropic" may here mean "warm": Dickinson referred to herself as the "Tropic [warm] Bride" who would be manacled to Death's icicle (*1771, "'Twas here my summer paused"). It has also been suggested that Dickinson might use "tropic" in this context to mean "using tropes, figures of speech" (a definition found only under "tropical," not under "tropic," in Dickinson's 1844 Webster and in the *OED*). "Typic" and "Tropic," as choices, had the distinct virtue of alliterating with the two "T" nouns in the line: "Had but the Tale a [typic] / [tropic] Teller - / All the Boys would come - ". "Spacious" is also an adjective of manner, and suggests a Telling that would possess breadth of vision and grandeur of reference. "Magic" introduces a non-Christian supernatural power: it was to "magic Perpendiculars," not to God, that the poet's spiritual traveler ascended in "The Road was lit with Moon and star - " (*1474). In finishing her poem on the Bible, Dickinson will ultimately discard both divine power and supernatural "magic" in exchange for a "Teller" with a tinge of both.

As we know, in making her final copies of "The Bible is an antique Volume - ", Dickinson chose to distinguish her Teller as a "warbling" one. This adjective refers to manner, but a manner that bears no relation to the hearty personality or attractive looks of the Teller, nor to his enthusiasm or his literary manner (typic, tropic, spacious), nor to the sort of content that is being purveyed (whether sacred or secular), nor to a supernatural power. In choosing her final adjective, Dickinson must (it seems) be recalling Milton's characterization in "L'Allegro" of Shakespeare "warbling his native woodnotes wild." "Warbling"—uttering a melodious song—is persuasive no matter what the looks or the personality of the Teller may be, no matter whether the content is typic or tropic, the manner spacious or not, the Tale biblical or not. "Warbling" is a purely aesthetic word, ethically and substantively neutral.

But once Dickinson settles on the content-neutral "warbling," she elevates it to the archetype of all music making, as the divine Orpheus (the son of Apollo) with his lyre trumps, so to speak, the Christian preacher. All the reluctant Boys would come to hear what Dickinson mischievously ascribes to Orpheus: a captivating "Sermon." Only by returning, now, to the list of Tales do we see that in naming them Dickinson reveals how "Orpheus" (or she herself) would have interpreted the Bible from a secular pulpit: as a boys' adventure story, offering an American "Homestead" (the Dickinson house in Amherst was often called "the Homestead") along with dashing characters such as a "Brigadier" and a "Defaulter," and an Orpheus figure, the "Troubadour." Such a humorously colloquial list reminds us that Dickinson and Mark Twain were contemporaries.

Dickinson's thirteen-member list is merely a conspicuous instance of what her verbal imagination lavishly suggested for any temporary gap in composition. Thirteen written alternatives exist here—but their profusion awakens us to the incalculable number of unrecorded alternatives that passed through the poet's mind as she invented her poems.

[J 1545]

# 1581

Those - dying then,
Knew where they went -
They went to God's Right Hand -
That Hand is amputated now
And God cannot be found -

The abdication of Belief
Makes the Behavior small -
Better an ignis fatuus
Than no illume at all -

Literalizing a religious metaphor, Dickinson is at her most shocking. In countless carvings and paintings, at the Right Hand of God sits his Son, with the saved gathered around Him. (On the left side, the damned are driven into hell by devils). The concept of the place of honor at God's right hand goes back to Psalm 110: "The Lord said unto my Lord, Sit thou at my right hand." It is frequently alluded to in Paul's Epistles, where Paul says to the faithful, "If ye be risen with Christ, seek those things which are above, where Christ sitteth on the right hand of God" (Colossians 3:1). Dickinson has witnessed the touching belief of dying Christians that they will be "risen with Christ" and sit with Him at the right hand of God; anyone "dying...now"—in modernity—can have no such relief.

Her bitterness at such deprivation erupts in her searing retort to Paul's confidence: "That Hand is amputated now." The clinically surgical metaphor assumes for a moment that the rest of God still exists, with a bleeding stump where a Hand used to be. The pious believer, who has never really thought in any literal way about the religious metaphors he has absorbed, is taken aback when one of them is so viciously embodied before him. Dickinson moderates the image of an amputee-God by adding that the whole of Him has now disappeared entirely: God "cannot be found." There is no place for ambiguity here. These statements declare a creed opposite to that of the church, and are stated as absolutely and forthrightly as the assertions in the

Nicene Creed (which says of Jesus that he "sitteth at the right hand of God").

Tired of her bitterness, and knowing she cannot will herself into Belief (since it has abdicated of its own accord from her soul), Dickinson faces the consequence of her intellectual position. Where does one find, after belief is gone, standards of behavior to compare with those embodied in the Christian virtues of Faith, Hope, and Charity, or the Christian advocacy of works of corporal and spiritual mercy? Where is there a set of ideals as compelling as those of the Beatitudes? Who will be one's guide after one has rejected institutional Christianity?

A "lapsed" (fallen) Christian is usually said to have "lost" his faith. In both of these formulations—"to lapse," "to lose"—the "sinner" is responsible for, and blamed for, his fall. Dickinson does not accept the blame suggested by such verbs. She did not "fall," she did not "lose" her faith; rather, it left her, abdicating from the throne of Belief. She refuses to chastise herself for her present conviction of final annihilation; if there is no Right Hand of God, in fact no God at all, death is simply a fact of animal life. The nostalgia she feels for the old uprightness of the "Perpendiculars" of Christianity—and the consequence that disbelief may allow the countenancing of "small" (unworthy, mean, ignoble) behavior—lead her to a sardonic conclusion in favor of denial (a choice she can scarcely endorse for herself).

As so often, the poet turns for her closing epigram to a proverbial form: "Better X than Y." If there is in fact no leading "kindly light" (John Henry Newman's phrase), most people nonetheless search for any substitute, and follow a deceptive *ignis fatuus* rather than live without belief altogether. (An *ignis fatuus,* Latin for "foolish fire," sometimes called a "will-o'-the-wisp," is a phosphorescent light that flits over swampy terrain; those who follow its illusory light become lost.) Dickinson's ironic recommendation "Better an *ignis fatuus* / Than no illume at all - " rings precisely and dismissively because it is a relief unavailable in her own case; but her distaste for "small" behavior leaves her ambivalent toward those who still rely on the grand aspirations of belief. Nonetheless, the resemblance of "illume" to "illusory" hovers at the close.

[J 1551]

# 1593

He ate and drank the precious Words -
His Spirit grew robust -
He knew no more that he was poor,
Nor that his frame was Dust -
He danced along the dingy Days
And this Bequest of Wings
Was but a Book - What Liberty
A loosened Spirit brings -

The "precious Words" that in the Book of Common Prayer accompany the dispensing of the Communion bread and wine are drawn from Matthew 26:26–27: "Take, eat; this is my body" and "Drink ye all of [this], for this is my blood." In the preliminary prayer before Communion, the priest not only uses the words "eat" and "drink," but also implores that "our souls [may be] washed through his most precious blood." "He ate and drank," says Dickinson, continuing with the priest's word "precious"; but for the substance consumed—in the Prayer Book the "body and blood of our Lord"—she substitutes "Words." The heartening of the spirit expected as a consequence of Communion happens in Dickinson's protagonist, too: "His Spirit grew robust - ". What the Spirit lifts him away from, however, are two Christian doctrines: that we are poor creatures, and that from dust we came and unto dust we shall return.

In her philological version of the most sacred rite of the Christian church, Dickinson presents herself in the persona of a male consumer of Words. Because the priest partakes of the bread and wine before the congregation, I think Dickinson may be imagining herself here not merely as a communicant, but as the (necessarily male, in her era) priest-communicant. Once the philological communicant has dismissed the depressing poverty and Dust of the Christian idea of man, which had rendered his Days "dingy," he becomes an angel, his Wings a "Bequest" from the exhilarating Book. The "Good Book" (as the Bible was sometimes called) was supposed to elevate the Spirit;

but to Dickinson, any Book, a mere earthly Book, can be a Good Book. She specifies no content—religious, philosophical, or aesthetic—with respect to the "precious Words"; all she asks is that the book "loosen" the Spirit into Liberty. The word "loosen" implies that the Spirit has previously been tethered or shackled, has lacked the freedom of independent movement.

The soul's declaration of independence is, one could say, an earthly form of conversion, and the elation consequent upon a "Great Awakening"—like the salvation promised by Jonathan Edwards—is precisely what Dickinson brings to the close of the poem, marveling that it was "but a Book" that gave the Spirit Wings. The last line of the poem seems at first tautological. Would not any "loosened" Spirit have "Liberty"? The line would indeed be redundant if it were a statement—but it is an outburst: "What Liberty - " exclaims the unshackled being, free not only to wander the earth at will, but also to rise on the newly acquired Wings.

Dickinson's usual skeptic mockery of conventional religion can be seen in her rhyming the dingy Christian "Dust" with its antonym, the energetically "robust" Spirit gained from "the precious Words." The happiness of the liberated spirit is mirrored in the alliteration animating every line of the second quatrain (phonetically if not graphically in "Wings" and "Bequest," pronounced "Be-kwest"). It is as though, to the accompaniment of this transforming Book, Dust animated itself into dance. In the competition of "a" Book and the "Good Book," the earthly Book wins. Yet by analogizing its "precious Words" with those of Jesus and of the Communion service, Dickinson confers on secular writing the highest dignity available within her cultural repertoire.

[J 1587]

# 1618

There came a Wind like a Bugle -
It quivered through the Grass
And a Green Chill upon the Heat
So ominous did pass
We barred the Windows and the Doors
As from an Emerald Ghost -
The Doom's Electric Moccasin
That very instant passed -
On a strange Mob of panting Trees
And Fences fled away
And Rivers where the Houses ran
Those looked that lived - that Day -
The Bell within the steeple wild
The flying tidings told -
How much can come
And much can go,
And yet abide the World!

Dickinson's naturalization of the Day of Doom is announced by Gabriel's trumpet in the wind, and by an ominous transformation of the surroundings of the poet's house. It has been a hot day in midsummer, the grass flourishing, but the wind brings a "Green Chill" as the temperature precipitously drops and the sky takes on a peculiar greenish color (compare Coleridge's "Dejection" and its sky with a "peculiar tint of yellow green"). Any moment now, the dead will rise from their graves. Barricading themselves in the house, the inhabitants await the arrival of an "Emerald Ghost." And at the very moment of their fear, their apprehension is confirmed. The dispersed and dead local tribe of Indians, creeping up unnoticed, is taking back its stolen land; its "Electric Moccasin" brings lightning, a lethal revenge, in its wake.

Those two quatrains are the overture to Dickinson's tone poem. The next quatrain—revealing the unnatural upheavals in the landscape—is written (suitably) backward. Rearranged to a natural grammatical order, with its el-lipses filled in, the quatrain would read: "Those [who] were alive [on] that day looked on a strange mob of panting trees, and fences [that had] fled away, and rivers [running] where the houses [also] ran in flood waters." The odd phrase "Those . . . that lived - that Day - " tells us that the Day took place in the past; only some persons were alive to see the spectacle. The day has so lived in memory, however, that even those who never witnessed its derange-ment of the normal have a bequeathed knowledge of its dislocation of time and space. Dickinson has in mind various biblical passages about the end of days, with manifestations such as earthquakes, hail, and falling stars. These are drawn in part from Mark (13:24–25) and Luke (21:25), but the clearest source is Revelation 16:18–21: "And there were voices, and thunders, and lightnings; and there was a great earthquake. . . . And every island fled away, and the mountains were not found. And there fell upon men a great hail out of heaven." Dickinson echoes Revelation's "every island fled away," in her "Fences fled away," and the thunder and lightning of Revelation also make their way into her poem (although in her summer storm she substitutes wind and torrential rains for Revelation's icy hail).

Dickinson had originally written, "The Living looked that Day - ". In re-vising the line to "Those looked that lived - that Day - ", what did she gain? The original, in its "Living looked," already had the alliteration she wanted, so she was not aiming to improve that feature by her rephrasing the line into "Those looked that lived - ". Is there a difference in meaning between the two lines? After all, who could have witnessed the stormy panorama except the "Living," or "Those . . . that lived - that Day - "? Dickinson has in mind, I believe, Jesus' account of "the abomination of desolation" (Mark 13:14–20) which will fall so suddenly upon the land that those who wish to escape death must flee. Jesus also prophesies (in Matthew 16:27–28; also in Mark 9:1) that at the end of the world, when the Son will come in judgment, some of his present hearers will still be alive: "For the Son of man shall come in the glory of his Father with his angels; and then he shall reward every man according to his works. Verily I say unto you, There be some standing here, which shall not taste of death, till they see the Son of man coming in his kingdom." In Dickinson's revision, those who remained living at the Last Judgment, and who had not fled, were "Those . . . that lived - that Day - ". Dickinson's boldness appropriates the affliction of the biblical Doomsday for a description of a summer storm in Amherst, no mean act of literary bravado.

In describing the storm, Dickinson uses an unusual degree of enjambment both in her overture (lines 2–6) and in the storm as beheld (lines 9–12). She, who could hardly end a line without her characteristic dash, lets the storm rage on unhindered. She draws on the usual word for a revolutionary assault ("Mob"), but in her tempest it is trees who are rioting, "panting" from the beating of the rain and wind. The deregulation of all borders (not only Fences but also Rivers "where the Houses ran") speaks of a chaos both of persons (the panting Trees) and places (the village) that may not be reparable. We are left (in line 12, when we finally reach the end of the storm-sentence) with the spectacle of aghast survivors gazing at the disruption of their lives and landscape.

How will Dickinson put a coda to this apocalyptic narrative? She borrows Tennyson's "wild bells" from *In Memoriam,* Section 106 (1850), and recalls a line from "O Little Town of Bethlehem" (1868) to usher in the news of a ravaged world awaiting a new beginning. Tennyson's New Year poem reads, in part,

> Ring out, wild bells, to the wild sky,
> The flying cloud, the frosty light:
> The year is dying in the night;
> Ring out, wild bells, and let him die.
>
> Ring out the old, ring in the new,
> Ring, happy bells, across the snow:
> The year is going, let him go;
> Ring out the false, ring in the true.
>
> Ring out the grief that saps the mind,
> For those that here we see no more;
> Ring out the feud of rich and poor,
> Ring in redress to all mankind.

Perhaps because this is one of *In Memoriam*'s three Christmastide poems, the angelic "good tidings of great joy" (Luke 2:10, alliteratively modified by Phillips Brooks in "O Little Town of Bethlehem" as "We hear the Christmas angels / The great glad tidings tell") may have contributed to Dickinson's alliterative "tidings told." There is no atmosphere of "great glad tidings" in the dark apocalyptic texts the poet depended on for the storm. But when she arrives at the tongue of the Bell, the joy of her identification with the Bell's utterance is palpable: her assonance in long "i" ("wild," "flying," "tidings") is a "bright" sound entirely unlike the heavier phonemes of "The Doom's Electric Moccasin" or the "strange Mob of panting Trees."

Once the Bell's "tidings" have announced the end of the storm's scourging of the earth, Dickinson can look about her at the altered village scene, and make her closing summary: "How much can come"—a Wind, a Chill, a Ghost, an Electric Moccasin, a strange Mob of Trees, fled Fences, running Houses—"And much can go"—peace, quiet, order, stationary trees, borders, riverbanks—"And yet abide the World!" She could not have written such a summary when she was younger and thought that one could never recover from such a disaster. Fortunately for both herself and her poetry, her primary ecstatic response to natural phenomena never failed to return—even after the many "funerals" in her brain.

She looks for a verb to suit her exclamatory wonder that the World always will . . . will what? Remain? Survive? It was an important word she was seeking—the last verb, the one that stands behind all the coming and going of phenomena. She first wrote "remain," but with quick genius exchanged it for "abide." Not only does "abide" suitably assonate with the wild flying tidings; it expresses (as "remain" does not) the connotation of waiting and expecting. And while "remain" is Latin in origin (*remanere*, "to stay behind"), "abide," with its Teutonic root, is an antonym etymologically in keeping with the swiftness of Dickinson's very non-Latinate ending as things "come" and "go." Finally, and most conclusively, "abide" is a biblical word, with two contexts relevant to this poem of restoration: perhaps Jesus' command to his disciples, "Abide in me, as I in you" (John 15:4), but certainly Jesus' promise that he will not leave the disciples comfortless: "And I will pray the Father, and he shall give you another Comforter, that he may abide with you forever" (John 14:16). That abiding presence was for the disciples the Holy Spirit, but for Dickinson the ever-remaining World.

[J 1593]

# 1668

Apparently with no surprise
To any happy Flower
The Frost beheads it at its play -
In accidental power -
The blonde Assassin passes on -
The Sun proceeds unmoved
To measure off another Day
For an Approving God -

Innocuously entitled "Death and Life" in the 1890 *Poems,* this poem should have been called "God's Assassin"—or something equally brutal. In "Those - dying then" (\*1581), God's Hand had been "amputated" (with no evil agent named as the one responsible for the severing), but here an active agent, the Frost, actively "beheads" the happy Flower. The Flower is a child still at play in early Autumn; then comes the first "killing frost," and behold the be-headed result. Yet Dickinson ascribes no blame to the Frost for its "acciden-tal" act of beheading, nor does she impute any surprise to the "happy Flower." Unlike plants that cry out when wounded (in myth, in Dante's wood), the Flower utters no protest. Such is the self-contradicting narrative of the first quatrain. Is it by design or is it by the exercise of "accidental" power that the Frost beheads the Flower? One might expect a white space as preparation for Dickinson's conclusion after this pitiless narrative. But because the conclu-sion is inseparable from the annihilating act, Dickinson conjoins them seam-lessly in order to leave not so much as a chink for doubt.

And so the second quatrain revises the first. The Frost's act is not "acci-dental." He is an "Assassin" (that sinister word, meaning "hashish-eater," was borrowed from the Arabic centuries ago). Since an Assassin is "one who un-dertakes to put another to death by treacherous violence," Dickinson is now representing the Frost's power as evil, murderous, and treacherous. The usual literary and pictorial "Assassin" is dark-haired; it seems particularly under-handed to locate the fatal scimitar in the hand of a "blonde" killer, who will not awaken suspicion. But who has employed the Assassin? To what authority will he report his success?

At first we do not know; the Frost merely "passes on" to his next victim. And now that the day's assignment has been completed, the celestial time-clock can register day's end. The Sun has watched (no doubt) any number of beheadings, but now, as before, he remains "unmoved." His obligation is simply to keep time accurately, and he too has an authority to whom to report. Only in the final word of the poem does Dickinson utter the incriminating name—"God." In the biblical story of the Creation, we see only two aspects of God: his power to bring new things into existence, and his approval as he sees that what he has done is "good." The self-approbationary "good" is repeated seven times in Genesis 1 (verses 4, 10, 12, 18, 21, 25, and 31). In Genesis, God never disapproves of anything he creates, which is, of course, the problem raised by Blake in "The Tyger." (Dickinson probably noticed that the only created being that did not garner an approving "good" from God was Eve.)

The second quatrain (except for the conspicuously foreign "Assassin") begins in a distinctly latinate way, because Latin is often Dickinson's grand diction for abstractions (including the Christian God). But perhaps (it occurs to her) we don't know the quarter in which that God really lives, and so she turns away from Latin to an inextricable Teutonic trio for this unmerciful "Approving" God. "God," the biblical "good" (implied in "Approving"), and "Day" make up a non-latinate reprise of Genesis: "On the first day . . . God saw that it was good."

"Apparently with no surprise" anthropomorphizes a common garden-loss happening every autumn, but its literal beheaded Flower (over which Dickinson, with her love of Flowers, would have grieved) stands in for the tragedy of premature death. Dickinson's adored nephew Gilbert had died rapidly, at the age of eight, in 1883, of a short and severe fever; Dickinson was "alarmingly ill," according to her sister, for months afterward, and never (says Sewall) entirely recovered. This 1884 poem is surely a product of Gilbert's death (if perhaps also of other deaths), and its irremediable grief is voiced in the chilly and detached narrative which ironically imitates the distant voice of a complacently approving God.

[J 1624]

# 1715

A word made Flesh is seldom
And tremblingly partook
Nor then perhaps reported
But have I not mistook
Each one of us has tasted
With ecstasies of stealth
The very food debated
To our specific strength -

A word that breathes distinctly
Has not the power to die
Cohesive as the Spirit
It may expire if He -

"Made Flesh and dwelt among us"
Could condescension be
Like this consent of Language
This loved Philology

Like "Shall I take thee, the Poet said" (*1243), this is a poem analogizing the human word embodied in a work of art to the Johannine Word, the incarnate Jesus. Neither poem is about Christ; his "condescension" to become human is merely a metaphor for the "consent" of Language to give words ("Philology") to the poet's interior contours of feeling.

Dickinson, as we know from a draft which is "related" to "A word made Flesh" (according to Ralph Franklin's note), had pondered John's obscure opening of his Gospel in sufficient depth to be repelled by a Preacher who "broached" the topic of the Incarnation without having any intimation of its "import":

The import of that Paragraph
"The word made Flesh"
Had he the faintest intimation
Who broached it yesterday!

Dickinson had intimations of the "import" of John's phrase beyond what she had heard from a superficial preacher:

> In the beginning was the Word, and the Word was with God, and the Word was God. The same was in the beginning with God. All things were made by him; and without him was not any thing made that was made. In him was life; and the life was the light of men. And the light shineth in darkness; and the darkness comprehended it not. . . . That was the true Light, which lighteth every man that cometh into the world. He was in the world, and the world was made by him, and the world knew him not. He came unto his own, and his own received him not. But as many as received him, to them gave he power to become the sons of God, even to them that believe on his name: which were born, not of blood, nor of the will of the flesh, nor of the will of man, but of God. And the Word was made flesh, and dwelt among us (and we beheld his glory, the glory as of the only be-gotten of the Father), full of grace and truth. (John 1:1–5, 9–14)

The only begotten Son "became flesh" (New Revised Standard Version) and "condescended" to leave his heavenly realm and take on an embodied pres-ence on earth.

It seems to Dickinson that the creation out of nothing of a poem (or any other work of art) makes the poet's creative force analogous to God's own. But is the poem truly "created out of nothing" in a process analogous to Gen-esis' narrative of God creating all things *ex nihilo?* The poem, after all, does employ a raw preexistent material: words. But a poem is not merely a collec-tion of juxtaposed words (or what Coleridge would have called an assem-blage made by "Fancy"). Something (apparently from no source) has to have happened to the words for them to coalesce into a single new totality. This coalescence—or, as Dickinson called it, "Cohesive[ness]"—was ascribed by Coleridge to an entity he named the Imagination. In "Shall I take thee," we have seen that in Dickinson's view sustained work and determined will alone do not suffice for the fusion of words into poetry. The poet, too impatiently seeking the *mot juste,* must wait until the contour of her mental "Vision" suf-ficiently comes forward to prompt the right word.

In rewriting the earlier poem "Shall I take thee" into "A word made Flesh," Dickinson changes her own role. In "Shall I take thee," she is the would-be creator who has to learn patience. But in "A word made Flesh," she is no longer the maker but the partaker, a member of the poet's audience. She therefore adds the analogy of Communion (used in "He ate and drank the precious Words - "; *1593) to the analogy of the Word made Flesh. Remembering the revelatory reading-moment of being pierced by a poem, she wonders how its author knew it was exactly what she needed in the way of spiritual nourishment. The poet is the creative spirit who prepares for us food precisely "debated / To our specific strength"—that is, sustenance professionally weighed against our capacity to digest it. Just as a patient will be prescribed the quantity of medicine suitable to his age and weight (more for an adult, less for a child), so the reader has the eerie feeling of being precisely prescribed for by the poet. The physician/poet, says Dickinson, "debates" (estimates) exactly what is necessary in each case. It seems miraculous that one should receive, like manna from heaven, the very food that matches one's own specific need and capacity. Dickinson expresses her wonder at the miraculous *individual* accommodation of word to need by the singling out of "Each one of us," by the intensifying adverb "very," and by the particularizing adjective "specific."

Dickinson's own initial experiences of aesthetic transport came from books that she perhaps had to read in "stealth" (her father would buy books she desired and then implore her not to read them). We know from Thomas Wentworth Higginson's letter to his wife (L 342a), written the day after he met Emily Dickinson for the first time, that the poet had told him that the sensation of reading a poem shook her to the core: "If I read a book [and] it makes my whole body so cold no fire ever can warm me I know *that* is poetry. If I feel physically as if the top of my head were taken off, I know *that* is poetry. These are the only way [*sic*] I know it. Is there any other way[?]" There is no reason to suspect Dickinson of hyperbole. Her "glittering Retinue of nerves" ("Severer Service of myself"; 887, J 786) must have trembled in passionate physical sensation during her early encounters with poetry. When, as a young person, she reads, let us say, Shakespeare, her appetite—despite its intensity of desire—partakes of the banquet of embodied words seldom and tremblingly; nor does she tend to "report" to others her discoveries and her responses. There is something in Shakespeare for her every mood, her every intuition. The poet has found that she is proffered precisely what she was hungering for at the time of reading. In another decade, the "food debated / To [her] specific strength" might be found on another page entirely.

Dickinson doubts the immortality of the soul, but not the immortality of a word given life. The strongest assertion of the poem emerges from that first shaken encounter with "A word that breathes distinctly." Such a poem-word "Has not the power to die," because its hitherto scattered phrases have been raised into a linguistic coalescence that issues from, and matches, the cohesiveness of Spirit itself. Such a word, Dickinson says, will expire only if Spirit expires. When the conceptual Language of inner Vision reaches its apogee, and then "consents" to incarnate itself as a breathing poem-word, it is (alliteratively) behaving like Christ, who "condescended" to dwell among us. (As Milton writes in the proem of the "Ode on the Morning of Christ's Nativity," Christ "laid aside" his "far-beaming blaze of Majesty" in Heaven, "and, here with us to be, / Forsook the courts of everlasting day, / And chose with us a darksome house of mortal clay.") "Condescension" (from "descend") is used here by Dickinson in its (now rare) positive sense—a gracious kindness to those of humbler status. The word has been used of the Incarnation from at least the seventeenth century. The *OED,* in its first definition, cites (from Hale's *Contemplation of the Lord's Prayer*) "Give us a sense of thy Great Condescention [*sic*] to thy weak and sinful Creatures" (1677) and (from Whitlock's *Zootomia*) "He [Christ] was to expiate man's Pride in the lowest Condescentions [*sic*] possible" (1654). The burning question for Dickinson is whether Language—her "loved Philology"— will condescend to her page and consent to be embodied in poetry, in the manner of the Word of God consenting to become man.

Rendered into prose, the sense of the last two stanzas would read:

A word that breathes distinctly has not the power to die; it is as cohesive as the Spirit, and it will not expire unless the Spirit itself does (an impossibility). If one can compare earthly things with legendary ones, then what I have experienced of the extraordinary consent of Language, this loved Philology, perhaps justifies the tale that Jesus indeed, in his own great "consent" and "condescension," was "made Flesh and dwelt among us."

Or, condensed as are Dickinson's lines: "That he was 'Made Flesh and dwelt among us' is credible if his 'condescension' resembled this consent of Language to philological embodiment (which to me appears miraculous)."

Dickinson's use of the Communion service as an analogue to reading is visible here, as in "He ate and drank the precious words - " (*1593). To "partake" (*OED,* definition 5a), transitively used, is "to take (food or drink) in company with others," with citations from 1602 on, including an 1876 citation (from George Ticknor's *Life, Letters, and Journals*) referring to Communion: "When the cardinal had partaken the sacrament he administered it to her."

In daring to appropriate the Incarnation as a metaphor for her own experience of the "consent of Language," Dickinson reverses the usual homiletic procedure, in which the preacher mentions doctrine first, and then finds a human exemplum to illustrate it. The Preacher might say, "Now, in trying to understand the Incarnation, we might think that it is like the action of a King who comes to share the dwelling of one of his humblest servants." Dickinson, by contrast, mentions first the human exemplum—the poem made possible by the "consent of Language" to its embodiment in words—and then uses the Incarnation as a metaphor of that experience. Whereas the preacher coopts the human to illustrate the divine, Dickinson coopts the divine to illustrate the human. And her reduplication of "love" closes the poem: *Philo-logia,* in Greek, is the love of words. "This loved Philology" means "this beloved love of words."

[J 1651]

# 1742

In Winter in my Room
I came upon a Worm
Pink lank and warm
But as he was a worm
And worms presume
Not quite with him at home
Secured him by a string
To something neighboring
And went along -

A Trifle afterward
A thing occurred
I'd not believe it if I heard
But state with creeping blood
A snake with mottles rare
Surveyed my chamber floor
In feature as the worm before
But ringed with power
The very string with which
I tied him - too
When he was mean and new
That string was there -

I shrank - "How fair you are"!
Propitiation's Claw -
"Afraid he hissed
Of me"?
"No Cordiality" -
He fathomed me -
Then to a Rhythm *Slim*
Secreted in his Form
As Patterns swim
Projected him.

That time I flew
Both eyes his way
Lest he pursue
Nor ever ceased to run
Till in a distant Town
Towns on from mine
I set me down
This was a dream -

Dickinson only rarely transcribed dreams, so she must have considered this one significant. It is hard for us to see it except as a sexual dream about a limp penis (worm) which then becomes erect (snake); the climax comes at "He fathomed me - ". The snake seems to become once again "Slim" as he then projects himself forward toward her, and she escapes in terror, looking ever backward "Lest he pursue." She runs until she arrives at a distant Town, where she sets herself down. Only after telling us the whole story does she admit, in the last line, "This was a dream - ".

As we read the poem, we realize its fictionality, but do not, I think, guess its origin in nightmare. This is not a story the poet has "thought up" (as we might have imagined), but a dream-story projecting itself out of her, passing from the unconscious mind to the conscious one. Shorn of a "Freudian" reading, the poem still seems bizarre—a reworking perhaps of her encounter with "A narrow Fellow in the Grass" (*1096)—from which she in fact borrows, at a crucial moment, the word "Cordiality." The worm/snake's menacing question (which I repunctuate here)—"Afraid," he hissed, "of me?"—is answered by the poet in a propitiatory fashion: she says not the "Yes" that would be truthful, but rather the understated, "[Well, I feel] No Cordiality [for you]." Although the poet has already made one self-abasing gesture, shrinking and telling the snake "How fair you are!" and extending not a hand to be shaken but "Propitiation's Claw," he merely hisses back at her his intimidating question.

Is Dickinson inventing a macabre variation of Eve in Paradise? Does the apparently harmless "worm" swell to a deadly snake "ringed with power" (his rings like the rattles of a rattlesnake, his scales mottled) as he begins to exert a

Satanic temptation? After finding the worm in her "Room," she has claimed him as her tame worm, and, having "Secured" him by a string outdoors to something in the neighborhood, has gone her way. The worm then reappears in the form of a menacing snake in her very own "chamber" (the former "Room," now specified as her bedroom), and in his enlarged form asserts his identity with his former worm-self by wearing the "very string with which / I tied him - too / When he was mean and new"—"mean" (in this context) indicating "of low status." The poet seems to have been complicit in some way (via the weakness of the string) in her own seduction, or rape (if that indeed is what she means to convey by "He fathomed me - "). That Dickinson consolidated this dream-event by commemorating it in a poem suggests she wanted to understand it further by giving it a formal structure and verbal embodiment.

She has created a "worm-structure," long and thin, in stanzas of varying numbers of lines (9, 12, 10, 8), since the snake is of varying lengths depending (I adapt the poet's words) on whether he is "fathoming" her or "projecting" himself. The "widest" lines come in stanza 2, when the worm has swelled into the snake. The rhymes are irregular, like the snake's unpredictable motions: couplets, tercets, single unrhymed lines. Three stanzas—1, 2, and 4—end with an unrhymed line; only stanza 3, unwilling to interrupt the serpentine self-projection, ends in a rhyming quatrain ("*Slim,*" "Form," "swim," "him"), by which we recognize the snake as the former worm, who also was allotted a rhyming quatrain ("Room," "Worm," "warm," "worm"). (These are the only two rhyming quatrains in the poem.) When the last line of a Dickinson stanza is left unrhymed, there is something existentially amiss. Closure cannot occur here except in stanza 3, when the snake is in charge of his own motion. The speaker can achieve no closure of her own—not outdoors, nor indoors, nor in the "distant Town." The only closure is conferred by her denying the actuality of her own story: "This was a dream - ".

In stanza 1, the speaker performs a cruel act: she tethers the worm (who has done nothing to her) "to something neighboring," in her fear that he will "presume." The first stanza indicates her fear by the recurrence of "worm-ish" line-endings ("Room," "Worm," "warm," "worm"—in addition to "worms" within line 5). By the second stanza, she is terrified by the lethal snake's size and his invasion of her chamber: she retells her story "with creeping blood."

Nonetheless, she continues to be fascinated by every detail concerning the snake: that he has "mottles rare," that he is "ringed with power," that he still wears her string, that his rhythm is "*Slim*," and that his mottles make swimming "Patterns" as he projects himself.

Unlike Eve, she escapes the threat, but not the fear that makes her run until she reaches "a distant Town / Towns on from mine." Like Eve, she is alone with the snake. But perhaps the snake, to her, is not Satan but Adam, and this is a virgin's dream of masculine sexual approach rather than (or in addition to) a dream of Satanic temptation. Dickinson does not provide a sufficient number of clues to establish what she herself understood by her dream-poem. Why, for instance, does she grow an aggressive talon—"Propitiation's Claw"—when she attempts to mollify the snake? In what emblem-book would Propitiation exhibit a Claw? In her six other poems using the word "claw," Dickinson offers it within a more plausible context; only when she is a bird does she offer a "Claw" *in propria persona* elsewhere. And we wonder how the social protection available in a distant Town exceeds the social protection in her own Town. Is she running toward a different kind of society? (Hardly, since the Town is Towns on from her Town; they seem tautologically identical.)

Is this dream related to her other fantastic poem ("I started Early - "; 656, J 520), in which she is physically pursued by the masculine Ocean, and gains safety only when they meet the "Solid Town," where there was "No One He seemed to know - "? Or is it related to the poem "The waters chased him as he fled" (*1766), in which a man is killed by "The waters," who attempt to seduce him as he flees? These poems all invite sexual interpretation, but they frustrate interpretation even as they invite it.

[J 1670]

# 1766

The waters chased him as he fled,
Not daring look behind;
A billow whispered in his Ear,
"Come home with me, my friend;
My parlor is of shriven glass,
My pantry has a fish
For every palate in the Year," -
To this revolting bliss
The object floating at his side
Made no distinct reply.

When we perceive that a poem rhyming in quatrains has only ten lines, or two and a half quatrains, we recognize that half of the third quatrain is "missing." Dickinson ends with a mere couplet, following the two quatrains, just as she had in "The Rat is the concisest Tenant" (*1369). We see the reason for the truncation of the last stanza when, at the end, no "reply" is forthcoming from the drowned man. Dickinson has "written" two lines of silence.

This gloriously macabre poem examines the appeal of death by giving death—in the person of the Ocean (represented by the masculine "billow")—a gruesomely seductive speech of invitation. Dickinson may have known that Wordsworth had written down, in the 1850 *Prelude,* a dream concerning an Arab who carries a stone and a shell. He explains that the stone is Euclid's *Elements of Geometry* and the shell is poetry. He is intending to bury them so that they will be preserved against a coming destruction:

His countenance meanwhile grew more disturbed,
And looking backwards when he looked, mine eyes
Saw, over half the wilderness diffused,
A bed of glittering light; I asked the cause:
"It is," said he, "the waters of the deep
Gathering upon us."
. . . . .

[He,] with his twofold charge
Still in his grasp, before me, full in view,
Went hurrying o'er the illimitable waste
With the fleet waters of a drowning world
In chase of him; whereat I waked in terror.
[*Prelude*, Book V, lines 126–131, 134–138]

When Dickinson writes, in "I never saw a Moor" (*800), that she knows "what a Billow be - ", she chooses the word "Billow" for its buoyancy and gaiety. Now, in the context of death, the "billow" becomes a threatening presence, about to overwhelm the man but affecting harmlessness by calling his prey "Friend." The poem rewrites Keats's "La Belle Dame sans Merci," in which the seductress feeds the hapless knight with "roots of relish sweet, / And honey wild, and manna dew," enticing him into her "elfin grot." The billow has his own elfin grot, which includes a pantry of gourmet nourishment (with "a fish / For every palate") and his own elegant parlor (of "shriven glass"). The billow, however, does not know how to speak English; there is no meaning to the phrase "For every palate *in the Year*" (italics added). Equally, in English we wouldn't speak of anything but a person being "shriven" (absolved of sin). Dickinson probably borrowed the shriving from "The Rime of the Ancient Mariner": "O shrieve me, shrieve me, holy man!" begs the Mariner of the Hermit (but the Hermit in fact never responds to the plea). It is as though the Dickinsonian billow has heard the Mariner's ballad recited, was pleased to note that it concerned the Sea, and therefore stole the "human" word "shriven" from it without knowing its accurate meaning. Similarly, the billow has somewhere heard the phrase "in the Year," and has mistakenly attached it to palates instead of, say, feasts (as in Shakespeare's Sonnet 52).

The narrator, having heard this billow-speech, comments on it: to the "revolting bliss" proposed in the invitation, the dead man made no answer. It is at the side of the billow (male, like the sea) that the man-drowning-into-object floats, the billow perhaps becoming his "pillow." There may be a dying gurgle in the man's throat, but there is no "distinct" reply. And even the gurgle dies in the silence of the two "missing" lines at the end. For all the cartoon comedy of pantry and parlor, we are nonetheless left to ponder, here, as elsewhere in Dickinson, the relativity of taste: the billow would ask nothing more in the way of happiness than to eat a fish in his glassy parlor. Even in the withering oxymoron "revolting bliss," the narrator admits that to some creatures such an invitation would afford "bliss." To make her point about the relativity of taste, Dickinson wickedly rhymes "bliss" with "fish."

[J 1749]

# 1771

’Twas here my summer paused
What ripeness after then
To other scene or other soul
My sentence had begun.

To winter to remove
With winter to abide
Go manacle your icicle
Against your Tropic Bride

Even more unnatural than the billow's pantry and parlor in "The waters chased him" (*1766) is this wedding of Tropic Bride and Icy Winter. The poet begins in bitter memory of her last moment of joy, as she stands at the very place—"here"—where her life "paused" for good, leaving her emotionally dead. After that irrevocable "pause" in the normal procession of the seasons, what ripeness could exist for her, she asks, in any other scene or any other soul, in any new landscape, with any other lover. She has received her life sentence, and it suspends her in perpetual paralysis until she will die in the flesh. With a straightening of shoulders, she articulates her fate: "To winter to remove / With winter to abide." We assume she is speaking of the grave, but she is not. She is describing a posthumous life, as it were, one to be endured within her remaining living years.

We grow to understand this stopped life as she allows the seasons to progress, unfolding her defiant challenge to Winter in her two concluding lines: "Go manacle your icicle / Against your Tropic Bride." The preposterous jolt as "manacle" and "icicle" collide is exceeded only by the vista of the Bride (still warm from the Summer where she "paused") manacled to Winter's icicle, the manacle a parodic wedding ring, the icicle a parodic penis. "If I have to live with you," the poet says defiantly to Winter, "Go, do your worst." By assuming "command" of her future, giving "permission" to her inner Winter to take her when he will, she claims the small amount of control she still has over her life.

The phallic implications of the "icicle," like those of the worm/snake of "In Winter in my Room" (*1742), may seem evident to us, but they may not have been to Dickinson. "Your icicle" may have seemed to her to be a plausible allegorical attribute signifying Winter, as flowers signify Spring or as a wheat-sheaf and sickle signify Autumn. In Dickinson's culture, the usual expectation at death was "To Heaven to remove, / With Jesus to abide," and Dickinson is perfectly aware that such expectations are awakened by her hymn-like stanzas. She takes a distinct delight in her perverse revisions of cliché.

For all the wit and dash and wintry malice of the last tableau, for all the energy thrust into devising a way to talk disrespectfully to Winter, Dickinson's first line—her own epitaph—lingers in memory; and her closing glee—the revenge for sadness—begins to seem sad itself.

[J 1756]

# 1773

My life closed twice before its close;
It yet remains to see
If Immortality unveil
A third event to me,

So huge, so hopeless to conceive
As these that twice befell.
Parting is all we know of heaven,
And all we need of hell.

In a Christian poem that began as this one does, with tragedy, the lament would lead to the expectation of a better life in Heaven: "It yet remains to see / If Immortality unveil / A third event to me, / [To compensate for all the grief"], etc. The only things Immortality is supposed to unveil are good things. "To unveil" (like "to uncover") is an English version of the Greek-derived word "Apocalypse," borrowed by Christianity to signify the End of Days, when all that was hidden on earth shall be uncovered, revealed, in order that it be judged. Dickinson, conceiving of Immortality as a hellish continuation of life, with further deadly closings lying in wait, expects "A third event," more "hopeless" than the first two, bringing the final loss of everyone she has loved.

By reserving the suspense of what Immortality might unveil until after the white space between quatrains, and by repeating the "twice" of stanza 1 in stanza 2, she reiterates the (essential) history of her life: that it has had only two hopeful episodes, each of which ended with the death of a beloved person. The implied five phases of her life have been Solitude, then Love, then the first loss (huge and hopeless), then renewed Love, then the second loss (as huge and hopeless again). Conventional Christianity would reassure her that in Immortality she will meet again her lost dead; she intimates that no such reunion will ever take place. The epigram on Parting equates heaven and hell. Whatever Heaven takes away from us in this life, the discovery that Immortality is a fiction creates the hell of the future.

The perfect rhymes seem to leave nothing to chance; they chime like clockwork. Why do we not feel an effect of complacency in Dickinson's aggressively didactic ending? I think because the lesson it teaches is so dark that only a ringing epigram could rein it in. The word "hell" as the name for what "befell" us spreads out at the end so as to cover the whole poem and its three identical events: Death, Death, Death.

[J 1732]

# 1779

To make a prairie it takes a clover and one bee,
One clover, and a bee,
And revery.
The revery alone will do,
If bees are few.

Because no Dickinson manuscript exists for this little epigram, transcribed by Mabel Todd, Ralph Franklin places it among the undated works at the end of his edition. It seems to sum up (in fewer than thirty words) all of Dickinson's work. She records her delight in clover and bee, but adds that if nature will not provide real objects, she will make do with "revery" to create her prairie.

Why clover instead of daisy? Why bee instead of Humming Bird? Because bee and clover are a sexual couple exchanging "Balms" and "nectars": the bee enters the flower as the Humming Bird does not (see "Come slowly - Eden!" 205, J 211).

Why "prairie" instead of "garden" or "meadow"? Because only "prairie" rhymes with "bee" and "revery," and because "prairie" is a distinctly American word. And because it gives double value by reflecting, in its spelling, its etymological root, the Latin *pratum,* "meadow."

Why "revery" instead of "dream" or "fantasy"? Not only because the word hints at dream (it comes from the same French root, etymologically, as the modern *rêver,* "to dream"), but also because it has a plethora of definitions. Dickinson's 1844 Webster gives three relevant ones:

1. Properly, a raving or delirium; but its sense, as generally used, is a loose or irregular train of thoughts, occurring in musing or meditation; mild, extravagant conceit of the fancy or imagination. [Webster cites Addison's remark: "There are reveries and extravagancies which pass through the minds of wise men as well as fools."]

2. A chimera; a vision.

3. In medicine, voluntary inactivity of the whole or the greater part of the external senses to the impressions of surrounding objects, during wakefulness.

And the *OED* has a few more (I do not cite obsolete or rare uses) that Dickinson may have known:

4. A fit of abstracted musing; a "brown study" or day-dream.

c. *Mus.* An instrumental composition suggestive of a dreamy or musing state. (1880)

5. The fact, state, or condition of being lost in thought or engaged in musing.

Finally, the three-syllable "revery" is phonetically more "spread out" than the curt monosyllabic Anglo-Saxon "dream." A reverie can recall real things that have happened; it evokes memory, as the word "fantasy" does not. The more one contemplates Dickinson's diction, the more one respects her awareness of connotation and her fastidiousness and elegance of choice.

Dickinson's minuteness of scrutiny extends to the smallest particles of language. She plays, for example, a little linguistic game here with the indefinite article ("a") and the number "one," reversing their distribution in lines 1 and 2. She poses a little linguistic test:

Distinguish between the following two italicized phrases (the latter in context):
Line 1: *a clover and one bee*
Lines 2 and 3: *One clover, and a bee, / And revery.*

Answer: 1. <u>One</u> single bee needs only <u>a</u> (random) clover from which to sip nectar.
2. Here the first phrase has been rearranged so that the two originally named essentials (clover and bee) become separated by a comma; they are no longer engaged in a quasi-sexual union. And this second arrangement produces an effect of second thought, and third thought, in the specifying list of (now) three essentials as it unfolds: "Yes, <u>one</u> clover," "*and* <u>a</u> bee / *And* revery." (The bee and revery are now grouped

together by "and" as, in the first line, bee and clover were). The list —in choosing its third essential—has been made halting by the line break, which allows for "revery" to come up as the poet's third thought, arriving as a "surprise" even to herself, because of the category-difference between her first two material thoughts (both arising from the visual prompt of "bee/clover") and the third, abstract one—"revery."

This miniature poem could seem initially the recipe for a painting as well as a poem. To make "a prairie," the painter could depict an uninterrupted terrain of grass defined by a closeup of a single bee on a single clover. But as soon as the category break occurs with the addition of "revery," we recognize that Dickinson's bee and clover are not real but constructs in the imaginative creation of an equally mental prairie suitable to a poem. Dickinson's brisk New England self-correction in the last two lines—conceding that what is at the heart of creation is the reverie out of which it comes—is announced as a practical one by the verb "do." "Just a yard will do," one hears the seamstress saying at the fabric counter; "The revery alone will do," says the thrifty poet. The quick monosyllables of the last six words bring us out of dreamy reverie itself (here a clover, there a bee) into the poet's argument for the power of reverie alone, even when it is unsupported by correlative natural images. Dickinson is a rapturous poet of nature's flowers and bees, but her more abstract meditations can arise powerfully from reverie alone.

The odd distribution of rhythms in this five-line poem suggests that we need to think of a structure—and its motivation—that would render Dickinson's rhythmic practice here intelligible. We could, for instance, read the poem as a two-couplet "recipe" for poetry, headed by the relatively unscannable first line, which lists (as is common in cookbooks) the necessary ingredients before the recipe proper.

Ingredients (laid out in "prose"):
    To make a prairie it takes a clover and one bee,

Rhythmic instructions revising the phrasing of the first two ingredients (clover and bee) and adding the indispensable third:

One clover and a bee,     (trimeter)
And revery.       (dimeter)
The revery alone will do, (tetrameter)
If bees are few.   (dimeter)

[ J 1755]

# Primary Sources Cited

Dickinson, Emily. *The Letters of Emily Dickinson.* Ed. Thomas H. Johnson and Theodora Ward. 3 vols. Cambridge, Mass.: Harvard University Press, 1958.

—— *The Manuscript Books of Emily Dickinson.* Ed. Ralph W. Franklin. 2 vols. Cambridge, Mass.: Harvard University Press, 1981.

—— *The Poems of Emily Dickinson: Including Variant Readings Critically Compared with All Known Manuscripts.* Ed. Thomas H. Johnson. 3 vols. Cambridge, Mass.: Harvard University Press, 1955.

—— *The Poems of Emily Dickinson: Reading Edition.* Ed. Ralph W. Franklin. Cambridge, Mass.: Harvard University Press, 1999.

—— *The Poems of Emily Dickinson: Variorum Edition.* Ed. Ralph W. Franklin. 3 vols. Cambridge, Mass.: Harvard University Press, 1998.

Hallen, Cynthia L., et al. *The Emily Dickinson Lexicon.* Online at edl.byu.edu.

Hawthorne, Nathaniel. *The English Notebooks.* Ed. Randall Stewart. New York: Russell and Russell, 1962; orig. pub. 1941.

Melville, Herman. *The Letters of Herman Melville.* Ed. Merrell R. Davis and William H. Gilman. New Haven: Yale University Press, 1960.

Sewall, Richard B. *The Life of Emily Dickinson.* New York: Farrar, Straus and Giroux, 1974.

White, Fred D. Approaching Emily Dickinson: Critical Currents and Crosscurrents since 1960. Rochester, N.Y.: Camden House, 2008.

# Acknowledgments

I thank John Kulka of the Harvard University Press for proposing that I write this set of Commentaries on poems by Emily Dickinson. I am grateful to the Carl Friedrich von Siemens Foundation of Munich for my 2009 appointment as a Siemens Fellow, and for the support I received from the Foundation. I owe thanks to those in Munich who made my stay a pleasure: Professor Doctor Heinrich Meier, Director of the Siemens Stiftung, and his wife Wiebke; Karen Osés of the Foundation, whose practical help made my life comfortable and my work possible; and Professor Meier's graduate student Anna Schmidt, who not only guided me through the bureaucratic procedures of visa and bank account, but looked after me so generously and delightfully that we became friends. At the Ludwig-Maximilian University, Professor Klaus Benesch welcomed me hospitably and offered to me the resources of the Library of American Studies; and his young Americanist colleagues Sascha Pöhlmann and Kerstin Schmidt became companions for coffee and conversation. I had the privilege of spending two evenings with Professor Willibald Sauerländer and his wife Brigitte, whose scholarly friendliness lighted up my time in Munich.

I owe thanks to President Derek Bok and President Drew Faust of Harvard University for allowing me a premature leave so that I could take advantage of the invitation from the Siemens Stiftung. I also owe a debt of gratitude to my kind chairman, Professor James Engell, for agreeing to my taking the leave.

The Emily Dickinson Lexicon has been an indispensable resource, as have the many efforts by scholars and critics to illuminate Dickinson's life and work. I especially owe a debt to Ralph Franklin for his scrupulous re-editing of Dickinson's poems. Domhnall Mitchell's painstaking reading of my manuscript contributed many insights to my final commentaries, for which I render profound thanks.

My assistant Kristin Lambert helped to ensure that the manuscript was properly formulated for printing. At the Harvard Press, I was fortunate in having Maria Ascher as my keen-eyed copyeditor. I am grateful also to the designer, Tim Jones, who discovered the photograph for the book jacket.

And I thank my dear son David, whose phone calls were a lifeline to this scholar in far away Germany.

# Index of First Lines

Numerals in parentheses refer to the poem number; those that follow refer to the page numbers. Poems that receive a full discussion in the text are indicated with an asterisk.

Did the Harebell loose her girdle (*134), 45–
    46
Doubt me! My Dim Companion! (332), 112
Dust is the only Secret. (166), 16

Essential Oils - are wrung - (*772), 7–8, 323–
    325, 402
Experiment to me (1081), 192
Exultation is the going (143), 116

Four Trees - upon a solitary Acre - (*778),
    326–329
From Blank to Blank - (484), 10–11, 168–169
Further in Summer than the Birds - (*895),
    361–366, 373, 411

Go thy great way! (1673), 221, 347
God is a distant - stately Lover - (*615), 16,
    269–271
Growth of Man - like Growth of Na-
    ture - (*790), 336–338

He ate and drank the precious Words - (*1593),
    498–499, 508, 510
He forgot - and I - remembered - (*232), 69–71
He preached upon "Breadth" till it argued him
    narrow - (1266), 14, 283
He put the Belt around my life - (*330), 135–
    137
He scanned it - Staggered - (*994), 384–385
Her - last Poems - (600), 215
"Hope" is the thing with feathers - (*314), 12,
    14, 118–120
How many times these low feet stag-
    gered - (*238), 75–77, 124, 279
How sick - to wait - (410), 94

I can wade Grief - (*312), 115–117
I cannot live with You - (*706), 4, 19, 21, 132,
    297–303, 304, 319–320, 346, 465
I died for Beauty - but was scarce (*448), 216–
    218, 302
I dreaded that first Robin, so, (347), 310

I dwell in Possibility - (*466), 222–224
I felt a Cleaving in my Mind - (*867), 196, 357–
    360
I felt a Funeral, in my Brain, (*340), 141–143,
    155
I found the words to every thought (436), 480
I got so I could take his name - (292), 136
I had been hungry, all the Years - (*439), 205–
    208, 209
I had not minded - Walls - (554), 203
I have never seen "Volcanoes" - (*165), 50–53
I heard a Fly buzz - when I died - (*591), 4,
    266–268
I know that He exists. (*365), 165–167
I like to see it lap the Miles - (*383), 177–179,
    392
I measure every Grief I meet (*550), 220, 250–
    254, 316, 355–356
I never hear that one is dead (*1325), 449–451
I never lost as much but twice - (39), 14, 244,
    280
I never saw a Moor. (*800), 12, 13, 343–344,
    516
I play at Riches - to appease (856), 316
I reckon - When I count at all - (*533), 246–
    249
I saw no Way - The Heavens were
    stitched - (*633), 275–277
I shall keep singing! (270), 95
I shall not murmur if at last (1429), 51, 288
I should have been too glad, I see - (283), 242
I sometimes drop it, for a Quick - (784), 310
I started Early - Took my Dog - (656), 514
I stepped from Plank to Plank (*926), 369–370
I taste a liquor never brewed - (207), 116
I thought that nature was enough (1269), 18
I tie my Hat - I crease my Shawl - (522), 232
I would not paint - a picture - (*348), 148–150,
    213, 322
If any sink, assure that this, now stand-
    ing - (616), 319
If *He dissolve* - then - there is *noth-
    ing - more* - (251), 18–19